"This book is an incredible resource for anyone v.
autism or who works with a child with autism. I wish I'd had this book when I first started working with my child. It would have been invaluable in supplementing the work that others were doing with my son. Joyce gives practical and concrete examples of HOW to work with your child, not just what needs to be done. This book addresses a hierarchy of skills needed for children who are severely impacted with autism to children that are high functioning. I am going to give this book to everyone who works with my son and will use it as a constant reference as my son gets older and acquires new skills. This is the absolute best book, most inclusive book, most practical book regarding working with children with autism that I have ever read."

—Kathy O'Rourke, parent of a child with autism and special education specialist, College View School, California, USA

"With love, grace, and skill, Joyce Show shines a light of hope and healing during a time for families which is often filled with uncertainty. Whether you are personally touched by autism or not, you will be transformed by Joyce's devotion as a mother and her commitment to improving the lives of others."

—Gwennyth L. Palafox, Ph.D., Clinical Psychologist and Director of Meaningful Growth, California, USA

"A work that is well researched and detailed: Joyce Show shares her extensive knowledge of autism gained by teaching her autistic son, Peter. But this book contains much more than a personal encounter with autism; it is also a structured and comprehensive teaching manual that can be used by parents seeking to develop essential skills for their autistic children within a home setting."

—Penny Kershaw, autism manager and outreach service leader for a special school in East Sussex, UK, author of The ASD Workbook: Understanding Your Autism Spectrum Disorder

"This lovely book offers an intimate story about raising Peter, a child with autism. Joyce's warmth and insightful reflections are inspirational, and her wisdom will provide reassuring guidance for many. Love, joy, and faith triumph over the many hurdles they encounter."

—*Diane Cullinane, M.D., Developmental*
Pediatrician and Executive Director of Pasadena Child
Development Associates, Inc., California, USA

"Joyce Show's comprehensive and profound command of the subject matter, as well as the different treatment modalities, is infused with the love, compassion, and the understanding that can only be mustered by a parent. She also accomplishes what few other books on autism have, which is to seamlessly use each modality as a tool without the rigid dogmatism that pervades books written about a particular therapeutic method, creating a truly holistic educational approach. It is sure to become an indispensable guide and a beacon for parents on their autism journey."

—*Anita Ghazarian, O.D., parent of a child*
with autism, California, USA

Teaching Your Child with Love and Skill

of related interest

Key Learning Skills for Children with Autism Spectrum Disorders
A Blueprint for Life
Thomas L. Whitman and Nicole DeWitt
ISBN 978 1 84905 864 3
eISBN 978 0 85700 467 3

Hints and Tips for Helping Children with Autism Spectrum Disorders
Useful Strategies for Home, School, and the Community
Dion E. Betts and Nancy J. Patrick
ISBN 978 1 84310 896 2
eISBN 978 1 84642 877 7

Playing, Laughing and Learning with Children on the Autism Spectrum
A Practical Resource of Play Ideas for Parents and Carers
2nd edition
Julia Moor
ISBN 978 1 84310 608 1
eISBN 978 1 84642 824 1

Everyday Activities to Help Your Young Child with Autism Live Life to the Full
Simple Exercises to Boost Functional Skills, Sensory Processing, Coordination and Self-Care
Debra S. Jacobs and Dion E. Betts
Foreword by Carol A. Just
ISBN 978 1 84905 238 2
eISBN 978 0 85700 482 6

Motivate to Communicate!
300 Games and Activities for Your Child with Autism
Simone Griffin and Dianne Sandler
ISBN 978 1 84905 041 8
eISBN 978 0 85700 215 0

Parenting Across the Autism Spectrum
Unexpected Lessons We Have Learned
Maureen F. Morrell and Ann Palmer
ISBN 978 1 84310 807 8
eISBN 978 1 84642 506 6

Teaching Your Child with Love and Skill

A Guide for Parents and Other Educators of Children with Autism, including Moderate to Severe Autism

JOYCE SHOW

Jessica Kingsley *Publishers*
London and Philadelphia

Basic Curiculum Guide on page 114–121 reproduced with kind permission from Gwennyth Palafox.

First published in 2012
by Jessica Kingsley Publishers
116 Pentonville Road
London N1 9JB, UK
and
400 Market Street, Suite 400
Philadelphia, PA 19106, USA

www.jkp.com

Library of Congress Cataloging in Publication Data
A CIP catalog record for this book is available from the Library of Congress

British Library Cataloguing in Publication Data
A CIP catalogue record for this book is available from the British Library

ISBN 978 1 84905 876 6
eISBN 978 0 85700 569 4

Printed and bound in the United States

I dedicate this book to
my beloved mother,
whose gentle and accepting love will forever be
an inspiration to me,
and to my dear husband Vinh,
who exemplifies "deeds, not words."

Contents

Acknowledgments

Peter, thank you for writing this book with me, as we practiced the games and worked out the principles together, step by step.

I would also like to thank the innumerable people who have blessed Peter with their love and talents, especially:

Dr. Gwennyth Palafox and Belinda Wulke, you are my dream team. Gwen, you are a brilliant psychologist, gifted with a sense of fun, joy, and humor that makes everything seem possible, and intuition and wisdom far beyond your years. Belinda, none can match you in resourcefulness, fortitude, and patience. You are a naturally brilliant teacher, Peter's second mother, and my best friend and support.

To our gifted teachers Jeannette Pound and Gabriela Ziolkowski, you have stuck with our family since Peter was a tiny tot, and your love is woven into the fabric of who he is.

To Dr. Diane Danis, Dr. Diane Cullanae, Dr. Susan Spitzer, Dr. Mona Delahooke, and Dr. Shakeh Mazmanian, you are everything one could hope for in a doctor, compassionate, more than competent, and always going beyond the call.

Susan Hollar, you are the best of professors because you are always learning, and in that constant search for knowledge, you found relationship development intervention (RDI) and saved my child with it.

Dr. Bodil Sivertsen, thank you for leading us through those early dark days with your brilliance.

Cynthia Cottier, you opened a whole new world for Peter with your outstanding teaching in assistive technology (AT).

Thanks to Drs. Robert and Lynn Koegel who graciously provided training for Peter and me in Santa Barbara when we arrived on your doorstep, desperate.

Thanks to my friends and fellow struggling parents, Caren and Charles Gale, who threw me a life jacket when I first heard Peter's diagnosis; Dr. Anita Ghazarian who gave me a push when I needed it; and the board of the Foothill Autism Alliance for their provision of outstanding parent education.

To Dr. Tamara Jackson, Kristen Angelica, Diana Yuen, Leslie Maine, Raissa Choi, David Wulff, Emily Felong, Wendy Watts, and all the loving, dedicated, and talented staff in our school district, there is no other district in the country that would have done what you've done for Peter. God bless you!

To my little army of angels, all the dear young people who have poured their talents and energy into loving Peter—Frances, Laura, Charlie, Teresa, and Joseph Wulke, Alison Joe, and Jessica Lam, I feel you are my sons and daughters.

To Dr. Cullanae and all the lovely developmental interventionists from the Pasadena Child Development Associates, especially Felicie Standley and Wynai Tsing, thanks for many wonderful hours of floortime. You have been at the heart of Peter's social and emotional development.

Thank you Tao Zhen Yu, Lydia Lam, Sargis Akopyan, and the Mountain High Disabled Ski staff for all your contributions to Peter's growth.

Thank you Claudia Lara and Marjorie Gell for the support of Lanterman Regional Center.

Thank you Dr. Palafox, Dr. Cullanae, Dr. Danis, Dr. Spitzer, Susan Hollar, and Beverlee Paine for lending your expertise in looking over various chapters of my manuscript.

To my inspiring teacher friends, Stephanie Joe and Bonnie Hine, and wonderful friends at the San Gabriel Valley Inklings, including Jane Rumph, Marilyn Woody, Yvonne Ellfeldt, Sandee Foster, Sharon Pearson, Marianne Croonquist, Muriel Gladney, Susan Skommeta, Debby Allen, and especially my mentor Pat Stockett Johnson, warm thanks for your edits, encouragement, and most of all, your prayers; I know our meeting was providential.

To all my beloved extended family, especially Jane and Matthew Wada, for faithfully walking the journey with us by showing up every single week, you hold us up with your loving support. Jane, you told me long ago when Peter was first diagnosed, that we would do this together, and you kept your promise.

Thank you Yeye for supporting Peter, and Yiyi Judy for many comforting phone calls, prayers, and many long drives to bring my talented niece Rosie to tutor Peter.

To my dear children, Judy, Jeffrey, Stephen, Joseph, Teddy, and Luke, each one of you have lovingly poured some of your giftedness into your special sibling, in your own special way.

And most of all to my beloved Vinh, the finest husband and father anyone could ever have, who always impresses me with all he observes and humbles me with all I miss, I thank God for you!

And I thank God for His gracious provision, and for giving us Peter, our beautiful treasure.

I have a special heart for you parents with highly impacted children. That is my child—very few areas of his brain are untouched by autism. I read book after book, but no one teaching method sufficed. There was too much damage in too many areas. Each method in isolation would fall short because while it might be good at remediating one or two areas of deficit well, it depended on other areas of the brain functioning that weren't working in my child. I felt discouraged because I thought there was something wrong with what I was doing. I didn't realize that the problem was missing pieces and missing steps.

I discovered that you have to identify, understand, and support each and every area of deficit, lest the deficit you overlook become the rate-limiting step in your child's progress. You therefore have to have a comprehensive understanding of all the areas involved, and a comprehensive strategy to tackle many areas simultaneously. You need to have the breadth of educational methods or tools to handle each problem. You will need to use many tools all at once, and work on all the rooms of your child's house simultaneously. If you only have part of the information, you won't get far.

This is the book I wish I had had when I began my journey over ten years ago. You might call it "the book of the missing pieces." I have tried to include the missing steps I wish someone had pointed out to me, and had to figure out through research and lots of trial and error. It will guide you on how to assist your child to form his earliest interactions to nurturing the emergence of abstract and reflective thinking. The principles work for children with all degrees of autism. Indeed they also apply for neurotypical children. You'll just get through the stages faster if your child is less impacted, but the missing steps are all there for those who need them.

The emphasis is on your truly understanding what's wrong in the brain of your child so you'll know what it will take to rebuild it. That way if you hit a wall, you'll know what next direction to take, and what areas of difficulty might need addressing first. Knowledge is enabling, and gives hope because you can see what needs to be done, even if you see it's going to take a long time and require a lot of practice.

The book is arranged in order of the steps you need to take to work with your child from the most fundamental stages on up. First you need to understand your child's needs, learn how to observe and attune, identify and accommodate sensory differences, and enable motor processing. Then you should engage your child in fundamental interactions, work on motivation, create a strategy for cognitive development, develop a system of communication, address nonverbal communication, and work on the fundamentals of social and emotional development. The final chapters help you guide your child into higher levels of cognitive and social and emotional development, and support every step of the learning process. I include chapters on self-help skills, routines, and behavioral challenges, including self-injury and aggression. If you read the chapters in sequential order, you will gain an understanding of child development and how to nurture it from the ground level up. Each chapter may also be read as a stand-alone to gather helpful tips on particular topics.

I'm a mother of seven children, the sixth of whom has been heavily impacted by autism. I received my BA with a Magna Cum Laude in Biochemistry from Harvard University and my MD from a joint program in Health Sciences and Technology from Harvard University and the Massachusetts Institute of Technology. I'm dually board certified in internal medicine and geriatrics. I left my private practice in internal medicine of over ten years to stay home to help my son, because even with all the outside educational resources we could muster for him, he was not making progress. I loved my work as a doctor and received a lot of love and joy from working with my patients. I always felt that I was one of the luckiest women in the world. However, I knew that a rewarding career in medicine would not make me happy if I left my son behind. I wanted to do everything I could to help him develop to his greatest potential so he could live a meaningful life.

My son, Peter, is now 12 years old, and he still has severe autism, but I offer a message of hope. We have not discovered any quick or easy fixes, but do not despair. With hard, persistent work and understanding, even children with severe autism can make significant progress. Peter's language skills test out at the six-year-old level when given access to his assistive technology (AT) communication device. He dresses himself, eats with utensils, bikes, skis, and helps out with chores. He is frequently better behaved when we go to church and other outings than his nonautistic little brother. Most importantly, Peter is active and joyful, and has a sweet sense of humor. A while ago, to keep him occupied in church, I made a flower, with a stem and leaves, out of pink and green strings of wax. I put it on the church pew between us. We stood up for prayers, and when we sat down again, I noticed that, laid carefully beside my wax flower, was a straight wax string for a stem with one bent into a simple circle on top for

Chapter 1

What's Wrong with My Child?

> I watched from my bedroom window as Peter ran in circles in the back yard. We had just returned from seeing his pediatrician, Dr. Maz. Peter was 18 months old. My dear friend, Mrs. Yu, was watching him. I needed a moment away. My heart felt like a heavy stone in my chest. The scene replayed in my mind. Dr. Maz had banged a pan right behind Peter. He didn't turn his head. He was just smiling to himself, and didn't even flinch. Dr. Maz sympathetically wrote a prescription for a hearing test. Was my child deaf? But sometimes he seemed able to hear, such as when he'd come running when the theme song to "Thomas the Tank Engine" played on TV. All those times I had cuddled him and told him I loved him—could he hear it? The tears streamed down my face, but worse was yet to come...

What's wrong with my child? This is the heart-wrenched cry of every parent when the symptoms of autism finally force themselves upon our consciousness. The lack of eye contact, pointing, checking back for reassurance or approval—we pass off these early signs for as long as we can. Those of us who have children who have regressed may experience residual sparks of abilities such as a burst of babbling or running to the door to greet us until even these small signs of hope quietly slip away. At some point, we realize we have lost our child, and not even had the cognizance to say goodbye.

WHAT IS AUTISM? UNDERSTANDING IS THE FIRST STEP TOWARD HEALING

Autism is a disorder of brain development that results in profound social and communication difficulties. Problems with body coordination ("motor planning"), the filtering and processing of sensory input ("sensory integration"), and dealing with emotions ("affect regulation") occur frequently. Also characteristic are restricted interests and the persistent repetition of apparently senseless acts or words ("stereotypy," called "self-stimulation," or "stimming" for short), such as flapping the hands or squealing. Autism is a spectrum disorder, which means that different areas or domains of the brain are affected to different degrees in each individual.

No one knows what causes autism. There may be a genetic predisposition in some cases, or it could be as a result of flooding our environment with tens of thousands of new chemicals each year—their potential biologic harms are largely unstudied before their release. Since we don't know the biologic cause or causes, neither can we offer standard biomedical cures that work for most children with autism. Some parents have been fortunate in trying various biomedical interventions that seem to make a dramatic difference for their children. However, large-scale studies are still to be done to prove their effectiveness when compared with placebo treatments. Autism is so devastating that many parents are willing to experiment with some of these biomedical treatments, even those with potential side effects. But after spending a lot of time, energy, and money on these treatments, many families find their child remains uncured. So then what?

The brain is fortunately a quite plastic organ, which means it is capable of substantial remodeling and change. Since the 1970s, substantial progress has been made in developing educational methods that attempt to fix the brain (called "rewiring" or "remediating"). When best attempts at remediation don't work, other methods teach how to compensate (support or use another part of the brain) for the affected brain domains. Regardless of whether or not you are also working on biomedical treatments for your child, you'll want to get started right away on educational treatments. The young brain is the most plastic, so early intervention results in the largest gains. (If your child is older though, don't despair as the brain keeps developing, albeit at a slower rate, until 50 years old and probably beyond!) Before learning how to remediate and compensate, it is important to find out what exactly needs "fixing."

Neurobiologists are just beginning to explore how the brain works, and autism is a very complex and comprehensive disorder. Some vocabulary and concepts used throughout this book might sound a little technical, but will be useful for you to learn so you can communicate with your consultants more efficiently. I also use some medical terminology, defined in the Glossary at the end of the book, in some of my explanations, for those of you who are interested.

While it is not really essential to understand the medical pathophysiology of autism, much of which is speculative anyway, what is important is to get a general understanding of what's working and not working so well in your child's brain so you will know how to best help him. If a child is blind or crippled, his disability is easy to identify. We don't expect him to do things he can't, and we automatically provide compensations and supports to help him function more independently and effectively—we would never make the mistake of thinking that using punishment and reward would be useful in helping a blind child to see, or a lame child walk without braces. No amount of motivation will make a child do what he cannot do. Offering rewards that are impossible to earn, or punishing the child when he's coping in the only way he knows how, is enormously frustrating for the child, and totally unfair. It adds insult to injury, and results in low self-esteem and oppositional behavior.

Children with autism have physiological deficits just as real as being blind or lame. But these deficits are hidden in the brain underneath an apparently normal physical exterior. Furthermore, the behavioral manifestations of these deficits are very complex because what you see is the result of interplay between different domains of the brain working together. The stronger regions are reacting to and trying to compensate for the processing deficits of the weaker ones. Inexplicable tantrums may result from sensory overload. Mysterious self-stimulation behaviors may be the child's way of feeling where he is in space. Maddening echolalia (repetition of the last words heard) may be the result of poor development of the speech production center in the brain. Impenetrable aloofness may also be misinterpreted as willful, whereas it's probably due to deficits in facial processing and mirror neuron dysfunction (see pp.28–30).

If you understand what domains in the brain are often affected in autism, you won't blame the child for what he can't do, and you won't blame him for compensating in the only way he knows how. If the music is too loud in a church, for example, and your child throws himself on the floor, you'll understand that he can't filter out the sound. He's in pain, and distracts himself from the pain by rolling on the floor. Perhaps it's the only way he can tell you to get him out of there because when he experiences such pain, it's too hard to come up with words. Understanding autism will save you a lot of grief in the end—knowledge is not only power, but also healing. Don't make the mistake of taking it personally, and thinking that the child is intentionally trying to hurt you.

The goal of this chapter is for you to learn to identify your child's areas of challenge in a systematic way. As you observe and interact with your child, you'll get a feel for what brain domains are more impacted and on what level to begin working on each. You'll learn how to use your child's strengths to work on his weaknesses. Instead of getting frustrated with your child, you'll learn to adjust your expectations, provide more support where needed, and set more achievable goals, step by step.[1]

CHALLENGES WITH SENSORY INTEGRATION

Start by looking at the world from your child's perspective. We all take in information about our environment through channels called "senses," and everyone is familiar with the "five senses" of vision, hearing, touch, taste, and smell. Another one of the senses that isn't as commonly taught is called "proprioception." This is the ability of the brain to sense movement and position. Sensory receptors for proprioception reside in muscles, tendons, and ligaments. This sense is often affected in autism.

Children with autism often seem to have what are called "sensory integration" issues, meaning difficulties taking in, filtering, processing, and integrating environmental information through their senses. Many seem to pay more attention to sensory input closer to the body like smell, taste, and touch (called "proximal" stimuli) than visual and auditory input that gives information about things located farther away from the body (called "distal" stimuli). Thus, when preoccupied with proximal stimuli, they may ignore important (salient) distal stimuli in their environment, for example, the child busily flapping to satisfy a deep sensory need, totally ignoring a sudden loud sound that makes everyone else in the room turn to look.

Some of the "channels" seem to be turned up too loud or too soft such that a child may seem oversensitive ("hypersensitive") or undersensitive

---

1   In the example above, of the music being too loud in a church, start on a remediation program to gently desensitize your child to gradually increasing volumes of sound. In the meantime, compensate. Bring noise cancellation headphones or earplugs and teach your child how to use them ahead of time. Sit in the back to make a quick getaway if necessary, and teach your child to hand you a "let's go" card instead of throwing himself on the floor. Or adjust your expectations altogether and enroll him in a special needs Sunday school class instead of sitting in church together. If he has cognitive strengths, talk to him ahead of time or read a story you make up with pictures about what to do in church if the music gets too loud.

("hyposensitive") to certain sensory input. Some individuals with autism have described their experiences in overstimulating environments, such as those that are too loud or too bright, as actually being painful. My son Peter will bury his head into my arm when we step outdoors into bright sunlight, and cover his ears with his hands when the audience claps after a show or when someone turns on the blender or vacuum cleaner.

Some children seem to be hypersensitive to tactile stimulation such that they are extremely picky about what fabrics they feel comfortable wearing. Others seem to have a decreased sense of pain such that they seem not to care when they fall. I heard one adult with autism say that he would flap in order to feel where his body was in space, as if he had a decreased sense of proprioception. Certainly my Peter flaps and taps on everything, and craves squeezes, hugs, and crawling into tight spaces as if constantly seeking out ways to satisfy an understimulated proprioceptive sense.

Some children seem orally hypersensitive, and are extremely picky eaters. I know one child with autism who eats only one flavor of yogurt and no other foods. Others seem to crave strong or unusual flavors and smells, such as the child who will work for a whiff of blue cheese or another who loves to smell his mother's hair.

A child may have any combination of sensory differences. It takes careful observation of an individual child to know how to tailor accommodations (refer to the Glossary at the end of this book) to help "regulate" him, so that the child isn't overwhelmed, but can calmly take in and function in his environment. A quiet, uncluttered environment with indirect lighting, and the child facing away from any windows, seems to work best for many children when required to focus and concentrate.

A decreased speed of processing sensory information is another common problem. At an autism conference I attended an interview of a young man with marked autism named Tito Mukhopadhyay. Tito, who communicates by typing, described how he experienced water from a faucet filling a bucket, and how long it took him in stages to put together what he was seeing and hearing to identify what was happening. He first heard the sound of the water filling the bucket. A few seconds later he noticed the blue color of the bucket. It took even longer for him to put together the sounds and sights and realize that water was filling the bucket. The problem with slow processing is that in real life, many a stimulus will change or disappear before the child has had enough time to process and comprehend it, making his understanding of the environment patchy and distorted.

For example, an airplane goes by, and I ask, "What do you hear, Peter?" By the time Peter tunes into the new sound in his environment, I am frantically pointing to the sky, saying, "Look, look, an airplane!" Chances are that by the time Peter understands my signal and looks up, the plane is gone and has vanished out of sight. The opportunity to put together the sight and sound of an airplane is lost.

I sometimes wonder what it must feel like to have stimuli popping in and out of one's consciousness without the time required to identify and understand them. It must feel like being constantly assailed. It's no wonder that many of these children cope by seeking to control their environment with regimented routines or withdrawal. There's a lot of noise and jostling in the passing interval between class periods at Peter's school. When Peter gets caught in the crowd, he throws his arms up around his head and buries it in his tutor's arm. He looks exactly as if he's defending himself from attack.[2]

CHALLENGES WITH SUSTAINING, DIRECTING, AND SHIFTING ATTENTION

Attention problems are common in children with autism. Some are highly distractible and seem to be captured by the stimulating qualities of each object in their environment. They flit from one thing to the next without being able to select, concentrate, and focus on any one thing meaningfully on their own initiative.[3] There are other autistic children who seem to have the opposite problem. As one father put it, "My son

---

2   The physiologic basis of these observed sensory integration deficits is not completely understood. However, in studies comparing the brains of individuals with and without autism, a part of the brain called the cerebellar vermis appears smaller in size in autism. There appears to be an underdevelopment of a kind of cell in the cerebellum called large integrative and projecting pyramidal neurons, most especially to those that project to the frontal cortex. Therefore, there is an imbalance in neuronal numbers between the front and back of the brain. It may be that the neurons that process sensory signals at the rear of the brain are trying to communicate with too many frontal neurons, resulting in the connections being too diffuse, impairing the ability of the frontal cortex to integrate sensory information.

The cerebellum regulates the rate, rhythm, and force of movement, and may analogously function the same way in regulating socioemotional and cognitive behavior. Hence cerebellar dysfunction may contribute to problems with both "overshooting" such as circumlocution and tangential wordiness, and "undershooting" such as paucity of language (Koziol and Budding 2009).

3   Arnold Miller (2007) refers to these children as having a "systems forming disorder."

has 'overattention' disorder, as opposed to attention deficit disorder."[4] These children seem captured by one activity such as lining up cars, flicking lights on and off, or flushing the toilet. They do these activities repetitively, when nonautistic ("neurotypical") children would long ago have moved on to do something else. Some children are so captured by one stimulus in their environment, such as a bright window or the spinning of a fan, that they cannot attend to anything else until the stimulus is removed.[5]

CHALLENGES WITH DETERMINING *GESTALT* (THE BIG PICTURE) AND SALIENCE (WHAT'S IMPORTANT)

Many children with autism seem to focus "on the parts instead of the whole" so that they will repetitively spin the wheels on a toy car instead of making it drive around. Related to this problem of integrating and processing information, many children cognitively find it difficult to get the *Gestalt*, the big picture, or "see the forest for the trees." Donna Williams (1999) writes about her sensory and perceptual differences as an adult with autism—when she looks in a mirror, she sees parts of herself rather than the whole.

When I ask my son Peter to wipe the table, he takes a towel and dutifully wipes the table, but only a small part of it, missing many of the spills and certainly not going over the whole table. This problem with getting the *Gestalt* may contribute to why children with autism are often very concrete and don't generalize what they learn automatically. When Peter learned to label his body parts, I thought I would help him

---

4   Arnold Miller (2007) refers to these children as forming "closed systems" in their object of concentration.

5   Current theory speculates that dysfunction of the basal ganglia may be the cause of some of these attention problems. The basal ganglia have a gatekeeper role in attention, deciding when to release automatic behavior or inhibit it in favor of higher order control. For some children, habitual, automatic responses may be released in situations that require more frontal cortex input (the frontal lobes deliberate, plan, and analyze). Think of the child who speeds through a page of equations without noticing that some require addition and some subtraction. For others there may be not enough automaticity such as the child who hates writing because the physical act of writing requires too much cognitive effort, or the child who has to consciously remind himself to give eye contact and smile in a greeting. The basal ganglia may also control starting and stopping, as well as not starting and not stopping. Hence dysfunction of the basal ganglia may result sometimes in a lack of initiation. One example is the child who just can't begin his morning bathroom routine without prompting despite innumerable trainings. In other children it may present as perseveration, as in a child who gets stuck on one problem on a test and can't move on to the next, or requires a lot of encouragement to transition from one activity to the next.

generalize his knowledge by giving him a washcloth during bathtime and playing a game. I sang, "This is the way we wash our (arm)," and watched to see if Peter would wash the body part (for example, arm) that I labeled. What followed was fascinating, though frustrating. Peter immediately placed the washcloth over the exact spot he was used to pointing to when doing his labeling exercises. However, he washed that one small spot only instead of the whole arm. That experience certainly confirmed the importance of working on generalization.

When I first started cooking with Peter, I remember baking a cake together. Peter loves to crack eggs. When he was just getting the hang of it, I remember him cracking the egg into the batter and then very carefully and deliberately placing the eggshells in the batter as well. Although he had seen me bake cakes many times before, he had not absorbed the concept incidentally as most children would have that the shells are always discarded. He had not gotten the *Gestalt* or common sense of the process.

With this difficulty in constructing an integrated concept (*Gestalt*) of what they are perceiving and what they are doing, it is not surprising that many children with autism cannot seem to pick out what's important to pay attention to (salience).[6] When we are stuck in a traffic jam because of a car accident along the side of the road, Peter doesn't turn his head to look. He appears uninterested even when we try to point it out. It took many months of practice for Peter to learn to pick out the crumbs on the floor to vacuum up under his place at the table.[7] Therapists who work with children with autism learn early on to simplify their visual teaching materials lest the student focus on the background instead of the main subject. For example, given a photo of therapist Anne in front of a brown wall and another of therapist Janet in front of a white wall, the child might simply learn to associate "Anne" with brown and "Janet" with white instead of paying attention to differences in their facial features.

---

6   The basal ganglia may also control what gets in and what gets thrown out of working memory, so the right information is kept on line in a given context. If it doesn't do its job as "bouncer" of the brain, too much information may get in for the frontal cortex to process (Awh and Vogel 2008; McNab and Klingberg 2008).

7   For some individuals with autism, the problem may lie in visual processing deficits. Donna Williams (1999) describes how as a child she saw only patterns and colors. When she put on tinted glasses (Irlen Lenses), she finally perceived that the colors and patterns in the room were identifiable objects such as the window, curtains, and furniture.

CHALLENGES WITH MOTOR PLANNING AND COORDINATION

Children with autism not only commonly have problems with how they take in and process sensory information (sensory integration) and what information they pay attention to (attention problems), but also with body awareness, coordination, and motor planning. In other words, they have problems both with intake and output. Motor planning means putting together all the body movements needed to accomplish a task, including gross motor tasks, like shifting the body to go down a slide, and fine motor tasks, like holding a pencil correctly and drawing a circle. A deficit in motor planning is not surprising considering we know that autism is associated with abnormalities in the cerebellum, which coordinates motor actions.

Chantal Sicile-Kira writes about Tito Mukhopadhyay in her book, *Autism Life Skills* (2008, p.7):

> Motor planning difficulties are also explained in such experiences as trying to ride a tricycle. Tito says that he tried to order his legs to move (to pedal the bike), but that they would not move. His mother had to do a lot of hand over hand with any tasks requiring muscle groups, such as teaching him to ride the tricycle. I remember her telling me how she sat him on a chair, and over and over for most of the day, she would put her son's legs through the motions until he could move them on his own.

When Peter was a toddler, he took a long time to figure out how to apply enough pressure on the handle of the toilet to get it to flush. Now the challenge is spreading butter on bread. Peter would play with his Thomas trains and seem to want to grab a train a few feet away on the other side of the tracks. I would have to give him lots of encouragement and specific direction to get him to move his body position so that he could reach the train, even to the point of marking exactly where to sit with a carpet square or pillow. Children with autism need a lot of work to become aware of how their bodies move and what they can do, so that they gain confidence acting upon their environment and becoming doers and explorers.

So autism affects both input, that is, sensory integration, and output, that is, motor planning. These issues are usually the first to be addressed in early intervention. For sensory integration, compensatory and desensitizing techniques can be tried. For motor planning, a lot of rough and tumble play and gross motor activity enhances body awareness. We discuss these strategies further in later chapters (see pp.49–58, 61–3). Managing the sensory issues is at least partially under your control as you can manipulate your child's environment, and gross motor work is usually inherently fun and motivating for the child. The hardest work in treating autism is actually in addressing the more complex core features of the disorder, namely impaired social interaction and communication.

CHALLENGES WITH SOCIAL INTERACTION

Even in a carefully controlled, not overstimulating environment, with minimal motor planning requirements, the lack of natural interest in social interaction is striking in children with autism. What is different in the brain of a child with autism that may be responsible for this? There is some evidence that children with autism are deficient in the mirror neuron system, a domain in the inferior frontal gyrus of the brain. This mirror neuron region lights up on functional MRIs (magnetic resonance images) both when performing goal-directed actions and while observing the same actions performed by others.[8] Another area called the insula seems to act as an interface between the frontal component of the mirror neuron system and the limbic system, the emotion center of the brain. In other words, the mirror neuron system may be what enables an individual to experience an observed action in his own mind on an immediate emotional level.

Let's take an example watching the Olympics. We might hold our breath as we watch a figure skater doing a triple axel on the ice. If she lands well we feel relieved and triumphant, as if we had succeeded ourselves. If she falls, we feel dismayed. Our mirror neurons are firing like crazy as we perform together with her, and our own limbic system fires in concert, making us feel for her what we would feel ourselves if we succeeded or failed. But children with a deficiency in these mirror neurons might be having a very different experience. They might be interested or even fascinated with the graceful movements of the skater, but not automatically be skating along with her or feeling what we would if we were in her place. Hence Peter might be watching the same skater as I am, but seems to care so much less. He would probably make a most objective and impartial judge, but the excitement and emotional investment is missing.

---

8 Functional MRIs image blood flow. Greater blood flow marks areas of greater metabolic activity in the brain.

This relative deficiency in mirror neurons therefore might explain why individuals with autism might not be as naturally empathetic or interested in what other people are doing.[9] They may not experience what they see in the same vicarious way that other children automatically do. The same reason may explain why children with autism do not seem to have a natural inclination to imitate what they see others doing. They may not perceive the potential for a rewarding experience because they aren't experiencing it vicariously in their own minds first. Perhaps also related to this is what observers have labeled in children with autism a lack of "theory of mind," meaning a natural understanding that other people have different minds and therefore don't know what you are thinking and feeling. If you believe that others already know what you know, there is less motivation to share your thoughts. Theory of mind in neurotypical children leads to the discovery of the joy and fun of guessing and sharing those different thoughts and feelings, which is a major motivation for social functioning.

Furthermore, researchers have discovered that individuals with autism have differences in the posterior portions of their brains that recognize faces and interpret emotions. Nonautistic people use part of their brain called the fusiform gyrus to recognize faces, and a much less sophisticated part of the brain called the inferior temporal gyrus for objects. Robert Schultz and colleagues (2000) at Yale found that people with autism used their less discerning object recognition area for both objects and faces. As Malcolm Gladwell (2005) put it in his book, *Blink*, the difference in sophistication between those two regions explains why you can pick out a long-lost friend from a crowd but have trouble finding your luggage on the airport carousel. We recognize faces and interpret facial expressions automatically and instantaneously.

These abilities require deliberate effort and training for people with autism. Imagine talking to a friend. Think of the number of facial expressions your friend has during the course of a conversation. What if you had to work at interpreting each of those changing facial expressions? Social interaction would be so exhausting and frustrating, it might not be worth the effort. Multiply the effort by going to a crowded party. Besides the noise and sensory overload, think of all the people you'd offend because you couldn't recognize them out of context, and they thought you were ignoring them.

---

9   What Dr. Bryna Siegel (2003) describes as "affiliative orientation."

The problem begins at a very young age. Many babies with autism tend to look at the mouth and lower part of the face instead of the eyes for information. Impaired reciprocal social interaction shows up early on with *a lack of eye contact*, and later with a lack of awareness of the emotions of others (called "mindblindness"). Without an automatic capacity for empathy, the child may rarely seek out other people for comfort and affection nor offer these to others when they appear distressed. Without theory of mind or a natural ability to understand perspective taking, another early sign of autism is *the absence of pointing* to engage the parent's attention, and later the usual "Look at me, Mom!" remarks. He may seem to *fail to share his enjoyment or achievements* with others.

Unfortunately the lack of inclination to be interested in what other people are interested in, to imitate, and to please, not only impairs social interaction but also spills over into the cognitive realm, as these are major motivators for learning. Add in the sensory integration issues that make a child withdraw from his environment, and motor planning challenges, and it's no wonder that children with autism fail to explore novelty, but rather restrict themselves to repetitive and stereotyped interests and behaviors that they can control, comprehend, and execute.

As Koziol and Budding (2009, p.144) put it, "Behavior resulting from damage to a particular brain region does not reveal the function of that brain region. Instead, the resultant behavior reveals how intact brain areas perform the behavior without the affected brain region's input or contributions." Consider a hypothetical child with autism at a carnival. Say his mother is trying to interest him in the merry go round. The sounds of the music and people talking are crashing in his ears, while bright colors are flashing by, and the crowd is jostling him. His cerebellum cannot coordinate all the sensory input to give him an integrated understanding of all the causes of the sensory bombardment he is experiencing. His basal ganglia cannot screen out all the background information and allow him to focus on his mother. And his lack of mirror neurons makes him unable to self-regulate by emotionally appropriating his mother's excited and happy responses. He doesn't have the language to express a desire to leave. What are his options? He may have a meltdown and scream and cry. Or he may try to control the situation by withdrawing into himself, covering his ears, and start humming and rocking to try to drown out the excessive external stimulation with his own internally driven stimulation.

As a toddler, if left to himself, Peter spent most of his time engaging in self-stimulatory behaviors ("stimming") such as flapping, jumping, squealing, and wiggling his fingers off to one side or the other of his visual field. It was as if he were entertaining himself by experimenting with different self-generated sensory stimuli, withdrawing into his own world that he could comprehend and control, as opposed to the unpredictable and incomprehensible outer world of his environment.

How did we eventually coax Peter out of this state of withdrawal? I discuss this further in later sections (see pp.84–95). For now, suffice to say we first simplified his environment, trying to avoid overstimulation. Then we started out with many repetitive, simple interactions centering round gratifying his sensory needs, such as swinging him up on our legs or squishing him in pillows. Eventually, Peter learned to associate pleasure with his relationship with us. Neurotypical children automatically reference their parents, using their parents' emotions to regulate themselves, and imitating their reactions to learn how to react to their environment. Peter eventually learned to do this, but only after we had worked hard to help him learn to enjoy us. My point is that a biological disadvantage does not mean that a capacity such as emotional connection with others or empathy cannot be learned and developed to a significant extent. But you must make this a constant, conscious goal in your interactions with your child. In Peter's case, that ability to connect with us became his bridge to the outside world, and the key to teaching him both to want to learn and how to learn about the world on his own.

CHALLENGES WITH COMMUNICATION

The other major deficit that defines autism is in communication. Both nonverbal and verbal communication is impaired. Some of the problem is related to the social deficits discussed above. Because of their challenges in processing facial expressions and interpreting emotions, children with autism are not getting all the expected information from their conversation partner's face. Because of their frontal and prefrontal cortical deficits, nor are they able to automatically empathize or guess the other's mental state in order to make a reply that is meaningful and interesting to the other party. This leads to difficulty maintaining a conversation back and forth (what speech and language pathologists call "pragmatics").

One study by Dr. Baron-Cohen, a pioneer in research on theory of mind, looked at a group of intelligent individuals with autism. They took an extensive course on theory of mind skills. To pass the course they had to pass a final exam to demonstrate reasonable skills in understanding how other people think and perceive things. However, to the researchers' dismay, they did not apply their newly acquired social skills in their daily lives (see Gutstein 2000, p.51). Without that automatic connection between sharing mental states and emotional gratification, there just didn't seem to be enough reward to put in all the effort required for socializing. That is why a key goal of therapy is to work to tie affect or emotional gratification in your child with his relationship and interaction with you. Without that foundation, social skills training will be meaningless to your child.

But the problem with communication can be even more basic. The part of the brain that processes auditory input and understands speech (called Wernicke's area—see the Glossary at the end of this book) may be much impaired. Although the child may be able to detect sounds well enough to pass a hearing test, left on his own, he may act functionally deaf. The sounds come in as "white noise," and the child can make no sense of language.

Furthermore, the part of the brain that controls expressive speech (called Broca's area—see the Glossary at the end of this book) may also be damaged; certainly in some functional MRI studies, it appears to be shifted from the left to the right side in some subjects with autism. Some children additionally have a severe speech dyspraxia with extreme difficulty coordinating all the complex motor movements necessary to articulate the sounds of language. Whether they are unable to clearly process the sounds they are hearing or perform the motor planning necessary to articulate, these children find even imitating monosyllables a major challenge.

Some children may also have auditory memory difficulties such that even if they learn to understand and say a word, they need prompts and cues to retrieve the word to use it spontaneously. Children with intact articulation but suffering some degree of impairment with word retrieval will often try to compensate with echolalia. Although they repeat the last part of what was just said to them, as if to say they are with you on the topic, they are unable to come up with their own words to reply. Others might use repetitive or stereotyped speech, lifting phrases or lines they've heard from TV, and applying them to their current situation. One such bright child with autism greeted his aunt at the front door with a line he had recently heard on a Barney video, saying, "Now, let the fun begin!"

CHALLENGES WITH EMOTIONAL REGULATION

Other areas of the brain that seem to function differently in autism include the regions that control emotion and memory (the amygdale, hippocampus, and temporal regions). Many individuals with autism suffer from fear and anxiety. They almost seem to have a heightened memory for situations that trigger such emotions. We call it "one time learning" for Peter, as he can develop a strong avoidance reaction if he has had even one negative experience, especially in a situation of high emotional relevance. For example, he used to love skateboarding at high speeds with his brothers' assistance, but after tripping once over a crack, he didn't want to go skateboarding again. When we do now manage to coax him onto the board, he makes a complete stop before that crack, and very carefully and slowly walks the board across it every time. As a toddler, he used to love to hike around his aunt's terraced back yard, but when he slipped once, he did not want to go into her garden again. We had to make many trips venturing into her back yard together carefully and slowly. We repeatedly recollected successful trips into her yard using photographs of our successful attempts, to rebuild positive associations. Eventually, Peter was able to enjoy exploring her garden on his own again.

Obsessive compulsive disorder (OCD) is a neurosis marked by compulsions to repetitively perform certain acts or rituals. It is very common in individuals on the autistic spectrum. Hence one child might insist on his mother driving the same route to school every day. Another might have to retrace his steps twenty times between the front door and the car. Another might throw a tantrum if the teacher changes the classroom routine. Deviance in expected routines or interruption of compulsive behaviors frequently results in massive meltdowns, with kicking, screaming, hitting, and sometimes even self-injury.

SUMMARY

This long list of brain differences and the challenges that ensue from them is daunting. Not all children on the autism spectrum manifest all of these features, and not all features are equally severe in degree. Children on the milder end of the spectrum have large areas of the brain intact. Early and intense intervention can remediate their deficits to a considerable extent. Children more severely impacted can also make great gains, but they may continue to require varying degrees of compensatory support in multiple areas. Remediation entails hard work and detailed, careful analysis. Determine which of your child's brain domains you can build upon as strengths. For the weaker areas, you need to determine what your child is capable of, and work up from there. Break down the skills you want to teach into tiny learnable steps. Isolate the problem you want to work on in learning tasks so that you are focusing on one area of weakness at a time. Provide enough repetition and motivation for the child to make the effort to learn, and work on all the different domains of the brain in concert to give him the building blocks he needs to make future progress. Challenging, yes. Lots of hard work, yes. Impossible, no!

Chapter 2

Attitude First

So now, take a deep breath. You know that your child has a very serious brain problem, and that it will not be easy to change, but the situation is not hopeless and you can help your child. Before you begin, I invite you to first look within yourself.

I had weathered what I thought were disappointments and difficulties in my life, but I never knew what the word "brokenhearted" really meant until Peter was diagnosed with autism. You see before you, every day, a beautiful child, so beloved, afflicted with a mind that is held captive, imprisoned, and bound by an implacable disorder. I don't know how many times my husband Vinh and I looked at each other in sorrow and dismay as we watched our child struggling with the simplest of tasks or skills, what our other children seemed to learn automatically and effortlessly. It's better now, but it still happens. With all the challenges our children with autism face, progress can seem to move at about the rate of a glacier. So how do you keep from getting discouraged? Battling autism is not like a one-time deal. Every day, every moment, you seem to feel the grief anew as you watch your child struggle, give up, or not even try.

> The Spirit of the Lord God is upon me, because the Lord has anointed me to bring good tidings to the afflicted; he has sent me to bind up the brokenhearted, to proclaim liberty to the captives, and the opening of the prison to those who are bound… to comfort those who mourn… Instead of your shame you shall have a double portion, instead of dishonor you shall rejoice in your lot…yours shall be everlasting joy. (*Isaiah* 61:1–2, 7)

I love the wording in the above quote from Isaiah. It matches my experience. Although I can't help but be brokenhearted, I do feel held together by that spirit of love working in the actions of all the good people who help me every day. Life is completely different after autism.

You have to learn to swim or sink. For me, learning how to swim meant living "by faith and not by sight" (2 *Corinthians* 5:7).

What does this mean? That I couldn't survive my child's autism on my own power. As another special needs parent once told me, "We're only human, but these kids take superhuman patience." She was right. Actually most parents would probably say that parenting is a very humbling experience because the child will push you to your limits and beyond, and make you realize how much you have to grow in patience, wisdom, and love. But as the challenges are magnified a thousand-fold in our children, it's all the more true for parents of children with autism that superhuman grace is required.

I feel like I live off of prayer—the hard-nosed scientist in me would have given up long ago. Many times, I've put on my doctor's hat and thought, "If this were my patient, would I continue treatment? Is there enough objective evidence that it is working? Haven't we given it a long enough trial?" But raising a child is not "evidence based." For me it's a matter of the heart and the spirit. So when I feel like giving up, I pray instead. And I am always surprised, and encouraged. It gives me that extra inspiration, that bit of intuition, that creative idea I need to get me through that next difficult step. If you embrace the task and keep getting up and beginning again and again, you will grow and learn. It's actually not a bad way to live, putting all your love and creativity into the present moment. You just do the best that you can, with what you have, with the time that you have, in the place that you are.

I say this to encourage you. The mountain looks highest as you stand at the foot, but once you start climbing, it's not so bad, just one step in front of the other. Try not to overthink this journey, and don't burden yourself with preconceptions and pessimistic projections into the future. Various people along the way, even professionals, may try to give you dire prognoses or get you to "accept reality," but the truth is that no one can predict what your child will or will not be able to do in the future. Disability, even mental retardation, is not a fixed entity. Keep attuning to your child and working at his pace, comprehensively, on all the different domains of the brain. Many children with autism seem to take two steps back for each one forward, but they really do make progress, and will surprise you with what they learn. Be patient. Learning is a funny thing. It doesn't always occur linearly. Sometimes you think you see little progress for eons, and then there is a big jump.

Perhaps what we are really grieving is the loss of our dreams of the child we hoped for. These are hard to relinquish. This is one place where you must try to be realistic and objective in order to best help your child. It may be very painful, but try to see your child's present abilities realistically so you can determine what he needs right now. You've got to work at his current level and set appropriate goals he can reach to make progress. I am always struggling to rein myself in and not charge ahead of my child. It seems Peter and I are always going back to the fundamentals of emotional attunement, regulation, and interaction, but that's where we need to be. If you do keep going back to the basics your child needs, your child will indeed build a strong foundation, making remarkable achievements in development possible.

There are a few more essentials I'd like to share with you as you begin your journey. The first is to give yourself enough time. Our children with autism take more time to raise—a lot more time. As another parent of a child with autism told me, "It is remarkable how much time one child can consume of your day and your life." Our children don't do things on schedule. They don't hurry. They march to the beat of their own drummer. They need more time to process, to interact, and to motor plan. You need to spend a lot more time planning everything you do. So from the beginning, be realistic and plan your life and schedule accordingly. If you schedule in too many other obligations and goals for yourself, you set yourself up for massive frustration, and may alternate between feeling guilty for not spending the time with your child that he desperately needs, and feeling resentful of your child for consuming more time than you have.

Be sure to pace yourself. You're in for a marathon, not a sprint. Reflect upon your schedule and make those hard choices to clear it so you have the time you need to take care of your child and to take care of yourself. In general people do not have any inkling of the amount of time and energy it takes to raise a child with special needs, so expect to have to gently educate them on why you must say "no," and claim your time firmly and unapologetically.

You can give only what you have, so take care of yourself, get plenty of exercise, and make time to be with your partner and other children. Time invested in maintaining close and joyful relationships one on one with the other members of your family is the best investment you can make for your child, because those relationships create the home and family he depends upon. We all need to refresh and restore. When you do decide to go out together, it's helpful to include the interests of the rest of the family as well as your child's in selecting activities. We've gone on many hikes, and spent a lot of effort trying to help Peter learn to swim and garden, because those are all activities my husband and I enjoy, and are ones we can do together over a lifetime. I've been taking him to concerts and church since he was tiny, and worked steadily on appropriate behavior in those settings so we can enjoy these activities together for the long run. Sometimes it works the other way too—Peter tried skiing in an adaptive program and loved it, so I have been trying to learn to ski as well. Putting in the effort to find common ground and nurturing those interests is a way to invest in your future together, while enjoying each other right now.

Second, don't put the expectation upon yourself that you can provide everything your child needs—remember the proverb, "It takes a village to raise a child." Remember that disability is a product of a mismatch between environment and ability. From the beginning, your goal should not only be to help your child to improve as much as possible, but to build a community of good people who can relate to, accommodate, and assist your child. In this way you will be developing an environment for your child so that his challenges are less of a handicap because of the support and understanding of the people in his world. Also, you personally will be in great need of the support over time.

My sister Jane told me several years ago that in prayer she felt inspired to help me with Peter once a week. True to her promise, despite being a very busy person, she has made time to play with Peter, his brothers, and me every Sunday afternoon. That precious hour or two a week has been a great encouragement. She is not an expert in autism, but that is not necessary. I know what to do with Peter, but for me, interacting with him often feels like hard work. So what Jane brings is that critical catalyst of a joyful, positive attitude and fresh energy. Together, we attempt to do much more ambitious games and interactions, and are able to involve Peter's siblings as well. She has become much closer to my entire family because she has been here every week, and she says she actually enjoys coming. Trying to help Peter gets her out doing things like biking and swimming, which she would not otherwise do. I believe she would say that Peter enriches her life. So will it be for the other friends and family you invite into your life. Do not be afraid of accepting help. You are not burdening others. Rather, you are enriching their lives.

Finally, I would ask you to forgive yourself. There will be many times you lose patience, even come "unglued." You may tell yourself over and over that you mustn't blame your child for his behaviors because you can see that they are due to autism. But even though I know that, when Peter breaks a delicate lamp by tapping on it, rips the stitching from the sofa by climbing on top of the backrests, or tears up a book or important paper, I feel very angry. The emotion of anger is there for a reason—to give you the energy to set things right. Eventually you will learn to use that energy constructively. You'll be able to reset your expectations, and therefore provide for the household modifications and level of child supervision needed. You'll learn how to do a "functional behavioural analysis" (p.307) to help your child meet his sensory needs in an acceptable way. You'll even find you can turn these kind of situations into opportunities to teach your child to recognize some basic emotions (such as "mad!"), begin to distinguish "bad" from "good," and begin to internalize limits.

In the meantime, when you feel your blood boil, take a few deep breaths. Try to get everyone in a safe place. If you have screamed or yelled or said terrible things, try to apologize to your child as soon as possible. Explain why you got angry, that you did not mean what you said, and that you are deeply sorry. Even if he doesn't understand all the words you say, he will understand your tone of voice and change of attitude. Ask for forgiveness. Then forgive yourself. Everyone makes mistakes, and every mistake is an opportunity to learn, even if the lesson is in reconciliation and humility.

A friend once gave me a card she keeps in her purse to look at whenever she starts a negative spiral of thinking. She is a very conscientious, hard-working person, and has the kind of mind that is always analyzing a situation. What happened? Why did it happen? What could I have done differently? What can I do next time? This kind of analysis is usually very useful, but she was often too hard on herself. She used to blame herself all the time when anything went wrong, which happened daily as her child also has severe autism. So her card reads, "Stop. Life happens. Change happens. Mistakes happen. Accidents happen. IT'S OKAY."

That's the last thought I'd like to leave you with in closing this chapter on attitude. Believe it will be okay. I know many a wonderful, heroic family dealing with autism, and have never met one who hasn't discovered a unique and lovable person in their child. My hope is that it will be a beautiful journey for you, full of love and faith. I hope that you will be given the wisdom, fortitude, grace, love, support, and resources you will need to help your child. May we have the humility and serenity to accept and love our children as they fundamentally are, with the courage and strength to work to improve what is possible.

Chapter 3

Observation
The Essential Starting Point

"Okay, Joyce, I want to see how you play with Peter. Feel free to use any of the toys in this room. Pretend I'm not here." Dr. Danis, Peter's developmental pediatrician, settled into a corner of the room and watched quietly. Peter was not yet three years old. I found a plastic mountain set, trains, and Little People dolls. I made up an exciting drama of a great race of dolls to get around the mountain. Dolls screamed and laughed, trains crashed and derailed, and there was a zany climax to the finish. It was brilliant! The only problem was that Peter just sat there. He didn't even pick up a train. Dr. Danis diplomatically said, "I see you like to create themes and stories." She smiled and went on with her testing.

It should have been obvious to me, but it was not. For successful interactions, you have to meet your child at whatever level he's at. At nearly three years old, Peter had no language. He did not have a natural understanding of competitive social interaction like racing. He didn't even like the loud sounds of the trains crashing. The drama I was performing in front of him had no meaning for him. You cannot reach your child if your play goes over his head. Therefore, good treatment starts with good observation. Your goal is attunement, to tune into your child and try to see things from your child's perspective. But what are you looking for?

ATTUNING TO YOUR CHILD'S PHYSICAL AND SENSORY NEEDS

The first thing to observe is your child's physical needs. All parents soon discover that you can't teach a child who's cranky because he's hungry, thirsty, cold, wet, tired, sick, or needs to use the bathroom. You have to take care of the basics, and you have to take care of your child's bodily needs so that he can be calm and attentive. However, our children present special challenges at this level.

First of all, they usually can't tell you what they need, so you have to guess based on observation and context (for example, how long has it been since he last ate or went to the bathroom, etc.). Second, they have unusual sensory profiles. You can't use yourself as a standard, but have to key into and anticipate your child's reactions to the environment. Furthermore, what is tolerable to your child one day may bother him another depending on his mood and circumstances. For example, the other day I was playing one of Peter's favorite children's music CDs in the car. I looked back in my rear view mirror, and noticed he was hunched over, cringing, with his hands over his ears. That particular day, his sound hypersensitivity was worse than usual. I turned the volume down, switched to a quieter song, and he was fine. I'm glad I checked that rear view mirror.

I've had plenty of experience where I haven't checked, with dire consequences. Peter may suffer in silence with noise, hunger, or whatever the unmet need, until he explodes in a tantrum. You can't depend on the child to even know what he needs, let alone tell you. Until your child develops the capacity to identify and communicate what his body needs, you will need to assist him in regulating himself. So get into the habit of tuning in and observing your child for his sensory and bodily needs, and anticipating them.

ATTUNING TO YOUR CHILD'S EMOTIONAL NEEDS

The next thing to observe is your child's mood, what I call "deliberate common sense." Use common sense to note your child's mood, and adjust your behavior accordingly. If your neurotypical child looks dejected coming home from school, you'll put on a concerned expression, and speak in a gentle and soothing tone as you ask what happened that day. A child running to meet you with a big smile, jumping up and down with excitement, will elicit a big smile from you and animated expression and voice.

Our children with autism just need more of this kind of help with "mood regulation." Because part of the disorder is to be out of touch with one's feelings, you can help your child by putting to words how you think he feels. If he's overexcited or upset, you can calm him with a quiet and soothing voice. If he's lethargic or withdrawn, you can gradually warm him up with your energy and "high affect" (big smiles, animated voice, and expression). So when Peter flops down on the couch after a hard day's work at school, it would probably be counterproductive for me to charge in with a booming voice and five different games I want to push him through. Instead I might say, "Oh hi, Peter! You look tired," and let him be for while. When I sense he's had a long enough rest, I might say, "Closer I come!" and sit closer and closer to him, until he might just find Mom lying on top of him pretending to sleep. That usually elicits a giggle, and an opening to warming up to some "people games" that we discuss further in Chapter 6 (pp.73–4).

You need to be "deliberate" about this kind of mood regulation, because it's easy to skip this step or hurry through it. Your more flexible and adaptable nonautistic children can bounce back on their own, and quickly pick up your mood cues and adjust automatically to them. Your more verbal nonautistic children will use words to get more help from you. Not so with our special kids. If you try to push onwards to the next activity without helping them regulate their mood first, beware! You are likely to run into resistance. Your withdrawn child might dive behind the couch and make himself impossible to extricate. Your overexcited child might start racing up and the down the hallways, literally banging into the walls. If you continue to push, you might get an outright tantrum, self-injury, or aggression. The behavior feels like hostility and rejection, but your child's behavior may be his only way to tell you he needs help at this basic level of emotional regulation. So get into the habit of deliberately observing your child's mood. Factor in the time it will take to calm down or warm up your child. Your investment at this step is critical for the success of your subsequent interactions.

OBSERVING YOUR CHILD AT PLAY

So say you've got your child in a regulating environment, meaning one in which none of his sensory channels is overwhelmed, so he can tune into it. Say you've got him warmed up and in a reasonably calm and attentive mood. Now you're ready to do some observations to assess his developmental level. Gather some toys in a quiet room for just the two of you. Choose toys that are roughly age-appropriate such as simple cause-and-effect toys like rattles, a jack-in-the-box, push-and-go cars, balls, balloons, and a blanket for an under-two-year-old. For the preschooler, add a set of blocks, a big car he can get in and use his feet to drive, dolls, puppets, or stuffed animals, and a set of little trains, cars, or play food/dishes.

Next spend some time quietly sitting and simply observing what your child does. Does he quickly narrow down onto one activity and repetitively play with that? Does he flit from one thing to the next, maybe picking up one toy briefly or tapping it before moving on? Does he manipulate objects with dexterity, and does he move and adjust his body position appropriately? Does he use the objects functionally, meaning drive or crash the little cars, set up the play food on plates, or bounce the ball, or just spin the wheels, and tap the other toys? Does he ever try to engage you to play with him, look back at you for reassurance, or to check if it's okay to pick up that doll or get into that car?

Next try to interact with your child. Does he try to move away from you, withdraw, or seem to ignore you? Does he ever look at you to see what you're doing, look at your face for your reaction, or follow your eye gaze? Can you join him in whatever he's doing and get any back-and-forth interaction (what Stanley Greenspan calls "circles of interaction"; see Greenspan and Wieder 2006, p.85), meaning you do something, and he does something in response? Does he try to imitate you such as shaking the rattle or pushing the ball or car? Does he try to get your help to repeat a pleasurable experience such as turning the crank on the jack-in-the-box? Can he coordinate actions with you (for example, hand you blocks as you build a tower), anticipate what's happening next (for example, giggle before you lift up the blanket he's hiding under in a game of peek-a-boo), or repair an interaction (for example, go and get the ball when you're rolling it back and forth and it gets away)? Does he ever initiate a variation of a back-and-forth game you've got going (for example, push the cars back and forth under the table instead of over the table)? Does he pretend to eat the food (as opposed to mouthing it because he's exploring it), or use toys symbolically, such as pushing a block as if it's a car? Does he use themes in his play where he is connecting ideas such as feeding the doll and putting it to bed, or "cooking" the play food and "eating" it?

Each observation will give you information on your child's strengths and challenges, and tell you what you need to work on. We now take each set of observations to see what they reveal about your child's developmental level.

How does he interact with his environment?

Watching how your child interacts with his environment alone helps you assess his attention. If he flits from one toy to the next without ever exploring or using it, he may have what Arnold Miller calls a "systems forming" disorder (Miller 2007, pp.24–5), in which the pull of the environment upon the child seems to turn everything into a distraction, and the child seems unable to focus on anything to make meaning of it. You may need to drastically reduce environmental distractions (closing the curtains, reducing the number of toys out, etc. so he can focus on you), and take the lead in pulling him into meaningful patterns of interaction with you. If he narrows down too quickly into a repetitive activity, he may have what Miller calls a "closed systems" disorder, and your best tactic may be to gently intrude into the activity to gradually and playfully expand and vary it.

If your child displays poor motor planning and doesn't shift his body position to access toys appropriately, or seems clumsy with manipulating them, he might benefit from physical and occupational therapy to work on his gross and fine motor skills, respectively. In the meantime, you will need to slow down to explicitly teach your child how to move and position his body and try to select toys and other materials that are easier to manipulate (for example, DUPLO® blocks instead of LEGO®).

Pay attention to the environment and where you position things, including yourself. Sitting at a 45 degree angle to your child often helps him to simultaneously reference you and the toy or book you are looking at together. It's worth the investment of time and energy to set up the room thoughtfully before a playtime session. Is there too much clutter, or not enough variety of toys? Are the toys easily accessible and the table and chairs the right height? Perhaps you could put a picture book and blanket on a beanbag in one corner, a train set in another, and several windup toys on the table. Presenting the toys in several distinct stations of different activities instead of one big heap on the toy chest may help to organize your child.

Next observe how your child plays with the toys. If he makes the car go or stirs the play food in the pot, you can play pretend games with themes and stories like crashing cars or eating in a restaurant. If he bangs, taps, and spins toys instead of exploring them to use them functionally, you know he's at an earlier developmental stage of thinking. You may need to create interactions around sensory experiences that he enjoys, and work up gradually to pretend play as he comes to understand it.

How does he interact with you?

Observing how your child interacts with you will give you information as to what developmental stage he's at socially. It's helpful to know what normal social emotional development looks like so you know what you're looking for. Development for neurotypical children begins with paying attention to you and regulating their emotional state with yours, such as, the baby cries, a parent soothes by hugging and speaking softly and reassuringly, and the baby calms down. Neurotypical babies seem to have an innate circuitry for looking at the human face, reading the emotion, and adjusting their own accordingly. If your child does not look back at you for reassurance or permission, you know you will need to spend time working with your child at this fundamental stage of emotional engagement. We go over the details of how to intervene in Chapter 6. You will learn how to woo your child by observing what gives your child pleasure, and creating situations in which you insert yourself as part of the pleasurable experience, slowing down your interactions, and accentuating and holding your emotional expressions (using high affect) so your child can process them.

After emotional regulation and engagement, neurotypical children learn what Dr. Stanley Greenspan calls two-way communication (Greenspan and Wieder 1998), and this is what you are looking for when trying to play with your child. Does he *respond* to your initiations? So you pull a blanket off your head, and a neurotypical baby laughs and giggles in response. Better yet, you put the blanket back on your head, and he *initiates* pulling it off.

The next stage would be *multiple circles of interaction*, where you alternate putting on and pulling off the blanket. The child may demonstrate *anticipation* by giggling before you lift the blanket off. As he progresses developmentally, you will see him taking on more and more of the work of the interaction. He may make *variations* by peeking out from different sides of the blanket. He may even start *repairing interactions* by reaching for the blanket to pull it back on when it accidentally falls off before you've had the chance to tug. If you're not seeing these kinds of interactions with your child, you know you will need to create simple games where he can practice all these kinds of skills repeatedly, but always playfully and with high affect, so the child will learn the joy of relating to you.

In later stages of development, the child learns to chain these circles of interaction into *solving problems* together, and coming up with his own initiations and variations. He learns that objects can be used for different purposes and functions, and starts using toys *functionally*, such as setting out a tea party of plastic food and pretending to eat it, and then *symbolically*, such as using a toy block as a substitute for a toy train or a banana for a telephone. Finally, he starts linking ideas *associatively* and then *logically*. If you're playing with the plastic food, he might think of taking out the toy cash register because he associates these with the grocery store. Later he might enjoy linking a whole series of actions logically and be able to play a game of pretend shopping with you, laying out the toy fruit and vegetables, selecting some in a basket, and checking out at the cash register.

INVESTING IN A STRONG FOUNDATION

Don't be disheartened if your child displays few interactive skills. I purposefully did not list the ages that nonautistic children reach these developmental milestones because development is not a race. Most of our children need a great deal of work at the very earliest stages of social and emotional development. Laying a solid foundation of emotional engagement, coregulation, and interaction can take many years. But it can be done.

Mastering the skills of each developmental stage lays the foundation for moving on to the next stage, and it is critical not to rush past or try to skip the basics. Observation will tell you what stage of development your child is at so you know where to begin in your play and what next stage to gradually aim for, step by step. You will not repeat my mistake—I was creating logical dramas with symbolic and representational play, when Peter had not even learned to complete one circle of interaction.

Instead you will use good observation as your starting point. It will become second nature to attune to your child's sensory, physical, and emotional needs. Through careful observation, you will be able to interact with your child at his level of development. You will learn to observe what your child is interested in as your starting point for engagement, thereby getting your child interested in interacting with you. Note what motivates him and how he learns best. Constantly observe his reactions to gauge his understanding and adjust your next moves accordingly. There will be more on how to do the adjustments as you read on (see pp.64–78). For now, the goal is to get into the habit of taking time to observe.

Chapter 4

Sensory Integration

My husband Vinh and I were playing with Peter. Peter's excellent floortime specialist was there for support. The room was a bit noisy because the TV was on quietly for another child. Peter spent the whole session mostly looking out the window, despite the high energy and affect of all of us "therapists." After the others left, Peter and I went into a smaller room. With his back to the windows, he did great with games we could not get him interested in only just before. I learned then the power of environment. You cannot fight Mother Nature, and you cannot fight windows and TV in the background.

Sensory issues loom large in the lives of our children. As discussed in Chapter 1 (see pp.22–4), individuals with autism typically have profound differences in the over- and undersensitivity of their sensory channels, and how the brain processes and puts together sensory information. The brain's ability to integrate all the information coming in from the various senses is frequently impaired. The result is a piecemeal understanding of the environment, which severely impacts a child's ability and desire to explore and interact. Taking in information about the world through the senses is step one in development. It is critical that you identify your child's sensory differences, accommodate and train them so that your child can learn.

WHAT'S IT LIKE FOR OUR KIDS? LEARNING FROM THE EXPERIENCE OF OTHER INDIVIDUALS WITH AUTISM AND SENSORY DIFFERENCES

Chantal Sicile-Kira (2008, pp.1–28) has an excellent chapter on sensory processing in her book *Autism Life Skills*. She includes many excerpts from adults with autism who have learned to communicate. They describe what their sensory processing feels like and how challenges in this area have impacted their lives. One young woman describes her visual processing disorder. She looks in the mirror and can only "see" one part of her face at a time as she deliberately focuses in on it. Another young man, when presented with light and sound at the same time, cannot even see the light unless it is presented a full three seconds after the sound. A child with visual processing issues uses his feet to feel each step as he descends the stairs because he cannot "see" the beginning or end of the step. Another young woman with both auditory and visual processing issues needs to concentrate all her energy to decipher the sounds of a conversation and translate them into meaning. If she also tries to look at the speaker's face, she gets mesmerized into trying to decode the ever-changing expressions and cannot understand what's being said. Another young woman says that without conscious effort on her part, voices just sound like running water. A man who finds light touch irritating gets anxious about people standing close to him because he is afraid they will brush against him. Showers feel like pin pricks on his skin. One young man with oral undersensitivity constantly put foreign objects in his mouth and chewed them.

The ability to process internal bodily sensations may also be impaired. One young woman could not distinguish being hungry from her bladder being full. It took over 40 years before she could sense temperature well enough to run a bath without scalding herself. Peter has taken over ten years to reliably know when he needs to head toward the bathroom.

These adults with autism talk about how they struggle to deal with their sensory processing disorders. Before she learned how to communicate, one woman recalled biting and screaming when overwhelmed with sensory information. During his junior high school years, another individual spent most of his mental energy just getting through the crowds to find his way to the next class. Another spoke about the impossibility of learning in a classroom with fluorescent lights which to her flickered like a disco dance floor, with the sound they made feeling like a dentist drill hitting a nerve. The good news is that many of their sensory issues did improve over time. They also learned strategies of how to accommodate their sensory differences, communicate to ask for help, and use their strongest sensory channel to learn.

ASSESSING YOUR CHILD'S INDIVIDUAL SENSORY PROFILE

Each child has his own unique profile of sensory differences. One child might be oversensitive to touch and have marked visual processing difficulties. Another might be undersensitive to movement and oversensitive to bright light and sound. You can spare your child some grief if you take careful note of these differences. Make a table of the five senses, and add in proprioception. The other sense to add in is vestibular, which detects rotation and movement of the body through space via receptors in the inner ear. Then make a note if your child is over- or undersensitive in any of these sensory channels.

Dealing with hypersensitivities

Children who are oversensitive will dislike or avoid stimuli to that sense. Hence a child who is visually oversensitive may avoid the sun and shrink away from bright light. Keeping a visor and sunglasses in his backpack, and using incandescent instead of fluorescent lights may be helpful. He might concentrate better in class with minimal visual distractions on the wall. If he's oversensitive to sound, he will cover his ears often and may appear distressed when the vacuum cleaner, blow dryer, or blender is in use. A quiet learning environment is essential. Put a pair of acoustic noise cancellation headphones in his backpack. Warn your child to put them on or cover his ears before turning on a noisy appliance or entering a loud environment. Children who are oversensitive to smell and taste may like bland foods and dislike perfume. Children who are oversensitive to movement may get carsick easily or show inordinate fear on escalators, steps, and slides. The child who is oversensitive to touch may be very picky about wearing only soft fabrics. Tags on clothes may need to be cut off. He may dislike sticky things like playdough, mud, or paint on his hands.

Dealing with hyposensitivities

Children who seem undersensitive to a particular sense tend to crave stimuli for that sensory channel. Additionally, some children seek sensory stimuli to help modulate sensory hypersensitivities. The child who has a vestibular hyposensitivity will seek out movement by jumping, rocking, spinning, or running back and forth. Such a child might need plenty of breaks to climb on a jungle gym, swing, or jump on a trampoline.

He might find adaptive gymnastics a satisfying source of recreation and exercise.

Children who are tactilely undersensitive like to tap,[1] enjoy long, big bear hugs, like to lie flat on the floor, and enjoy squeezing into tight spaces. Deep pressure, a weighted vest, a heavy blanket, sleeping bag, or body sock are comforting. A child like this may enjoy helping you carry things, move furniture together, and play games where he gets wrapped up in blankets like a human burrito or squished between beanbags and pillows like a human sandwich.

A proprioceptively undersensitive child may enjoy isometric exercise breaks, pushing his palms together with both elbows pointed outwards, doing standing pushups against the wall, doing sitting pushups pushing down on hands placed on either side of the chair and lifting the bottom off the seat of the chair, or hanging from a bar. A resistance band tied across the front legs of his chair will give him something to put his foot behind and pull up against.

Build upon your child's strengths and support his weaknesses

It is equally important to note which sensory channels are the strongest. Many children with autism are visual learners. They learn better by seeing things rather than by hearing them. They do better when spoken language is paired with written language and pictures, and may be attracted to picture books and videos. But not everyone with autism is a visual learner. Some children have profound visual processing difficulties, and do better with auditory instruction. For the hands-on learner who loves to push buttons, swing doors back and forth, and touch all the walls and furniture, using a lot of tangibles and tactile materials while teaching may be helpful. Experiment with teaching your child using different modalities, and try to figure out which sensory channel is the best learning channel for your child. A combination may be best, with one kind of processing supporting the other, as long as you give enough time for the child to take in all the information.

Some children are practically "monochannel," meaning they can only focus on the information coming in from one sense at a time, so if you present information in too many ways at once, it might be overwhelming. The key is to SLOW DOWN the rate at which you present information, so that the child can process it at his speed. You might need to present

---

1   Tapping may also be a way to seek auditory and proprioceptive sensation.

information through different sensory modalities in sequential layers instead of simultaneously (for example, show a picture of a dog for a few seconds before you add the barking sound of the dog). Observe for feedback and understanding before you introduce something new, and adjust the pace of teaching to the child's processing speed.

Some of your child's sensory challenges will change over time—some sensory issues may improve with maturation and training. Occasionally an individual may develop talents as an adult in what were areas of difficulty in childhood, such as Donna Williams (Sicile-Kira 2008, p.12), who had auditory processing difficulties as a child but now composes and plays music. Peter had such severe auditory processing difficulties that he appeared functionally deaf as a toddler. Then as a preteen he developed a marked oversensitivity to sound. Nonetheless, with a lot of training, his auditory processing has developed to the point where it sometimes supports his visual processing (see Chapter 9, pp.123–5; Peter sounds out words in order to write down their spelling). It's not a good idea to make assumptions about a developing child. It's better to continuously adjust your sensory accommodations based upon open-minded observation.

DEALING WITH THE INSATIABLE SENSORY APPETITE

Accommodating sensory differences is a balancing act. There are some children who seem to benefit from "sensory diets" or regularly scheduled breaks of sensory activities, such as swinging, deep pressure, and bouncing up and down on a large ball. That may be helpful in some children, but may lead to a craving for more and more in others. Sensory seeking may evolve from a need to a habit to a compulsion. How do you distinguish a sensory need that you need to accommodate from a habit you might want to work on inhibiting?

Often, you need to do what in medicine we call "an empirical trial." That means you try out a treatment based upon a presumed cause, and if it works, you figure you probably guessed it right. If it doesn't, you figure you guessed wrong, and change course. (This is commonly known as "trial and error"!) Therefore, to figure out if sensory seeking is a need versus a habit, try accommodating it, and see if that helps or not. Many stims decrease with direct occupational therapy using a sensory integration approach, especially when the child is younger. The other measure of whether accommodation is working is how well the child is able to concentrate and perform in his work and other activities afterwards. If stims decrease after a sensory break and the child focuses better, you probably guessed correctly. The stimming is due to a sensory need, and you should continue your strategy of sensory accommodations.

If your sensory accommodations don't seem to reduce sensory seeking or improve concentration, you can't immediately assume that your child does not have a sensory need. The first step is to make sure you are providing the right accommodation for the particular sensory system at issue, at the right intensity. Many children need structured sensory breaks, not just "free play" in order to benefit. An occupational therapist can help you design an appropriate sensory diet. If a child has high needs, it can be valuable to take long breaks at appropriate times such as before school starts, during recess and lunch, and right after school to see if greater time and intensity meets the sensory need. Try timing a structured sensory break right before activities that require more effort and concentration to see if it prepares the child and prevents maladaptive behavior. The key is to really watch and determine if the child is now able to come back and do the work. If so, this type of sensory break is appropriate.

However, children frequently resort to sensory seeking not because of a primary sensory need but because they feel stressed emotionally or physically for some other reason, such as illness, a perceived excessively high demand, or an overstimulating environment. Providing the sensory stimulation the child seeks in these situations may not hurt, and may actually still have a role in soothing, but must not delay or distract you from addressing the primary reason for the distress.

What do you do if sensory accommodations are not working, and instead seem to be feeding a sensory habit that keeps growing? What if you are doing your best to provide plenty of exercise and structured breaks targeted correctly to the sensory need at appropriate times and of sufficient intensity, and your child still constantly wants to stim, to the point of distracting him from work and other activities?

Sometimes the trick is to be aware of the context in which you are providing the sensory breaks. If your child is stimming and not focusing during circle time, and the aide takes him out for a sensory break, he may learn to stim more at circle time as you have reinforced that behavior by rewarding him with a sensory break. However, if you use the sensory break itself as a reinforcer (for example, telling the child he can take a five-minute break on the swings if he does some achievable number of math problems), then you might see some decreased stimming during work as the child tries to focus to get it done.

If you feel stimming has become a habit or compulsion, interfering with his work and overall progress in learning, is there a direct way to work on inhibition? One useful strategy is to reward progressively increasing periods of abstinence from sensory activity. Start by taking a morning or two to record the child's baseline. On average, how long does the child last between sensory breaks? Once you've determined how many minutes he can work at a time, gradually increase that time period by a few percent every day until you hit a reasonable "recess" frequency. For example, say your child needs a sensory break every 20 minutes. You might set a timer with a promise of bouncing him on a big ball when it goes off. Set the timer for every 20 minutes the first day, then 21 the next, and 22 the next till you hit your goal of, say, working straight through a 30-minute session.

My son had such severe sensory seeking that I had to start with asking him to inhibit it for just one-minute intervals, having my son check off boxes every time he made it through a one-minute hourglass (with a tiny pretzel), and giving him the sensory break he craved after checking off ten boxes. At this point, Peter understands that he is supposed to inhibit stimming while working. If he stims, we stop working and do a learning readiness "Three–Two–One" countdown (see Chapter 8, p.101). We only continue working once he's inhibited his stims and gathered his focus back. He's highly motivated to get on with and complete his work because of the reward he knows is coming at the end (which frequently is a sensory break). My point is that even the child with the most insatiable sensory appetite may improve over time if you persistently and consistently work at it together. (For more strategies on managing this common problem, see Chapter 15, pp.310–22.)

DESENSITIZATION VERSUS ACCOMMODATION

One more word on sensory differences—you can gradually "desensitize" a child over time *to some degree*, and should make a reasonable attempt to do so. For example, children who are extremely picky eaters can gradually expand their list of edibles by having new foods introduced gradually, a morsel at a time, to be quickly followed by a favorite food, with imperceptibly increasing amounts in subsequent meals and less frequent reinforcement. It's best to try this at the beginning of a meal when the child is hungriest, with foods that are closest in texture and taste to those he prefers.

The tactilely hypersensitive child may find playdough initially too sticky, but tolerate plasticine. If he gets to like sculpting shapes in plasticine, he might be willing to experiment with small bits of playdough, perhaps to add a few finishing touches to his plasticine sculpture in a favorite color that's only available to him in playdough. Fingerpainting might be too overwhelming, but he might be willing to try a paintbrush. If he likes art, he might gradually learn to tolerate a little paint on his hands.

It's a generally known fact that stimuli are perceived differently depending on many factors, such as emotional state, expectations, and distractions. A junior high school kid getting tackled in football may claim it doesn't hurt, but complain loudly when his big sister punches him in the arm for teasing her. Therefore, if you want to try stretching your child's capacity to tolerate some kind of stimulus, try doing it in a relaxing, friendly environment in the context of putting up with it in order to do something highly motivating. A child who hates vegetables might tolerate a few if cut up cleverly to create a happy face on a pizza that he puts together himself. Peter loves classical music so much that he enthusiastically goes to concerts with me, even though he needs to wear his noise cancellation headphones to turn the volume down. He puts up with the amplitude of sound because he enjoys the quality of the sound (music).

How much you bend over backwards to accommodate and how hard you try to desensitize is a balancing act. We spent a great deal of time and effort sitting at the kitchen table with Peter stretching his ability to tolerate a healthy variety of foods by waiting for him to consume morsels of new foods before offering preferred foods. Peter's teacher struggled for a while to try to move him out of an isolated but quiet side room into a cubby in the main classroom. He was able to get through some of his already mastered academic exercises ("maintenance activities") in the new setting, but could not learn new material well. The teacher moved him back into the quiet side room. In that case, we decided that his energy was better spent learning than fighting to filter out background noise.

Indeed the first thing to consider in a session during which your child just can't seem to learn is sensory processing. You might also have to break down your teaching into smaller steps, but first rule out sensory distractions; you may then need to present information through another stronger or additional sensory channel.

PASSING THE BATON TO YOUR CHILD

It takes constant observation and vigilance to monitor the environment and your child's reaction to it. Eventually, you will be able to anticipate problems and plan your environmental manipulations and accommodations. You might be asking yourself if you need keep this up forever. The answer is yes and no. Unfortunately, sensory challenges may last a lifetime. Your child may be operating at high levels of logic and reasoning some day, and still experience meltdowns because of unanticipated, overwhelming sensory bombardment. If you remember to return to working on these primal sensory needs at those times, you may help your child to calm down a lot faster.

The goal, however, is for your child to eventually develop self-awareness and take over the work of anticipating environmental sensory challenges and proactively accommodate for them. With that end in mind, teach your child how to do this by explicitly commenting on your thought processes and actions as you accommodate your child's sensory profile. When you notice your child not paying attention to his lessons because he's staring at a bright window, say, "I see it's hard to pay attention when that window is so bright." Then walk over and close the blinds, or better yet, teach your child how to close the blinds or move his seat so his back is turned toward the window. The next time, you might ask your child, "I see it's hard to pay attention when that window is so bright. What can we do about it?"

Children have an inherent incentive to learn how to accommodate for sensory hypersensitivities. Peter is oversensitive to sound. When we first bought him a pair of noise cancellation headphones, we were unsure if he'd tolerate them since he dislikes putting anything on his head. But when he tried them in a noisy environment, he was so pleased with the result, that he quickly learned how to take them out of his backpack on his own as needed (see p.168).

Following are some commonly used accommodations for auditory and visual processing challenges. In the beginning, you will be doing the hard work of tuning into your child's sensory differences and accommodating for them. It takes effort because you can't use yourself as the standard—you need to constantly think of how your child would perceive the environment. But with practice, serving as your child's sensory filter will become more second nature. As your child develops more language and thinking skills over the years, however, don't forget that your goal should be to teach your child how to anticipate and accommodate his sensory needs on his own. Self-awareness is a key to future success.

Accommodations for auditory and visual processing challenges
Auditory processing disorder
Individuals with auditory processing disorder have difficulty making sense of information taken in through the ears although hearing is intact.

Suspect when the child:

- has difficulty with hearing and discriminating the sounds in language
- has trouble paying attention and remembering information presented orally
- needs more time to process information
- can't carry out multistep directions
- has difficulty with language, vocabulary, and spelling.

Accommodations:

- Reduce unnecessary, distracting noise in the environment (for example, fluorescent lights, humming from computers, close the door to eliminate hallway noise). Adjust the volume. Provide seating up front to allow the child to watch the speaker's gestures and face, and to read the board easily. Provide noise cancellation headphones. Consider getting an assistive listening device such as an FM system for large meeting rooms (a receiver with headphones and a wireless mic for the speaker that transmits the speaker's voice directly through the headphones while eliminating most extraneous noises). Ask people to speak one at a time.

- Provide multimodal teaching including visuals, demonstrations, and hands-on learning. Provide assignments, directions, and other information in writing. Communicate with emails and text messages as opposed to phone calls. Use the closed captions (subtitles) option when showing videos or watching TV.

- Provide agendas, notes, and textbook chapters for students to preview ahead of time.

- Slow down the rate of speech. Allow for processing time. Simplify what you say—use shorter, simpler sentences and vocabulary. Cue prior to asking questions or giving directions. Give directions one step at a time; post directions and provide checklists. Paraphrase rather than repeat when the child doesn't understand. Frequently check for understanding (for example, "Can you repeat back what I just said?"); request feedback. Use gestures.

- The first step is getting an audiological exam (hearing test)!

Visual processing disorder

Individuals with visual processing disorder have difficulty making sense of information taken in through the eyes although vision is sharp.

Suspect when the child:

- has difficulty tracking, such as frequently losing his place when reading, taking a long time to copy from the board, following the ball in sports, or following the course of an animal running or flying when viewing nature

- has difficulty with visual discrimination, meaning he misses visual details or has difficulty recognizing letters, numbers, symbols, words, and pictures, especially when the print is small and the page is busy

- misses the overall concept in a picture and has difficulty recognizing the important information in assignments and tests

- feels confused or agitated working with material that is too visually stimulating, such as too much on a page or too many posters on the wall

- has problems with gaining information from pictures, charts or graphs

- asks for verbal directions despite the presence of clear written directions

- has poor visual memory, meaning he can't remember what he sees.

Accommodations:

- Reduce visual distracters. Choose picture books with simple line drawings instead of busy artwork. Use enlarged print with less information per page. Some strategies include covering all but one line with blank paper, cutting a window in a sheet of paper, or using a ruler to follow text. Use note cards with short blips of information on them, rather than long, detailed paragraphs. Put one word list or poster up on the child's cubby with the information he needs to concentrate on for that day, and change it as needed. If you put up too much, he'll ignore all of it.

- Highlight important information more prominently. Use simplified worksheets.

- To make visual tracking easier, add more structure to a paper with darker or raised lines.

- Provide multimodal teaching including lots of auditory support, demonstrations, and hands-on learning. Pair visual information with auditory input, record lectures, and use books on tape or textbooks on CD.

- Request information by telephone instead of email or text messaging.

Chapter 5

Motor Planning

Our local YMCA has a circuit room of simple exercise equipment that works out one muscle group at a time. By the time you've finished using the dozen machines or so, you've exercised your whole body. Peter is always seeking out pushing and pulling movements, so I thought he might enjoy the gym. When I first took Peter, I demonstrated how to use each machine, and then let him try. I was astounded at the number of incorrect ways the machines could be used.

Instead of flexing and extending arms or legs, Peter's whole body would attempt to rock back and forth to move the levers. The weights would return to baseline position with a loud clang with each repetition. The wrists doubled back as his biceps flexed to lift a bar. The only way to get both Peter and the equipment through a circuit without major damage to either was for me to continuously "spot" and coach. I would hold his back to the backrest to prevent his torso from rocking. I held out my hand as a marker for Peter to reach so he would know how far to move a lever. I would chant a rhythm "slowly back!" and put my hands over his to teach him how to let a weight back down without losing control. I used my hands as splints to keep his wrists straight while he flexed his biceps to move a lever up.

Even in gross motor (large muscle movement) activities, what is intuitive and simple for neurotypical individuals may require explicit instruction and support for our kids.

THE MYSTERY OF DISORDERS OF MOVEMENT AND MOTOR PLANNING

Other parents have echoed my experience. Chantal Sicile-Kira (2006, pp.96–7) writes about having to teach her son Jeremy since he was a baby how to do even the simplest motor tasks such as getting into a sitting position, crawling, and putting his arm out when pushed so he wouldn't fall over. When he was older and trying to learn how to push the buttons on the microwave, he told her that he understood what to do, but could not get his body to follow through. Tito Mukhopadhyay (2003), another remarkable individual with autism who learned how to communicate through typing (see pp.23 and 27), described how he knew that his hands were made of voluntary muscles, but when he tried to order his hands to pick up a pencil, they would not obey. Both individuals made progress when their mothers rapidly motored their limbs through the physical movements they wanted to teach, repetitively, for up to several hours at a time (with breaks).

Arnold Miller (2007), in his book *The Miller Method*, describes a child who was having difficulty learning how to gesture for her mother to come to her, despite many attempts by her therapists to teach her the simple sign. Dr. Miller suspected the problem might be a motor output problem rather than a comprehension problem, and had her practice pushing phone books off her body to learn how to intentionally use her arms and hands. After learning that she could use her arms purposefully to affect her environment in this way, she was finally able to use her upper limb to gesture "come," and have her mother come to her.

We know that many areas of the brain work in concert to affect movement. The motor cortex of the frontal lobe gives the command, the cerebellum coordinates the muscles, and the basal ganglia plays a role initiating and terminating actions. Yet movement is still a mystery. There are dozens of neuromuscular disorders in neurology, and different diagnoses within the autism spectrum have associated movement disorders to varying degrees. For example, Asperger's syndrome is associated with clumsiness. Nonverbal learning disabilities are commonly associated with poor balance and motor coordination. Childhood disintegrative disorder is associated with a loss of motor control. By and large, however, no one really understands the exact physiologic deficits that cause our children such problems with controlling their bodies. One young woman with an insatiable urge to flap and tap poignantly told her father she wished he could spend just one day in her body to understand how it felt.

That being said, the good news is that for most children with autism, gross motor function is relatively spared. In general they walk, jump, and run around, although more complex movement may be problematic. They may need a lot of work on motor planning, meaning explicit teaching on how to sequence their actions with lots of repetition. Complex sequences such as riding a bike or swimming may take much longer to teach than for nonautistic children, and require much more intensive and persistent instruction.

PRACTICAL TIPS ON IMPROVING MOTOR PLANNING

Improvement comes with practice. It's worth trying to get your child involved with some kind of sport. Just as you'd do for a nonautistic child, expose your child to a variety and see what he seems to like. Many children with autism shy away from team sports because of difficulties with processing speed, coordinating actions with teammates, and anticipating the opponent's next move. Individual sports may be less frustrating. My son enjoys the sensory feedback he gets from swimming and gymnastics. He has a naturally good sense of balance and enjoys skiing and biking.

You need to start early while your child is small enough in size to be physically assisted and supported. Frequent practice is essential to acquire motor memory. Don't get discouraged when your child seems to take one step back for every two forward. Lapses in motor memory are common and do not mean learning is not possible. The key is patient repetition and persistent practice. Remind yourself that development is not a race. In the long run, it doesn't matter if it takes your child longer to learn yoga, swimming, or riding. The goal is for him to have some form of exercise that he can enjoy and practice lifelong for his physical health. If you can manage to maintain a steady, positive, nonjudgmental attitude, your child may surprise you with what he can accomplish.

Do not assume that your child is being lazy or uncooperative because of seeming inconsistencies. Peter can climb to worrisome heights up trees or on the roofs of play structures, but until recently, he could not hang from a bar. I learned the consequences of unrealistic expectations from an incident at the park when he was five years old. Peter became enamored with the zipline. The problem was that he would not hold onto the bar tightly. I had to close his fingers around the bar and hold onto his body while walking across to the next platform.

I could not understand why Peter would not hold onto the bar himself. I thought I'd let him learn by natural consequences and let him fall. We tried again, and he still fell. It was not a big drop to the rubber mat below, but it hurt enough to destroy Peter's interest in the zipline. I still remember the puzzled look he gave me when I let go of his hands, so that he dropped to the ground. It was as if the thought dawned upon him that Mom would not always protect him. Instead of learning to hold on tighter to the bar, he learned it was dangerous to try something new. It took many trips back to the park with lots of encouragement to regain Peter's trust that I would support him on the equipment.

Possibly because of their cerebellar and proprioceptive deficits, many of our children have a lot of difficulty with motor planning, including gauging how much force to use to accomplish an action. Strangely enough, the problem seems worse if they think about it. Peter had no difficulty holding onto tree branches as he climbed out of my reach. But when instructed to close his hand around the zipline bar and hold on, he couldn't. Similarly, Peter likes yoga, but it takes a lot of effort for both him and me to get him into a yoga posture correctly. However, when we go hiking, he gracefully boulder hops and positions his body fluidly and effectively without thinking. The situation seems analogous to stuttering—people stutter more when consciously making an effort not to. So when unsure if your child's difficulty is organic or due to poor effort, in general you'll be right in giving your child the benefit of the doubt.

Fine motor control refers to skillful use of the small muscles of the hand. Most of our children receive occupational therapy early on to work on holding a pencil, using utensils, cutting with scissors, etc. Give your child lots of opportunities to practice. Bake with your child and let him knead, roll, and pinch the dough. Make thick dark lines on paper for your child to cut along, and roll your strips into loops for a colorful paper chain. Fold some laundry together and teach your child how to make a ball of socks. Preschool manuals are full of great ideas for improving fine motor skills (see Myers 1992, for example).

Knowing how to move your own body is essential for a child to initiate and act upon the world. We need to empower our children with lots of opportunities to learn how to do that. Lots of rough and tumble play is great if your child enjoys and tolerates it. Playgrounds provide lots of opportunities for swinging, climbing, jumping, kicking balls, sliding, and pouring (sand). Make it fun by taking turns pushing each other on the swing, jumping and climbing together, or pretending to "get" your child, in slow motion of course, so your child is successful at getting away. If your child enjoys playing with balls, simplified soccer and basketball are great, and for the slow processor, balloons naturally move in slow motion. Creating obstacle courses with fold-out tunnels or futons, chairs to climb over, and tables to crawl under provide gross motor fun indoors. The great thing about working on gross motor skills and body awareness is that most of the time the activities provide their own inherent sensory reinforcement—that is, they provide their own "payoff" or motivation that grabs the child's interest. In fact, because they are inherently fun, these kinds of activities provide outstanding opportunities to also work on problem solving and social interaction goals. More on that in Chapters 6 and 11.

Chapter 6

Engaging Your Child (How to Get Your Child to Play with You)

It was time to play, and I had set up several stations of toys in the family room. Peter, however, firmly planted himself in the rocking chair and started rocking. My heart sank as I noted the averted gaze and watched his feet determinedly push hard back and forth against the ottoman. The floortime coach tried to coax him into looking at the other toys and games, but Peter wouldn't even look up at her. I said a quick silent prayer and braced myself.

I quickly removed the ottoman and replaced it with a big sofa seat cushion. Peter pushed it with his feet. I sat opposite to Peter, caught the cushion with my feet and pushed it back. Peter kicked it back. After several rounds, I started chanting "tick-tock" as we kicked the cushion back and forth. After we had a rhythm going, I substituted a large exercise ball for the seat cushion, continuing the same chant. The floortime coach positioned herself diagonally. We worked her into the game so that we were kicking the ball around rhythmically in a triangle. We varied the pattern to alternate kicking the ball to Peter.

Occasionally, I would miss my target so Peter would have to reach over to retrieve the ball, giving him the opportunity to repair the interaction. After a while, we substituted balls of different weights, sizes, and numbers, trying to get up to kicking around three balls simultaneously. At the end, we transformed the action into pulling Peter by the arms and draping him over the big exercise ball and letting him walk out with his arms as far as he could go. He was moving! He was smiling! We even finally got him out of the rocking chair, ready to try something new.

Getting your child's attention has got to be one of the hardest parts of parenting a child with autism. Although you may tell yourself over and over that his apparent lack of interest in you is not personal, but just part of his autism, it's still painful. And it's still hard work. But steel yourself! It will take fortitude, but I have lots of tricks to share, and you will succeed. If you keep practicing, and never give up, your child will come to not only pay attention to you, but also love being with you and want to interact with you.

REMEMBER THE ESSENTIAL PRELIMINARIES

Start with observation and attunement. Quickly go through your mind all the contextual things. What has he just been doing? How's his mood? What does he seem to be interested in doing right now? Before you try to engage your child in play, attending to some preliminaries may be in order. Take care of bodily needs first like hunger, thirst, using the bathroom, being too hot or cold, or needing to lie down for a nap or rest.

FINDING YOUR WAY IN: CAPTURING YOUR CHILD'S INTEREST

Once your child is in a reasonably calm (therapists call this "regulated") and alert state, you're ready to play. Set up the room with a few toys. I use the principle of "limited choices," meaning I only put out toys that I can imagine building an interaction around. For example, a ball, balloon, and train and track set open you up to more interactive possibilities than a Game Boy® or pogo stick. Sit back and give your child a few minutes to relax and explore. Nonautistic children are naturally motivated by social interaction. Not so with autism. To motivate your child to play with you, you need to tie interaction with you to something that is naturally motivating to the child. Therefore, follow his interests. If he gravitates to a particular toy and gets interested in playing with it, there's your chance to enter his world.

If the object of interest is a ball or balloon, then it's pretty obvious how to enter your child's activity. Sooner or later, the ball or balloon will get away from him, and you can start by graciously fetching it to hand it back. Ever so gradually, you might have the child use more effort by making him reach a bit to get the ball out of your hand or have to take a step or two forward to get it. Eventually you might try rolling the ball back a short distance. You might stretch your arms open wide with an animated expression and see if you can entice the child to roll the ball back. The key is to insinuate yourself bit by bit, interfering, interrupting, or obstructing your child's solitary activities playfully and tactfully to entice him to respond purposefully to your initiations.

When you do something (such as roll the ball to your child), and he does something back (such as roll it back to you), this is what Dr. Greenspan calls one "circle of interaction." In *The Child with Special Needs* (1998) and *Engaging Autism* (2006), Greenspan and Wieder give detailed descriptions on how to do "floortime" (otherwise termed "DIR" for a "developmental, individual-difference, relationship-based" approach). The goal is to play by building more and more circles of interaction around the child's natural interests.

Once you get a pattern going such as rolling the ball back and forth, keep going as long as the child finds it fun and interesting. When you sense that you need to "spice it up" to keep the child's interest, you can add variations. A helpful mnemonic to think up variations is PLOP (Miller 2007), for position, location, object, and person. Using our ball example, start passing the ball from behind you or between your legs standing facing backwards. Shift your location between each pass to move in a circle round your child. Switch between different size and weights of balls or try to substitute rolling a truck instead of a ball. You could ask a sibling or other parent to join the game, or make a stuffed animal "come alive" and ask to play.

In our example at the beginning of this chapter, at first Peter only seemed interested in rocking his feet against the ottoman. Therefore, I playfully interrupted by substituting a big sofa cushion. We added "tick-tock" to aid motivation, as rhythm and music usually have a positive emotional impact. I varied my location, introduced different balls, and included another person. We ended by transforming the action from using our feet to roll the ball to rolling Peter on a big ball.

Let's take another example. Say your child starts "stimming" off of a little toy train by spinning its wheels repetitively. One approach might be to sit next to your child and hold up another train right next to his, and start spinning its wheels. If the child glances over at you, smile and wink and offer your train's wheels for the spinning. If the child brushes the train away, at least he's responded. Your train might protest, asking for the child to spin its wheels. It might creep closer and closer till it jumps into the child's hands, as your other hand deftly removes the child's original train that lands on your head. This maneuver will hopefully be met with a smile and a reach to retrieve the train, which could lead to a number of circles as you vary the landing spot of the child's train to various amusing locations (your head, your pocket, behind your back, etc.). You could pull back a little so the child has to reach farther for that train on your head. A few circles later, try taking a few steps back so your child has to walk over to get the train. Try working up to getting him to have to chase you down short distances to get that train.

Remember when we talked about children with "closed systems disorder" (see pp.25 and 43–4), who get obsessed with an activity such as lining up cars or opening and closing a door? The "overattention" of these children, their intensely focused interests, may actually provide opportunities for interaction. Edge into your child's attention by first perhaps copying what your child is doing, and then playfully obstructing him. For example, have your line of cars cross your child's line of cars, or "accidentally" get stuck in the door he's repetitively opening and shutting (Greenspan and Wieder 1998).

But what if your child has more of the "systems forming disorder" (see pp.24 and 43–4) when it comes to attention? Greenspan and Wieder have a clever game where you pretend you're a fence blocking your distracted child as he flits from toy to toy. They say not to be discouraged if the child gets irritated with you, pushes your arms away, or ducks. At least you've had a meaningful interaction, and the child has done some problem solving.

This is true, but when Peter was a toddler, he was so determined to withdraw and run away, that we could only get in so many circles of "playful" obstruction before it was not fun for either of us. He also had very severe language deficits and such limited interests that most of the time he seemed to just want to run back and forth and squeal or rock and tap. He had little purposeful activity and few interests, and there seemed to be little to work with.

WHEN THERE ARE NO MEANINGFUL INTERESTS: CREATING THEM WITH CIRCUITS

This is where I think Dr. Miller's (2007) insights are very helpful. He noticed that many children with autism seek an "edge" experience. Possibly because they are constantly trying to define themselves in space, they tend to explore the edges or periphery of a play yard. They collide into walls, one after another, or squeeze their bodies through narrow spaces. Miller thought to make use of this natural interest in exploring boundaries and simultaneously focus the child's attention in a highly defined space. Hence he created the elevated square, a microenvironment made of four wide pillars two-and-a-half feet off of the ground connected by four 14-inch wide planks with a removable small staircase and removable slide attached. Being elevated off the ground seemed to focus and direct the child's attention. It also dramatically reduced toe walking, flapping, or other self-stimulation behaviors. He made a work station at each pillar, with each consisting of an inherently interesting, simple activity such as pouring water into a bucket or dropping a coin through a slot into a metal can to make a nice clinking sound. Going from station to station created circuits of activity for the child to do.

Start the child at the first corner station. A parent, standing at the second station, gestures, "come," and hands the child a cup. The therapist, standing at the third station, gestures "come," and prompts the child to dip his cup into a bucket of water. At the fourth station, where the parent has moved to, the child may get to pour the water over a water wheel, or pour water back and forth into the parent's cup. Before long the child learns what he's supposed to do in the circuit, and is enjoying joyful smiles and congratulatory comments as he's successfully pouring water back and forth. Voilà! You've got the child engaged and paying attention.

Then you're ready to add variations to challenge and interest your child. For example, instead of simply handing the child a cup at the second station, hold the cup off to the side or up or down to make the child have to reach for it. Similarly, you can vary the position of your cup when pouring back and forth at the fourth station to make it more fun and challenging. You and the therapist could switch positions periodically so different people are interacting with the child at different stations. The therapist could step back from the third station and see if the child knows the circuit well enough to initiate filling his cup himself without a prompt. Obstacles could be placed in the child's path so he would need to kick or push them out of the way. A big shower cap could mysteriously appear over the bucket so that the child would have to problem solve to get the cover off. Instead of using cups, try using pots or big ladles or even a sponge on a plate.

Instead of using an elevated square, you could create your own circuits on the ground, providing interest by being lively and animated. In your circuit include a "payoff," an activity your child inherently enjoys, such as a favorite sensory experience like pouring water, tickling, swinging, or knocking down a tower of blocks. Use masking tape on the ground, beanbags and pillows on the floor, and move the furniture in such a way to create visual boundaries. Initially the stations might be placed in a square-shaped formation, and then randomly. Once the child is engaged and having fun interacting, you can use the circuit to stretch your child in all kinds of ways. You could put a heavy object on top of the lid on the bucket so your child has to coordinate actions with you to lift it off. Pause and wait so that the child anticipates and initiates the next step. You could lay out different containers to pour with together and allow your child to choose which to use. Turn your back or duck and hide behind a station at a step you know your child will really want or need you (like getting the heavy object off of the bucket). That way your child will have to tap you to get your attention or look for you. The variations are endless. Remember "PLOP"—vary position, location, object, and person (Miller 2007).

The key is to have fun. Do lots of nodding and smiling. Wait for eye contact and give your child time to problem solve. Keep the pace or rhythm of the game going with prompting when the child gets distracted or lost. Spotlight the climax of the game (pouring water back and forth) with a joyful, "We did it!" comment and high fives. Work on that "edge" where the child is challenged but successful so he is learning while having fun.

The most helpful aspect of the play circuit to me has been the structure, or framework. When you are working with a child with very little repertoire and few interests, the circuits suggest or provide your child with meaningful responses. If your child has very little initiation or purposeful activity, you can create a pattern of activity that you think he will enjoy. My experience has been that Peter may take a while to "warm up" to the play activities I put into the circuit. I may have to give a lot of instruction (therapists call this "prompting") at the beginning, but he usually does finally enjoy it as he learns the pattern, and starts anticipating the fun "payoff" activity at the end.

HOW DO YOU TEACH YOUR CHILD HOW TO PLAY THE ACTIVITIES IN THE CIRCUIT?

So how do you provide the instruction, or prompting? What do you do when your child doesn't come when you gesture, or know how to pour water back and forth with you? The most important thing you can do is to wait. Some parents actually count to 45 seconds (which may feel like a very long time). I have actually done that, and sometimes waited even longer. But usually, I base my timing upon observation. You want to give your child enough time to process, but not enough to get "lost." If he starts wandering off or "stimming," I realize he's become distracted or forgotten what we were doing. Time your prompting and keep the pace going to avoid that. It's tricky, but you will get the hang of it with practice. It's like a dance between you and your child—the more you practice, the better the two of you will get at capturing one another's rhythms.

So, after an appropriate pause to give your child the opportunity to respond on his own, how do you instruct or prompt your child? Prompting is an art. The goal is to provide just enough support to enable the child to learn how to do something eventually by himself. Thus you provide help, but at the mildest level necessary for the child to succeed. Upon subsequent repetitions, provide less and less strong prompts, until you can withdraw help, thereby providing the opportunity for your child to perform independently.

The word "scaffolding" conjures up a very helpful image, and the term is used to describe this kind of instruction, support, cueing, and prompts given to the child to assist him in maintaining an interaction. Imagine you are building a structure. (In fact you are building an internal organizing structure in the child's brain.) You provide enough scaffolding to support the work you're doing at a particular level, and constantly remove scaffolding as you complete your work. It is just as important for you to remove the scaffolding as you go as it was to provide it in the first place. Providing the scaffolding enables the child to build that internal structure, but from the beginning your goal should be to gradually remove it. Withdraw support as slowly as necessary to allow for adequate consolidation or mastery. Keep moving in the right direction, or instead of becoming more independent, your child will learn to become "prompt dependent," and will come to see your prompt as an inherent part of the activity. Therefore, the longer you provide unnecessary scaffolding, the harder it will be to withdraw it.

How do you withdraw scaffolding? Fortunately, there is a systematic way. All autism teaching methodologies provide some kind of "order of prompts." The box that follows details a very helpful schema adapted from ABA (see Cooper, Heron and Harard 2007, pp.401–4; Millenberger 2004, pp.198–206; Palafox 2006) but which is generally applicable to all kinds of instruction. It's worth reading it, but the general gist is that it is common sense.

Primer: The art of prompting

The greatest and most intrusive degree of support is called the physical prompt. In our earlier example of the water pouring circuit, a physical prompt might be assisting the child to pour water hand over hand, that is, wrapping your hand around the child's hand to show him how to hold the cup and pour it. Lesser degrees of physical prompting include placing the cup into the child's hand and letting go to let him pour the water out, and less still would be tapping the child's hand with the cup to remind him to pick it up.

The second highest level of prompting is demonstration. Show the child how to hold the cup and pour it by demonstrating the action yourself, and then offer your child a turn. Alternatively, another person (preferably a peer) demonstrates the response or next step you want the child to take. For example, if the child reaches the water pouring station but forgets what he is supposed to do there, the therapist and a neurotypical sibling could pick up cups and pour water back and forth, smiling and demonstrating how fun it is. Then the sibling could offer her cup to the child to carry on.

The third degree of support is the gestural prompt where you might just point to the cup to remind the child to pick it up and pour with it, or lesser still, look at your child to grab his attention, point to the cup with your eyes by gazing at the cup, then look back at the child to make sure he got the message. This is called the "three-point eye gaze." It's a great nonverbal communication tool to aim to teach your child to use, and a marker for what therapists call "joint attention."

The fourth level is a verbal prompt. Some verbal prompts are stronger than others. "Action-oriented directions" are direct, simple imperatives such as "pick up the cup." These kinds of directives are useful when the child is struggling with motor planning, and can't seem to get the body to move. If motor planning is not an issue, however, the goal is to move down to a milder verbal prompt, which models a more respectful way of speaking. Gutstein (2000) promotes the use of declaratives instead, like "Let's pick up the cup," or better yet, "That cup looks good for pouring," or even better yet, "I wonder what we could do with that cup." Such language is both more respectful and inviting, as long as the child has the language capacity to process it.[1]

---

1   Using declarative language in conversations with neurotypical individuals has been shown to elicit more initiative and lengthier and more robust responses than questions.

Many therapists would reverse the order of gestural and verbal support for highly verbal children, who might find the verbal prompt easier to attend to, so the therapist might use that as the greater level of support and fade it to gestural to make the child attend to nonverbal body language.

The fifth level of prompt is the proximity/location prompt where you place the item you want the child to choose closer to him. For example, if the child gets to the pouring station and starts aimlessly self-stimulating (flapping or squealing), you might pick up the cup and place it deliberately in front of him. Modifying size can also be considered a proximity prompt. Make the cup you offer your child reasonably large and perhaps brightly colored.

The sixth or least intrusive prompt is making use of "previously learned responses." In the example of the water circuit, just repeating the circuit over and over provides a prompt for the child to learn what to do next. If a child is writing a story and trying to remember how to spell a certain word that you have previously helped him with, pointing to that word he previously correctly spelled on the page as a reminder to refer to it would be a previously learned response prompt.

Speech pathologists frequently make use of previously learned receptive language to prompt expressive language in their students. For example, say the speech pathologist asks the child what a toy dog wants to do next, and the child has difficulty retrieving the words he needs to answer. The speech pathologist might use words the child has previously learned receptively by asking, "Does the dog want to eat the bone?" The child might nod or say, "Yes." Then, when the speech pathologist asks, "What does the dog want next?" the child is more likely to be able to answer, "The dog wants to eat the bone," because he has just heard the words he needs in the previously presented question.

Think of how you go about teaching naturally. If the task is completely new and difficult for your child, you might put your hand over your child's hand to show him how to do it. This is called a "physical prompt." If the task is less demanding, you might point or gesture. This is called a "gestural prompt." If the task is easier or more familiar, you might just tell him to do it. This is called a "verbal prompt." When teaching your child a new play activity, you might start off with a physical plus verbal prompt. Upon the next repetition in the play circuit, you might try a gestural plus verbal prompt. On a subsequent turn, you might try words alone, or gesturing alone. With enough repetition, with an appropriate pause to wait, the child might just do his part on his own without any prompting. The beauty of making circuits or play patterns is that the child has multiple, predictable turns to practice and learn his response so that he can master it. If you keep on highlighting the payoff step with smiles, high fives, and a lively, warm tone, your child will come to anticipate taking his turn with pride and joy.

HELP ME! I'M NOT THAT CREATIVE!

Fortunately, Gutstein (2002a, 2002b) has produced some excellent manuals that are full of creative circuits that work your child up from learning to engage through higher and higher levels of relationship development. (These take place on the floor for the most part, not requiring an elevated square!) His books detail innumerable games you can play with your child that use the fun of gross motor/sensory stimulating activities to entice your child into a circuit of playful interaction with you. Some favorites include sitting face to face with your child, holding hands and pushing and pulling back and forth, playing airplane, "flying" your child on your knees, swinging your child on a beanbag with an adult on either end onto another pile of beanbags, and building beanbag mountains together and sliding down them. The goal is not to learn the game; the games just provide a structure or framework for you and your child to work on coordinating actions and nonverbal communication, and the real emphasis is on the shared enjoyment of the interaction, in other words, to have fun together! The smiles, hugs, high-fives, and warm glances are what you go for.

Fern Sussman (1999), a speech and language pathologist, proposes lots of what she calls "people games." These are physical games in which the parent is the main toy. You can play "up, up, up" and "down, down, down" as you lift your child up and down, horsey, chase, tickle, and tug of war. They give the child lots of opportunities to tell you what to do, such as go "up" or "down," what body part to tickle next, or to "stop" or "go" when playing horsey. Both Gutstein and Sussman's books are organized by developmental level, so it's easy to find games that your child can do. If you just keep practicing, playing with your child will become second nature. When your child demonstrates particular interests, you will be able to think up your own circuits to build around them. Your child will be so used to associating you with fun that he will readily engage. Playing and interacting will then become spontaneous and integrated into your daily life, so that you can do, as Greenspan puts it, "floortime anytime, anywhere."

FLOORTIME VERSUS RDI VERSUS HANEN PROGRAM: HOW DO YOU CHOOSE?

I should make some clarifications here. What I teach in this chapter is actually a blend of several methods. As previously mentioned, Greenspan's method is called "floortime" (see p.66). His emphasis is on following your child's lead in order to harness the motivational power of your child's interests. His central insight is that emotion is ultimately the engine that motivates a child to make the effort to interact, learn, or communicate. In other words, if you want to motivate your child to do something, you must make it meaningful to him. A child is much more likely to learn what "a lot" means if you are giving him a choice between "a little" or "a lot" of cookies. He's much more likely to try learning colors if he's naming colors in order to select the next color M&M® to get from you. He'll want to play with you if you're playing a game he likes.

Gutstein's method is called RDI, relationship development intervention. Like Greenspan, his method tries to build that neural connection in the brain between pleasure and playful interaction by using high affect (the smiles, whoops, and high fives), and including activities that are inherently enjoyable to your child (such as swinging your child in your arms, pouring water, or blowing up a balloon). He adds Miller's insight about using circuits to provide structure and repetition. His genius is in creating a diverse array of fun circuit activities to work on different interactive skills for all levels of development. Some of these skills include coordinating actions, referencing eye gaze, using head nods, and anticipating actions (more on this in Chapter 11, pp.171–7). All these fundamental skills require hard work and lots of repeated practice for our children to learn, so Gutstein has designed the games to focus on one interactive skill at a time.

RDI is parent-led rather than child-led in the beginning, to get the child used to making the effort to tune into the parent. Once the child masters following play patterns, he is encouraged to initiate variations within the pattern, and eventually to transform and co-create new patterns of interaction on his own. In other words, the child starts out having to tune into the parent, but eventually they take turns taking the initiative.

I found starting out by establishing the expectation that Peter had to follow my lead was very helpful in breaking through my child's compulsive, repetitive, and self-absorbed play. That expectation helped draw him out of his "stimming" into a play circuit. As the "hook," I always included some kind of rewarding sensory or gross motor experience (swinging, tickling, jumping, etc.). Looking forward to the "hook," Peter would put up with the rest of the circuit. With enough repetitions, he would gradually warm up and end up enjoying all the activities in spite of himself.

Sussman's Hanen Program uses the same concepts of incorporating your child's interests, tuning into each other, and providing plenty of repetition and turn taking. Her emphasis is on using opportunities in play to elicit communication. For example, in the previously described elevated square circuit, the parent could hold the pouring objects and wait, requiring the child to request the one of his choice. If the child is unable to come up with the words himself, he could be prompted with a choice, such as "red cup or blue cup?" or "big cup or little cup?" If the child can't imitate sounds, you could have him point to a picture of a red versus blue cup, or big versus little cup, or teach him how to sign for red or blue, big or little.

In other words, don't worry about deciding between floortime, RDI, or Hanen. Just practice their common principles of attunement, including your child's interests, insisting, and supporting your child to take his turn, creating circles and circuits of interaction, and making it fun. Work in language demands, but not so many that it disturbs the rhythm and fun of the interaction. Follow your child's lead whenever possible, but be ready to create a framework of play around his interests should he start getting disorganized. Take a look at the books recommended here (see the References section at the end of the book), and pick out the games and ideas that look appealing for your individual child.

Leading versus following

So do you follow your child's lead à la floortime,[2] or insist your child follow your lead, à la RDI? I would say the answer is both. To interact well, your child has to know how to both follow and initiate. Emphasize one or the other to balance your child.

If your child is assertive with lots of ideas and interests, following his lead could potentially be very motivating for him. However, if you see the interaction deteriorating because he stubbornly follows his own drummer, and doesn't include or build off of your responses, at least take turns in leading. When it's your turn to initiate the play, insist your child learn how to stay with the pattern so he learns how to follow.

If it's too confusing for your child to switch between leading and following, I recommend you follow Gutstein's advice, and insist the child learn how to follow first, and gradually take on more of the initiative in the context of fully engaged interactions with you. Otherwise your floortime sessions may consist of following a child around the room as he ignores you. Your primary goal is to draw out your child from his self-absorption into a world of interaction and communication. Explain to your strong-willed child that playing is fun only when you can both follow and lead. He's already good at leading, but needs to work on following. Once he's good at following (this might take months of consistently practicing being the follower), he gets to take turns leading again. You can still include his interests by creating play circuits around activities and toys he likes (it's best to choose activities that are enjoyable but not yet obsessions). If you are able to keep insisting and practicing, he will eventually learn that following is also fun. You might even expand his interests.

If your child is passive, and rarely initiates, following your lead provides content. You can expand his repertoire by teaching him new activities that he has to get through to get to the fun payoff activity. But whenever this type of child initiates even the tiniest of meaningful variations on his own, be alert and prepared to encourage it by transforming your play pattern to include it.

TO TALK OR NOT TO TALK: HOW MUCH DO YOU DEMAND?

Play is indeed a great opportunity to teach language naturally. However, be careful to introduce speech demands in the right way and at the right

---

2   Actually, floortime is not only about following a child's lead, but really aims to create reciprocal, balanced interactions. Its emphasis on enticing a child to take the initiative is a worthy long-term goal.

time. This means that you must wait until your child is fully invested in the game and willing to put forth the extra effort to give you language. If you demand words that are "too hard," meaning too difficult to articulate or perhaps not introduced or taught before, you might tip the balance of work and fun to too much work, and your child may withdraw.

And remember that understanding body language is not automatic in children with autism. As 70 percent or more of communication occurs nonverbally, it is critical for children to learn to both understand and use gestural communication. Nonverbal communication skills include following another's eye gaze, natural eye contact to reference faces for feedback and information, understanding and using gestures like pointing, waving, and raising one's hand, orienting and positioning the body to show attention, and interpreting the emotional meaning of facial expressions and body postures (happy, angry, sad, etc.).

So at least in the beginning, talk less and act more. Allow your child to invest his energy in consolidating his newly learned skills in gestural communication. Allow him to repeat those play circuits nonverbally many times, and have fun doing it before even considering the introduction of new speech demands. As always, observation is the key. Meet the child where he's at, and make additional demands only when you see he's ready for them.

SUMMARY

What are the steps to engaging your child? First comes observation. Assess your child's sensory and physical needs and accommodate them. Attune to his mood, and buffer his emotions with your tone of voice, gestures, and facial expression.

Once he's in a "regulated" state, meaning calm and ready to pay attention, observe your child to see what he's interested in. Set up the room to eliminate distractions like TV, bright windows, and clutter. Put several toys or materials for other activities out like crafts or books in order to offer your child some choices.

If your child "forms his own system," meaning, he engages himself in an activity, you can join in as described by Greenspan and Wieder (2006), by copying, gently intruding, and playfully obstructing and then expanding the child's play with variations (think Miller's "PLOP") to create multiple circles of interaction. If your child is aimlessly engaging in self-stimulating activities, assist him to form a meaningful circuit of interaction by introducing a pattern that culminates in some intrinsically fun, usually sensory and/or gross motor activity like pouring water, knocking a tower of blocks down together, crashing cars or sliding them down a ramp or a poster tube, rolling your child in an accordion fold-out tunnel, flying paper airplanes, letting the air out of a balloon, or swinging (which can be done without a playground with two adults holding on to either end of a sturdy beanbag upon which the child is sitting).

Use the order of prompts to support your child through the interaction. Systematically withdraw scaffolding to move him toward responding on his own. Wait an appropriate time to give your child the opportunity to take his turn. Pair high affect and verbal praise or encouragement with every pleasurable, reinforcing sensory experience to spotlight the fun and to help your child develop the desire for social interaction he was not born with. In other words, you develop emotional bonding, engagement, and attunement by constantly pairing social interaction with fun and pleasurable experiences.

Conversely, when your child gets emotionally dysregulated and has a meltdown, try to help your child associate you with affect regulation, meaning calming down and feeling comforted. This is much easier said than done, however. It might be helpful to start with a checklist in your head of unmet physical needs including hunger and pain (which may come from a hidden medical problem like heartburn, headache, constipation, or toothache), and frustration from working too hard or too long. Consider lowering the difficulty of your demands so your child can feel successful, offer more help, or give more breaks. Whether you end up comforting your child with soothing words, distraction, or just being there, every time you successfully help him ride through an emotional storm together, you put "money in the bank" in terms of building trust. Building positive affective memories between you and your child is how you build the foundations of both social interaction and emotional regulation.

Before we go on to discuss the development of affect (emotional) regulation and social interaction, we need to look at building cognition. The different domains of the brain should not be worked on in isolation, but need to be built together, as progress in one depends upon the other. The development of language and cognitive skills such as problem solving, categorization, ordering, and sequencing will greatly enrich social interaction. Conversely, emotional regulation, engagement, and joint attention are prerequisite to and serve as the motivational engine for cognitive learning.

Chapter 7

Building Motivation

SPECULATING ON THE NEUROLOGICAL BASIS OF WHAT MOTIVATES US TO LEARN

Let's step back a moment and reflect upon how a child learns. Siegel (2003), in her excellent book, *Helping Children with Autism Learn*, points out several inborn tendencies of neurotypical children that motivate them to learn. They have a natural affiliative orientation, meaning they are drawn to be interested in what other people appear interested in. They naturally tend to imitate what they see others doing, and have an inborn curiosity and desire to explore the identity and function of novel items and activities.

The first two motivators may have something to do with those prefrontal cortical mirror neurons that appear to fire when a primate observes another acting, such that the observer appears to be practicing in his own mind what that other actor is doing. At least in humans, the firing of these mirror neurons is apparently accompanied by a consciousness or realization that the experience is only vicarious, and an automatic understanding that different minds perceive and experience things differently. Because of the reward of vicarious experience and the understanding that it can be enjoyed through sharing the experiences of others, affiliative orientation and imitation are natural behaviors in neurotypical individuals. The mirror neuron theory may serve as the neurological basis for "theory of mind" and explains what makes social interaction inherently interesting and motivating to those without a deficiency.

The third motivator, curiosity, also has a neurological basis. Curiosity requires the neural connectivity to seek the *Gestalt*, or big picture, of the purpose of things, and also the motor planning skills to explore. These two capacities are also deficient in children with autism.

So does that mean that the learning motivators are broken in children with autism and cannot be fixed? Is it possible for children with autism to learn to want to learn? The good news is that some of these tendencies can be developed and strengthened, at least in part by a backwards approach.

Building affiliative orientation

Let's take the first motivator, affiliative orientation. Is there a way to get your child to become interested in what other people are interested in?

As discussed earlier (see Chapter 6), if you constantly pair interactions with you with fun sensory "payoffs" in your activities and circuits, your child will gradually associate you with fun. Therefore, he will learn to be drawn to you. Being interested in you, though not the same, is certainly a big step closer to being interested in what you are interested in. Even neurotypical children tend to learn better from teachers they like and have a good relationship with. The importance of that relationship is just so much more important to children with autism in motivating them to make the effort to learn.

Peter loves his primary tutor at school so much because of all the fun and affectionate interaction she provides. He so looks forward to the tickles, clapping games, smiles, hugs, and praise with every effort and each step he progresses, that he loves to get to work. I now believe that because he has experienced the satisfaction of mastery and accomplishment, he has truly learned to love to learn, even apart from her reinforcing interactions. He shows real pride when he's finally got a new concept down, looking up at us with a big smile and happy sounds. All the different tutors and specialists who work with Peter are impressed with his readiness to learn, and that he's such a hard worker. But I am quite sure he could not have got there without his tutor's constant pairing of the warm happy feelings of interaction with learning. His love of learning started with his love for her.

Building imitation skills
USING DISCRETE TRIALS TO JUMP-START IMITATION SKILLS

Can you teach your child to imitate? You can certainly teach your child how to go through the motions of imitation. The discrete trial method of teaching uses "tangible reinforcers," such as tiny pieces of edible treats, stickers, or a minute or so to play with a favorite toy to motivate children to perform imitation exercises such as "touch nose," "stand up," "sit down," or "clap." For example, give the instruction, "Touch nose," and go through the order of prompts (see "Primer: The art of prompting" in Chapter 6, pp.71–2) to get your child to touch his nose. When he does it, reward him with a tangible reinforcer. Because he wants the reinforcer, your child will probably fairly quickly learn how to "do this" or imitate your action. Discrete trial training (DTT) can certainly "jump-start" teaching your child how to imitate.

MOVING TO INTRINSIC REINFORCEMENT

However, to teach your child to want to imitate on his own initiative requires that the payoff be intrinsic or inherent to doing the imitation. For example, say the therapist places a parent at one end of the room, and stands at the other end with the child. The therapist gestures with her hand for the parent to come, and the parent comes, delivering a big hug and smile to the child. The parent returns to her spot at the opposite end of the room. The child may then be motivated to imitate the therapist (perhaps needing to start with a hand over hand, following the order of prompts) so the parent will come again to give him a big hug and smile.

Take another example. Say you get your child to imitate you in building a block tower. If when completed the two of you get to knock over the tower together and say "crash!" with lots of whoops and laughter, then the child will see the "payoff" in imitating you. He learns that imitating can be fun, and may be more inclined to put in the effort to imitate your next block tower. Similarly, if the child is imitating you build a simple LEGO car (get two sets), be sure to spotlight all the fun in playing with the car together at the end, so that the child sees the point of imitating. Highlighting the rewarding consequences of imitating you doing all different kinds of activities is how you teach a child to want to imitate.

WHY YOUR CHILD MAY NEED TO TASTE THE REWARD FIRST

Neurotypical individuals without mirror neuron deficiencies may feel some of the satisfaction or pleasure you feel on task completion just by watching you, and thereby feel motivated to imitate what you did to get there. A child with autism, however, may need to be helped to go through the steps and experience the reward himself before he sees the point of imitating what you just did. If you pair this process of imitation with satisfaction repeatedly, your child will learn that imitation is usually rewarding. He will come to imitate you more readily and automatically, without necessarily having to taste the reward first.

USE BACKCHAINING TO REMIND YOUR CHILD OF THE REWARD IN IMITATING YOU

Even once your child starts imitating more spontaneously, keep using the concept of *backchaining* for motivating him to imitate longer task-oriented sequences. Backchaining is when you do the initial steps of the sequence yourself, and have your child just imitate the last one or two steps, so that the motivating "payoff" of task completion is readily achieved. That way the child understands quickly that imitating the sequence is worth the effort. Then gradually lengthen the number of steps the child imitates before the payoff.

Cooking is a great opportunity to practice backchaining. Your child will quickly learn the value of imitation as long as you are making something you know your child enjoys eating. You might start out with a very easy recipe like making Gatorade, a sports drink, from Gatorade powder. All the child has to do is imitate you scooping up a big spoonful of Gatorade powder and then stir it into a glass of water. If that is too hard, do all the initial steps and just have the child stir and drink. If the child can do the last step, back up one more step and have the child spoon in the powder, stir, and drink. Once he's got that down, have him imitate you pour water into the glass, spoon in the power, stir, and drink. At the very end, have him imitate you get a glass, get a spoon, pour water into the glass, spoon in the powder, stir, and drink.

Try longer recipes like making a peanut butter sandwich or fruit smoothie. Your child will learn to tolerate imitating more steps before he tastes the reward as you backchain increasingly longer sequences (for example, making a fruit salad, putting together a LEGO car, or puzzle with more and more pieces). Don't forget to compliment your child on his persistence and patience as you celebrate eating or playing with the results of his hard work.

Facilitating curiosity

Theoretically the way to "teach" curiosity might work similarly. The starting goal is for the child to own the idea that exploring objects is fun and rewarding. But how do you get your child to "explore"? Your child might need direct teaching on how to use all his senses in identifying and understanding objects, paired with modeling how enjoyable it is. Gather up some simple cause-and-effect toys and lay them out on the floor to explore together. Some good choices might be squeeze toys, windups like a moving train or jumping mouse, toy instruments, and cause-and-effect toys which work by the child pushing a button or pulling a lever to produce a sound or make a popup toy appear. Others include see-and-say wheels, jack-in-the-boxes, "busy boxes," and a simple flashlight. Follow your child's lead and see what he reaches for. Let him spend some time figuring out how to use each toy. If he figures out how to use the toy on his own, celebrate his success with high fives and hurrahs.

The next step is to help expand his exploration of the toy. For example, if he figures out that the stuffed bear has a string to pull that makes him talk, you can also demonstrate how cuddly and soft the bear is, how fun he is to hug, and how you can move his arm to point to his string as the bear asks to have his string pulled. You might notice how hard and square that jack-in-the-box toy is, and how it might be fun to rap on his lid and listen to the sound that makes, or try shaking the box to make the clown come out. While it is delightful to pull the lever and listen to the sounds of the see-and-say wheel, there are also colorful and funny pictures to examine. You could put a few of the toys in a pillowcase, and see if the child can reach in and find the square toy or the soft toy or the squeaky toy.

The vegetable garden and kitchen are natural multisensory exploratory laboratories with opportunities to taste, smell, and explore all kinds of textures. Tracing letter shapes in a layer of sticky pudding, squishing dough, pouring rice, or shaking beans in a can are typical preschool activities that invite sensory exploration. Living room sofa cushions and bedroom futons, blankets, and pillows offer opportunities to explore big and little, in and out, shapes, sizes, textures, putting caves and tunnels together and reconfiguring them, and problem solving as tunnels cave in and pillow "debris" happens to obstruct passageways.

CAN YOU FIX A BROKEN MOTIVATOR?
Intensive intervention helps many children

If you constantly provide experiences for your child that pair imitation and exploration with positive natural and social consequences (smiles, hugs, high fives, etc.), can you expect your child to develop his own innate desire to imitate, explore, and look into what others are interested in? Even if you pour in all this effort, is an apparently broken motivator ever truly fixable? I don't know of any studies that directly answer this question, but there is some indirect evidence that interventions that work on motivation and initiation do result in global developmental gains. Greenspan and Wieder (2006, p.381) cite that out of 200 children diagnosed with autism whose families brought their children to Greenspan's center to receive intensive DIR/floortime intervention (many also used other teaching methodologies in addition), all but eight showed significant progress in global emotional, social, and intellectual development scales, with 58 percent having "good to outstanding" outcomes.

Hope for the slow to progress

But numbers won't mean much when you're feeling discouraged. What if you've been doing your best to draw your child into high affect interactions, but he continues to lapse into perseveration and withdrawal? Is there anything more you can do for your child who seems to be falling outside that 58 percent of "good to outstanding" outcomes? What do you do with a child with very limited natural interests, other than the pull of sensory seeking and self-stimulatory behaviors?

What follows is a more detailed explanation of motivational strategies for such a child. The principles actually apply to teaching all children, but for those of us with children most highly impacted by autism, we need to go back to them time and time again. I am convinced that my son would have qualified for Dr. Greenspan's most severe type IV category of NDRC (neurodevelopmental disorders of relating and communicating)— the aimless and unpurposeful child who has the most severe challenges in all processing areas with severe difficulties with shared attention and engagement unless they are involved in sensorimotor play. These children tend to make very slow progress.

But very slow progress does not mean progress is not possible. By doggedly applying the motivational principles that follow, Peter has come a long way, step by tiny step. Concentrate on getting your child motivated to do that little step you want him to take right now. No matter how little motivation he displays for what you want him to do, insist on some effort. You can make that next step as tiny as need be, but make it an opportunity for success. Celebrate those little victories, even when they occur fortuitously. Your child just might develop a taste for success.

MOTIVATING HIM TO TAKE THE NEXT LITTLE STEP: WHAT DOES THAT LOOK LIKE?

Say you're holding a box of crackers, and your child wants one. Show him the sign for "more" (touching the fingertips of both hands together repeatedly). He continues to pull on your arm instead of signing "more." Put your hands over his, make him sign "more," and then celebrate, "You signed 'more'!" as you hand him a tiny piece of cracker, just enough to whet his appetite. He eats the cracker, then pulls on your arm again. "More?" you ask, as you demonstrate the sign again. Say he accidentally brushes his hands together as he lets go of your arm. "'More!' You signed 'more'!" you say excitedly, as you do another hand over hand demonstration to pair the correct action with the word, and hand him another cracker.

Perhaps the next time, you forego the hand over hand maneuver, and just demonstrate the "more" sign. Over time, with many repetitions, your child will realize that making the sign for "more" is associated with getting more crackers, and he will purposefully bring his hands together spontaneously to get a cracker.

> The other day, my husband Vinh and I were practicing for our upcoming ballroom dance class on the kitchen floor. Peter was watching us dance the rumba from a distance. My husband caught him looking at us out of the corner of his eye, and invited Peter to join us. To my delight and surprise, he eagerly came over. I used masking tape to make a square on the floor to give him a visual reminder as to where to put his feet. I put his arm around my waist, took his hand, and started moving my feet. Peter imitated the steps perfectly. He wanted to learn the rumba! He laughed with delight, and intently followed my steps. He had learned the fun of imitation. Another time we danced, he spontaneously initiated a turn, lifting his arm up abruptly, looking into my eyes, and ordering me, "Turn!"

It only took ten years to get there, but Peter did learn to be interested in what we were interested in (affiliative orientation, see p.79) and to want to imitate. Let's take a look at the principles of motivation that got Peter to love to learn, and that may get your child there too.

PRACTICAL PRINCIPLES ON HOW TO MOTIVATE YOUR CHILD

The following principles have been compiled from several teaching methods, including floortime (Greenspan and Wieder 1998, 2006), pivotal response training (Koegel and Koegel 1995), the Hanen Program (Sussman 1999, 2006), and ABA (Cooper *et al.* 2007; Fovel 2002; Leaf and McEachin 1999).

The first step: Getting your child's attention

Half the time, the reason Peter gets an answer wrong is because he's not paying attention. If your child is staring out the window or humming to himself and rocking, it's a waste of time to present a question or instruction. Because it takes effort and time to focus and pay attention, give your child a head's up before you start asking something of him. Warn him with a "Get ready to listen," "Are you ready?" "Three–Two–One" countdown, or whatever attending routine you establish between the two of you to signal him to focus. This also means using your legs, not your voice. Calling to your child from across the room to set the table is much less likely to be effective than approaching him, kneeling down to his level, tapping him lightly to get eye contact, and then saying specifically, "Time to put your fork and napkin on the table, please."

INCLUDE YOUR CHILD'S INTERESTS

One basic principle common to all teaching methodologies (floortime, pivotal response training, or Hanen) to maximize motivation is to *include your child's interests*. When deciding what to play, spread a few toys around the room and see what your child gravitates toward. Alternatively, take photos or create pictures of your child's favorite activities and places, and offer him several options on a choice board that are also acceptable to you. When deciding what to teach, consider what is most useful for your child to learn. What items does he need or want to request most often? Teach those words first, so he learns how useful it is to talk. Create a *functional curriculum*—teach what matches the child's interests and needs at his level.

SELECT ENTICING TEACHING MATERIALS

In the classroom, lend the teacher teaching materials that are interesting to your particular child, such as using Thomas trains to teach counting and colors for a child who loves Thomas, or a Hoberman Expanding Ball or balloons to blow up to teach big and little.

Outside the classroom, constant observation and paying attention to your child's interests will enable you to take advantage of the many incidental learning opportunities that occur naturally in daily life. Create learning opportunities around those interests. For example, whenever your child wants something such as a toy, activity, or something to eat or drink, you can withhold the desired item briefly while looking expectantly at the child to verbalize his request.

Pouring or giving *bit by bit* (Sussman 1999) is a great way to create many incidental (natural) learning opportunities. When your child asks for "ju" (juice), pour just a little, let him drink it, then pause and look expectantly at him to request it again. When your child is into lining up cars or doing a puzzle, you can be the "keeper" (Sussman 1999) of the cars or puzzle pieces and occasionally pause for your child to request "car" or "puzzle piece" before handing one over.

When swinging, stop the swing periodically and pause to get your child to ask for "swing." When he's having fun just running around, periodically playfully make a fence with your arms around him to stop him until he says, "go" or "move." One of Peter's favorite games when he was little (and lighter) was to hold hands with his father and me while walking between us as we would count, "one, two, three…(pause)." Peter would fill in the blank with the command "up!" and we would swing him up in the air. Rough and tumble games are great opportunities to elicit "up" as you lift up your child higher and higher, bit by bit, or "down" as you hold your child's hands and lower his head backwards farther and farther while sitting on your lap.

Balance success and challenge

The trick to maximally capitalizing on naturally motivating opportunities is to *balance the challenge with plenty of success* so that the activity is fun, and therefore remains motivating for as long as possible. Thus if you are pouring juice, make sure you are pouring enough to make it worth the effort for your child to communicate his request, yet little enough to give you as many repetitions as possible. Similarly, wait to pour the juice until the child has made a reasonable effort to approximate the word "juice," such that you aren't rewarding backsliding (that is, a poorer attempt than he has established as his current baseline), but do not make your standard too high such that the child gets frustrated and gives up.

Keeping an interaction going is always a balancing act between challenge and reward. A little challenge adds to the fun if the child feels generally successful, but too many challenging instructional demands can swing the balance between fun and effort to too much effort for the child to find continuing worthwhile. In general, adjust the level of difficulty in your questions and demands so that your child gets at least twice as many correct answers as incorrect, and is successful easily twice as often as he has to struggle.

Another way to say this is to *intersperse lots of easy demands with your challenging ones* (Koegel *et al.* 1989). In ABA parlance, we would say it's a good idea to intersperse maintenance (mastered) tasks with target (to be learned) tasks. For example, say your child knows how to retrieve a rolled ball, but is just learning how to catch a thrown one. If you intersperse just one throw for every two or three rolled balls to him, he is much more likely to enjoy the game and put up with the difficulty learning how to catch those occasional thrown balls than if he missed one thrown ball after the next.

When reading bedtime stories with Peter, I alternate pointing out what I see that's interesting on one page with asking him a question on the next, so a demand isn't made on him for every page. When I ask questions, I try to ask a couple of easy questions such as "What color is the…" (since he knows his colors well) for every more challenging question such as "What is the boy doing?" (which requires use of a verb that he knows less well than colors). I also let Peter turn the pages which gives him lots of opportunities to participate successfully and take the initiative. My taking a turn also allows me to use vocabulary I anticipate Peter will need to use answering my next question, so that he gets a kind of prompt built into the process should he need it. For example, if reading *The Three Little Pigs*, on my turn I might point out that nice yellow straw on the picture depicting the first little pig's house made of straw. On his turn to answer a question, I might ask "What color is the first little pig's straw house?" (easier question), or "What kind of house did the first little pig build?" (harder question). The answers to the first ("yellow") and second ("straw") questions were both imbedded in my previous comment.

BUILDING MOTIVATION **89**

Give your child some choice

Of course, it would also make it more motivating if Peter had chosen the book. In general if you look for opportunities to give your child choices, you'll create many more naturally motivating learning opportunities. Even when you have a teaching agenda in mind, there can still be "shared control" (Koegel *et al.* 1989; Sussman 1999). If I have several books I'd particularly like to read with Peter, I offer only those particular ones for him to choose from. If there are certain floortime activities or RDI games you'd like to practice, set up the room with several "stations" with the toys or equipment you plan to use, and then follow your child's lead as he gravitates first to the game he feels like playing. If you have several worksheets or academic tasks on your lesson plan, create file folders or icons for each one and let your child pick the order in which he does his work.

Using shared control to encourage independent working

What is a file folder? A file folder is just a folder, plastic bag, shoebox, drawer, or any container that contains one work task in it. You might put laminates of some of the upper case letters of the alphabet with Velcro on the back of each letter in a plastic ziplock bag, and laminates of the same lower case letters of the alphabet with the corresponding Velcro® on the back of each letter in another, and put them in a folder with directions written on the front saying, "Match." This is an example of a file folder. Another file folder might contain Velcroed laminates of all the numerals of your child's phone number, a sheet of cardboard with a Velcro strip with seven blank lines underneath, and the written directions saying, "What's your phone number?" Another might have a spelling puzzle inside for your child to put together, a set of LEGO to construct a pictured vehicle, or a worksheet and pencil.

First teach the child how to complete the work in each file folder. Once the tasks are familiar and mastered, they become "maintenance tasks." You can pull them out when your child needs something to do to keep productively occupied. They are better than "busy work" because they enable your child to practice concepts and skills you want him to keep up.[1]

---

1 For outstanding file folder activities, see Eric Schopler, Margaret Lansing and Leslie Waters' *Teaching Activities for Autistic Children* (1983), a compilation of sample activities from the famous TEACCH program (see the Glossary at the end of this book).

A great way to encourage initiation and independence is to set up your file folders in an "independent work station" for your child. The station may consist of a set of plastic drawers or bins next to a table and chair. Place several folders in a bin labeled "Start." Label the other bin "All done." Teach your child to take out a file folder from the "Start" bin, complete the work, and place it in the "All done" bin. He can do the work in any order he chooses. In order to encourage completion, offer a treat at the end, such as a favorite activity. Rotate the mastered material in your file folders to maintain those concepts in your child's repertoire.

To encourage timely work initiation and completion, you can give this activity an added twist. Play "Beat the clock." Have your child turn on a timer (sand timers or other visual timers are especially helpful), and use "differential reinforcement" by offering a bonus treat should he complete his work on time.

Offer rewards

The point of including your child's interests and sharing control is to harness the intrinsic motivation of doing what he wants. However, many of our children have very limited interests or interests that are not strong enough to have to do work for.

Body parts (for example, eyes, nose, mouth, arm, tummy) are important to teach so a child can identify what's hurting them—but what if your child just isn't interested in learning them, even when you've put them to the usual songs or games (for example, "Head, shoulders, knees and toes," "Let's do the hokey pokey," or "Simon says")? It may not always be possible to find or engineer naturally rewarding consequences for important concepts you need to teach. In that case, remember "Grandma's Principle,"—"No dessert till you eat your vegetables."[2] You might have to motivate your child to do something he doesn't care to do (like eat his vegetables, name a body part correctly, or sit on the potty) by pairing it with an extrinsic reward. Extrinsic rewards can be anything the child likes such as dessert or other favorite edibles, stickers, bubbles, songs, or activities like time on the swing or trampoline, time to play with a favorite toy, or time to get bounced on a big ball, squished in a beanbag,

---

2   This ABA principle is also known as the Premack Principle—a behavior with a low frequency of occurrence (like naming or eating vegetables) can be reinforced by the contingent presentation of a behavior that has a high probability of that occurrence (like wanting to eat ice cream).

or tickled. Make a list of your child's rewards or "reinforcers," and put them in hierarchical order, from least to most preferred. In general, use the mildest and smallest amounts of reinforcement possible to provide sufficient motivation, and reserve your strongest rewards for the most challenging tasks or to reward the greatest accomplishments, especially spontaneous ones.

Increasing motivation with a masterful use of extrinsic reinforcement: A case of potty training

Siegel (2003, pp.292–4) describes a method of potty training that is a masterful example of making the most of a reinforcer. Say your child displays signs of toilet training readiness like clutching at himself or showing you he wants his diapers changed, but resists potty training. However, say he loves Thomas trains. They would be at the top of his reinforcer hierarchy. To further increase their motivating power, make your child "Thomas-deprived" by removing all Thomas trains and paraphernalia from the house except the stash of trains you keep in the bathroom cabinet. When you think he needs to urinate because it's been a while since the last time, or he's clutching or dancing around, seat your child on the potty and immediately pull out a Thomas train in a child-proof transparent jar. He only gets the jar if he stays seated on the potty. If he gets up before urinating, immediately put the jar away. By taking out and putting away the jar immediately, you make the reward (getting the jar) clearly contingent upon the behavior (sitting on the potty).

By giving the child the jar so he can see Thomas, but not touch Thomas, you further heighten his desire, increasing its value even more as a reinforcer. Of course, as soon as he does urinate, immediately open the jar and let him play with the train for five or ten minutes (use a timer). Then say goodbye to Thomas till the next time, and put it back in the jar and away in the cabinet again so it retains its motivating power. If your child just can't urinate despite sitting on the potty for a long time, put Thomas away and get your child up from the potty. Try again later. Alternatively, you can try pouring some body temperature water over the perineum as he sits on the potty to give him the idea of what he needs to do to get Thomas, and immediately open the jar to reward tolerating that.

Encouragement and praise

Of course, the most important and potentially most powerful reward you can give your child is your warm encouragement, meaningful praise, and attention. At first, you may feel that your child pays no attention to you, and does not care how you feel. But keep pairing your social praise with those tangible edibles, tickles/sensory games, or other primary, inherently pleasurable rewards he loves, and over time it will gain equal or greater reinforcing value.

Keep your praise meaningful by making it commensurate with your child's effort and achievement. If you monotonously say "good job" for everything, it won't mean much. Vary your words, tone of voice, and actions. Accompany your "Well done!" "Good talking!" "That's right!" and other comments with different actions like smiles, squeezes, tickles, high fives, hugs, clapping games, and "Gotcha" games, depending on what your child likes.

Your tone of voice and body language alone convey most of your message. You can use the words to be more specific with your praise to make it more meaningful. This can range from "Nice pointing!" or "Good building!" to "I saw (or heard or liked) what you did (be specific), and that was great!" You can also use your words to add a bit of back-end teaching. If your child just said "ju" for "juice," smile warmly and repeat "Juice" as you pour a bit of juice for him.

Rewarding wisely by systematically fading prompts and shaping better responses

You can get a lot more mileage out of your rewards, whether intrinsically or extrinsically motivating, by administering them skillfully. *Fading prompts* is an important concept. Let's go back to the example of your child reaching for juice. Say he has never said the word "juice" before. Hold up the pitcher and his cup so he knows you understand his request, look expectantly at him, and say, "Juice?" If the child makes any approximation, for example, "ju," go ahead and pour a bit of juice in the cup for him to enjoy. That bit of juice serves as a natural reinforcer or reward for your child to make the effort to say "juice." When your child finishes the bit of juice and looks up for more, you might repeat the procedure a few times. If readily successful each time, next time prompt with the initial letter sound "j" as you hold the pitcher up, and after a few successful trials, always rewarding with a bit of juice, prompt with just forming your mouth into the letter "j" sound, and wait expectantly. If successful, you can move on to no prompting and simply holding up the pitcher and looking at your child, waiting for him to vocalize his "juice" approximation spontaneously. Once he readily does that, reward with a nice helping of juice. Your child now has a verbal approximation for "juice" and can use it to request juice independently.

What you did is systematically withdraw prompting support for your child. First you demonstrated saying the entire label, then made the initial sound of the label, then shaped your mouth for that first sound, and then just waited, working down to provide the least support necessary for your child to produce the desired word. Consolidate this stage by rewarding your child with juice whenever he says "ju" until you feel he's really got it down.

Once he requests juice reliably with "ju," it may be time to demand a little more. *Shaping* means withholding a reward unless the child meets progressively higher standards. No longer reward all speaking attempts, but gradually make the reward contingent upon better and better approximations of the word as your child gets more capable. In this case you might wait to pour the juice only upon getting the ending consonant sound as well. You thus help "shape" the child's attempts into the ability to say the whole word "juice" spontaneously.

Let's take another example. Say you're trying to teach your nonverbal child to communicate "up" when he wants you to pick him up. At first prompt him to raise his arms up by doing a hand over hand maneuver and physically lifting his arms up before picking him up. After a number of repetitions, demonstrate by lifting up your arms to get him to lift his. Once he's got that down, just gesture for him to lift his arms. At first pick him up with any slight upward movement of the arms. After many successful repetitions, gesture for him to raise those arms up a bit more to get picked up. Each time, wait for a bit more effort to get those arms up till he gives you a nice, clear signal, getting those arms up for you to pick him up.

Rewarding wisely with differential reinforcement

The concept of "differential reinforcement" is also useful. It means you should deliver the amount of reinforcement that is commensurate with the behavior that was displayed. For example, back to the pouring juice—if your child suddenly spontaneously comes up with the word "juice," without any prompting, you would probably want to pour a whole cup of juice at once accompanied by lots of praise: "You said 'juice'! Great talking!"

When Peter first walked into the kitchen in the morning having fully dressed himself, even with some of the clothes inside out or backwards, we were thrilled and demonstrated that with hearty congratulations and favorite breakfast food choices. Again, highly reinforce those behaviors you want to happen again, especially those that are independently displayed without prompts.

Conversely, poor effort or backsliding should not receive reinforcement, but should quickly be followed with giving another opportunity for the child to succeed. Say the child has been saying "juice" and then goes back to "ju." Withhold the juice and wait expectantly. If he says "ju" again, say, "Do you mean 'juice'?" emphasizing the last consonant. When he says "juice," promptly pour that juice.

Rewarding wisely with careful timing

It is also critical that you reward immediately after your child does or says the right thing. You want him to associate the reward with the right answer, not the wrong answer. In psychological jargon, *reinforcement must be contingent upon the desired behavior.* For example, Peter often misspeaks. If I show him an apple and a mango, and ask, "Do you want a mango or an apple?" he might point to the mango because that's what he wants, but say "apple" because he's echoing the last word he heard. If I just give him the mango anyway, I would be reinforcing an incorrect label. If I give him the apple, he'd probably get frustrated, since he pointed to the mango. It would probably be best if I said, "No. Not apple. That's a mango. What do you want again?" If Peter then pointed to the mango and said "Mango," I should then say, "Oh, you want a mango! Good talking, Peter!" and give him the mango.

As another example, if Peter started banging on his chin as I was starting to give him the mango, I should take away the mango, stop the chin banging, and start again rather than inadvertently reward chin banging with the mango. I might hold his hands, say "Mango?" and hand him the mango after he says, "Mango."

Finally, if I offered Peter "Mango or apple?" and he said the name of his favorite fruit, "Orange," it would be best if I could reward his spontaneous vocalization and give him an orange. If I protest, "But I offered mango or apple," I would lose the opportunity to reward his initiative and teach him that his words do affect his environment. In each case, give the child what he wants only after he asks for it using the correct label. Reward the correct answer and be careful not to inadvertently pair reward with an incorrect response or behavior.

SUMMARY

Your child may not be born with affiliative orientation or an innate desire to imitate, but he can develop these to some degree. As he experiences many warm and fun interactions with you, he becomes interested in what you're interested in because he loves you and wants to be with you. As he repeatedly experiences the positive consequences of imitating you in games and routines, he learns to trust that if you want him to imitate, it's probably worthwhile, even if he doesn't have the mirror neurons to give him a foretaste of the reward by watching you. In other words, his loving and trusting relationship with you will help him develop some of the underpinnings of motivation he wasn't born with. I say "some" because biology presents its limitations. You mustn't attribute your child's lack of motivation to something lacking in your relationship with him.

For your part, the principles of motivating your child are intuitive. Get your child's attention. Give clear, concrete directions or instructions. Include your child's interests and offer him choices. Pair tangible reinforcers with social praise so that it becomes as or even more rewarding. Use rewards wisely by rewarding bit by bit, fading prompts systematically, shaping, creating a hierarchy of rewards and using them differentially, and timing reinforcement immediately after the right response. Intersperse more challenging demands with lots of easy ones to keep the balance between effort and reward tipped toward success.

Chapter 8

Creating a Strategy for Cognitive Development

> When Peter was a toddler, my floortime specialist and I used to joke
> that Peter seemed allergic to toys. Whenever we brought one out,
> he withdrew and turned away from us. He had few interests. Despite
> using high affect and enticing games and toys, I felt that I was doing
> all the work of interaction. When left to himself, Peter spent all his
> time rocking, tapping, flicking his fingers on one side of his visual
> field or the other, or squealing. As he grew older, he developed
> compulsions to climb on shelves and other furniture, tap objects,
> shake lamps so hard that the light bulbs broke, maraud the kitchen
> pantry to eat insatiably, and run back and forth along the hallways
> squealing, literally bouncing off the walls.
>
> Peter's RDI therapist told me that he was the slowest to make
> any progress in her entire practice. His floortime supervisor just
> listened quietly when I spoke of nearing despair and giving up the
> constant effort to engage. Perhaps I should just accept the fact that
> we were hitting a biological wall. She made no attempt to persuade
> me to persevere.

I read and re-read Greenspan and Wieder's (1998, pp.132–90) chapters
on level one and two engagement and two-way communication. I literally
tried every trick in the book. They suggest making pretend fences with
your arms around your child as he's walking away to avoid you, to make
a game of him trying to slip under your arm. Put the toy or object he's
perseverating with on top of your head or between your teeth to get a
smile or effort at retrieval. Hide treats in your hands or around the room
for a treasure hunt. Play horsey and have your child direct where you go
and when to stop or start. If he lays down on the floor and won't move,
put a blanket over him and turn off the lights, to see if he throws the
blanket off. Try lying down and putting your head on him as if he were

a pillow. Playfully obstruct by putting your hand over the cars he's lining up, or line one up perpendicular to get him to react.

We tried all these ideas innumerable times, but would only get a few circles of interaction before Peter would walk away, or have a meltdown if we tried the fence idea more than a few times. Greenspan and Wieder's writings made me expect that if we tried hard enough to engage Peter, eventually he would progress, and we could get multiple circles of joint attention and joyful shared experience. But why wasn't it happening?

I realize now that the main reason was the severity of Peter's cognitive deficits. He needed to be taught how to think. He needed more cognitive abilities such as imitating, matching, sorting, constructing, sequencing, and problem solving. He needed better motor planning and more language. Peter needed to learn to think and move if we were ever to get beyond purely sensory interactions. Social interaction is all about communication, but you must have some content to communicate; if not original ideas, at least repertoire.

That is why it is so important to have some strategy for the cognitive development of your child. The good news is that you do not need to figure out how to teach your child to think. There are many good books (Fovel 2002; Leaf and McEachin 1999) that provide detailed descriptions of cognitive development programs. In general a reasonable approach is to start by looking up the neurotypical developmental goals for each level, see where your child's baseline is with respect to each of the domains (cognitive, language, social, etc.), and start working on the next step up.

SETTING GOALS FOR COGNITIVE DEVELOPMENT

A good resource for speech and language developmental milestones up to the seven-year-old level is the "Speech and language development chart" by Addy Gard *et al.*, available online through a company called Pro-Ed based in Texas.

I have two favorite resources that I use every year to help create the goals for Peter's annual review meeting (see Glossary entry for "IEP"), during which all the educators involved with a child (parents, teachers, and therapists) meet to determine his educational goals and services. These are the California educational standards adapted for special needs children (available at www.k8accesscenter.org/training_resources/iep. asp) and the ABLLS-R, *The Assessment of Basic Language and Learning Skills* by James W. Partington (2006, available at www.behavioranalysts.com).

The step-by-step goals listed in the ABLLS-R systematically cover every domain of the brain. It starts with the basics of cooperation and learning readiness, imitation, visual performance (matching, categorization, patterns, sequences, puzzles, seriation, and mazes), and receptive and expressive labels. Then it lays out goals for teaching adjectives and prepositional phrases, making requests, using carrier phrases (such as "I want" or "I see"), and answering and asking "wh" questions (what, who, when, where, why, and how). The goals go all the way up to spontaneous conversations and retelling stories. It includes academic goals in reading, writing, and math. The ABLLS-R is comprehensive, including play and leisure skills, self-help skills (dressing, eating, grooming, and toileting), and fine and gross motor skills. I use this outstanding reference to construct Peter's curriculum as we advance several goals in each cognitive area each year. The ABLLS-R doesn't tell you how to teach each goal, but it does guide you as to what you need to teach next. In the cognitive and academic realms, the ABLLS-R has served as our roadmap for teaching our child how to think, showing us our next destination as we progress along the developmental journey.

HOW DO YOU TEACH THE GOALS?

Knowing what your child's baseline is, and doing your reading so that you know what the next reachable developmental goals are specifically for each of your child's cognitive domains, is the first step. Next comes developing a teaching strategy. How do you teach that next goal? Learning labels for commonly requested items may be your next destination, but how do you get there? As parents we do a lot of "incidental teaching," teaching when the opportunity naturally presents itself. We withhold the desired toy or food until our child makes some approximation of the label to request it. We send our children to preschool or arrange playdates to have them hear other children use the labels. But many of our children have so many challenges with motivation, attention, processing, memory, and dyspraxia that they need more help than they can get even when we try to make the most out of natural learning opportunities.

I assume you may be reading this book because your child is one of these children. Say you've done your observations, accommodated his sensory preferences, understand his baseline strengths and weaknesses, and have come up with a list of specific cognitive goals. But even with some one-on-one tutoring and trying to make use of all the incidental teaching opportunities that present themselves in daily life, your child is not making progress. He just doesn't seem to be learning. Is there some kind of power tool you can use to help him learn?

USING DISCRETE TRIAL TRAINING WHEN INCIDENTAL TEACHING IS NOT ENOUGH

Fortunately, there is. ABA is the most extensively researched treatment for autism, and children enrolled in intensive ABA programs demonstrate significant cognitive gains. Discrete trial training, or DTT, is a method of teaching used extensively in ABA programs. It has received some criticism because it's not effective when used as a sole teaching method for learning social interaction, and requires generalization to become meaningful and useful to the child. However, it is an extremely useful power tool for introducing new concepts that you can then generalize with all the incidental teaching opportunities you encounter in daily life and interactive games you play together.

The discrete trial is just a distillation and concentration of all the common sense you use in good ordinary teaching. Reduce distractions, get the child's attention, break down concepts into one learnable step at a time, elicit constant feedback from the child, and use that feedback to adjust the difficulty of your instruction, provide enough repetition till you ascertain mastery, and move on to new material systematically.

As in your incidental teaching, try to use materials naturally interesting to your child, allow the child some shared control in selecting reinforcers and the order of activities, try to use intrinsic rather than extrinsic reinforcement when possible, intersperse challenging new exercises (target tasks) with mastered ones (maintenance activities), and use a lot of high affect and social interaction initially paired with your reinforcement and later serving as your reinforcement.

Parents often mistakenly believe or are led to believe that DTT is for the experts to use on their child, but not for them. It is true that companies that specialize in administering DTT programs to children with autism have a lot to offer, including a curriculum, trained staff, and lots of experience. However, parents are totally capable of learning how to do discrete trials, and should have this power tool available to use as desired. I firmly believe that the basic discrete trial method is a helpful tool for any parent to learn, even if your child is already enrolled in a DTT program. You can augment your child's program with more hours if funding doesn't cover all that he needs, do "homework" with your child, and generalize what he's learned in his program with similar materials at home.

For children with severe learning disabilities such as Peter, we use DTT as the primary format of his structured teaching at school, but this method can also be used for shorter segments of the day for children who would just benefit from some focused teaching on certain problem areas. As a parent, you may want to pull out this tool here and there when your child has particular trouble learning a certain concept. Once your child learns the basic format or contract of earning reinforcers by attending to your instruction and making better and better responses, you will find that you can weave in sessions of discrete trials into your instructional day as needed. Here is an overview of this "power tool" of structured teaching, the discrete trial.

A PRIMER ON DISCRETE TRIAL TRAINING[1]

The term "discrete trial" sounds technical, but don't let it turn you away from this common sense teaching tool. Here are the basic concepts. The idea behind DTT is that what you want to teach your child can be broken into little steps, called "trials." The steps are taught systematically and separately, that is, "discretely," as you get feedback from your child after each trial to make sure he's mastered it before you teach more. Each trial is structured as a choice between the right answer and wrong answer(s), also called the "distracter(s)." That way, you automatically get the feedback you need from your child. If the child gets the right answer 80 percent or more of the time on two or more sessions,[2] you may assume he's mastered that step and move on to teaching the next. If he gets the answer wrong, you know you need to support him with more prompting or break down the learning into smaller steps (see "Primer: The art of prompting," pp.71–2).[3]

---

1   This primer is based on a seminar presented to the Foothill Special Education Local Plan Area under the auspices of the "La Canada Unified School District on DTT" by Gwennyth Palafox, PhD (www.meaningfulgrowth.com).

2   Some mastery criteria calls for 80 percent correct across three sessions across two different therapists.

3   You may rearrange the hierarchy depending upon the child's profile. For highly verbal children, a verbal prompt is stronger than a gestural prompt.

The essential preliminaries: Addressing physical needs and sensory issues

Before you even get started teaching, you need to get your child ready to learn. Many of our children find focusing their attention extremely difficult, especially when also fighting massive distractions such as motor issues like tics and restless legs, and sensory integration issues that turn up the volume on background visual and auditory stimuli. You must get your child's attention before you can teach him anything. First help him get his body ready by taking care of hunger, thirst, toileting, heat or cold, and any medical needs. Accommodate his sensory needs, such as providing a calm, quiet environment facing away from windows and other distractions. If you have a fidgety child, make sure he's had his sensory break and exercised his muscles. Make lists of sensory and gross motor activities that work for your child. Sensory breaks might include hiding under a heavy blanket or stretching inside a body sock, swinging, or bouncing up and down on top of a big ball. Exercise breaks might include jumping with or without a trampoline, squats, sit-ups, jumping jacks, pushups, flexing and extending against a resistance band, or throwing a medicine ball ten times. Keep those lists handy and consider offering sensory and exercise breaks periodically and routinely throughout your DTT session. If your child enjoys them, you may also offer them as choices when your child earns a reinforcer.

Teaching learning readiness with a "Three-Two-One" countdown

Most DTT programs begin with learning readiness exercises. The child gets rewarded for sitting tall, with a quiet mouth, and hands on his lap. If he can't keep his hands in his lap, draw an outline of where the hands should be placed on the table, and reward him for keeping them there for ten seconds. Pair the steps with a countdown like, "Three, sit tall. Two, quiet mouth. One, hands down" (see more about the "Three–Two–One" countdown on pp.156). If you do this routinely, the steps will become ingrained in your child, and you can fade the reward. Eventually you will also be able to just give the countdown without needing to demonstrate at the same time.

Mass trials and errorless learning

Grab the moment your child is paying attention and finally ready to learn. Say you want to teach your child what the word "ball" means. Do a little "pre-teaching" (also termed "priming") and hand him the ball several times, each time saying, "Ball. This is a ball." Then place the ball in front of him and say, "Ball. Give me ball."[4] Say he hands it to you several times in a row each time you give the instruction. This is called "a mass trial." At this stage, you are giving your child many opportunities all together (en masse) to actively pair the real ball with the word "ball" in order to form a neurological connection between the object and the label. There's a basic principle in neurology worth remembering: "What fires together, wires together." You don't want any mispairings at this point to mess up the connection you are trying to build, so that is why you only present the correct choice to your child, the ball, without any other distracter to choose from. The goal of this initial teaching phase is "errorless learning."

Adding distracters

The next step to strengthen this new budding neurological connection between a ball and the label "ball" is to challenge your child to make a more active choice with each trial. Instead of just presenting the ball, now present the ball with an untaught item like a clothespin in front of him. Again ask for the "ball." Each time the child selects the ball instead of the clothespin to hand to you, he is discriminating the ball from the distracter. This kind of trial is called a "mass trial versus distracter." You are demanding discrimination between the right and wrong answer, but isolating the variables the child has to discriminate between to one easy choice. That is why you select an untaught, novel item for the distracter that makes for a ridiculous alternative—in other words, something unfamiliar and uninteresting that the child would have no reason to gravitate toward, like a clothespin. It's still a mass trial because you are asking for the same target over and over. Every trial is an opportunity to work on the same neurological connection repetitively, the connection between a real ball and the label "ball."

---

4   When teaching a severely dyspraxic child, it may be helpful initially to use simplified telegraphic speech, but eventually, as long as the child demonstrates continued understanding, you can and should switch over to normal speech, including articles, using voice inflection to stress the important words.

Say your child gives you the wrong answer twice in a row, meaning he hands you the clothespin instead of the ball a couple of times when you've asked for "ball." The next time you ask for "ball," make sure your child hands you the ball even if you have to put your hands over his hands to select the ball. Then try letting your child choose the right answer himself a couple of times. If he continues to select the wrong answer, the clothespin, when you've asked for "ball," go back to errorless learning and take away the distracter. You don't want your child to make too many mistakes in a row. Otherwise, each time he selects the clothespin when you've asked for "ball," he may be miswiring clothespin together with the word "ball" in his brain. After many errorless mass trials of presenting only the ball and requesting "ball," you can try adding back the distracter (a clothespin or other untaught item) again, and ask him to choose between it and ball when you ask for "ball."

Block trials

After your child selects the right answer over 80 percent of the time, challenge your child further. See if he can hold the newly learned word "ball" in his memory and use it alternately with another word he knows. This method is called "block trials." Say your child has already mastered the word "cup." Put the cup and the ball in front of your child and ask for the ball many times in a row (say four times), so he gets to practice the connection between ball and the label "ball." Then switch to asking for "cup" four times in a row. If your child can do this, try gradually decreasing the number of repetitions—ask for the ball three times in a row instead of four, and then the cup three times in a row. This phase of teaching is called a "block trial," because you present the same instruction repetitively in blocks before you switch the instruction. The goal is to gradually decrease the size of your "blocks," meaning the number of times you repeat the same instruction before you switch. Next ask for the ball twice in a row, followed by asking for the cup twice in a row. Finally ease into full *random rotations*, asking for the ball or cup in any order.

Expanded trials

Another way to challenge your child and both test and strengthen that neurological connection between ball and the label "ball" is the "expanded trial." The idea is to successively expand the amount of time he has to hold that connection in his memory between distracters. Start out by alternately asking your child for a ball or a cup (or other mastered distracter). Then ask for the cup twice in a row between asking for the ball. Then ask for the cup three times in a row, and then four times in a row between asking for the ball. When the child gets the right answer over 80 percent of the time, again, move into random rotations.

Increasing the size of the field

You may also challenge your child further by *increasing the size of the field* of choices you present to your child, increasing the number of items on the table. Rotating the items stretches your child's ability to process language, in essence to be able to discriminate, by having to switch from word to word while retaining the newly learned word. Lay the ball on the table along with multiple mastered distracters like a cup, spoon, and apple if he's familiar with those labels. Test your child by asking for each of the items in random order. If he has difficulty with random rotation, drop to block trials and ask for each item several times in a row before switching to the next.

Mastery and maintenance

Mastery criteria is when your child gets the right answer over 80 percent of the time in random rotation in which you present the target instruction in random order with other mastered materials. Aim for a score of over 80 percent correct over at least a couple of sessions. Also see if your child can score 80 percent or higher with at least a couple of different people, in case one of the presenters is unconsciously giving nonverbal prompts the child is cueing into, such as a special inflection of the voice when asking for "ball" or inadvertent glance at the correct choice.

Once your child has accomplished these criteria, your child has mastered understanding the word "ball." It's important to adhere to mastery criteria so that you don't move on too quickly or slowly, avoiding frustration or boredom, respectively. Even after you move on to teach new words, you should periodically review the word in "maintenance" exercises. You may use the word "ball" as a distracter in future discrete trials when learning a new word, which also keeps the word "ball" in practice. But the best way to consolidate your child's mastery of "ball" is to *generalize* use of the word "ball" in different settings and circumstances. If your child discovers the word "ball" is useful and relevant, he's more likely to remember it. In the swimming pool, you could put out several different floating toys such as a rubber duck, ball, and plastic fish, and ask your child to swim for the ball. Hold onto him if he starts reaching for the wrong item, but let him swim if he heads for the ball.

How to correct

So what do you do when your child gives you the wrong answer? What if you ask for "ball" and your child hands you the cup? It's important to be clear and simple in your correction. Say "No," in a neutral tone of voice. Have your child put down the cup, and pick up the ball, as you say, "Ball."

Don't say, "Good try. But that's a cup, not a ball," because that's too many words. If the answer was good, was it right or wrong? Were we talking about a ball or a cup? What does "not" mean, anyway? Excess information may create brain scramble.

Despite a clear correction, what if in the next trial your child still gives you the cup instead of the ball? Again, deliver your simple, clear correction. Say "No." Show him the ball and say "Ball," as you did before. You've presented the correct pairing again, but be prepared to help your child more during the next trial. After you give your instruction, "Give me ball," prompt him by placing your hand over his to select the ball. With each successive trial, fade your prompt to a less strong one (see pp.71–2). The next time, say, "Give me ball," and point to the ball. Then just place the ball closer to him than the distracter cup. Fade your prompts only as your child keeps getting the right answer. When he makes a mistake, go back to the next stronger prompt that he was successful with before. You are using your child's feedback after each discrete trial to determine how you deliver your next instruction, that is, how much prompting, how many distracters in your field, and whether to go back or move on to a mass, block, or expanded trial.

It sounds complicated when explained, but DTT does become second nature with practice. The theory is actually simple—if the child gets the answer right, make it harder. If he gets it wrong, make it easier. Because you adjust your teaching systematically and responsively, it's an efficient way for your child to learn.

Examples of different kinds of DTT trials

Type of Trial	Example	Abbreviation ("B" for "Give me ball," "C" for "Give me cup," assuming "ball" is the target word to be learned, and "cup" the mastered distractor)	Comments
Mass Trials (MT)	"Give me ball. Give me ball. Give me ball. Give me ball."	BBB	Initially present the ball alone; later present the ball with a novel distractor, unknown to the child, for the child to choose from when asked for "ball." Wait for mastery before progressing to a block or expanded trial.
Block Trials (BT)	"Give me ball. Give me ball. Give me ball. Give me ball. Give me cup. Give me cup. Give me cup. Give me ball. Give me ball. Give me ball. Give me cup. Give me cup. Give me cup. Give me ball. Give me ball. Give me cup. Give me cup."	BBBBCCCCBBBCCCBBCC	Only progress to smaller blocks after the child successfully chooses the correct item in larger blocks (for example, wait for the child to correctly give you the correct item in a BBBBCCCCBBBBCCCC patttern before you move to a BBBCCCBBBCCC pattern of instruction).
Expanded Trials (ET)	"Give me ball. Give me cup. Give me ball. Give me cup. Give me cup. Give me ball. Give me cup. Give me cup. Give me ball. Give me cup. Give me cup. Give me cup. Give me ball."	BCBCCBCCCBCCCCB	Successively expand the amount of time the child is asked to select/perform the distractor between being asked to select/perform the target. Only progress to longer periods of distraction after the child demonstrates ability to correctly select/perform the target with shorter distraction periods (for example, wait for him to correctly select/perform in a BCCBCC pattern before you move to a BCCCBCCC pattern).
Random Rotation (RR)	"Give me ball. Give me cup. Give me ball. Give me cup. Give me cup. Give me ball. Give me ball. Give me cup. Give me ball. Give me cup. Give me cup. Give me ball. Give me ball."	BCBCCBBBCBCCB…	The RR tests the child's ability to discriminate the target from among other mastered targets. Ease into RR after the child has passed ETs or BTs with 80% accuracy.

What does a basic discrete trial training curriculum look like?

You can teach an entire basic curriculum with this DTT method, such as the sample one appended to this chapter (see pp.114–21). A typical beginner's curriculum includes teaching colors, labels of items commonly requested by your child such as favorite foods, toys, and activities, body parts (for example, mouth, eyes, hands, etc.), numbers, and letters of the alphabet. Real items or photos can be used when teaching vocabulary. Sorting into categories can be taught by laying out several paper plates labeled with the category name and icon (small pictorial representation) with perhaps a couple of sample items or photos already sorted into each plate. The child may be given an item or photo with the instruction, "Sort," or "Put with same." Imitation skills include imitating actions like stand up, sit down, raise your hand, give me, and point to. One way to teach your child to understand action words is to verbally label your actions as you get your child to imitate you. Gradually fade your demonstration of each action, and see if your child can perform the correct action given the verbal labels alone. Hold up the alphabet letter corresponding to the sound you are teaching during vocal imitation exercises, and you will be teaching the beginnings of phonics as well as articulation. Imitation also includes right-brained exercises in spatial relationships as you get your child to imitate simple block formations you construct by stacking several or more blocks in different configurations. For more ideas, Ron Leaf and John McEachin's *A Work in Progress* (1999) is an excellent "how to" DTT manual that offers a typical beginner's curriculum for cognitive development plus sections on play, self-help skills, and behavioral challenges.

Generalization and intrinsic reinforcement

No matter how much your child learns in DTT sessions, it's only the beginning. Generalization is a critical part of the teaching, and that's best done outside the classroom. Every time your child learns something new in his DTT sessions, try to immediately use it in some meaningful way in real life. If your child just learned to say "ball," have your child request "ball" in many different settings with different sizes and colors of balls. And don't just roll the ball to him when he says "ball." Kick it, throw it through a hoop together, do different things with it. If your child doesn't particularly like playing ball, you can always use it as the first activity that starts off a play circuit that ends in an activity your child does really like, such as being spun around or thrown in the air.

If your child learned to label colors in class, at home open a little bag of M&M's or Skittles and get him to tell you which color candy to give him next (you can use a pill cutter to quarter them if you don't want him to have too much sugar). If he learned some body parts in DTT, at bathtime sing "This is the way we wash our ____," and wash that part as he fills in the blank. Give him that favorite food item he just learned to say bit by bit so that he has many opportunities to verbalize his request. Use action verbs in daily life or use them in a game like "Simon says." Helping you get items at the grocery store is a great opportunity to practice quantities, colors, and receptive language as you ask him to get a certain number of certain items of a specific color. Stopping in front of his favorite foods is a great opportunity for him to practice expressive language as he makes his requests. We used to keep updated lists of new vocabulary that Peter had just learned in school on the refrigerator door to remind us to look for and engineer opportunities to use and elicit those words from him in our daily routines and interactive games.

You can work on reading along with talking. I know parents who print newly learned vocabulary labels on index cards and tape them around the house to the corresponding objects. I used to put Velcro under familiar items on the pages of Peter's favorite picture books so he could Velcro written labels to them that I would prepare ahead of time and display on a plastic sheet insert for each book. Peter would stick the correct label to different items pictured on the page we were reading together. Take a lot of photos sequentially throughout your family outings. I made homemade picture books out of the photos, then I made menus of labels of people, activities, and places, and had Peter Velcro the labels to the corresponding pictures.

Your mantra at home for generalization might be, "Use it or lose it." Affect drives learning, and your child must see the usefulness and relevance of what he is learning to retain it. If you break up what you teach into small enough steps with enough repetitions, it's amazing what your child will be able to learn.

Motivating your child with enticing materials and intrinsic reinforcement

"Well and good," you might be thinking. "Now I know my part, but what do I do if my child doesn't know his? What if he just doesn't want to cooperate?" Learning readiness is a whole separate issue from the learning process itself. All the principles of motivation discussed in the last chapter apply. First you've got to get your child's attention, and the best way to do that is to present something you know he's interested in. Select enticing teaching materials. If you know your child loves Thomas the Tank Engine trains, teach colors using the different train characters, that all have their distinctive colors. When you ask him to "Get blue," and he correctly reaches for Thomas, letting him play with Thomas for half a minute is natural or *intrinsic reinforcement*. When selecting vocabulary to teach, start with his favorite foods and toys, items he'll want to request. When you ask him to "Get cracker," and he correctly reaches for the cracker, letting him eat it is another example of intrinsic reinforcement, or a natural positive consequence. To teach your child to "Sit down, please," select an irresistible chair like a swivel chair if he likes spinning, or a big ball if he likes to bounce, and spin or bounce him as a consequence of sitting when asked. If he loves to topple things, when you practice imitating block constructions, make your models into towers. If he imitates yours correctly, say "Ready, set, go!" and topple your towers together. In other words, try to include your child's interests in the curriculum.

The use of extrinsic reinforcement

Sometimes it's too hard or not possible to work your child's interests into the activity you need to teach. In that case, use extrinsic reinforcement, meaning prizes or rewards. *Tangible reinforcers* include edibles like tiny bits of cut-up fruit or crackers and little prizes like stickers, bubbles, or toy parts that your child can collect to put together a whole toy like a LEGO car or puzzle. Other rewards include playing or singing a song of your child's choice, a favorite clapping or tickling game, or getting a specified amount of time to do a *favorite activity*, like blowing bubbles, a sensory activity like bouncing on a big ball, or hiding under a heavy blanket, or playing with a favorite toy. To end the reinforcement period and signal time to get back to work, use an objective timer of some sort like a sand timer or alarm clock, and get your child to start the timer himself.

Carry out periodic *reinforcement surveys* to find out what rewards work for your child. Create a reinforcement hierarchy by ordering them from least preferred (weakest) to most preferred (strongest). Differential reinforcement is a useful principle to increase the effectiveness of your reinforcers. Use small doses of your rewards to avoid satiation and decrease dependency on extrinsic rewards. Although you might need to start with rewarding every time a correct response is given, your goal should be to move toward an *intermittent reinforcement schedule,* to decrease the chance of satiation and decrease dependency on extrinsic rewards. Check off a certain number of boxes for correct responses or work completed to earn a reward your child chooses ahead of time. Another idea is to create a *token economy* in which your child can earn tokens for correct responses that buy prizes or time to do favorite activities like playing computer games. And if you use coins for tokens and attach price tags to your rewards, your child has an opportunity to inadvertently practice math as he figures out what he can buy with what he earns.

Shaping

An important concept to use when administering rewards is shaping. This means getting a child to make progressively better attempts at fulfilling an instruction by only rewarding progressively better attempts. For example, say you are teaching your child how to say the word "ball." You and your child are sitting opposite one another. "Ball?" you say as you hold up the ball. At first you might reward the child for just imitating your face as he puts his lips together in the right configuration to make the "b" sound, rolling the ball to him back and forth several times. Periodically hold onto the ball and say, "Ball?" as you look up at him inquiringly. Wait for him to make an attempt to say ball before you recommence your rolling back and forth game. Once you feel he's got the lips configuration down, the next time you stop to wait for him to request "ball," don't give it to him until he makes a better attempt, like "bah." Recommence your rolling game, holding onto the ball periodically until he requests "bah." Once you feel he's got "bah" down, try to hold out for that ending consonant if you feel he's capable. Hold onto the ball until he manages "Ball." Then celebrate with high fives and more of your rolling game. If your child is ready for it, try not to backtrack and start rewarding for "bah" or the "b" lip configuration—by rewarding only for a certain standard, you shape your child's response to meet that standard.

Setting standards

How you apply the concept of shaping will be noticed and tested. In general, children learn to size up teachers over time to figure out what their standards are. They will try harder for a teacher who has the discipline and fortitude to hold out for higher standards. Setting the standard is always a balancing act. As a teacher, you are constantly making educated guesses about what a child can achieve. If you set too high a standard, the child may get frustrated and give up. If you set too low a standard, the child achieves less and gets used to getting away with low effort. But it doesn't hurt to probe and give a child a more difficult instruction now and then to see how he does. If your child can't make that final consonant and asks for "bah" repeatedly, try making the trial easier by having him make two separate sounds, a "bah" followed by an "ll" sound, and go ahead and roll that ball. Set your teaching standards so that your child is generally walking that line between challenge and success, and he should make progress.

You can set an appropriate standard by gradually increasing the demand on your child till you discern the effort required may exceed his motivation. And maintaining that balance between challenge and success is the key to successful teaching. Determining where to draw the line requires careful observation of and attunement to the child. Guess what the child is capable of reaching to set the level of difficulty of your next target instruction. That depends upon several factors. It depends upon what *prior level of difficulty* the child could handle. In our example, the child could say "bah" for ball easily, and "ba" plus "ll" with help. If your goal is to shape adding an ending consonant, you might want to go for "ba" "ll" for the next instruction.

However, the level of difficulty you aim for also depends upon the child's *motivation versus effort* required. If he just barely mustered the ability to say "ba" "ll" using all his concentration and might, he might not have the energy to do it again right away. He might need a lot of free ball rolling with smiles and laughter to celebrate the last time he managed "ba" "ll" successfully. Once his "energy tank" is refilled and restored with your fun interaction, try "ba" "ll" again. Warn him ahead of time, "Just one more, and we're done!" Intersperse plenty of easy demands using "maintenance" words he's already mastered, such as holding the ball and asking, "Go?" These are all strategies to decrease the cost, or the effort, to try. If your child just isn't that interested in rolling the ball, you could also try tipping the balance by increasing the reward. Substitute a clear hamster ball, and put one of your child's favorite tangible reinforcers in it. That way, he will see that if he manages to say "ba" "ll" he will get the prize when you roll the ball. Or set up a token system in which rolling the ball a certain number of times is tied to a desired prize.

Sometimes, you need to examine your agenda to see if it is reasonable. During DTT sessions remember that you as the teacher get to decide on the next reasonable target to hold out rewards for when shaping. If the child only says "ba" "ll" with huge effort, you may decide to keep rewarding for "ba" (such as with a tiny piece of cracker), but give an extra large reward whenever he manages "ba" "ll" (such as with a whole cracker, accompanied with a hearty congratulations). Wait until your child demonstrates at least 80 percent mastery of a new word in DTT sessions before you start insisting on ever more proper use of the word label in natural settings. If your child just managed to say "ba" "ll" during DTT sessions once or twice only when offered his favorite reinforcer, it is unreasonable to expect him to say "ba" "ll" every time he wants to play with it in everyday life.

You teach the child, and never some predetermined agenda. If your child is tired, sick, hungry, or having a bad day for whatever reason, be flexible in setting lower, more achievable targets. On such a day, you might be lucky just to get the ball rolling with "bah." Use your instincts to decide on the next reasonable target *depending* on how your child is doing. When he's on a roll, alert, calm, learning and enjoying learning, aim for higher targets. This is not the time to allow backsliding. Actually, you never reward for less than you know the child is capable of—you just need to be observant, flexible, and responsive in deciding what he's capable of at the present moment.

Tipping the balance toward success

It is never worth "winning a battle to lose the war." Don't be so stuck on pushing your child to accomplish some target that you lose his trust and desire to follow your instruction. Both teacher and student should feel as if they've "won," as if both have accomplished something. Even if you could push for one more trial, try to end a session on a good note, as that last success or failure will probably be the first thing your child remembers when he returns to the table. When setting a target for shaping, it's better to undershoot slightly and keep your child's love of learning. He'll still get to the higher target, just a bit more slowly as you allow time and practice for consolidation. To nurture that love of learning, he needs to feel successful. Keep the balance between effort and reward, challenge and success worthwhile.

Fading extrinsic reinforcement
SUBSTITUTING SOCIAL PRAISE FOR TANGIBLES

Once your child tastes the pleasure of success, especially paired with your warm praise and smiles, he will be more and more willing to cooperate and work, and will need less and less tangible reinforcement. Aim to reach the point where your child will work for just social praise, high fives, hugs, or tickles.

USING A VISUAL SCHEDULE TO ENLIST COOPERATION

Often a child cooperates better simply by knowing what to expect. Therefore, once you've developed a repertoire of teaching activities, make a *visual schedule* so your child knows what to expect, when he can look forward to his sensory and exercise breaks, and sees the end in sight. For example, say your repertoire includes practicing colors with Thomas the Tank Engine trains, labeling favorite foods, and doing block tower imitations. Make labels of each activity—for example, write "Naming colors" and draw some colorful Thomas trains next to it, write "Naming foods" with pictures of some of the foods, and write "Crashing towers" with drawings of block towers. Attach Velcro to the back of each label, and get your child to select the order of activities, as he sticks the first, second, and third label on his visual schedule. Make sure you stick on the label "Fun choice" at the end, so your child knows he'll get to choose a sensory or exercise activity after completion of his work (see Chapter 7, pp.89–91). When your child knows what to expect and has helped select those expectations, you enlist his cooperation.

GOOD INSTRUCTION ENLISTS COOPERATION

A child is generally more willing to put in the effort to learn if he feels successful. Therefore, the most important motivator is a well-designed curriculum with thoughtful instruction. With all the learning challenges our children have, it's easy to make the mistake of presenting an instruction that seems simple but is actually too difficult for them. I presented "ball" versus "cup" hundreds of times to my child before I realized his auditory processing was so poor that at that stage he was functionally deaf. Once I added sign language to my presentations, he quickly learned to discriminate between them. Peter could not hand me one versus two blocks even when I signed by holding up one versus two fingers. But when an ingenious tutor used blocks with holes in them, he learned to thread the blocks upon her held-up fingers through the holes. She was eventually able to fade the holes and use normal blocks, but that physical matching was the intermediate bridging step he needed to understand quantities.

Learning how to do discrete trials well enables you to present information clearly, systematically, and repetitively, but at the end of the day, it's only a method. The teacher has to figure out the steps to take to teach each goal, and how to present the instruction for each step. You, along with your teaching team and your consultants, need to be creative in breaking down the concepts you want your child to learn into learnable steps. Cookbook approaches to DTT cannot replace the thoughtful, creative teacher who observes and listens to the child, and constantly adjusts and individualizes the program accordingly.

Basic Curriculum Guide by Gwen Palafox PhD

Attending skills

1. Sits in a chair independently
2. Makes eye contact in response to name
   a. Face to face
   b. Activity to adult
3. Body is quiet, oriented, and ready (sensory needs met)

Nonverbal imitation skills

1. Gross motor actions
2. Fine motor actions
3. Oral motor actions
4. Object manipulation
5. Block imitation
6. Grapho-motor imitation
7. Imitate peer play behavior
8. Learn through observation

Receptive language skills
1. Follow simple one-step commands
2. Receptive object identification
3. Receptive picture identification
    a. People
    b. Pictures
4. Receptive action identification (self)
5. Receptive action identification (pictures)
6. Receptive categorization
7. Receptive prepositions
8. Receptive identification of possession
9. Receptive function of objects
10. Receptive pronouns
11. Follow two to three-step directions
12. Receptive identification of functions
13. Receptive identification of emotions
14. Retrieving items out of view
15. Receptive understanding of "wh" questions

Expressive language skills
1. Talk program (response time)
    a. Within 5 seconds
    b. Within 3 seconds
    c. Within 1 second
2. Verbal imitation
    a. Vowels (V)
    b. Consonants (C)
    c. CV combinations
    d. VC combinations
    e. CVC combinations

      f. CVCV combinations

      g. Words

      h. Phrases

3. Labeling

4. Requesting

5. Yes/no

6. Describing familiar items

7. Labeling familiar people

8. Reciprocating greetings

9. Social questions

10. Expressive action identification (self)

11. Expressive action identification (pictures)

12. Expressive action identification (others)

13. Expressive pronouns

14. Expressive categorization

15. Expressive prepositions

16. Expressive identification of functions

17. Labeling emotions

18. Labeling functions of objects

19. Answering "wh" questions

20. Reciprocating social information

Pre-academic skills

1. Matching

      a. Object to object identical

      b. Picture to picture identical

      c. Object to picture identical

      d. Picture to object identical

      e. Object to object non-identical

      f. Picture to picture non-identical

2. Colors

   a. Match

   b. Receptive

   c. Expressive

3. Shapes

   a. Match

   b. Receptive

   c. Expressive

4. Letters

   a. Match uppercase

   b. Receptive identification uppercase

   c. Expressive identification uppercase

   d. Match lowercase

   e. Receptive identification lowercase

   f. Expressive identification lowercase

   g. Match uppercase to lowercase

5. Numbers

   a. Matching

   b. Receptive

   c. Expressive

6. Counting

   a. Rote count to 10

   b. Count 10 objects

   c. Give quantities

   d. Match number to quantity

7. Identify written name

   a. Match

   b. Receptive

   c. Expressive

8. Understanding size concepts

   a. Match by size

   b. Receptive ID big/little

   c. Expressive ID big/little

9. Understanding first/next/last

10. Match written words to objects

11. Match categories

Object manipulation

1. Puzzles

2. Stringing beads

3. Simple toys and games (e.g., "Barnyard bingo," "Don't break the ice," etc...)

Oral motor actions

Smile	Chomp teeth
Smack lips	Fog mirror
Puff up mouth with air	Blow bubbles
Open mouth	Tongue up
Pucker	Tongue down
Stick out tongue	Tongue to one side
Bite lower lip	Move lower jaw left to right
Bite upper lip	Lick top lip
Pout	Lick lower lip
Blow air	Bite tongue
Kiss	Wink

Object imitation

Put block in cup	Drink
Push car	Read book
Hug doll	Open box
Bang hammer on table	Blow bubbles
Put on hat	Shake maracas
Put on glasses	Play piano
Answer telephone	Brush hair
Eat	Brush teeth

Gross motor action (prime for receptive commands and play skills)

Arms up	Touch elbow
Sit down	Ride bike
Jump	Throw ball
Clap hands	Sleep
Wave	Stand up
Pat knees	Jump
Touch nose	Touch head
Turn around	Pat table
Touch shoulders	Touch belly
Lie down	Stomp feet
Hands on hips	Touch floor
Walk	Cross arms
Touch ears	Hug
Dance	Skate
Crawl	Roll ball
Run	Read book

Fine motor activities (prime for receptive commands, play skills, and functional skills)

Touch eyes	Touch mouth
Point	Index finger to index finger
Shake head yes	Shake head no
Touch teeth	Thumbs up
Peace sign	Salute
Open and close hand	Blow kisses
Index to thumb	

Receptive and expressive objective identification (select meaningful items)

Cow	Shoe	Bear	Cookie
Boat	Hat	Duck	Juice
Cup	Elmo	Mickey	Phone
Pig	Tape	Dog	Apple
Hammer	Ball	Money	Video
Towel	Coat	Chair	Baby
Spoon	Banana	Bike	Train
Bag	Crayon	Puzzle	Cracker
Cake	Blanket	Pencil	Big bird
Nose	Cookie	Chip	Pillow
Car	Brush	Fish	Bed

Plate	Book	Balloon	Water
Truck	Peach	Fork	Potty

Social questions (priming for self-awareness, safety, and independence)

1. What is your name?
2. How old are you?
3. How are you doing?/How ya doin?
4. What is your mommy's name?
5. What is your daddy's name?
6. What is your sister's name?
7. What is your brother's name?
8. When is your birthday?
9. What do you like to play with?
10. What is your favorite toy?
11. What school do you go to?
12. What grade are you in?
13. What is your last name?
14. When is your birthday?
15. How do you go to school?
16. Where do you live?
17. What is your phone number?
18. What is your favorite color?
19. What did you eat for breakfast?
20. What did you eat for lunch?
21. What did you eat for dinner?
22. Who is your friend?
23. What do you wear on your feet?
24. What do you do when you are thirsty?
25. What do you do when you are hungry?
26. What do you do when you get tired?

27. Where do you sleep?

28. What do you wear on your head?

29. What do you use when it's raining?

Source: www.meaningfulgrowth.com

Chapter 9

Developing a Means
of Communication

WHY AN ECLECTIC APPROACH?

My husband Vinh and I were not sure at the beginning if Peter even had the capacity to learn language. His auditory processing was so poor that although a medical test called "auditory evoked potentials" confirmed that his hearing was normal, he acted functionally deaf. He would not turn his head if you banged a pot behind him, let alone respond if his name was called. We tried sign language, and discovered that Peter was capable of understanding some simple signs, but his motor dyspraxia prevented him from being able to form more than a few clumsy signs himself. In any case, knowing that Peter's hearing was intact, we were loath to resign him to a world of meaningless sounds. Was there any way to teach him how to make sense of auditory input?

I reflected upon my own experience trying to learn Chinese. My parents were always puzzled as to why I never picked up Chinese although they did speak it in the home, and my sisters were much better at it. To me, the sounds and tones were too difficult to distinguish at first. I felt I could relate to how language might sound like incomprehensible static or noise to Peter. But when I took Chinese in college, I was introduced to a magic key. That key was a phonetic code called pinyin that assigns sounds in Chinese to letters of the English alphabet. Once I cracked the code, meaning once I had learned it thoroughly, I could pronounce any Chinese word by reading the word in pinyin. To speak Chinese, I simply visualized the words written in pinyin, and "read" them out loud. I could also finally understand Mandarin because I could translate the sounds I was hearing into pinyin, and reconstruct the words in pinyin in my mind. After some practice, I could comprehend and speak Chinese without the step of visualizing the words in pinyin first. However, whenever I wanted to learn a new word, I had to spell it in pinyin in my mind to register it.

So perhaps Peter could use the English alphabet as his magic code. The strategy of his teaching team was to have him understand that visual symbols—written words—represented objects, and then to learn that sounds were associated with those written words. We began getting him to match written words to objects in his DTT program, and to our delight, discovered that he indeed had the capacity to understand that written words symbolically represented real objects. When presented with the written word for "ball" or "cup," he would accurately hand us the corresponding item.

We then laboriously began teaching him phonics, how letters represent certain sounds that put together make audible words. We did "vowel circles," exercises in which you write down a consonant in the middle of your paper with the five vowels around it, and had Peter read aloud each pairing of consonant-vowel in turn. We went through the Nancy Kaufman Speech Praxis Workout (2006a, 2006b) that provides a home program for childhood apraxia of speech. Peter did indeed slowly but surely learn to read out loud phonetically, and that was how he learned how to talk.

To this day, he depends heavily upon written word cues. Without a written word menu in front of him, he cannot spontaneously recall words well enough to speak, except for foods and activities he frequently requests. When given word choices verbally, he often just repeats the last word spoken to him (echolalia). Even echolalia is a big advance for Peter, as it demonstrates good vocal imitation, which required major work on both his auditory processing (ability to hear the sounds in any meaningful way) and speech dyspraxia (ability to make the muscles of the face, tongue, and vocal cords coordinate and move to create verbal speech).

What has been most gratifying is the faster development of Peter's ability to understand spoken language. It's as if learning how to phonetically decode the alphabet enabled him to meaningfully "hear" spoken language. He still needs to see a new vocabulary word written as well as spoken to learn it. However, he understands enough of what we say to get by receptively, without requiring us to write down everything we want to tell him. It's as if the brain uses a roundabout visual pathway (reading) to encode a new word and be able to "hear it" and store it in memory, but thereafter there appears to be a direct or at least faster connection between hearing the word and comprehending it.

How the brain creates associations and lays down memories is sometimes surprising. Peter and I love to watch Rachel Coleman's outstanding "Signing Time" DVDs (www.signingtime.com) together. The music and visuals are entertaining and delightful. The signs are clearly paired with verbal language, either said or sung. Interestingly, without formal teaching, Peter's brain has incorporated many of those pairings, not just receptively, but also expressively. When Peter is trying to tell me something but can't retrieve the word spontaneously, I make the sign for the word I think he wants. Then he can say it verbally. In other words, Peter can retrieve a word from his memory and speak it with the support of sign language, which has no phonetic code. Is the brain circuit between the visual sign and auditory memory or some kind of musical memory site that's easier to retrieve words from? We can't predict what areas the brain may recruit to access language, nor what circuitous routes it can create to bypass poorly developed language areas.

Neither can we assume that apparently damaged areas cannot improve. Peter's auditory processing and auditory memory have improved to such a great extent that he now occasionally uses verbal language to support written. For example, in order to spell words, he has to say most of them out loud slowly, writing each letter down as he phonetically encodes it. If shown a picture of a cat and asked to spell it, he mutters "c–a–t" to himself under his breath as he sounds out each letter and writes it down. When searching for a word on his AT device, he sometimes mutters the names of the categories and subcategories he needs to navigate through to find the target word. In a great neurological turnaround, the auditory and verbal is now sometimes supporting the visual and written.

It's clear that one part of the brain can support and even help develop another. As different areas of the brain become stronger, circuits created to bypass weaker areas may be replaced with more direct routes. Your child may need to use an eclectic approach at first to communicate. Advancements in one brain area may lead to further developments in others. More possibilities will open up for your child as he gains new footholds to climb up the developmental ladder. Over time, it's likely that whatever mixture of visual and auditory supports you find useful in the beginning will change over time. The only way to know what will work for your child is to try and test it.

We have used sign, singing, picture exchange, verbal and written language, and AT in combination and at different times to assist Peter to communicate. Verbal communication alone did not work in the beginning. Pairing verbal language with written words and teaching the phonetic code eventually led to Peter being able to comprehend verbal language. Pairing verbal language with sign language led to Peter being able to retrieve expressive spoken language with signing prompts. The use of picture exchange enabled Peter to make his first requests without any prompting. Getting used to reading pictorial icons with picture exchange and written words in DTT matching exercises eventually enabled Peter to make use of AT, which talks for the child once he presses the buttons displaying the corresponding written words +/- icons.[1]

To this day, we continue to find every tool useful in different situations. Verbal communication is fastest and most convenient, but Peter can only auditorily retain short instructions and spontaneously request in short phrases. He uses his AT device to compose longer sentences to us, and as a reference to retrieve words. When we forget to bring it, or it needs recharging, we still find paper and pencil to write word menus a great way to assist Peter in word retrieval, or for us to relay longer messages or multistep directions to him. And sign has been a great way to emphasize what I want to say without raising my voice, and is handier than paper and pencil to support Peter in word retrieval.

My point is not to be afraid to explore and use different approaches. Every child is so different, and different means of communication work better for some than others. Many children have deficits in several of the multiple areas of the brain that have a role in communication. Supporting and developing each of these areas may require an eclectic approach, using multiple methods. And different communication tools work better in different settings and situations—the more tools you have, the more flexible you can be to enable your child to communicate in all kinds of situations.

You might be thinking, "Glad it worked out for you, but what about my child? How do I start with my child?" If you've been trying the simple play circuits and interactions described earlier, the truth is you've already started teaching your child how to communicate. What is communication anyway but two people exchanging responses that require tuning into one another, with the formation of one response dependent upon the other's response?

---

1   "+/-" means "with or without" ("plus or minus"). AT keys usually come labelled with both the written word label and a pictorial icon (tiny diagrammatic picture representing the word). Some words like "a" or "the," however, are better represented with the written word alone. Pictorial icons can also be gradually removed from the keys when literacy for the written word is the goal.

ACTION-BASED AND GESTURAL COMMUNICATION

Consider the steps in a play circuit. Observe your child's interests, and create an interaction around it, in which you have a turn and your child has a turn. Prompt your child through his turn, and with every repetition of the interaction, gradually, systematically fade your prompts as he takes over doing his turn on his own. The goal is for the child to find he enjoys the interaction so much that he wants these exchanges, and looks forward to his turn. Eventually, he will correct "mistakes" in the interaction, then initiate his turn on his own, and finally come up with his own variations which you incorporate into the circuit. Because you tune into your child and select an activity centered round his interests, he enjoys it, and therefore learns to tune into you. Each person's action depends upon the other having taken his turn. The desire to interact in this way forms the fundamental motivation to communicate, what speech pathologists call the "intent to communicate." Your play circuits are really your child's first conversations.

Step One: Find that element of fun

It cannot be emphasized enough that the foundation of communication is interaction. The best way to prepare your toddler to talk in the future is to find as many opportunities as possible to interact in play, outings, and daily routines like dressing, bathtime, mealtimes, and bedtime. The key to creating opportunities for interaction is to figure out what you can use as a payoff. What interests your child? That's your hook. Play is wonderful because you can create your own activity circuit around sensory payoffs that you know your child enjoys. Outings provide novelty, new sights, sounds, textures, smells, and tastes to point out to your child for him to explore, and new experiences. Payoffs can be built into daily routines, such as preferred foods at mealtime, warm water and bubbles to splash in and toys in the bath, and cuddling and colorful books at bedtime. You can find an element of fun in even mundane toileting and dressing routines if you insert songs ("This is the way we…") and imitation games (try playing stop/go while brushing teeth together) into them.

Once you figure out what interests your child, use it to get him interested in you. Find the fun and engage your child with it. After a "free sample" of the payoff, make your child pay for more by doing the work of interaction and communication with you.

Next steps: Create a conversation in actions and gestures

Fern Sussman (1999, pp.92–110), founder of the outstanding Hanen Program, talks about the four fundamental steps of getting your child to communicate with you. She calls them the "four I's." Sussman applies the four "I" principles to verbal conversation, but they also apply to the earliest stage of action-based and gestural communication, and for all types of everyday interactions, including play, outings, and routines. Let's take an example from a playtime situation. First, *include* your child's interests. Say your child is running aimlessly around the yard. His interest at that moment is to run around. Second, *interpret* for your child. As Sussman puts it, "Model what your child would say, if he could say it." You might say, with or without signing, "Run! Peter likes to run!"

Third, *imitate* your child or *introduce* something new (your turn). You might imitate him and starting running after him. After a while, he might notice you copying his every move, and start trying new moves like running in another direction to see if you follow. If he's looking back at you, you know you've been successful at turning his aimless running into an interactive game. You might even be able to get him to run after you. Alternatively, you might catch your child as he's running and say, "Gotcha!" If he likes it, try spinning him around in your arms, and then let him down to go running again.

Sussman's last "I" is to *insist* or *intrude*. Even if your child struggles out of your arms the first couple of times you catch him, be patient and persistent. Keep playfully inserting yourself into his activity. If you've tried spinning a couple of times, and he really doesn't like it, try different actions like lowering his head back, tossing him in the air, or just giving him a gentle hug and smile before putting him down. Go with whatever seems to get a happy response. With any luck, after a while, he'll get hooked on the payoff experience. Then you'll be able to put a communicative demand on your child, such as teaching him to raise his arms up for you to pick him up and give him that preferred experience. Use your order of prompts, starting with physically putting up your child's arms before spinning him, then gesturing and modeling, then perhaps giving a verbal instruction, like "Arms up!"

Learning to communicate with words

Let's take another example in which the payoff is a favorite food. Say your child grabs your hand and leads you to the cookie jar. He tries to put your hand over the cookie jar. Your child is interested in getting a cookie. You interpret his actions by saying what your child should say if he could, "I want cookie," or simply, "Cookie." Take a cookie out of the jar, get down to his eye level, face to face. Hold the cookie up and say, "Cookie." Give him a little piece. He's sure to want more. He's hooked. Now it's your turn. Hold the cookie up again, say, "Cookie," and wait expectantly. If he says "cookie" or makes whatever communicative attempt meets your target for his level at that time, give him a little piece of the cookie. Let him eat it, providing the smiles and head nods to show you are celebrating with him. You might even add, "Cookie!" in a warm tone of voice to show your approval and sneak in some back-end teaching by letting him hear you say "cookie" again.

Keep the "conversation" going. His turn is to give that target communicative attempt again, even if it's only an "oo," pointing at a picture of a cookie taped under the cookie jar shelf, or your helping him sign for cookie. Your turn is to acknowledge and affirm his effort by showing you understand and interpreting for him. "Cookie!" you reiterate, and hand him another little piece. You are introducing a keeper/requester game, and establishing a repetitive pattern or circuit that serves as the "conversation" framework for your child. By withholding the piece of cookie, you insist he take his turn in the conversation, and that he make another communicative attempt.

Moving from actions to gestures to words in conversation

What content you put in your exchanges depends upon your child's level of cognitive ability. Initially, the exchanges are the actions in your play circuits. If your child makes no communicative efforts at all, your initial target may just be to engage. In the first example, it would be great if your child did like being spun around or tossed up in the air. You might be able to set a target of waiting to get him to look into your eyes before you give that next spin or toss in the air. "Aha! I see you're looking at me! That means you want a spin, right?" you might say as you deliver that spin.

If he doesn't want to do anything but run again, help him express his protest as his communicative attempt. As he struggles in your arms, teach him to shake his head "no," or better yet, prompt him to gesture "down," and let him down as soon as he makes any recognizable attempt to gesture. Developing a repertoire of gestures is a worthy goal for the preverbal child, and requires this kind of explicit teaching in children with autism, as they do not develop gestural communication automatically. If even gesturing is too hard, make a fence with your arms around him, and let his turn be pushing your arm away or lifting your arm to duck under. Check out the "people games" in Sussman's *More Than Words* (1999, pp.139–88) or play circuits in Gutstein's *Relationship Development Intervention with Young Children* (2002a).

It's important to emphasize that you need to stay at this action/gestural level of interaction and communication for as long as your child needs. Just as it would make no sense at all to drill an infant on using scissors or saying the alphabet, you should not be constantly trying to communicate at a level beyond your child's current developmental cognitive capacity. At best such efforts are a waste of time and at worst a cause of immense frustration for both you and your child. You will know you're working at the right level if your child is usually successful at taking his turn in your interactions, and is eager to engage with you.

Of course you need to occasionally probe by making a higher communicative demand on your child, such as waiting for your nonverbal child to point down before you put him down, or waiting for your child to not only push away your encircling arms, but to look into your eyes before you let him go. If he's successful, but it takes so much effort that you can see he's getting frustrated, go back to lower demands for several more turns before you try again. Adjust the difficulty of the content of your exchange by your child's reactions, and he will make progress at his own pace.

COMMUNICATING WITH OBJECT EXCHANGE

As your child's cognitive abilities grow, you set different targets for your child's communicative turn. In general, cognitive development progresses from the concrete to representational to symbolic (Siegel 2003). Say your child eats the last cookie in a box and wants more. He might communicate that to you by handing you the empty box. You take the empty box and hand him a cookie you take out of a freshly opened box. Leave the empty box next to him, and when he wants another cookie, have him hand you the empty box again. If you give small enough pieces of cookie, you might get many exchanges out of his hunger for cookies. You are teaching your child the most concrete level of communication, "object exchange." Similarly, if your child has a special cup, you might turn that cup into his "requesting drink" cup. Whenever he wants a drink, have him hand you that cup, and exchange it for one with a drink in it. If he has a special spoon, you might have him hand it to you whenever he wants to eat (Sussman 1999).

REPRESENTATIONAL COMMUNICATION: USING PICTURES

Exchanging a picture for the desired item is the idea behind PECS, the picture exchange communication system. The picture representations can start out being concrete and gradually switched to being more and more symbolic. Your initial representation of "cookie" might be a real cookie taped to a card. Once your child gets good at using that, you might switch to card with a cut-out of the picture of the cookie on the package taped to it. Then you might go to a photograph of it, a color drawing, and finally a diagrammatic line drawing, or picture icon. The less concrete the representation, the less specific, the easier to generalize.

The key part of PECS is to make sure your child gets down the communicative process of handing you a picture representation of the food, toy, activity, place, or person he wants. You can make it easier for him by locating his PECS cards conveniently. Put a strip of Velcro on the refrigerator and pantry, and hang picture cards of his favorite food choices on them, so he can easily pull off a choice and hand it to you. He's more likely to use the PECS if he doesn't have to walk over to find his book of PECS cards, especially at first. Hang PECS cards of his favorite toy choices on his toy closet, book choices on his bookshelf, videos on the video cabinet, songs on the MP3 or CD player, and places on the front door or on a ring attached to your keys.

After your child works out the process of picture exchange and gets used to reading pictorial icons, many families move on to using dedicated communication AT devices or communication applications for smart phones or tablets, such as the iPad, iPod, or iPhone. These AT aides store and organize up to thousands of picture icons in a portable fashion that saves the whole family from the perennial frustration of misplaced or lost PECS cards. However, as with PECS, you do need to practice categorization with your child, as the icons are generally organized and accessed by category.

To find "cookie" the initial screen might show a number of category icons. If your child pushes the button or touches the icon for "food," subcategories of snacks, fruit, breakfast, lunch, and dinner foods might pop up. If he selects "snack" or "dessert," a range of choices would then appear, including cookies. Some AT devices have additional benefits like voice output so that the device verbalizes your child's picture selections. If the waitress at a restaurant asks your child what he wants to eat, he can press the button for French fries, and the device says, "French fries" out loud for him.

SYMBOLIC COMMUNICATION: USING WORDS

Of course, the least cumbersome, fastest, and most efficient means of communication are symbolic. Speaking, writing, and sign language are all forms of symbolic communication.

Using sign language as a bridge and visual aide

Sign language may be a useful bridge as many signs are somewhat representational, and it is obviously readily available as you always have your hands with you. The sign for cookie actually looks like the action you use when you cut a cookie with a cookie cutter. To sign for banana, you hold up your index finger on one hand to represent the banana, and use your other hand to pretend to peel it. Signs for coming and going mimic natural gestures. When your goal is just to get your child to take his turn in a "conversation," sign language is a useful default for his communicative attempt as you can always fall back on doing a hand over hand prompt. The problem with sign language is, however, that many people are unfamiliar with it and don't understand it. Also, many children with ASD (autism spectrum disorder) are a little dyspraxic, and don't get beyond making more than a few somewhat sloppy signs. However, signing can be a useful adjunct while you work on other forms of symbolic communication.

Incidental teaching for verbal and written communication

Speaking and writing are clearly the most readily available, universally understood forms of symbolic communication. Some children may be able to make the leap to symbolic communication through just the day-to-day incidental opportunities you provide to pair picture representations to the spoken or written word. Say your child is already adept at using PECS. If your child hands you the PECS card for "cookie," say, "Oh, cookie! You want a (pause)." Let him fill in the blank with some vocal approximation for "cookie" before you give him the cookie. Eventually, he may just skip handing you the PECS card, and just ask you for "ootie." Celebrate and hand him the cookie. Over time, with many repetitions, he may spontaneously use his word approximation for cookie, and you may put away the PECS card. Over time, one word at a time, you may make the transition from PECS to spoken language.

Similarly, if you always pair your pictorial representation with the printed word for cookie, your child might eventually make the leap to sight reading. Try to make the printed word on your word cards progressively larger as you make the pictorial icon progressively smaller. Someday, your child may be able to hand you a symbol, a card with only the word "cookie" printed on it and no picture, to tell you he wants a cookie.

Using discrete trials to prime your child

However, many children need more practice than they can get through incidental teaching. Drills using discrete trials (DTT) may be necessary to provide enough repetitions to enable the child to make the connections between the spoken and printed words for "cookie" and a real cookie. A typical series of drills might consist of the child first having to match several different items, including a cookie, to their printed word labels. Then to work on a receptive understanding of the written or spoken word "cookie," you might do a "Give me ____" drill in which he hands you the correct item when labeled verbally or with a written word card. Finally, to work on expressive language, you might ask your child, "What is this?" as you have him verbally label or hand you the appropriate written word card for various items.

These kinds of drills may be critical in forging those initial neurologic connections between the word labels and the real items, but you still need to keep up the incidental teaching. The key to making the drills stick is for you to generalize what's been taught in your child's daily life. Keep close tabs with your child's tutors, and be sure to grab every meaningful opportunity to use the new words he learns. Once he discovers that in the real world he immediately gets a piece of cookie when he says a verbal approximation or hands you the printed word card for "cookie," he is much more likely to remember the connection. For learning to be remembered, it has to be meaningful.

Supporting word retrieval

Even when you do your best to make words useful and meaningful in real life, your child may still have difficulty with word retrieval. He may remember the meaning of a word when you say it or when he reads it, but he may not have the capacity to retrieve the word from his memory when he wants to express it. In other words, the connections your child learns by pairing and remembers by meaningful use may not be retrievable without ongoing support. Hence a child may always need some kind of reference, such as a word bank, PECS book, or AT device with words organized by category.

The best and most efficient reference is, of course, you. Because you know your child so well, you can usually guess what he wants or is interested in. Narrow the field of word/picture choices to as few as your child can handle. Instead of having to scan long lists of word or picture icon choices in a word bank, PECS book, or AT device, your child can pick from a list of one to several word/picture choices. "What do you want to do next?" you might ask your child as you hand him three cards that read/picture "book," "TV," and "outside." Consider displaying your choices on cards Velcroed onto a choice board. That way, your child can clearly demonstrate his choice by peeling off his selected card and handing it to you. If your child transitions to written words without pictures, use laminated blank cards and a dry erase marker to create your word menus on the go. Once your child makes definite and clear choices, you may want to transition him away from the cumbersome process of unpeeling and handing over Velcroed cards to having him just point to or circle his word choice from a written list.

I try to remember to carry something to write on so I can offer Peter word choices he can circle or point to, so when at the park, I can ask, "What do you want to play first?" and offer him a word list such as "swing," "sand," and "slide." (For nonreaders, there are a number of pictorial icon-based applications commercially available that are accessible via smart phones or tablets.) If no visual supports are available, offer verbal choices. "Swing or slide?" For the child with echolalia who tends to repeat whatever word(s) he last heard, put the word you believe he's looking for first and the distracter word last to make him tune in and answer purposefully instead of automatically. If he loves the swings, but is afraid of the slide, but answers "slide" because it is the last word he heard in your question, go ahead and start bringing him to the slide. That gives him a chance to make another communicative attempt, "No!" Then gently repeat your question again, "*Swing* or slide?" Using your voice to emphasize the correct word choice, "swing," serves as another prompt. Patient insistence will help train your child to tune into your words.

HOW TO TEACH YOUR CHILD TO PUT WORDS TOGETHER (SENTENCE CONSTRUCTION)

Once your child uses a vocabulary of a few dozen words with or without supports, he's probably ready to learn how to put words together.

Categorize your vocabulary by parts of speech

It's helpful to teach your vocabulary in groups organized by parts of speech, as the groupings provide a nice set-up for phrase/sentence construction. Categorize your child's vocabulary into subjects (people, animals), object nouns (functional items of preference or necessity in daily life), verbs or "action words" (consider starting with the present progressive tense so that all verbs end with "ing," making them easy to recognize), prepositions (such as in, out, under, in front of, and behind), and descriptors (colors, number of, and opposite pairs such as big/little, up/down, and hot/cold).

Incidental teaching tools: Add one word, use carrier phrases, and employ music

In daily life, start using Sussman's (1999) rule of "*repeat, and add* one word." If your child stubs his toe and says, "Hurt!" consider saying, "Hurt. Hurt toe." If he wants a push on the swing, and calls you, saying, "Mama," reply, "Mama. Mama push." If he's up to two-word phrases, continue your "repeat, add one more part of speech" strategy. If he hears a siren and says, "Too loud," acknowledge his comment with, "Too loud. Fire truck too loud."

Teach *carrier phrases* like "I want," "I see," and "I went" because they are useful, versatile, and count as one unit in your child's mind (Sussman 1999, p.100). If your child requests, "Juice," say "Juice. I want juice." Then pause with the pitcher in your hand, and wait for your child to say "I want juice" before pouring some.[2]

---

2 Nancy Kaufman's (2006a) excellent book of dyspraxia exercises includes drills on the use of carrier phrases.

Music is another tool you can employ to teach language concepts and communication skills. Sussman (1999, pp.297–332) has an outstanding chapter entitled, "Make the Most of Music." Some classic children's songs already teach language concepts like body parts in the song "Head, shoulders, knees, and toes," body parts and prepositions in the song "Hokey pokey," and animals and animal sounds in "Old MacDonald had a farm." Some classics can be easily adapted to teach whatever language concepts you're targeting. I taught Peter how to shower to the tune of "Here we go round the mulberry bush." I sang, "This is the way we wash our (arm, leg, tummy, back, etc.)" so he could copy me as I demonstrated those actions standing outside the shower. I use the same song to teach dressing, combing, and toothbrushing skills. "If you're happy and you know it" is a perfect song to teach emotions. Sing in front of the mirror, "If you're happy and you know it, make a smile…" or "If you're sad and you know it, cry boo hoo…" (to the tune of "If you're happy and you know it"). Teach your child some social speech like "How are you today?" to the tune of "Happy birthday to you."[3] Music is great for eliciting turn taking, imitation, and language as many children can't resist "filling-in-the-blank" when the last word in a line of a song is left out.

How to use structured teaching to construct sentences
SELECT SOMETHING WORTH TALKING ABOUT

Once again, try to get incidental teaching done with every opportunity. However, some children will require more intense and focused practice initially to learn how to put words together. One low-tech strategy is to construct sentences that describe simple action pictures such as of a moving train, a fish swimming, or a baby eating. You can get such pictures from books, magazine cut-outs, and google images, or buy them from catalogs of educational teaching materials. Your child might be more interested in talking about the images if you select them together as the two of you go through family photographs, favorite books, and colorful magazines. You can also talk about little scenes you create with your child's favorite action figures or toys that you freeze in a three-dimensional still life or take a photograph of. Make use of your iPhone or other handy camera and take pictures of things your child takes an interest in during the day, or meaningful events. When you select or take

---

3   Sussman (1999, p.326). You can also teach, "How old are you…I'm (age in years), thank you," to this song.

pictures, do your best to keep them clear and simple, without a lot of distracting background images.

CREATE WORD MENUS FOR EACH PART OF SPEECH

Say your child seems interested in the cover of his Thomas video showing a train moving, a *National Geographic* picture of a colorful fish swimming, and an old photograph of his baby brother making a mess while eating. If your child can read, create word menus for each part of speech, such as subject word cards printed with "The train," "The fish," and "The baby." Velcro these words to a subject menu strip. Attach "is going," "is swimming," and "is eating" to a verb menu strip. If your child can't read yet, he can do the same procedure using PECS cards instead of printed word cards.

CREATING SUBJECT-VERB SENTENCES

Teach your child how to construct simple *subject-verb* sentences by making the correct selections from the menus and placing them on a Velcro sentence strip placed under the action picture. You can even put a label for "subject" under the first "blank," and "verb" under the second, matching the same headings on the word menu strips. Your child selects the proper vocabulary cards and Velcroes them to the sentence strip to describe the picture. Give your child the picture of the baby eating with the sentence strip under it with the blanks labeled "subject" and "verb." Then hand him a subject menu strip and a verb menu strip. Prompt your child (remember to follow the order of prompts and give him the least amount of help he needs) to select "The baby" from his subject menu strip and place it on the subject blank on the sentence strip, and select "is eating" from his verb menu strip to place on the verb blank on the sentence strip. Gradually fade the "subject" and "verb" labels on your word menu headings and then under your sentence strips, and see if your child can construct a subject-verb sentence such as "The baby" "is eating" without them.

For a higher-tech alternative, there are language applications and computer games by companies like Laureate that do similar exercises. AT devices naturally lend themselves to phrase and sentence construction, as the word menus are usually already organized by category and parts of speech. One of the benefits of AT devices is that the child learns to organize words in his head by parts of speech as he searches for words that way on his device, and learns to construct sentences by putting those parts of speech together.

USING MULTIPLE ATTRIBUTES

You might next try a similar procedure to teach descriptor-noun word pairings. Have your child match pictures with one and then two attributes to written descriptors such as "big, yellow square," "little, yellow square," "big, red square," "two, little squares," "one, big square" to make him *attend to multiple cues* as well as learn to use a variety of descriptors. Try playing *attribute games*, in which your child selects an enticing item from among several based upon the descriptors you present, and vice versa, in which he describes the item he wants in order to get to play with it. For example, have him choose from among a blue car, blue train, red car, and red train to put in your open hand as you say, "I want a blue train." Then switch roles. Take all the vehicles, and let him ask you for the one he wants by describing it. If he wants them all, you have the perfect opportunity to teach conjunctions and number modifiers. "I want the red train *and* the blue train." "I want *two* cars and *two* trains."

CREATING SENTENCES WITH THREE PARTS OF SPEECH

Once your child masters phrases with two parts of speech, move on to sentences with three parts of speech. Try constructing *subject-verb-object sentences* like "The boy is eating ice cream." The beauty of making your own word labels by hand is that you can group them flexibly to teach your child how to put more complex sentences together. If your child has no difficulty constructing simple subject-verb-object sentences, teach him how to add in descriptors. Show the picture of the boy eating ice cream. Ask your child to describe the boy (offering a descriptor menu like big, little, happy, sad) and perhaps get "little boy." You can ask him to describe the ice cream (offering a descriptor menu like pink, yellow, green, yummy, yucky) and perhaps get "pink ice cream." Make your subject card "The little boy" and your object card "pink ice cream." Then get your child to place the three parts of speech, now embellished with descriptors, on his subject-verb-object sentence strip, and he has created quite a long sentence, "The little boy" "is eating" "pink ice cream."

Transitioning into answering "wh" questions

I should mention that instead of using the traditional labels for parts of speech, I actually use less technical terms. Try substituting "who" for subject, "doing" for verb, and "what" for object. If your child gets used to seeing those words on his word menu headings and under his sentence strip blanks, it will help him in his transition to the next level of language development, answering "wh" questions.

Show your child the picture of the boy eating ice cream, with a blank answer strip under it. Hand him a subject menu strip labeled "who" that includes several words like "boy," "girl," and "baby." Hand him a verb menu strip labeled "doing" that includes words like "eating," "walking," and "swimming." Finally, hand him an object sentence strip labeled "what" that includes words like "ice cream," "popcorn," and "apple." Include pictorial icons[4] for "who," "doing," and "what" alongside your printed word labels if your child uses PECS or AT primarily, but also if you have a child who reads, but could use the pictorial support.

Present each "wh" question visually as well as verbally. Visually ask your question by writing it down by hand, using an AT device, and/or using pictorial icons (PECS). You may emphasize the "wh" word in your question by writing that word larger and perhaps in bold, and stressing the word when you say it. When you ask a "who" question (like *"Who* is eating ice cream?"), the child can go right to his "who" (subject) menu strip to select the answer. When you ask a "what is he/she/it *doing*?" question (like "What is the boy doing?"), he has only to match the word "doing" to know to reference his "doing" (verb) menu strip. When you ask a "what" question (like *"What* is the boy eating?"), he can reference his "what" (object) menu strip. With repeated practice, you may be able to fade the "who," "doing," and "what" labels on his word menus, and have him answer "wh" questions independently, without the help of matching labels.

TEACHING PREPOSITIONS

One of the most challenging but also fun parts of speech to teach is the use of prepositional phrases. Have your child climb on top of a slide or go under a slide, for example, so he can use his own body to follow directions using prepositional phrases. Enjoy treasure hunts with a chip

---

4   Such icons can be found on the website for Johnson-Mayer and in Sussman (1999, p.251).

hidden in a box, under the table, behind the computer, etc. (The treasure hunt idea is also very helpful to motivate a child to learn the names of the different rooms in the house, as you tell him which room the treasure is hidden in.)

For more advanced students, use action figures or stuffed animals to weave a little story of hide and seek. Take out a goldfish cracker, shark puppet or stuffed animal, and box. Ask the child, "Where should the little fish hide?" Let him choose from a menu of prepositional phrases, which might include, "under the box," "behind the box," and "on top of the box." Prompt him to place the fish there. Then have the big bad shark come along and look for the fish in several wrong places. Hopefully, the child will not be able to resist telling the shark where to look with a prepositional phrase, using his prepositional phrase menu as a reference if necessary to aide him in word retrieval. If the child doesn't take the initiative, have the shark finally ask the child, "Where is the little fish?" and prompt him to answer correctly, using his prepositional phrase menu as needed. When the shark finds the fish, have the shark share the prize with your child.

Your child may also switch roles and play the shark. Have him cover his eyes while you hide the goldfish cracker, and have him ask you where it is. You can repeat this game with any cast of edible characters you can find, such as gummy bears and animal crackers. If your child gets into the game at a faster pace, it can morph into a game of chase. "Where should the fish swim to next?" Of course, if your child likes to play hide and seek and you can find another person to play with, practice prepositional phrases when you ask him where the two of you should hide or where the two of you should look, depending on whether your team is hiding or seeking.

I should clarify at this point that all these sentence constructions can be done using whatever method or combination of methods of communication work best for your child. Your child may select words by choosing from among a menu (list of choices) of printed word cards, PECS cards, or pictorial icons with or without written labels on an AT device screen. I suggest, however, that you encourage your child to do his best to try to verbalize the sentence he's made, as speaking is so useful, even if he can only manage a few favorite or urgent requests. A little verbal speech can go a long way, and with time and practice, his repertoire may increase.

HOW TO HELP YOUR CHILD TO VERBALIZE: A METHODICAL APPROACH

A child with speech dyspraxia has a lot of difficulty producing verbal speech. The mechanism may include motor planning difficulties (coordinating the muscles of the lips and tongue and breathing to produce speech), problems with memory and word retrieval, and problems with word order and grammar. Treatment includes all the accommodations discussed such as PECS, signing, and AT devices, and lots of practice with articulation and sentence construction. You can help your child with all these tools and exercises, and most of all by providing a warm, supportive environment to encourage your child's efforts and demonstrate a patient determination to help your child make himself understood.[5]

Kaufman (2006a, pp.120–1) describes an excellent *order of speech prompts* that she calls "scripting functional language" to coach a speech dyspraxic child to verbalize words, then phrases, and then sentences. As usual, the idea is to give just enough prompting as necessary, fading your support as your child improves. Say your child looks up at the cookie jar, and hands you the picture/word card for "cookie." If your child is just learning picture/word card exchange, immediately reward the child's communication with the cookie at this point. However, say your child has the concept of card exchange down solid. He's ready to learn something new. If you want to teach him to verbalize as the next step, there is an order of cues or prompts you can follow to challenge your child in a methodical way.

Prompting and shaping words

The least intrusive prompt is to simply wait. Say your child hands you the PECS/word card for cookie. You say, "I see you want a (pause)." Hold the cookie card he just handed you, point to it and look at him with an expectant look. If you get no response, add a gestural prompt and sign for "cookie." If no response, say, "Cookie," and don't hand over the cookie until your child tries to imitate you. Kaufman makes the point that it's important to reinforce a child for his best attempt at a word approximation, even if it's barely intelligible. For example, at first, go ahead and enthusiastically reward your child with a cookie (or piece of cookie) even if all he can say is, "uh-ee." As he gets better with practice,

---

5   Some children with speech dyspraxia falter when they perceive pressure to speak. Withholding desired items might feel too demanding for some children. Your child's speech pathologist should be able to guide you on the best method of teaching.

wait to reward for successively better approximations: "tootie," perhaps, and then "kuh-ee," and finally "cook-ee" (Kaufman 2006a). Kaufman's Speech Praxis Treatment Kit (2006b) includes shaping cards that list an order of approximations for each word beginning with the easiest of word "shells" (approximations) to articulate. Teaching and rewarding the simplified approximations enables a child to feel successful at each step of the shaping process.[6]

Adding carrier phrases

To teach your child to make a whole sentence, try adding an "I want" PECS and/or printed word(s) card to your choice board, and prompt him to place it on his sentence strip with verbal instruction, a gesture, or hand over hand maneuver, whichever is the least intrusive level of support he requires. Then have him place the "cookie" card after it, again providing the least intrusive level of prompting he needs. To help him verbalize his sentence, try the Kaufman order of speech prompts. Ask him a yes/no question that includes the vocabulary he needs for his answer. "Do you want a cookie?" Help him say "yes" with his best approximation or head nod. Then give him a verbal instruction that includes the words he needs for his answer. "Tell me, 'I want a cookie.'"

You might take "Ah wah" for "I want" initially, then withhold the cookie for better and better approximations, such as "Ah-ee ahnt" or "I oo-ahnt." You don't have to wait for perfect enunciation of "cookie" before putting words together. "I want," you say. "Ah wah," he says. "Cookie," you say. "Uh-ee," he says. "I want cookie," you say. If your child readily makes the approximation "Ah wah uh-ee," reward with a big cookie. Once he's demonstrated consolidation of that level of articulation by readily repeating the phrase whenever he wants a cookie, you can start shaping. If your child understands phonics, you can point to each word on his sentence strip as a visual cue to help him with his pronunciation.

Buildups and breakdowns

The concept of buildups and breakdowns (Sussman 1999, p.208) is very useful when working with a child to put words together. The example

---

6   Kaufman (2006a) also provides hand signal cueing techniques for vowels and simple consonants, and discusses a variety of other kinds of cues such as "mouthing a word" (oral postural cues), written cues (using phonics), and backward chaining cues (for "cookie" that would mean teaching and rewarding "ee" initially, then waiting for better approximations to reward in the following order: kee → ookee → cookie).

in the last paragraph was a buildup. "I want." (Child repeats, "I want.") "Cookie." (Child repeats, "cookie.") "I want cookie." (Child repeats, "I want cookie.") The opposite would be a breakdown. "I want cookie," you model to your child. If you get no response, break it down. "I want," you say. (Child repeats, "I want.") "Cookie," you say. (Child repeats, "Cookie.") You can always try another buildup then. "I want cookie." (Hopefully the child repeats, "I want cookie.") Use any combination of buildups and breakdowns. If your child falls down and hurts his knee, he may be anxious to tell you about it. "Hurt knee," you might say, pointing to his knee. "Peter fell down," you might add, gesturing "falling down" with both hands. "Peter fell down and hurt his knee."

Order of prompts for verbalizing sentences

If the chunks are too big in even the buildups and breakdowns, try the Kaufman (2006a, p.121) order of prompts for scripting functional language. Have your child repeat the whole sentence after you, one word at a time. Once he can do that easily, fade to giving each word of the phrase except the last word. "I want (pause)." "Peter fell down and hurt his (pause)." Once he can do that easily, withdraw another layer of support by just giving the first word of the phrase and the initial sound of the subsequent words. "I w…" (or "I w…c…" if he can't fill in that last blank without the initial sound prompt). "Peter f…d…and h…h…(pause)." Once he can do that easily, just model the mouth configuration for the initial sound of each word. Then just model the mouth configuration of the initial sound of the first word of the sentence. You can then probably just wait or say, "Tell me what you want," or "Use your voice" as he hands you his sentence strip, and point to the words/pictures as he says them or give sign/gesture prompts as needed.

A little goes a long way: Making it a priority to teach critical requests, yes/no, and social speech

Again, a little verbal speech goes a long way. Use your order of speech prompts to try to teach your child to verbally make a few critical requests like water, pee pee (or another word for bathroom), hurt, eat, and help, and use of the carrier phrase, "I want."

Teach him how to either say "yes" or "no" or nod and shake his head by offering him choices of things you know he doesn't want to get and things that you know he really wants to get. "Do you want this carrot for snack?" you might ask, as you place a carrot on his plate, and sit down with him to enjoy your popcorn. As your child reaches for your popcorn, ask your question about the carrot again, and prompt him to indicate "No." Then offer some popcorn. "Do you want some popcorn?" Prompt him to say "Yes" or nod his head, and then give him the popcorn.[7]

It will also help your child greatly to learn a few social words like "please," "thank you," "welcome," "sorry," "hello," and "bye." He can certainly learn to use them with PECS or an AT device, but it's worthwhile to also learn to vocalize or sign for them, as the opportunities to use them come up frequently and fast, and he may not always have the right cards or AT device with him. If you make it a habit, he will come to sign and/ or say these social words automatically or with minimal cueing. I often coach the people Peter is receiving something from to just hold onto the item he's requesting for a second till he says his "please" or "thank you." Often that tiny pause is the only reminder he needs. Acquiring these small social graces can make a big difference in how other people perceive and receive your child.

A game to practice social speech over the phone

I initially created this game to teach Peter how to use a telephone, but it creates many opportunities to practice polite social speech as well. I call it, "Down by the bay," after the silly song we love to sing to mark the beginning and end of the game. Peter and his little brother Luke sit up on the family room sofa, pretending it is an island in the "bay." I sit within eyeshot, but a bit away, in my store, "on the shore." I take the landline home phone, and the children use my cell phone. The children take turns calling me on the telephone. Peter knows the whole number. (We taught him by predialing the numbers minus the last digit, then the last two, then the last three, etc.) The children order what they want me to send from my store from an array of small treats I display on a tray (you may also give them menus). I put the treats in a "boat" (a laundry basket with a rope tied to it) that they pull in (they have the other end of the rope) to their island and enjoy. They have to remember their hellos, goodbyes, pleases, and thank you's as they practice their telephone manners.

---

7   It may take a long time for a child to use "yes/no" meaningfully. Even if the child knows what he wants and doesn't want, he may say the opposite word that he means because the part of his brain controlling speech betrays him and makes what are called "paraphasic errors," in which it involuntarily substitutes one word for another. Use PECS to enable your child to reach for his real choice, and then practice "yes/no" as described in the text.

SUMMARY: NOW YOU KNOW THE PRINCIPLES

At this point, you have the principles necessary to develop a basic system of communication for your child. The brain is a remarkable organ, and you cannot predict what areas the brain might recruit to bypass damaged language areas, which in turn may grow new circuits that later support the development of other areas. Therefore, it's important to be flexible and eclectic in your approach. Different forms of communication such as sign, singing, PECS, verbal and written language, and AT, work better in different settings and situations, and at different stages of the brain's ever-changing course of development.

The foundation of communication is interaction—expanding your child's desire for interaction expands his communicative intent. Your play circuits are therefore your child's first conversations. The content of these conversations grows with your child's cognitive abilities. As these progress from the concrete to representational to symbolic, your child's mode of communication moves from actions to gestures to pictures to words.

At every stage, the rules of conversation pertain. Begin with including your child's interest, finding the hook or the payoff for which your child will work to put in the effort of communication. Interpret for your child, "saying it the way he would if he could," thereby demonstrating your attunement to him. Knowing that you're listening and feeling understood will make your child more inclined to tune into you. For your turn in the conversation, present something your child likes such as an activity, something tangible (such as food, a toy, or prize), or a novelty (such as pointing out an animal at the zoo or float in a parade). Introduce a conversation framework such as a play circuit or keeper/receiver interaction that creates a communicative demand on the child, whether that be an action, gesture, or words using whatever mode of communication works for him (sign, PECS, AT, written or spoken language, or a combination). Insist on him taking his turn by making the payoff contingent upon his communicative effort.

You can support your child in his communicative effort in many ways. Use discrete trials to prime your child for incidental teaching—use drills to teach words so that your child can use them in the conversations of natural, daily life. Use structured teaching to help your child learn sentence construction—teach vocabulary in categories of parts of speech, use carrier phrases and subject-verb, subject-verb-object templates, and teach modifiers and prepositions. Support his word retrieval with word banks, PECS, or AT. Teach progressive word approximations to shape articulation. The Kaufman order of speech prompts may help your child verbalize sentences.

However, the most important way to help your child to communicate is with your warm encouragement and patient support. Find that element of fun, and base your interactions around that. That's how you keep the conversation going.

The fruitstand

Peter's floortime specialist brought over a new game called "The fruitstand." It consisted of an upright cardboard fruitstand that held a variety of colorful plastic toy fruit of all kinds. Each player spins the spinner on his turn that points to a color and number. The goal is to pick the number of fruits of that color with a pair of tweezers without making the rest of the fruit tumble down. The winner is the person who collects the most fruit. Wow! I thought of all the possibilities of getting Peter to count aloud, do math, and name different colors and kinds of fruit, plus all the social talk he could practice as we passed the spinner and tweezers and commented on each other's performance.

Unfortunately, Peter was not at all interested in the game. He just wanted to lie back on the couch and squish himself with the cushions. Aha! The payoff! "Come on, Peter! I'll race you! I get to sit on you if I grab the fruit first!" I said. I grabbed my pair of tweezers and went for a strawberry as the spinner fell on red. Peter saw what I was up to and grabbed his tweezers. We raced to the strawberry, and I beat him by a hair. "Ha! I win!" I said triumphantly, and dramatically sat upon Peter, making the pillows fly. Peter started giggling. "C'mon, Peter, no room!" I locked his hands around my waist like a safety belt, and we started scooting together with me on top to an open spot on the couch, for which I finally abandoned Peter's lap. "Okay, I wonder who's turn it is now?" I said, and Peter eagerly reached for the spinner.

In the end, we really did work in naming and math as I pretended not to know what fruit and how many to go for unless he told me. But the wave we were riding, what gave the game its momentum, was Peter's desire to scoot around the couch and squish Mom or be squished.

So find that element of fun, and focus your communication and other interactions around that. Affect and relationship drive learning and communication.

Chapter 10

Teaching Nonverbal Communication

I attended a brilliant demonstration by a Norwegian psychologist, Dr. Bodil Sivertsen, which has stuck with me. She invited a volunteer from the audience to come up and sit with her. In between the two was a table with some items of stationery on it. She started talking in an animated way in Norwegian, picking up items here and there, smiling, and gesturing socially. The volunteer had no idea what she was saying. Neither did anyone in the audience.

Dr. Sivertsen started over. She rearranged the items on the table to line them up neatly in a row. She picked up one item off the table, looked at the volunteer, named it in Norwegian, and gestured for the volunteer to repeat it. She repeated the process for each item, smiling with encouragement with each of her student's attempts. The volunteer understood exactly what she was saying, as she showed her each item as she named it, smiled and nodded with her encouragement and shook her head when correcting. The volunteer learned several words in Norwegian, and enjoyed the lesson immensely.

APPLYING THE FOUR S'S

Fern Sussman (1994, p.194) in *More Than Words*, talks about the critical importance of nonverbal communication. Her mantra for teaching children how to talk is the "Four S's: say less, stress, go slow, and show." That is exactly what Dr. Sivertsen demonstrated in her lesson. She established her authority as the teacher with her benevolent but commanding body language. She explained what she was teaching by her set-up of the environment with the table and a few items neatly arranged in a row. She used a gesture to direct the volunteer to sit at the table and look at the items. She delivered all of her instructions with gestures, picking up and holding up each item one at a time, and gesturing for her student to repeat after her when it was her turn. Her smiles, nods, and warm tone of voice provided the reinforcement, and resulted in a degree of emotional bonding and a sense of joy and fun. She used her eyes to point to items, indicate when it was the student's turn, and radiate emotion as she beamed at her student. She used her voice to verbalize the names of the items, but her tone and inflections were equally important in stressing the words she wanted to direct her student's attention to, and to convey insistence when she made corrections and encouragement when the answer was correct.

To many of our children with an auditory processing disorder, spoken language sounds as incomprehensible as Norwegian to us English speakers. We need to communicate with our children like Dr. Sivertsen did with that volunteer, making use of every nonverbal cue. Even though our children may not pick up these nonverbal cues as readily as neurotypical children, they definitely have the potential to respond to and tune into them.

Our job as parents and teachers is to make our nonverbal cues as big and clear as necessary for our children to learn them, gradually, over time, with constant repetition. If you consistently pair your gestures and words with high affect appropriate to the emotional context of the situation, your child will make progress in this critical area. Just remember Sussman's four S's. Especially in the preverbal stage, emphasize the showing, with gestures, voice inflection, and the visual cues you provide in your environmental set-up.

THE IMPORTANCE OF NONVERBAL COMMUNICATION

Even after your child learns to use some words, continue to work on nonverbal communication for its own sake. Nonverbal cues account for the great majority of our emotional communication. In fact, only 7 percent of emotional meaning is expressed in words. More than 50 percent is expressed through body language. The remaining 30–40 percent is expressed "paralinguistically," meaning through the tone, inflection, and volume of the voice (Shapiro 2003, p.237). Unfortunately, individuals with autism generally have a lot of trouble reading the body language of others. Neither do they automatically develop a repertoire of gestures to express themselves with. Lack of eye contact and pointing are two of the earliest signs of autism.

Because nonverbal communication is so important, and our children don't automatically acquire an understanding of it, it's important to consciously make the effort to help our children in this area. Nonverbal communication skills include following another's eye gaze, using natural eye contact to reference faces for feedback and information, understanding and using gestures like pointing and waving, orienting and positioning the body to show attention, and interpreting the emotional meaning of the facial expressions and body postures of others. Unfortunately, however, once verbal communication is acquired, some children may bypass learning these important skills altogether.

TEACHING NONVERBAL COMMUNICATION SKILLS WITH EXPLICIT COACHING IN DAILY LIFE SITUATIONS

Make the most of your child's preverbal years to develop his ability to give and receive nonverbal signals. Once he develops words (spoken, written, or pictorial), don't forget to keep teaching this other half of communication, both explicitly and by example. Model gesturing, showing, and voice inflections. When you have the extra moment to do so, deliver some explicit coaching. "Oh, so you're talking to *me*!" you might say after he finally looks up at you after making a comment, awaiting a reply. When he makes a request, pause, until he looks at you. "Oh, you want *me* to get it. Okay," you say as you hand him the desired item. As he stands next to his father waiting to ask him for something, prompt your child to tap his father on the shoulder to get his attention. As you see him out of the corner of your eye, waiting for something from you, don't ask, "What do you want?" Instead, try tapping yourself over the shoulder to prompt an imitation from him to tap you and learn how to get your attention nonverbally.

Above all, encourage his positive efforts. If he waves to you and a friend from across the school yard, wave back enthusiastically. Later, you might say, "I saw you waving at Gabby and me. That was a friendly thing to do." If he remembers to hold the door open for you, thank him. Later you might comment, "I love it when you open the door for me. Such a gentleman!"

CREATING MORE OPPORTUNITIES TO TEACH NONVERBAL COMMUNICATION

Include nonverbal communication goals in your child's Individualized Education Program

As in most areas, incidental teaching is usually the most meaningful way to teach nonverbal communication, but occurs sporadically. One way to get more practice in is to write a few goals for nonverbal communication in your child's Individualized Educational Program (IEP) so that everyone is looking for opportunities to practice the same gestures, eye contact, etc. both at home and at school. For example, the teacher could insist that your child greet her and one other student every morning upon arrival with at least a brief look and a wave. The teacher could make it a routine to ask the child to deliver a message to an aide or other adult daily, thereby providing an opportunity for the child to learn to get someone's attention appropriately by waiting and tapping lightly on the shoulder. However, a sure fire way to get repeated practice is to do it with games.

Play games that focus on nonverbal communication

Gutstein's (2002a) book, *Relationship Development Intervention with Young Children*, is full of exercises and games that work on following eye gaze and referencing the facial expressions and body language of others for information, using eye gaze to point and indicate attention, and coordinating and synchronizing actions. Each exercise concentrates predominately on developing one skill at a time to break down the complicated symphony of nonverbal signals used in daily communication into learnable components. In his initial exercises, Gutstein even forbids talking so the child can concentrate all his energy and attention on nonverbal communication. Michelle Garcia Winner's books (2005, 2007) also contain great ideas for working on this area in individuals with high functioning autism and Asperger's syndrome.

THE "EYES" HAVE IT!

What follows are a few favorite practical games and ideas I've found helpful to teach eye contact. Many are adaptations of games from Gutstein (2002a, 2002b) and others.

> *Peter was six years old when we visited his 84-year-old, very hard-of-hearing grandfather. I had been working hard with Peter to improve his eye contact. We had been playing a lot of stop and go games in which I wouldn't go until Peter both said "Go" and gave me eye contact. Because I was impatient, I had gotten into the habit of bobbing my head down to his eye level to make it easier and faster for him to make eye contact.*
>
> *At the end of our visit, I reminded Peter to say goodbye. To my surprise, he ducked down eye to eye with his seated grandfather, looked straight at him with eyes opened wide, and said, "Bye Yeye." I burst out laughing. It was a perfect imitation of my odd bobbing maneuvers. The old adage came to mind, "Teacher, beware of what you teach, lest your student actually learn it."*

Nowhere is that adage warning teachers to beware of what they teach more applicable than in teaching eye contact. The early methods of teaching children with autism on how to make eye contact sometimes led to highly undesirable results. The teacher would instruct the child to "Look at me" for a certain number of seconds in order to receive a reward. As the instruction was repeated over and over, what sometimes resulted was a child who learned how to stare in an unnatural and meaningless way. My head bob also resulted in Peter establishing eye contact with his grandfather in a rather odd appearing way, but at least it had a sweet communicative intent. Now instead of bobbing my head to search for Peter's eyes, I get down to his eye level and just wait for him to look. Peter's bobbing has not recurred, and his eye contact, though still effortful and occasionally still prompt-dependent, is more natural and functional.

The eyes communicate so much. In our culture, eye contact implies caring and attention. A lack of eye contact feels emotionally cold and distant to us. We make eye contact when showing respect. The eyes, eyebrows, and forehead convey much of our emotional expressions such as happy, sad, mad, scared, or surprised. We use eye contact to get someone's attention, and to demonstrate who has our attention and whom we are addressing. We "point" with our eyes.

PLAYING "LASER EYES" TO GET YOUR CHILD TO LOOK

The best way to teach your child to make eye contact is to teach him why to make eye contact through games and everyday encounters that demonstrate its usefulness. Initially, you might want to play games that exaggerate its power. When he was small, I used to take my son to the swimming pool a lot. As he quietly played by himself on the steps, I pretended to be a sea monster, warning him with splashing and lots of noise, "I'm coming closer!" If he turned around and looked at me, I dramatically fell backwards in the water and said, "Ahh, you *got* me with those laser eyes!" If he failed to turn around and look, I'd tickle him or grab him by the waist and spin him around in the water. After warming up, Peter tuned in more to me, and I would sneak up with successively quieter approaches. Gutstein (2002a) describes an analogous game on dry land in which a child's failure to look at an approaching person results in that person tickling him, or delivering some other mischievous action.

"I CAN'T SEE YOUR WORDS!"

Next consider teaching your child how eye contact is useful for getting someone's attention to signal a change or new action. The idea is to get your child engaged in a fun play circuit, and then wait for eye contact before you deliver the payoff. Say you and your partner are playing a game of stacking beanbags with your young child, swinging him on a beanbag up to the top of the stack, and on a count of three, sliding him down the stack on the beanbag like a sled on a hill. After your child gets used to the circuit, and is anticipating the fun part of sliding down, wait after that count of three for eye contact from your child. Once he looks at you, immediately nod, smile, and deliver that fun slide down. After counting to three together, if a pause is not sufficient, you may add a verbal prompt such as "I can't see your words!" (Gutstein 2002a).[1]

You can create such opportunities in chores and routines as well. Suppose you and your partner are unloading groceries from the car. If one parent is stationed at the front door and the other at the trunk of the car, you can have your child run back and forth between the two of you carrying the lighter grocery bags. Each parent can deliver a payoff upon the child's arrival such as swinging the child or a giving a high five. Once again, after your child comes to anticipate the fun upon arrival, wait for your child to make eye contact. Once he does, joyfully proceed to delivering the payoff.

EYE CONTACT THAT CREATES AN EMOTIONAL CONNECTION

The key is to make the most out of that moment of eye contact. If it's paired with a rewarding sensory experience plus a warm tone of voice

---

1   This is a phrase that Gutstein recommends to prompt your child to give you eye contact when he speaks to you.

and smiles, your child may learn to look into your eyes for love and warmth. When you start adding a demand for eye contact with social greetings such as when saying hello, goodbye, thank you, and excuse me, you don't need to insist on it with everyone—it only makes sense in the beginning for him to look into the eyes of people he cares about, and who will convey the warmth and affection that make the effort worth his while. What follows is an example of a beautiful greeting:

> Mrs. Patterson, the first grade teacher, had had Peter in her classroom a couple years before. When she saw him coming slowly down the hallway, she said, "Hi, Peter!" He continued down the hallway with his head down tucked into his shoulder. Mrs. Patterson stood in front of him, knelt down to his eye level, and gently held out her hand. "Hello, Peter. How are you?" Peter tentatively put his hand in hers and received a warm squeeze. Peter glanced up at Mrs. Patterson shyly, head still tucked into his shoulder, and smiled. "Hello," he whispered. "It's great to see you, Peter," said Mrs. Patterson warmly. She gave his hand one more squeeze, and stood aside. Peter continued on his way, head still tucked down, but with a smile on his face.

EYE CONTACT FOR POINTING

It's also worthwhile teaching your child to make eye contact for utilitarian signaling. Teach him how to point to things he wants with his eyes, and to follow the gaze of others to see what they're pointing to. Gutstein (2002a, p.86) describes a great game called "Non-verbal towers." The parent and child take turns playing the role of either architect or builder. Neither gets to talk. The builder can use his hands and build the tower, but has to look to the architect to find out which block he gets to pick up to use next. The architect indicates which block he wants the builder to use next by pointing only with his eyes, not his hands. In his game "Follow my eyes to the prize" (2002a, p.88), Gutstein describes treasure hunts in which the child follows the parent's eye gaze to the prize.

EYE CONTACT TO GET ANOTHER PERSON'S ATTENTION

It's also important to teach your child to use his eyes to get the attention of others. Toys with parts like vehicles or animals you put together, or even LEGO and puzzles work for teaching this skill. Say your child wants to build a little car made out of half a dozen parts. Display half of the parts in front of yourself and give the other half to the other parent to lay out before him. Then have your child shift attention between you and the other parent to request the parts he wants. After he gets into a rhythm with the game, don't hand over the part he's requesting from you without eye contact. The game gets to be an excellent workout when no words or pointing is allowed, and the child has to communicate solely with eye contact.

PLAYING "THE WAITER AND THE SILENT CUSTOMER" TO PRACTICE THREE-POINT EYE GAZE

Once your child gets good at these games, try teaching what's called the three-point eye gaze (see p.71 in Chapter 6). Look at someone to get his attention, look at the item of interest, and look back at the person to see his reaction and make sure he understands you. I created a game to practice this skill called "The waiter and the silent customer." Set out four or five bowls with different snack choices such as cut-up fruit, little crackers, nuts, or cereal. First make your child the waiter. Give him your bowl and a spoon, and say, "I am so hungry. Waiter, will you help me?" Then put your hands behind your back and do a three-point eye gaze, looking first at your child, then at the bowl with the ingredient of your choice, then back at your child. Someone else can prompt him if necessary to place a spoonful of that ingredient in your bowl. After several choices, thank the waiter, and switch places.

Now you're the waiter, and your child is the silent customer who has to point out his food choices with his eyes, hands behind his back. When he looks at an ingredient, narrate, "Oh, you want the _____." When he looks up at you, narrate, "Oh, you want *me* to get it for you!" If he needs prompting to choose an item, remind him, "I can't see what you want," or if that doesn't work, say," Point with your eyes!" If he forgets to look back up at you, say, "I know you want _____, but I wonder *who* should get it for you?" In that way you are explicitly teaching your child how to point with his eyes and how to signal for your attention.

PLAYING "TREASURE HUNT" GAMES TO TEACH FACIAL REFERENCING

Finally, it's worth teaching your child to reference your face for information. Toddlers naturally do this all the time, as they look back at a parent to make sure that what they're about to do next is okay. The treasure hunt is a perfect situation to engineer the need for your child to do this. Have your child select a toy or edible treat, and hide it. You can tell your child which room the prize is hidden in, but otherwise get someone else to prompt your child to reference you to know if he's getting closer or farther away. Start out by giving directions using pointing and other hand gestures, but after he gets the hang of that, move to only using head nods or shakes, and after that, make him reference your face alone for expressions of approval or disapproval.

TOWARD CREATING A REPERTOIRE OF GESTURES

It is a worthy goal to explicitly teach your child a repertoire of commonly used gestures. Put several in your annual IEP to get everyone at school and at home to find opportunities to use them with your child, and you can also practice with games.

Commonly used gestures

In *The Secret Language of Children*, Shapiro (2003, pp.261–2, 296–8) lists a number of common gestures that are worth teaching. High fives and tens, thumbs up, the okay sign (thumb and index finger forming a circle and the other three fingers up), clapping, and waving both hands raised over the head with the fists clenched (like at sports games) are great gestures for showing approval and praise. Thumbs down indicates disapproval. Head shakes and nods are basic, though surprisingly difficult for many children. (Try a game in which the family sits in a circle, and eye contact and a head nod are required before a player gets the ball sent to him/her.) Sign "all done" by holding the hands out, palms down and rotating the wrists while flicking the spread fingers outwards, and "stop" by extending the arm out holding the palm outwards and fingers up. Signal for help by raising your hand or waving both hands as if flagging someone down. Nod and smile or pat someone on the back to show you like him. Hold your index finger to your lips to tell someone to be quiet. Hold out your index finger to tell someone to wait a minute. Point to your wrist to show it's time to go or sign go by pointing away from you or using a "shooing" motion. Gesture "come here" by curling your index finger toward you, and pointing to yourself or beckoning with your arm toward yourself. Gesture "follow me" by moving the whole arm in an arc ending by pointing in the direction you're going in. Point and widen the eyes as you look at someone to tell him to look or indicate a chair for him to sit down upon.

Gesturing games

You can teach these by remembering to use them in the appropriate contexts, and by taking the time to have your child imitate you. You can practice "go" and "stop" by using gestures instead of words in "Red light, green light."[2] Another game you can try out that requires a lot of gesturing is called "Delivery truck directions." The customer pretends to call the store, which is across the room, to deliver a treat. The delivery truck driver, however, does not know the way, and asks the customer for directions. The customer then uses gestures to give blow-by-blow directions to the driver. When the driver reaches the customer, the customer gets to eat the treat. They may then switch roles.

Create an obstacle course with pillows and furniture so that the truck has to go forward two feet, then turn right two feet, then turn left two feet, etc. Say your child is the customer, and you are the driver. Someone else coaches your child to give directions. Your child gets to gesture for you to go, stop, point right, stop, turn left, stop, turn left, stop, etc. If you crash into a pillow along the way by not stopping in time, he gets to give you a thumbs down followed by a gesture for you to back up. After a final gesture to stop, he gets to give the thumbs up or okay sign when you arrive. The delivery truck driver can ham up the game with lots of other variations. After crashing into the furniture, you can pretend the truck is broken and frantically gesture for help. You can pretend to be sleepy, sign "all done," pull over, and pretend to sleep. If your child tries to wake you, you can hold up your index finger and give the "wait a minute" sign.

WORKING ON BODY LANGUAGE BASICS

Popular psychology magazines frequently run articles on how to posture one's body to express self-confidence, friendliness, or paying attention. Such nuances may be over the heads of many of our kids, but we can still work on body language. We can give our children a foundation in body

---

2   This is a classic game in which the caller stands a distance away from several runners with his back turned toward them. When he says "Green light," the runners start running toward him, but when he says "Red light" they have to stop in their tracks. If he turns around after saying "Red light" and sees anyone still moving, that runner has to go back to the beginning. The first runner to tag the caller wins and gets to be the caller next.

language basics by working on their awareness of others, control of their body posture, and identifying their own feelings and those of others.

Working on awareness of others

To get your child to learn to pay attention and tune into the body language of others, start with awareness of and accommodations for the locations of other people in space. Play silly sit down games with your whole family, such as musical chairs, or race your child to sit down with you in many different places, including some tight spots in which you have to squish together, or have your child sit on top of you (Sussman 1999, p.187).

Gutstein (2002a) describes games in which parents run with their children across the room and jump or fall into a pile of beanbags together, or synchronized walking games in which the child has to follow the pace of the parent as the parent stops, goes, and varies the speed of walking. Practice synchronized walking from the car where you parked to your destination; if you insist on going back to the car to start all over if your child gets significantly ahead of or behind you, reaching your destination becomes the built-in incentive. I taught Peter this game by walking arm in arm with him, then holding hands, then just giving verbal warnings of a change to come, and then just a mischievous smile and exchange of looks with Peter before a dramatic stop or sudden burst of speed.

Learning to demonstrate learning readiness with body posture

You can give your child his first lesson in controlling his body language by teaching him how to demonstrate learning readiness. Peter has enormous sensory integration issues and what looks like a body craving for self-stimulation. With all his flapping, squealing, and wiggling, he was distracting himself far too much to learn anything. As a purely practical matter, his first lessons had to be on how to listen and pay attention with his whole body. We taught him the "Three–Two–One countdown" (see p.101). Initially we demonstrated and did hand over hand physical prompts, we gradually faded to demonstration alone, and then counted alone. Now we just say, "Get ready to learn," and he counts down, says the steps quietly to himself (self-talk), and performs the steps independently.

IDENTIFYING AND EXPRESSING EMOTIONS THROUGH NONVERBAL COMMUNICATION

Identifying his own emotions

Finally, it's important to explicitly teach your child how to identify his own emotions and read the emotional expressions of others in their body language. Lack of a natural ability to do this is one of the core deficits in autism. So when your child gets really mad, explain to him that that bursting feeling in his chest and clenched fists is a feeling called being "mad." When he laughs and smiles, point out that he looks really "happy." You can even draw a happy, mad, or sad face on a card with the written label when he demonstrates the corresponding emotions to emphasize what his facial expression looks like. "Gee, Peter, your face looks like this. (Draw a simple line drawing of an excited face.) Does that mean you're really excited about something?"

Identifying the emotions of others

When reading books, watching videos, or observing strong emotions in other people in real life situations, grab the opportunities to point out how others feel. Thomas the Tank Engine videos are terrific because the faces on the trains are so simple and expressive. Press your pause button on the remote and talk about why Gordon looks mad or Percy looks happy. Flip through magazines to find pictures of people displaying various emotions, and cut them out to make books about "happy," "sad," or "mad."

Playing "Guess that emotion" to teach emotional identification and expression

You can play a game called "Guess that emotion" in front of the mirror in which you take turns drawing a card that says happy, sad, mad, or scared, and then act it out while the other players guess your emotion. "Drooping shoulders, corners of the mouth and eyes down—looks like you're sad." We often punctuate the correct labeling with a song (Sussman 1999, p.312), like, "If you're sad and you know it, cry boo hoo!" The game allows your child to practice how to read and accurately perceive the body language of others en vivo. It's equally important for your child to take his turn acting out emotions to become aware of how his body posture and facial expression are being perceived by others.

Point out discrepancies to teach the common "tongue"

Our children sometimes send nonverbal messages that don't truly match their intentions. It's important to point these instances out to your child and explicitly teach him how to speak the common "tongue" of body language. For example, if your child is excited and jumps several feet in the air right in front of someone, that could be perceived as threatening. Step in, translate, and teach an appropriate substitute nonverbal expression. "Oh Peter, I see you are excited to see Miss Cindy. We need to keep our 'bubble distance' though. Remember 'bubble distance?' We stay an arm's length away to give people enough room. How about giving her a high five and a low five instead of jumping?"

Using drama to teach nonverbal communication

Where we live we are fortunate to have a couple of institutions that offer drama classes for children with special needs. Drama is not just for more able, high functioning children. When you play with puppets, dolls, or stuffed animals with your child, you are giving your child the same kind of opportunity to try on and express different emotions. Angry Papa Bear uses a deep, serious voice and stands up tall when he asks, "Who's been sleeping in my bed!" and Goldilocks jumps up and trembles when she wakes up and is terrified to see the three bears. Aggressive Mr. Wolf steps forward and leans in when he huffs and puffs to blow the house down. The third little pig dances merrily when he tricks Mr. Wolf. The toys can't make the corresponding facial expressions, but you and your child can as you talk for them.

At home, we sometimes put on our own drama class in the form of skits. Peter's brothers will act out a simple dramatic scenario, and Peter guesses the emotion depicted. One brother acts "happy" as he plays with a cool toy. Another brother comes by, acts "mean," and snatches the toy away. The first brother then acts "mad" and demands the toy back. "How does he feel?" we ask Peter. The next skit may depict someone stubbing his toe and acting "hurt," dropping his ice cream cone (plastic play food) and acting "sad," or winning a game and feeling "happy." If you write down the scenarios and practice them repetitively, your child may learn these simple plots and be able to take his turn as the actor, with a shadow coach modeling and prompting. The other players can guess which emotion he is depicting, and offer hearty applause for better and better attempts.

NOT EASY, BUT DEFINITELY WORTHWHILE

I have to confess that despite spending quite a bit of effort and time trying to teach body language, our success is limited. Peter still walks past people trying to greet him. We have to coax gestures like waving and head nods out of him by waiting a while, and they still look dyspraxic. It takes him a while to process body language; when I get mad, he still smiles for a minute before he realizes how I feel and his expression changes.

However, I am so glad for every minute we've worked on nonverbal communication. It's taken that extra moment of waiting and effort to coach, but at least Peter is aware that this other layer of language exists and that he needs to pay attention to it. With a family of nine to get in and out, I really appreciate that he has the body awareness to scoot over in the booth in the restaurant or move to sit in the back of the car to make room for the rest of the family. He charms his teacher when he says "excuse me" even though she had to purposefully and repeatedly block his path for him to learn to say it. He charms me as he opens the door for me though I've had to make many loud protests when he forgot and closed the door in my face. Peter has stolen many a heart by the spontaneous shy, quick glances he makes into the eyes of people he especially likes.

Therefore, slow going as it is, don't give up! Persistently make your child aware of the nonverbal signals going in, and coach him so that the appropriate signals go out. Such efforts will make a bigger difference in your child's social life than any amount of verbiage you could teach.

Chapter 11

Fundamental Stages of Social and Emotional Development

My husband Vinh came home from work and flopped down on the couch opposite us, gesturing and saying, "Come sit with me, Peter." Peter instead turned his body away from Papa to me and buried his head into the couch beside me. I said, "Oh Peter, look at poor Papa! How do you think he feels?" Peter looked over at Papa, and said, "Sad." I said, "I think you are right. He looks so sad and lonely." Peter then got up and sat down next to Papa, laying his head on Papa's lap. Of course, Papa gave him a big hug, and thanked him from his heart.

What makes life worth living? In terms of the needs of the human psyche, Sigmund Freud answered that question simply. "Love and work are the cornerstones of our humanness." Applied behavior analysis (ABA) is great for teaching the instrumental, task-oriented skills our children need to work, but how do we teach them how to love? No matter how satisfying our work might be, take away the people we love the most and the prospect of building loving relationships, and few of us would want to live. And those on the autistic spectrum crave human love and friendship just as much as anyone else.

Gutstein, in *Solving the Relationship Puzzle* (2000), relates the story of one of his clients, a bright young man on the spectrum. He had worked hard to avoid painful teasing, and became adept at theory of mind (the understanding that other people think and feel differently from you) and perspective taking. He had the social skills to create the impression he wanted others to have of himself. But he fell into despair and expressed the desire to end his life. He had not learned how to be himself or how to create true friendships. Without relationships of love in his life, all his accomplishments meant nothing to him, and he saw no point to all the social skills he had learned.

So what is your goal? Most parents would answer that they want their children to be truly happy. If that's how you feel, remember this. *Loving relationships are the key to both your child's learning and his happiness.*

When Peter's younger brother was a first grader, he had the strictest teacher in the school with the highest standards. But she was so warm and loving that her students wanted to work hard for her. One could say, "Miss Zube loved them into shape." Likewise, Peter's ABA tutor, Belinda, is so loving and warm that Peter truly enjoys work. At first he worked for the pleasure of her genuine praise and warm hugs, and also for the fun tickle games they would play between discrete trials. He learned how to be proud of himself through her pride in him. He now needs less of the tickle breaks (though he still gets plenty!), because he gets so much satisfaction from and takes so much pride in his own learning accomplishments. Relationships motivate children to do the hard work of learning.

Learning aside, love makes us happy. Isn't it a goal of all of us parents for our children to experience the joy of true friendship? When your child grows up, how much happier will he be if he learns how to create true friendships on his own? If knowing how to make friends and have loving relationships is the ultimate social goal, how do we help our children get there?

Empathy is at the heart of all such relationships. But empathy requires a lot of steps. First you have to pay attention to and tune into another person. You have to understand what the other person is communicating and identify what he wants or needs. You have to want to meet those needs, and conceptualize a way to do so. The decision on whether and how to respond requires you to have an internal organizing principle, an identity or self-concept of values and interests. You then have to communicate or carry out that response.

Our children have many challenges to overcome to learn empathy. They have sensory distractions and attention deficits, making it hard to tune into other people. They may have mirror neuron deficiencies making perspective taking not automatic, but effortful. Their ability to understand both verbal and nonverbal language does not appear to be hardwired like it is in neurotypical children. Some of our children are early in their cognitive development, and may not be able to conceptualize another person's thinking or their own desires well enough to make a meaningful response. Even if they have meaningful responses they want to make, some have severe motor and language dyspraxia, making it hard to communicate them.

So try to have realistic expectations. Although your child's sensory issues and dyspraxia will improve to some extent with therapy, you may always have to provide some degree of support and accommodations to help him with these challenges. You have to respect the biology of the brain. Perspective taking and communication skills can also improve markedly with education, but you may always need more time and more patience to accommodate your child's processing speed. A turtle is a turtle—you can poke and prod to make it move a little faster, but only for a short burst, and then you've got a stressed-out turtle who gives up and withdraws. You can't push a turtle—you can only invite him to come out of his shell.

The big question is this. Even after we've struggled to support our children with all these challenges, and adjusted our expectations, knowing that our interactions are going to look different because of all those accommodations, can our children learn how to love and show their love?

After 11 years' experience with my child who is heavily impacted with autism, I can tell you without a doubt, that there is hope. There is definitely a real person locked in that miswired brain. Peter not only has the same feelings, thoughts, reason, and will that everyone has, but also a beautiful little soul. He tries so hard to do what he understands is right. When we want him to do something really hard although he can't fathom a reason for it himself, he still tries hard to do it because he loves us and trusts us.

> The other day, his tutor Belinda and I took Peter to the dentist. I had prepared Peter ahead of time by reading him books about visiting the dentist. I also had him practice being the dentist for his dinosaur collection, with a dental mirror, metal nut pick, and whirling electric toothbrush. He walked in and sat calmly in the dental chair. But when the dentist tried to work in his mouth, a look of sheer panic came into Peter's eyes. He sat bolt upright in the chair, and pointed to the door. He wanted to go home. Emotion drove out all reason.
>
> I asked the dentist for ten minutes. He walked away. I knelt down and told Peter I could see how scared he was. Peter relaxed slightly and looked at me. I explained how this was hard but good for his teeth so he could eat and chew just like his dinosaurs. I produced one

I had thrown in my purse that morning just in case. The dinosaur asked dentist Peter if he could help him. The dinosaur bumped Peter off of the patient's chair and settled in, while I handed Peter his instruments. Peter dutifully cleaned the dinosaur's teeth. Whenever the frightened dinosaur would try to sit up, Peter would gently push him back down. Then we played turn taking, bumping each other off the dental chair with mischievous smiles and lots of drama, until the dentist returned.

When he asked if Peter was ready, Peter was still afraid, but sat in the chair. He decided to make himself stay in that chair. He was holding our hands, but we were not holding him down. When he thought he was done, Peter jumped up and turned to the door. I stood up like a pillar between him and the door, and told him we still had the fluoride, but I'd help him through it. I turned him around and put my arms around him in a big hug. The dentist did a quick swish with his applicator, and Peter was free. I told Peter I was so proud of him because Peter was very brave.

Sure, the "play therapy" helped Peter work through his emotions, and changed his mood. No doubt it also reinforced his understanding of why he should cooperate. But ultimately, what motivated Peter to cooperate with the dentist despite every fiber of his being telling him to bolt? Our children may not think of picking flowers for us or running up to us with big hugs, but *their actions still tell us loud and clear that they do love us, and very deeply.* You just need to have the eyes to see it, because they show you indirectly. I told Peter I was proud of him because he was very brave. But in my heart I knew it was Peter's love for us and trust in us that enabled him to be brave, and for that I felt profoundly thankful.

To have the eyes to see, sometimes you just have to be quick on the take. I was standing in the kitchen, cooking while talking to another person. While I was still in mid-sentence and trying to stir something, he quickly reached over, took my hand, and leaned his head on my shoulder. I was so distracted that I almost missed the whole thing, but not till he caught my eye with a sparkle and smile before dashing away. Peter has taught me the necessity of keen observation, lest those fleeting, precious moments of initiation be lost. Timing the initiation of a social interaction is a tricky and multistep process. Until your child learns it by learning to tune into you, you will be the one who needs to tune in especially hard to your child, to capture his emerging communicative intents.

Grabbing the teachable moment

The ideal time to teach a social skill is when your child needs to use it to get what he wants. That moment when Peter took my hand was a moment he was seeking affection. Ideally, it would have been great if someone else had been available at the time. Say Vinh was also in the kitchen. He could have caught Peter as he was dashing away, and said, "Oh Peter, I think Mama really liked that. Look, I see she's done stirring; she's put down the spoon, and her arms are wide open. I think she's looking at you! Now's your chance!" Vinh could turn Peter around, point out my body language, and give him a gentle push to try again. After I reward the attempt with a satisfying hug and kiss and loving look, I could turn Peter around to face Vinh, and give him yet another chance to practice. "Oh Peter, look at Papa. He's looking at us like he would like a hug as well. What do you think?"

Another piece of advice is not to be quick to assume. One day, Peter had a change of classrooms at school. He kept telling his tutor he wanted to go home, softly saying "car" under his breath and gently pointing to the parking lot. She did not realize how anxious he felt because between these quiet communicative attempts, he tried so hard to cooperate with his work. Finally, when she went to microwave his lunch, he realized she was not going to take him home anytime soon. He totally lost it with a massive meltdown.

When Peter came home afterwards, I realized that he really needed to learn how to communicate the urgency of his feelings. I drew an emotional thermometer as shown (see Cardon 2004).

I created a story with various stuffed animals coming to visit Piglet and Pooh. The first was a stuffed lion who just came to talk. Piglet trembled a little and pointed to "not so good" to tell Pooh he was getting a bit anxious. Pooh asked the lion to leave. The next was a wolf with gruffer manners. Piglet shook harder and pointed to "upset" to tell Pooh he that his anxiety level was rising. Pooh bundled the wolf out the door. Finally, a blustery dragon burst onto the scene looking for someone

to eat. Piglet shook like mad and pointed to "very upset" to Pooh, who then chased the villain away. Then Pooh gave Piglet a big hug, and Piglet pointed to "OK."

I repeated the story a couple of times, and used a hand over hand maneuver to make Peter's finger point to the various degrees of feeling on the thermometer when that emotion came up in the course of the story. Peter showed little reaction or interest on his face. However, the next morning, his tutor Belinda brought out the thermometer at school, in his usual classroom. She asked how he was feeling. Peter clearly pointed to "OK." When she asked how he felt the afternoon before in the new classroom, *Peter emphatically pointed to "very upset."*

This story illustrates the truth of Dr. Greenspan's theory that *emotion drives learning.* When the emotional relevance of what you are teaching is high, your child will learn it much faster. In this situation, Peter learned how to use an emotional thermometer quickly. Its usefulness was clear because of what had transpired that afternoon.

My second point about that story is about not assuming. Our children frequently don't give us clear feedback about what they are thinking or feeling. Just because Peter looked uninterested did not mean he wasn't. Clearly, he was paying enough attention to have understood, processed, and learned the use of the emotional thermometer. Our children don't give us the signals we're used to in order to read them accurately. Don't let your misreadings discourage you. Making assumptions about what you think your child is thinking or intending can cause you to jump to the wrong conclusion. Keep yourself open to understand your child over time, and your child may surprise you with how much he's learning from you.

So don't give up. Every challenging situation that arises in the life of your child is also a potential teachable moment. With that perspective, I'm sure you would agree that life with these little ones abounds with opportunities to learn, and therefore to move forward. Keep trying, keep teaching, and you will discover that beautiful soul inside your child as well.

But keep in mind—our children are not born with an innate desire for social interaction. So, if you want your child to develop empathy, he has to have a reason to care. He has to learn to want to interact with you. You can help create that key connection between emotional gratification and social interaction if you make it worth your child's effort with your love and warmth. As Greenspan and Wieder (2006, p.60) put it, "Go for the twinkle in your child's eye." Forging that emotional bond should be an underlying goal in all of your teaching. Therefore, the love and warmth you put into your interactions are the most important ingredients you put into your teaching.

To teach the steps, you have to know the steps—there are no shortcuts to social and emotional development. Parents have tried through the years to use their children's strengths in language or cognition to bypass the development of emotional bonding and gestural communication that are so difficult for our children. But social scripts don't have the flexibility to deal with dynamic real life interactions. Even if you could do the impossible task of teaching your child great social skills for every situation, he won't be motivated to use them unless he learns the fundamental joy of emotional bonding. That neurological connection between pleasure and social interaction is best developed right from the start, strengthened and emphasized at every stage. It should be the cornerstone of your social skills programs throughout development, just as love gives meaning to every stage of life.

So we start from the very beginning stages of social and emotional development in infancy. In the following sections, I give a brief description of each stage of social development followed by some general teaching principles for the goals for that stage. This chapter provides an overview of the most fundamental levels of social and emotional development, from just becoming aware of other people to entering the world of pretend play. Chapter 13 provides an introduction to higher levels of social and emotional development, learning to reflect upon an inner world of thoughts and feelings, and becoming aware of those of others.

My overview of development is an amalgamation and simplification of developmental schemes created by and concepts derived from Greenspan and Wieder (1998, 2006), Gutstein (2002a, 2002b), and Sussman (1999, 2006). The numbering doesn't necessarily match the stage numbering of the above-mentioned authors, though I generally try to match the numbering of Greenspan and Wieder's developmental milestones (1998, pp.91–7). I highly recommend you read and reference their books directly, as they are outstanding resources. Their books contain a treasury of practical ideas you can pick and choose from to try out on your child. Many of Peter's favorite games described in the following sections are derived directly from or are adaptations or variations of games you can find in their books.

This chapter focuses on working on the core deficits in autism—emotional regulation and social interaction. Of course, we parents have a much more complicated task, as we deal with the whole child. It is assumed that you are concomitantly supporting your child's other areas of need—you should have strategies in place for sensory integration, have made accommodations for motor apraxia, and be working on some kind of communication system for your child.

STAGE ONE: CAN I BE CALM AND FOCUSED?

Stage One is the development of a child's ability to calm himself and focus so he can take in the sights, sounds, smells, tastes, and feel of his environment (including you). This ability to calm himself emotionally is called *emotional self-regulation.* The capacity to self-regulate enables the child to take in information about his world through his senses and thereby engage with it and learn about it. At this stage, you, as the parent, are teaching your baby to emotionally tune into you (this is called *emotional attunement*) as you gently rock, pat, massage, cuddle, and sing to soothe him. As you smile and talk to your baby, and try to catch his eye, you are teaching *shared attention.* As you instinctively adjust the amount of excitement and stimulation you give your baby according to his reactions, you are encouraging him to attend to you for novelty and soothing.

Because of distortions in how many of our children process sensory information, they may continue to require our support at this fundamental level throughout their lifetimes. It's not possible to learn or to interact calmly if under painful sensory bombardment. Observe carefully to learn your child's profile of sensory differences, and modify the environment to match it. At this stage, we're working to manipulate the environment and provide the accommodations necessary to make sensory integration possible for our children. You might want to re-read Chapter 4 that discusses intervention at this primary level in more detail. Children with autism have such profound sensory problems that it is crucial to get this right. Enlisting the support and guidance of an experienced occupational therapist can make all the difference. Tuning into your child effectively can be a difficult balancing act. A passive child will need high affect from you to energize him, but if he's also overly sensitive to sound, you'll have to express that high affect with big gestures and dramatic facial expressions while keeping your voice volume down. Your other option is to get noise cancellation headphones. Your hyperactive, distractible child may require lots of joyful jumping and gross motor activity with you at the start of a play session, and then a transition to an uncluttered environment with warm but calm interactions to help him focus. The sooner you get good at automatically and primarily addressing the individual sensory profile of your child, the better for his development, as you enable him to take in the external world.

In the beginning, you will be doing all the work of adjusting the environment, including the way you handle your baby, to get him into that *emotionally regulated* (calm, attentive) state that enables him to take in and process it. As your child grows up, the goal is, of course, for your child to eventually become self-aware, and to learn to make some of these sensory accommodations on his own. You can help him by explicitly teaching him your thought processes as you make those accommodations.

If your child enters the noisy school lunchroom, and cringes, covering his ears, say, "Too loud! Let's get out the headphones," as you slip on his noise cancellation headphones. Work toward teaching him how to anticipate sensory accommodation needs. Next time, before you enter the lunchroom, stop and say, "Do you think it might be noisy in there? What should we do?" You can *backchain* (see p.82) teaching the motor sequences involved in the accommodations. Next time, after asking "Do you think it might be noisy in there? What should we do?" hand the headphones to your child and let him slip them on himself. On subsequent occasions, open his backpack where he keeps the headphones and let him take them out and slip them on. Eventually, just point to his backpack. Once he has that down, after asking, "Do you think it might be noisy in there? What should we do?" shrug your shoulders, look at him expectantly, and wait. As putting on the headphones before entering the lunchroom becomes habitual, you can fade your verbal prompt, "Do you think it might be noisy..." Generalize this procedure to other noisy settings, and eventually your child may learn to anticipate when he needs to use the headphones and follow through independently.

STAGE TWO: CAN I ENGAGE AND RESPOND EMOTIONALLY TO MY PARENT'S OVERTURES?

Stage Two is the development of engagement, which means intentionally paying attention and responding to another person. Think of that classic game of peek-a-boo. Pop out from behind a blanket, and your baby laughs and kicks his feet in delight. If you come on too strong, your baby might start averting his gaze and whimper as if about to cry, but you then speak gently and reassuringly. Your baby might respond by signaling a desire to play again with a smile and gaze into your eyes with widened eyes. Then try popping out again, but more gently and slowly. This is the stage of emotional relating, in which the parent makes an overture, such as popping out from behind the blanket, and the baby responds, by either kicking happily or turning away distressed.

The parent is the one doing all the work of reading the baby's early communication. Hence the baby's smile and look for his parent signals his initiation of a new circle, which the parent responds to by popping out from behind the blanket again. His turning away leads the parent to wait, then initiate a gentler overture by popping out more slowly. The parent carefully regulates the amount of stimulation provided by attending to the child's reactions. By tuning in correctly, the parent encourages the child to continue in the interaction. Every time the parent reads the baby's subtle signals correctly, such as kicking his feet happily or looking away, and adjusts any actions accordingly, the parent rewards the baby's signaling. The signals grow stronger, and the baby learns the beginnings of nonverbal communication.

The baby is learning something else just as critical. After many such emotional exchanges, the baby accumulates a history of emotional memories of the parent. He learns the parent's love and warmth are predictable, and to anticipate the feelings of joy and comfort the parent's presence brings. Engagement leads to trust and relationship.

As for Stage One, we parents of children with autism cannot assume our children automatically master this stage. Rather, this critical level is one you have to come back to time and time again. Developing emotional intimacy should always be a primary goal because that bonding is your child's ticket to progress. You want your child to get addicted to your warmth and love. Once your child connects you with soothing and pleasure, he will let you lead him to learn all about the world. He will also let you help him develop emotionally. The deeper the relationship, the more he will be able to absorb your emotional reactions to regulate his. Because of his bond with you, he will also learn to look to you whenever he feels a big emotion to know how to handle it, and the more he will be able to trust your emotions to guide his.

Therefore, be happy with your child when he's happy. Hold that emotion with him as long as he's interested in holding it with you. Don't rush to move on. Similarly, when he's angry, sad, or upset, your calm and accepting demeanor will teach him that strong negative emotions are also okay, and he will survive them. So don't be in such a hurry to "fix it." You need to quickly remove or ameliorate environmental stimuli that are noxious to your child in the same way you would any physical source of pain, but if the child is frustrated because he isn't getting what he wants (as opposed to truly needs), hold firm to the limits you know he needs to learn, while sympathetically helping him ride through the big scary emotions. Those episodes are your opportunity to raise his level of tolerance for frustration (that is, patience), develop perseverance, and stretch what psychologists call "affect tolerance," meaning your child's ability to tolerate big emotions.

For the preverbal child, this can look like calmly standing by as your child throws a tantrum over not getting a cookie right before dinner. As he flails on the floor, say, "Wow! You're mad. I can really see how much you want that cookie. I bet you're really hungry, and that cookie looks super good. It's so hard to hear 'No' when you want something so badly." Be sympathetic, but stick to your guns. "Hey, baby, you must be getting tired of that floor. When you're ready, you can sit up here with Mom and try a bite of this yummy chicken. Bite of cookie coming after, guaranteed." He may not even understand your words, but he might absorb some of the calm friendliness in your tone of voice and body language. If you're consistent with your actions, he will eventually figure out that "no" means no. What is equally important is that he learns to soak in some of your calm when he's mad. Over the years he may learn that instead of having a tantrum when he feels mad, he might try some of that calming self-talk.

Say you have a child at a later stage of development who is more capable of forming ideas and understands a fair amount of language. Picture saying, "Peter, I can see you are really upset. Mama's not letting you break that stick off the tree. That's making you really mad! It's frustrating when you can't have something you really want." Identify the emotion. Sympathize, showing you understand how he feels, and you accept it without rejecting him. However, create a space between your child's emotion and his actions. Help him understand that his emotion is something he can label and identify as separate from himself—the emotion is something he has, but it does not have to control him.

The next step is to teach him alternative ways to handle his feelings. "Peter, would it help if we took a ride in the car? How about some of your favorite music? Remember that CD we played in the car this morning that you loved? How did it go? Ta, dum, la, la, la…" You can expect your child to continue to fuss for a while. Model calm understanding, but hold your ground. "I can see how much you really want that stick. You want it *too* much. You don't really need it, Peter. That's our neighbor's property. It's not ours. We have to let it go. I'm going to help you let it go. You're going to be okay, Peter. Let's just keep walking, and you'll see. You don't need that stick, and you're going to be okay."

Labeling the emotion, demonstrating understanding and acceptance with your demeanor and tone of voice, teaching self-talk to calm oneself down, separation from the inciting stimulus, and dissipating the emotion with music, taking a walk, or other soothing activity, like a car ride, are the usual steps to walk through to regulate emotions. Your child will see how you handle those big emotions, and learn how to regulate them from your example. The feeling is something separate from himself, and you are working as a team to deal with it constructively. When he sees that you accept those negative feelings while not loving him any less, he will learn to do the same. With repeated practice, he will learn to accept and love himself, while internalizing the process of "affect regulation."

STAGE THREE: CAN I RESPOND WITH PURPOSEFUL ACTION? TWO-WAY COMMUNICATION AND CIRCLES OF INTERACTION

What are circles of interaction?

The goal of this stage is to develop purposeful circles of interaction (see pp.66–7). Consider the baby in Stage Two who has robust responses to his parent's overtures, having mastered engagement and warm relating. However, the baby is just learning how to initiate an overture back to the parent. The parent is really the one who picks up on his look of distress or interest to gauge how and when to pop out from behind that blanket again. In responding correctly to the baby's reaction, the parent is teaching him how to signal for either more or less stimulation. When he gives the parent a certain signal (kicking and smiling versus turning away and looking distressed), the parent rewards him by adjusting the level of stimulation in the parent's actions.

The goal is for the baby to learn how to amplify those signals to get the reaction he wants more efficiently. With repeated practice playing peek-a-boo, the baby learns to initiate an interaction with the parent by giving bigger and bigger cues. Instead of just looking away when he wants less stimulation, he might push the parent away or hide his face. Instead of just looking at the parent with widened eyes for more fun, he might actually reach over to grab the blanket. When the baby can actually grab and pull that blanket away, or even try to put it over his own head, he's operating at Stage Three, the level of robust two-way communication. Now the baby is taking on more of the work of continuing the interaction, as he clearly initiates his own responses.

Chapter 6 was all about getting Stage Two going by creating circuits of interesting activities to engage your child, and then getting Stage Three going by using the structural framework of play circuits to elicit purposeful responses from him. As you gradually go down the order of prompts, decreasing the strength of your prompts and instruction, your child is taking on more and more of the work of interaction. As you look expectantly with excitement in your face and pause, you are encouraging your child to initiate his response, thereby moving him up the developmental ladder.

How do you encourage circles of interaction?

So much is happening in these play circuits. Let's go back to the peek-a-boo example. First your baby is learning how much fun it is to be with you as he enjoys the exciting climax of the game as you pop out from behind the blanket and laugh or tickle him. He learns how to anticipate the climax coming as you chant louder and louder, or sing on higher and higher pitches in thirds, "Here I come, here I come, here I come!" Help him pull away the blanket with a hand over hand maneuver at first, then perhaps pointing to the corner of the blanket, and then perhaps a little whispered instruction, "You can pull the blanket off now!" Finally, just wait. You are nudging your baby along to make his responses more robust as you withdraw your scaffolding and give milder prompts to direct his turn in the interaction.

Once the baby can pull that blanket off your head robustly on his own, spice up the interaction with some variations. Employ strategies to encourage initiation by making mistakes on purpose such as dropping the blanket on the floor to see if he'll pick it up, thereby repairing the interaction. You might do something surprising such as putting the blanket over his head instead of your own. Pulling it off his own head is another initiation. Substitute a different object for the blanket, like an oversized floppy hat that covers the face. Take alternate turns putting the blanket on your head or your child's head. If someone else comes by, give him a turn and pop the blanket over his head. Alternate hiding under the blanket or the floppy hat. Add variations to your game within the framework your child understands. That way he can still look forward to the climax, and is thereby still motivated to continue the interaction. Also, he still has a model in his mind of how to initiate his response, or his turn in the interaction. Once you've got a good rhythm going, you might even try to transform the game by changing the action. Introduce another funny hat. Put a floppy hat on each person's head. At the end of your countdown, instead of popping out from under the blanket, try switching hats instead. Continue highlighting the climax with laughs, giggles, and high fives.

Just think of all the goals you're hitting in a game like this. You're teaching your child how to respond and initiate to create multiple circles of interaction. He learns that actions can be predictable and sequential. He learns to anticipate what's coming. He learns how to reference your face because it's fun to see your warm, excited expression as you emerge from under that blanket or hat, and because you're giving him useful information as to your next move as you glance at the blanket or the hat. He learns how to maintain coordination in an activity by regulating his own actions based on the prior action of you, his play partner. If he's tolerating the variations and repairing the interactions, he's learning how to modify his actions to remain coordinated with you. As he continues to enjoy the game after you've transformed it to a switching hats action, he's experiencing the joy of creating a new game together, and that being flexible and introducing novelty can be fun. Most importantly, he learns the joy of acting together and being with you.

Consolidation takes a lot of practice

Play is very important. If you have a developmental strategy in mind, you can play with purpose. Don't get discouraged if you stay working on these early stages for a long time, however. You're wiring in a lot of important foundational circuitry in your child's social brain. You're challenging him to practice those fundamental components of social skills that seem to be hardwired and natural to nonautistic individuals, like facial referencing, anticipation, initiation, coordinating and repairing interactions. Peter and I have been working to make this stage solid for ten years. Even if your child shows fleeting or emerging capacities at higher stages, remember to keep coming back to work on these basics. The goal is for your child to not only show some ability at each stage occasionally and with support, but for him to master each stage so that he demonstrates those abilities consistently and independently, even under stress.

Practice circles in work as well as play

You can and should work on all these skills not just in play contexts, but also in work contexts. When you go about your daily chores and routines, make them interactive with your child. Remember the Mary Poppins' song, "In every job that must be done, there is an element of fun. You find the fun, and snap! the job's a game"? Those lyrics are a useful mantra.

When setting the table together, stand next to your child at the back of each chair. Set the table assembly-line fashion. Lay down the napkin, and your child places the fork. Make it fun with drama. Scurry over to the next chair together, stop abruptly and gracefully place the next napkin, and so on. You can create assembly lines with other chores like loading and unloading the dishwasher. Engage other family members and line them up when putting away toys in a toy box or books on a shelf, passing the item overhand, underhand, behind the back, under the legs, etc.

When you help your child make his bed, teach him how to grab the right-hand corner of the blanket while you grab the left, reference each other with a look and nod, and pull the blanket up together. One person tosses each stuffed animal to the other who places it on the bed, and after a few, switch roles. Vary the way you toss the animal, high, low, fast, to the right or left of the child, etc. so that he has to adjust his actions to coordinate with yours. Fold laundry cooperatively by one family member laying the clothing flat, another folding, and another putting it away in the proper pile. Your child can then play the delivery boy, delivering each pile of clean folded laundry to its proper owner with you as the navigator or dispatcher. Concentrate on coordinating actions, referencing one another, and joyfully completing each task, so your child internalizes the satisfaction of a job well done.

The great folding sock race

The goal of this game is to teach the concept of competition. It's an adaptation of a game invented by Arnold Miller (2007). Seat yourself opposite your child. Place something your child likes such as a potato chip or desired toy under a plastic cup in the middle of the table between the two of you. Each player must keep his hands behind the edge of the table. On the count of three, whoever grabs the cup first gets the chip or toy. After a number of trials, change the way the chip is won. Instead of placing the chip in the middle of the table, place two unpaired pairs of socks there. Place the chip on the side. Count to three, and give the chip to the child who grabs and folds a pair of socks together faster.

Once the children get good at folding one pair, make them each fold two pairs to win, then three pairs. They can learn to fold shirts and towels this way too, so that finally they compete by folding a small pile of laundry. You as the referee get to throw sloppy work back into that child's "to do" pile. You can of course substitute tokens for the chip, and assign different numbers of tokens to earn different rewards like a special outing or extra computer game time.

What does Stage Three look like?

By late Stage Three, your child knows how to maintain coordination in an activity by adjusting his own action based on the prior action of his partner, whom he references automatically without prompting. He eventually learns how to coordinate his actions without structured rules and roles, keeps the interaction going even with the rapid introduction of variations, and repairs interactions rapidly to maintain coordination.

> Peter came home from school one day, hungry, and asked me for chips. I suggested we play a game of treasure hunt for the chips. He covered his eyes and counted to three while I hid a chip. At the end of the countdown I sang, "I know where your chip is!" Peter asked "Where?" I then told him which room in the house it was (his bedroom). Once he got to his bedroom, he had to follow my eyes and gestures to the prize, frequently referencing back to me for more information. After the first few rounds, we started alternating roles, where he would have to hide the chip and give me gestural clues as to where it was. On my turns to hide the chip, sometimes I added a problem for him to solve such as placing the chip high up

on a shelf with a stepping stool in the vicinity, or out of reach under the bed with a rake close by. Sometimes when he asked, "Where?" instead of telling him which room I hid the chip, I told him to ask a certain one of his five brothers. Then he had to go to the right brother, get his attention, and ask "Where (is my chip)?"

Eventually, I varied the game even further. Instead of giving him gestural clues, I handed him a simple map of the room with a few of the main pieces of furniture drawn in and a big "X" over the location of the chip. I started by hiding the chip under one of three big pillows on the main sofa, and moved the chip to less obvious locations only after he got the hang of the map idea. There were long pauses as we waited for him to spatially process the maps. At times other family members would serve as assistants and give Peter more prompts. But the point in this and other games is that he participates enthusiastically, and transitions fluidly from one variation to the other, adapting to the new rules quickly and happily.

A worthwhile journey

If you can get your child to grow into Stage Three skills, you've already accomplished a lot. Instead of a self-absorbed child who isn't interested in paying any attention to you, and doesn't cooperate, a Stage Three child is easy to engage, looks to you for leadership and fun, references your actions and facial expressions, tries to understand your intent, knows how and tries to coordinate his actions with yours, and tolerates and even welcomes variations, change, and transformations (see Gutstein 2002b). This is a child whom you can bring on outings to explore the world together because he can follow directions and tolerate change. This is a child whom you can and should train to help you around the house, and who can internalize a sense of accomplishment and pride in doing good work at school and at home.

It may not look like interaction with a neurotypical Stage Three child because the pace may be much slower. You may need to make many more accommodations to reduce distractions and assist understanding with visual supports and AT. But as you learn how to make these accommodations and adjust your child's environment to match his needs, you can enjoy a rich, loving relationship with your child. Your child can enjoy a full life of loving relationships and work at school and at home that is challenging and satisfying.

Remember that disability is a product of a mismatch between environment and ability. If any one of us neurotypical city slickers were placed in the wilderness or a foreign country with a different language and culture, we would feel disabled and helpless. We all need accommodations, tools, and assistance to survive and thrive. When you enable your child to operate at the highest level of function he is capable of by providing those accommodations, support, and instruction, you may enjoy the greatest gratification a parent could ask for—the happiness of your child.

STAGE FOUR: THE BIRTH OF IDEATION AND PERSPECTIVE TAKING
Theory

Stage Four is exciting. The mind develops in many ways. There is now a space between perception and reaction—that space is called ideation (see the Glossary at the end of this book). The Stage Four child can separate perceptions from immediate reactions. He no longer sees a plastic cookie and automatically sticks it in his mouth, or a toy train and starts spinning its wheels. Now the cookie and train become ideas he can hold in his head. He can use past experiences and current modeling to manipulate different possibilities of what to do with these ideas in his mind. He can then act out these various possibilities in play. Maybe he can lay the cookies on a plate and serve them. Instead of spinning the wheels, he can roll the train to another person or on the wooden tracks. At this stage, most of the play is simple and concrete. The child uses real items to do what he's used to seeing them do in real life. This is called functional play. For example, the child may grab a cell phone off the coffee table, hold it to his ear, and start to babble. Representational play uses items that only represent real things, but still bear close resemblance to them. For example, a child may enjoy pretending to cook by cutting, serving, and pretending to eat plastic toy food.

INITIATION AND PROBLEM SOLVING

Children at Stage Four have their own ideas that they bring to their interactions with you. For example, in our previous peek-a-boo game, imagine how the Stage Four toddler would play it. He would not just be content to stick to you popping in and out from behind a blanket, but would no doubt be grabbing that blanket off of your head, experimenting with putting it on his own head, and then possibly climb off his chair to hide behind your chair and catch your gaze from alternating sides of the chair. In other words, the child not only makes intentional *responses* to your overtures, but also starts *initiating* interactions based on his own ideas.

Because the child can now conceive of actions as ideas, he can string them together to solve important problems. Picture a Stage Four toddler taking you by the hand to a stepping stool. He might look at you, look at the stepping stool and the cookie jar high upon the kitchen counter, and look back at you to see if you got the message. He might pull one end of the stool as you push the other to the counter. He might then reference your face to get permission and start climbing the stepping stool to reach for the cookies.

This toddler is exhibiting exciting developments of the mind. He can *logically sequence a series of actions to solve a problem.* He can picture and hold this plan in his head as he goes to get you. This cognitive ability to *conceptualize a logical sequence* of actions in his head, and hold it in his working memory as a plan, is called *executive function.*

THEORY OF MIND, PERSPECTIVE TAKING, AND JOINT ATTENTION

But the most exciting development of all is in how the child enlists help to solve the problem. As the child learns that he has ideas that precede action, he understands that you have ideas too. You have a mind that's different from his. This remarkable understanding is called *theory of mind.* It seems to develop automatically in neurotypical children, but requires some teaching in children with autism. Because the neurotypical Stage Four child recognizes that you have a different mind and don't know what he's thinking (a result of having *theory of mind*), he keeps checking your face to see if you understand what he wants correctly. He tunes into you as he figures out how to coordinate his actions with yours to drag the stepping stool to the counter. He references your face to check your reaction (*social referencing*) and get permission because he knows you might have a different opinion about the safety of this next step, thereby exhibiting both *perspective taking* and memory for past safety infractions. He adjusts his final actions—to climb or not to climb—depending on your signals, which he knows how to *read in your facial expression.* He not only understands but also uses an *extensive repertoire of nonverbal communication* in his gestures, pointing, and eye gaze. He looks at you to get your attention, looks at the object of his interest like the cookie jar, and then looks back at you to make sure you understand him. This three-point eye gaze maneuver marks a milestone in the development of a capacity for perspective taking and *joint attention*, the ability to seek out and direct another person's attention to what you're interested in, and to pay attention to their reaction.

Perspective taking begins when the child understands that different people want different things, perceive things differently from their various perspectives, and have unique reactions. The toddler is demonstrating perspective taking when it occurs to him that you may not want him to climb up, and references your face before ascending the stepping stool. He also demonstrates it when he initiates getting your attention and drawing it to his object of interest, the cookie jar, to consider it together. At first your child may use his joint attention skills to get what he wants, as in this example. Gutstein (2000) calls that an "instrumental interaction" because he interacts with you as an instrument to help him reach his goal, getting the cookies.

A deficit in joint attention is a signature symptom of autism. A child with autism may take your hand to lead you to the cookie jar, but typically then tries to put your hand over the jar to open the lid, as if you are an extension of his own body. Peter used to take my hand and place it over whatever body part he wanted to scratch as if my hand should be controlled by his mind. That kind of interaction does not represent joint attention, but rather a lack of understanding that we have separate minds. A neurotypical child demonstrating joint attention might look at you to get your attention, place your hand on his back for a scratch, and then check back to look at your face to see if you understand what he wants. He's demonstrating an understanding of theory of mind. That would be another example of a three-point eye gaze, and using joint attention for an instrumental goal.

EXPERIENCE SHARING

As the neurotypical child learns to enjoy a parent's unique reactions to shared experiences, he will use his joint attention skills not only to get what he wants, but purely to share emotion. Thus it becomes a delight to point out different things he sees on a walk to get a parent's reaction. At this stage the parent enjoys a lot of "Look, Mom" comments, as he's keenly interested in her reaction to what he finds interesting. The child wants to show his work to enjoy the parent's pleasure and pride in his efforts. Gutstein (2000) calls these "*experience sharing* interactions."

In neurotypical children with intact mirror neurons, this capacity is practically hardwired in the brain. The child sees an emotion on your face and experiences it himself to a large degree. When you smile with delight and pride, he feels and enjoys those same feelings. That degree of automatically shared feeling is far less in our mirror neuron deficient children. For our children to share our feelings, we have to make them bigger. Using high affect means we both animate our expressions more and hold them longer (see pp.41–2). It takes a lot of shared experiences, in which your highlighted emotions either increase your child's joy or soothe his pain or fear, for your child to learn to seek out your reaction. Therefore, joint attention for experience sharing represents a major developmental accomplishment for children with autism, and may occur much later, if at all. It requires a learned, not automatic, understanding that each person has his own unique inner world that is exciting and pleasurable to share.

UNDERSTANDING DIFFERENT PERCEPTIONS

There is another important aspect of perspective taking that is particularly challenging for our children to learn. Having different minds means not only having different preferences and reactions, but also different perceptions. In other words, just because I see something, doesn't mean you see it. It often takes explicit teaching for a child with autism to understand that seeing leads to knowing and that if he sees something that you can't see, he may need to give you some extra information, verbally or visually. Hence if you're reading a book together, and he's holding the book turned away from you, make sure you loudly protest, "But I can't see the picture!" so he'll understand he needs to turn the book toward you. Conversely, occasionally turn to block his view of the book, and teach him to take the initiative to ask you to do the same.

STAGE FOUR THEORY: A SUMMARY

The cognitive capacity to form ideas is momentous in its social consequences. The ability to form, hold, and manipulate ideas in his head enables the child to chain multiple circles of interaction together to solve problems. His ability to form ideas initially appears as a capacity to repair interactions in your play circuit (like fetching a runaway ball and throwing it back to you in a game of catch), then to introduce variations (like kicking instead of throwing), and eventually to co-creating new games (like running away with the ball, looking back at you to chase him). His ability to retrieve memories of past experiences to form ideas enables him to begin to engage in functional and representational play.

As he has his own ideas, he begins to understand that you have your own ideas that are different. You see things and think differently from him.

The capacity to understand that you may perceive and react differently to the same reality is just emerging. As you nurture that capacity, your child begins to develop perspective taking and joint attention.

Practice

Initiation, problem solving, joint attention, perspective taking, and functional and representational play are all emerging. But how do you nurture your child to make the most of each of these new cognitive capacities? How do you as the parent actually work with your child to help turn cognitive potential into social and emotional development?

ENCOURAGING INITIATION AND PROBLEM SOLVING IN ROUTINES, GAMES, SPORTS, MUSIC, AND THE VISUAL ARTS

Lack of initiation is one of the most discouraging aspects of autism. The reason is that initiation requires two things that our children have trouble with: creating ideas and acting them out (see Chapter 15, pp.325–334). For now, let's discuss the difficulty our children have with ideation. How do we bridge the gap from purposeless self-stimulation to creating ideas?

There is a step-by-step process you can try with your child. Start with teaching your child to follow directions and then to imitate. This may sound a little counterintuitive if you want to encourage initiation, but the reason it's important to get your child to follow directions and imitate is to get used to tuning into you, so that he can learn work routines and play circuits that automatically provide ideas for the next intentional action he could take. Your child's first initiations will therefore probably be to initiate the next step in a familiar routine, sequenced activity, or play pattern. His first original ideas are likely to be extensions or variations of familiar routines, games, and sequenced activities in work and play.

The first step therefore, is for you and your child to practice many routines, play circuits, and other sequenced activities together. Then provide lots of opportunities for your child to initiate by pausing during familiar routines and play patterns to let him take the next step without prompting from you. Make playful mistakes on purpose to give him a chance to correct or repair them on his own. Encourage your child to create his own variations by offering turns, pausing, and giving immediate positive feedback by praising and incorporating any new ideas he may introduce, even if he comes up with them accidentally.

Another way to elicit initiation is to offer him choices as to which game or toys to play with first. If he doesn't make a clear choice, lay the activity choices in stations around the room, and see where he gravitates. Build your play circuit around that station. Offer him toy, food, or clothing choices in which you know one choice is a favorite and the other something he definitely dislikes. Here's what this process might look like in daily routines, play circuits, sports, music, and the visual arts.

"IN ROUTINES"

Don't underestimate the value of the time you spend with your child doing ordinary chores or community outings. Inject warmth and enthusiasm into the little routines of each day, and then pause in the midst of one. Can your child do the next step in the routine? When you lay out his clothes at dressing time, place them in a row in the order he needs to put them on. Help him get started if necessary, and then pause to see if he initiates picking up the next item. Use your order of prompts to provide just enough support and no more. Take the time and effort to warmly and joyfully celebrate when the child does initiate and successfully completes an action. You may need to start out with warm encouragement for even picking up the next item of clothing. As your child does more, gradually wait for your child to do a bit more before celebrating.

Say your child isn't motivated by praise, and doesn't care about getting dressed. You can still encourage initiation by offering choices. Offer your child a scratchy sweater that he hates wearing as opposed to his favorite soft shirt. Good naturedly offer to help him put on the sweater, and give him the opportunity to protest, wave aside the sweater, and put on the soft shirt by himself. When packing a picnic lunch to take to the park, place some of his favorite food among least favorites to pack on the counter. As you ask your child, "What shall we pack next?" he'll be more likely to initiate a choice if he sees you reaching for his least favorite food items, and passing over his favorite ones.

When you want your child to initiate the next step in a routine, the way you set it up visually can make a big difference. Your child is much more likely to initiate if you make it easier. Therefore, when you lay out his clothes for him to get dressed in the morning, line up just a few articles at first, in the order he needs to put them on, and help him with the rest. When you pack that picnic lunch together, place those favorite foods in front at the edge of the counter where he can easily reach. The genius of the TEACCH method ("Treatment and Education of Autistic and related Communication-handicapped Children") developed in North Carolina in 1966 is in building motivation by visually setting up tasks to implicitly suggest the next step. I highly recommend Schopler *et al.* (1983) for all kinds of ideas to visually sequence both work and play activities to encourage your child to act independently.

Assembling a flashlight à la TEACCH and floortime styles

Get an easy to dissemble flashlight. Unscrew the end and take out the two batteries. Make a box with four compartments lined up in a row left to right. Place the body of the flashlight in the first compartment on the left. Put one battery in each of the next two compartments on the right. Place the end piece in the rightmost compartment. Place the box in front of your child. Show him how you assemble the flashlight picking up the parts from the left to right compartment sequentially. Finally, turn on the flashlight and enjoy playing a game with it (such as turning it on and off and shining it on various objects).

Once your child is really interested in playing with the flashlight, quickly dissemble it back into your compartmentalized box. Use an increasing order of prompts to assist your child in reassembling it. Let your child enjoy playing with it briefly. Playfully snatch it back, dissemble the flashlight, and present the box back to the child. Repeating the process in this game gives the child lots of opportunities to initiate putting together the flashlight himself. To further expand the fun of this game, grab a second flashlight yourself, and flash your light wherever he flashes his. Dissemble your flashlight, and have a race to see who can put together a flashlight faster—the winner is the first to flash his/her flashlight on the other player (when you lose, you might dramatically fall over and cry out, "Ah! You got me!").

Once your child knows his daily routines more solidly, you can encourage initiation by acting dumb, making mistakes, or doing something silly or unexpected.[1] Say you are setting the table together, and you are laying down a napkin followed by your child laying down the spoon. Try "accidentally" dropping a napkin. Then pause, hold an expression of surprise on your face, and look at your child expectantly. If nothing

---

[1] For more specific ideas, see Greenspan and Wieder (1998, 2006), Sussman (1999), and Gutstein (2002a, 2002b).

happens after an appropriate pause, use an increasing order of prompts (eye gaze, gesture, verbal, then physical) to assist your child to pick up the napkin and hand it to you or on the table at the next place setting. Continue with your coordinated routine of you laying down a napkin followed by your child laying down the spoon, and then try dropping the napkin again.

You can make silly mistakes as well, such as placing a banana down next to the spoon instead of a knife, or laying a napkin on the child's head instead of on the table. When getting dressed, try playfully handing your child his pants before his underwear, or mischievously put his socks on his hands instead of his feet. When he wants his food warmed up, stick his plate in the dishwasher instead of microwave. Then turn back to him with a confused look, shrugging your shoulders with your hands held out, palms up, the universal sign for "What now?"

Playing dumb or acting helpless are great techniques to encourage initiation. Say your child opens a door to pass through, and fails to hold it open for you. Don't open it yourself. Instead, cry out plaintively, "Help, help! I'm stuck!" and thank your child with relief when he turns back to let you out. When Peter wants something to eat from the kitchen, I pretend to be "Robot Mom" and need step-by-step instruction from Peter to walk to the pantry, open the door, be told what item to take out, and give it to him. Without clear gestures from Peter, dim-witted Robot Mom is likely to open the oven door instead of pantry, take out a boring box of fiber cereal instead of chips, or hand the chips to Peter's brother instead of to Peter.

Any situation in which your child clearly wants something can be an opportunity to play dumb and encourage your child to do some problem solving, from packing his lunch to getting a toy off the shelf. If your child wants a car ride, pretend you can't find the keys, need help putting on your jacket, or can't find your purse. Create little obstacles playfully, such as pretending a stuffed animal hid the keys. Let your child take the initiative to run around the house looking for the mischievous culprit (and keys).

"IN GAMES"

Games or play circuits similarly provide many opportunities for your child to initiate. Like routines, games and play circuits have patterns and rules that the child eventually knows by heart. Therefore, when the parent makes a mistake, forgets what to do, or breaks a rule or pattern by doing something silly or unexpected, the child automatically has a repertoire of correct actions to initiate with. The child's first initiations frequently occur in the context of repairing or maintaining coordination in your interactions. Hence when you roll a ball back and forth and let the ball get away from you, the child has an opportunity to initiate by going after the ball and putting it back into play. When you play a board game and move your piece backward instead of forward, your child initiates as he moves your piece forward where it belongs.

The added benefit of play is that as your child adapts his actions to your mischievous introduction of variations, he's bound to try a variation or just make a mistake of his own. You can treat such genuine mistakes as purposeful variations in your game, and reward his "initiations" by incorporating them into a new game. For example, say you and your child each have a ball and on a signal such as "Ready, set, go!" roll your balls to each other. If your child accidentally rolls the ball into your ball, you can delightedly exclaim, "Crash!" You can incorporate his new action by morphing the game into a "crash or no crash" deal, in which you ask him "Crash or no crash?" prior to releasing your balls, and follow his instruction. By treating his mistake as if it were purposeful and modifying your actions accordingly, you encourage him to intentionally initiate variations.

Let's take another example. Say you've got a fun interactive game going between the two of you. You're rolling a train back and forth to each other. Your child stands up and the train accidentally rolls between his legs. You can treat that as intentional, and say, "Wow, Peter, what a good idea!" Then roll the train back under your own legs. If he then deliberately spreads his legs apart to let the train roll under, you've encouraged him to come up with a new play idea. If you added a comment like, "Hey Peter, look, I'm a tunnel!" you've also introduced an element of pretend. Whenever your child introduces a variation on your pattern of interaction, it can be an opportunity to encourage creativity if you incorporate that new idea into your play circuit.

"IN SPORTS"

Sports is an obvious context to encourage initiation. Some children with autism love gross motor activity. Some may want to try sports. Once the child learns the rules of the game, he has lots of opportunities to initiate each time he takes his turn and decides to go after the ball, who to throw the ball to, or where to run. Adaptive sports take fun elements of traditional sports and some of the rules that provide structure and patterns to suggest your child's next move, but simplify and slow the game down. For example, for volleyball or tennis, you might use a balloon instead of balls. You might use a tee or pitch the ball slowly in baseball or kick ball and give other players handicaps like having to move in slow motion or run backwards. When playing "Around the world" in basketball, the child might get three or four instead of one or two tries per position around the hoop. Mark each position "around the world" that the child has to shoot from with chalk so he knows where to stand. Instead of rotating out when the child misses catching the ball in four square, just rotate positions in the square. Initiation is easier if you make the game easier to understand and success more within your child's reach.

Some children don't like adaptive sports, but movement games can still provide your child with opportunities to initiate. Take turns coming up with ways to throw the ball to one another such as underhand, overhand, with one or two bounces, or from behind the back or under the legs. Imitate each other's moves on the trampoline, or try making new ones together holding hands.

"IN MUSIC"

The arts provide another great context to promote initiation. Sing a favorite song, and let your child fill in the blank for the last word, then phrase, then line. Substitute a silly line in familiar lyrics, highlighting it with a dramatic pause and mischievous expression, and let your child correct you or laugh about it together. For example, after singing the line, "Old MacDonald had a cow, eeyi, eeyi, oh," follow with, "With an oink, oink here…," pause, and look at your child astonished with your hand over your mouth, "Oops!"

Encourage initiation by giving your child the opportunity to make choices. Listen to recorded music or sing songs to or with your child, and make picture icon/word labels for your child's favorites. Then put several of these labels on a board. Invite your child to select which song the two of you will enjoy together next. A more advanced activity (Stage Five rather than Stage Four) follows that also offers the music lover a chance to make choices.

Gutstein (2002b) describes musical games you can play with your child on the drums and a keyboard, in which you play a pattern together. Then vary it by starting or stopping, or playing fast or slow. Initially give your child verbal directions, calling out the change in tempo or whether to stop or play. Eventually try fading out your verbal prompts, so your child just has to pay attention to what you're doing and follow along. This game provides a natural context to encourage initiation. Take turns following each other's leads with a simple rhythm on the drum or a short pattern of notes on the keyboard. Your child will enjoy coming up with his own riffs. What makes this game magical is when you introduce some counterpoint or double time during your child's turn leading, so that the two of you co-create something completely new.

Teaching emotions through music

As you listen to recorded music or sing your own songs together, categorize them under emotional labels, like "happy song" (such as "If you're happy and you know it," "The more we get together"), "sleepy song" (such as "Rock a bye baby," "Sleep baby, sleep"), or "marching song" (such as "Here come the dinosaurs," "The ants come marching in"). Then take turns calling out what kind of a song you want the other person to select.

You can further accentuate the emotion expressed in the music by making masks or paper bag puppets wearing the corresponding facial expressions. Have your child help you draw in the matching facial expression. Dance to or act out the emotion expressed by the music while you wear the mask (or just hold it up, if wearing it is too scary for your child). Alternatively, make the paper bag puppets with the matching expressions come alive and act out the music.

"IN VISUAL ARTS"

You can do the same with visual arts. Get beads or macaroni of different shapes and/or colors. Have your child imitate the patterns you create as each strings a necklace synchronously, initially calling out your changes but later relying on the child to follow your lead without verbal cues. Then to encourage initiation, take turns imitating each other's short patterns as you string your separate necklaces. Finally, try stringing one long necklace together by taking turns synchronously copying each other's short patterns, working from opposite ends of the same string. The finished product will be unique and symmetrical.

You can do the same process with drawing designs on separate pieces of paper, and then working from either end toward the middle on the same sheet. Hang up your creation or use it as wrapping paper or a book cover. Depending on your child's drawing skills (the mechanics of which you can develop ABA style[2]), your designs can start out with patterns of colored dots or lines, progress to shapes, and include even simple representations. Again you can play "Follow the leader" and take turns following each other's short patterns or designs. Peter loves to tear paper, so we use bits of torn colored construction paper to make our alternating pattern designs.

Teaching the mechanics of drawing ABA style

Ed Emberley (1970, 1972, 1984, 2002) has an outstanding series of books that can teach even the most confirmed non-artist how to draw simple everyday endearing figures that your child will love. Let your child choose what to draw, and then take turns in which you draw two dots at a time, and he takes his turn by connecting the dots. It's a magical moment when the desired image emerges from the page.

Once you've drawn this figure many times, try leaving out the last two dots. See if your child initiates completing the drawing himself. Next time leave out the last four dots, and so on until he completes drawing an entire part of the figure himself. Emberley constructs his figures out of basic circles, rectangles, and triangles, so his figures adapt themselves readily to this kind of teaching scheme.

If your child enjoys drawing, you might teach him a small repertoire of figures that represent objects that are meaningful to him in his daily life. For example, Peter loves car rides, pizza, and skiing in the mountains. If he learns how to draw a stick figure on skis, a car, and a pizza, he might enjoy drawing these to recall happy events in his day, or to request them. Having such a skill would open up a whole new way for your child to initiate and communicate.

When your child gets more facile at drawing, a fun exercise in co-creation is to start out with a simple shape and then take turns adding to the picture. You can let your child select a model such as a picture he likes from a book or magazine, or a photograph you've taken of a meaningful event or family picture. Take turns drawing parts of the picture together.

---

2 Find ideas for structured teaching in drawing in Schopler *et al.* (1983, pp. 118, 126–8).

Someday you may get to the point where you don't need a visual model to copy, but can draw the ideas from your own imaginations. Keep an easy to follow manual of common figures and objects at hand to use as a reference, such as Emberley's (1972) *Make a World*.

If your child doesn't want your help, let him draw on his own— that's great initiation! Be available to help when he asks for it, though. If your goal is to create something together, if you let him draw the central figures, perhaps he'll let you supplement with contributions in the periphery. If, on the other hand, your child needs more help, you might draw in a part and let him initiate with the colors he selects to color it in. Or let him select the next part he wants to draw, and use your dot-to-dot technique to assist him. Let him select the model of the picture he wants to draw with you, or the next figure from Emberley's book. Ask him where he wants you to put the figure in the drawing.

With more advanced artists who don't need a visual model to copy, suggest illustrating a favorite scene from his own day or from a story he likes. Some children enjoy making their own "books" of drawings on a particular theme like sea animals or Pokemon®. Children capable of more advanced abstract thinking might enjoy drawing on a theme such as helping, sharing, or something that makes you mad or glad. For a talented artist, you can play a game in which you draw any shape, line, or curve and have your child make a picture out of it. You may learn a lot about what's on his mind from this game.

HOW TO TEACH PERSPECTIVE TAKING

This is an exciting stage. Your child is discovering that he can form his own ideas, and can act upon them. Now is the time to start pointing out that other people also have their own ideas. Point out that these ideas are different from his, and that different people have different *preferences*, *perceptions*, and *reactions*. Also point out the corollary that people are happy when they get what they want, and unhappy when they don't.

PRACTICE PERSPECTIVE TAKING IN DAILY LIFE

When your family goes out to a restaurant to eat, play a game pointing out what's the same or different about each person's order. Make a big deal about how Daddy likes pickles on his burger, but Mommy does NOT want pickles on her burger. Have Daddy playfully try giving Mommy some pickles. Mommy may then frown and emphatically tell

Daddy how he might like pickles, but she does not like them. She does not want them. If Luke and Peter want to watch different videos, and Luke gets upset because Peter got his choice first, I'll point out, "Luke wants a different video, so he's sad."

There are innumerable opportunities in daily life to help your child develop "theory of mind," an understanding that people can see the same thing and have different perceptions and reactions. Children with autism require explicit teaching to become aware of this. They need practice in perspective taking.

To capture opportunities to point out differences in perception, you need to catch yourself before making automatic accommodations for your child. If Peter accidentally bumps me or steps on my toes, I'll exaggerate a little and dramatically say, "Ouch, Peter, that hurt!" to make him aware of his actions. When reading a story to your child, turn away so he can't see the pictures. Have another family member coach your child to ask you to turn around so he can see the pictures too. When your child is reading aloud, complain loudly that you can't see the pictures. When he turns the book toward you, reinforce with praise, "Now I can see what you're seeing. I'm so glad you turned the book around!" You'll be encouraging your child to initiate as well as strengthening his understanding of theory of mind.

Don't be too good at getting into your child's head, and correctly guessing his every want and need. Pretend you don't understand or pretend to misunderstand, and let your child do more of the work of communicating what's on his mind. When Peter tries to squeeze past the teacher, she purposely blocks him and waits for him to tap her on the shoulder to say, "Excuse me." When your child takes your hand to scratch his arm, feign misunderstanding, saying, "Does this mean you want a tickle here?... Oops, maybe not...or perhaps a squeeze or shake?" Make a game of it until you finally prompt him by asking, "Scratch?" Wait for him to clarify and say, "Scratch, please," before you deliver the long awaited scratch.

Much of the joy of experience sharing derives from comparing differences in reaction to the same experience. This kind of perspective taking naturally becomes the favorite topic of conversation in family life. Hence after a trip to the amusement park, give everyone a chance to talk about their favorite ride. Share your favorite, funniest, or worst memory on your latest family vacation. Talk about your different feelings and opinions about events and characters in daily life and storybooks. Share interesting observations when you go on outings to the zoo or museum, or even out on a walk in the neighborhood. Highlight the perspective taking aspect on these outings by having the children take along drawing pads, journals, or cameras depending on what's fun for them. Have a contest of who found the most beautiful, unusual, or funniest exhibit, or simply enjoy sharing your discoveries at the end.

Ultimately, your child will only do the hard work of practicing perspective taking if it's worth his while. So be sure to highlight the payoff. Do complain loudly if he blocks your view when watching TV together. Do protest when you haven't made it through a door he's walked through first, and it's closing in your face. Stop him before he erases his work on his whiteboard before showing you. But when he complies when you ask him to move so you can see the TV screen, take a moment to give him a little squeeze and say, "Thanks for moving. Now Mom can watch with you!" When he notices you haven't made it through the door yet, and holds it open for you, give him that warm look and tone of voice as you thank him. When you ask to see his work on his ABCs and he comes over to show you, make your reaction big with a warm smile and high five as you say, "What a great job! Look at those great letters!"

As usual meaningful situations in daily life are the best time to teach perspective taking. However, perspective taking games provide repetition to help drive the point home. Here are a few of my favorite ones.

GAMES THAT TEACH PERCEPTUAL PERSPECTIVE TAKING

Realizing that seeing leads to knowing, and that people see things from different perspectives, is a big challenge for many children with autism. Even if your child has got to the point where he finds experience sharing inherently motivating, your child is unlikely to ever point things out to you if he doesn't even realize you might not be seeing them, that you have a different perspective. What follows are several game ideas to help drive the point home.

A time-honored classic is "Blind man's bluff." In this game, one player is blindfolded while the other players position themselves around the room. The "blind man" says "blind man's..." and the others cry out, "bluff!" The "blind man" tags them by tracking their voices. This game is fun in itself and highlights the use of the senses. However, you can adapt this game to more specifically make the point that seeing leads to knowing and that different people can see differently depending upon their point of view.

In the adapted game, one player is blindfolded or covers his eyes. Another player gives directions to the "blind man" on how to find and tag the other players who position themselves around the room. "Take three steps forward. Turn left and take one step. Reach down to touch Luke!" Tagging can result in a fun little interaction such as a joyful tickle or high five. If you don't have enough players, use stuffed animals or favorite toys for the "blind man" to find, and then have the stuffed animal interact with the "blind man" (the animal can even hand him a tiny edible treat if necessary for motivation) or play with the toy together briefly. Be sure to give your child the opportunity to be the caller. Even if he's nonverbal, he can use gestures or pictures and have someone "read" these aloud, translating them into spoken words. (Or you can play this game without the blindfold and just use gestures if the goal is to practice gestural communication instead of perspective taking.)

Gutstein (2000, p.138) has a clever adaptation of this game where one player is blindfolded, and the other player tells him how to navigate around an obstacle course. He has another game where two players stand on opposite sides of a barrier that prevents the player with the ball from seeing the basket on the other side. The other player gives him directions so he knows where to try to toss the ball over into the basket. You can try using coins instead of a ball, and a metal bin instead of a basket for immediate feedback from the sound of the coin hitting the container bottom to tell your child if he got it in or not. If he gets the coin in, he gets to keep it. I practice coin identification and counting money as well with this game by providing little treats Peter can buy with the coins he's earned marked with price tags of different amounts.

Arnold Miller (2007) has a brilliant, yet simple way to begin to teach perceptual perspective taking. Take a card with a different picture on each side. Show each side to the child and make sure he can label each picture. Then sit opposite the child and hold up the card between the two of you, one side facing you and one facing the child. Ask him what he sees, and after he labels it, ask him what you see. If he can't tell you, have him walk over to your side and see the card facing you from your perspective. Practice this game holding the card between two different people, and have your child answer what each person sees.

You can practice a variety of other skills while playing these types of games. Sussman (1999) describes "the barrier game," where you take turns guessing what object the other person sees on their side of the barrier. I do a variation of this idea by adding an element of pretend. Peter's beloved stuffed animals are laid out on his bed. Sometimes I pretend to be a monster that kidnaps one or two under the covers. To get the animal back, Peter has to identify which animal I stole. I start listing attributes such as, "I'm looking at an orange animal with black stripes who begins with the letter 'T'." If Peter says, "Tigger," Tigger bounds forth to hug him in a joyful reunion. To give him practice actively seeking information, instead of automatically giving him the attributes of the stolen animal, I'll sometimes have one of Peter's big brothers prompt Peter to ask "wh" questions, such as "What color is it?" "What does it eat?" "Where does it live?" etc. Then switch roles. Besides making the point that he can't see what you see, this game gives your child a chance to practice phonics, descriptors, and asking and answering "wh" questions.

TEACHING PERSPECTIVE THROUGH LITERATURE AND ART

Children's literature abounds with charming stories about perspective taking like the classic, *Seven Blind Mice* by Ed Young (1992), which is about seven blind mice trying to guess what the new animal is at the pond. They each explore a small part of the big animal, and make their guesses according to their perceptions from their various perspectives. The animal turns out to be an elephant, but for the one exploring the tail, it is a snake, and for the one exploring the leg, it is a tree. Turn reading the book into a game in which you show the picture showing the body part, and take turns with your child making your own guesses.

The visual arts provide deliberate practice in perspective taking. As your child learns how to depict a scene or object from different vantages, he learns to see from different points of view. If you position yourselves on opposite sides of your model, you and your child can compare what you saw in your drawings. For less able artists, an assistant can always help the child with his drawing, or the same point can be made using photography instead of drawing.

This next drawing game is not about learning to draw from different vantages, but how different people can see different possibilities from the same starting point. Start with a simple figure such as a geometric shape, line, curve, dots, or combination of any of these elements, outlined in bold or in a distinct color. Give copies to all the participants. Have them all make their own drawings out of that same starting figure, and compare the drawings at the end. Your child can see how different people see different possibilities and create different images out of the same starting point. For less able artists, you can still play this game, making use of Emberley's (1970, 1972) drawing books. Start out with a simple circle, rectangle, or triangle. Find several Ed Emberley figures (or draw your own) that make use of that shape for your child to choose from. Help your child draw the object of his choice. If you and other participants select different objects, you can all compare drawings at the end, and again celebrate how different people see and imagine different things to draw.

> *I took out Emberley's (1970) book on drawing animals from simple shapes. I drew a semicircle with a line connecting either end and each of us chose a picture to make from it. Peter chose a bird, I picked a porcupine, and our friend Chantal chose a turtle. After we drew our pictures, we showed them to each other, turning them around so everyone could see. I outlined the original shape in pink so Peter could see we made something different out of the same shape. Then we discussed whose was the best. I had Peter turn each picture around to show me one at a time, and voted for Peter's bird. Chantal had Peter turn each picture around to show her one at a time, and she voted for Peter's bird. Then we had Peter ask to have us turn our pictures around to show him. He said, "Mama's!" and pointed to the porcupine! "That's why I'm crazy about you, Peter!" I laughed, as I gave him a huge hug.*

TEACHING YOUR CHILD HOW TO BE MINDFUL OF THE NEEDS OF OTHERS

So far the games have emphasized perceptual perspective taking, meaning how different people perceive things differently. This final game teaches a child to think of what other people want or need and is an adaptation of a similar game from Miller (2007). It makes the child not only notice that his play partner wants something different, but to act upon it. I call this game, "Paying attention to the needs of others." Start out with a simple trading game. Select two different puzzles. Keep one and give the other to your child. Remove ten pieces out of your puzzle and give them to your child. Remove ten pieces out of his puzzle and keep them. Say, "Ready, set... Trade!" On "Trade!" you and your child exchange one puzzle piece and place the pieces in your puzzles. Hold out one of the puzzle pieces your child needs in one hand, and hold your other hand palm up to prompt receiving a piece you need in exchange. Do not release the piece your child needs until he gives you one in exchange.

After your child gets the hang of the idea of exchanging pieces, it's time to make the game more challenging. Put aside your original puzzle. Take out a distinctly different puzzle or any kind of put-together toy like a train made out of DUPLO blocks, from which several pieces are removed and placed next to your child. Give a verbal clue like, "I'm tired of doing that puzzle. I want to put together this DUPLO train." Then say the usual "Ready, set... Trade!" Don't release the puzzle piece the child needs until he hands you a DUPLO piece instead of a puzzle piece. Keep switching between the DUPLO train and puzzle, so that your child has to pay attention to which kind of piece to give you in exchange for another puzzle piece he needs. Once your child gets the idea, you can fade your verbal cues, and eventually switch between multiple different put-together toys. It's amazing how, after repeated practice, a child can keep up with noticing his partner's changing needs.

It's worth reiterating the critical need to generalize. Once you've got your child to notice and accommodate the needs of others in a game like this, have him use the same perspective taking skills in daily life. Thus when your child is assisting you as you cook, instead of directly telling your child to give you a mixing spoon, take a moment to pause. "Hmm... I wonder what I need to stir this with." When shopping for his little brother's birthday present, pick up a cool toy truck in one hand and a bottle of washing up liquid in another and ask, "Hmm... I wonder what your little brother would like."

As a general rule, using declarative instead of imperative language encourages the child to think more on his own, including perspective taking. So consider starting with comments beginning with "I wonder what I need to stir with." If your child doesn't respond, you can fall back to a direct question like, "What do I need to stir with?" and/or prompt with your eyes by looking at the spoon and back to your child, offer him choices, or move the spoon closer to him. You can always fall back on the most intrusive language, a direct order like "Spoon, please," if you're in a hurry.

Encouraging play
EARLY SENSORIMOTOR EXPLORATION

The complexity of a child's play typically develops over the years. A child begins with simple sensory and motor exploration, touching and feeling different objects and textures, tasting objects in the mouth, and enjoying climbing, swinging, and jumping. Many of our children get stuck in a perseverative version of this stage. They spend their free time "stimming," meaning they discover one sensory or motor experience that they enjoy, such as spinning, tapping, flapping, or rocking, and do it repetitively for long periods of time. This kind of obsessive "play" is not productive. The child gets drawn into a cycle of sensory craving to the exclusion of all other activity, and is neither connecting to his environment nor to human interaction.

TRANSFORMING SENSORIMOTOR STIMULATION INTO INTERACTIVE PLAY

Strategies to break such perseverative cycles include playfully joining and inserting oneself into the activity, or creating a new activity that includes similar pleasurable elements. For example, say you have a child obsessively jumping. Jump alongside your child, and eventually try jumping together, holding hands, and then using your arms to help him jump super high. For a child obsessed with tapping sticks gather a number of other long, thin objects like spatulas or drumming sticks and helpfully offer your child different objects to tap on, working up to a rhythmical game of exchanging objects. If the last exchange ended with everyone having sticks, the exchange game could morph into a tapping game of tapping sticks together rhythmically and perhaps finally playing the drums together.

The key to breaking a cycle of perseverative activity is to engage the child's frontal lobes. Peter loves to tear paper obsessively. As he was tearing, I started collecting his torn paper scraps to make a collage out of them. I asked Peter for a big rectangle or little triangle, for something long and thin or bigger or smaller depending on whether I was constructing a tree branch or flower petal. Before he knew it, Peter was working on his receptive language and fine motor tearing skills. What started out as an obsession became a friend's birthday card, which Peter proudly presented later that evening. Pretend your child's stimming or flitting is intentional, and turn it into a meaningful, interactive activity.

CAUSE-AND-EFFECT PLAY

Next in development, children typically make the leap of discovering the fun of actually acting upon their environment. They bang on pots and pans, roll balls, throw objects to watch them fall, and enjoy cause-and-effect toys starting out with simple rattles and moving on to toys that squeak upon squeezing, push-the-button popup toys, and windup or pull-the-string toys. As their fine motor skills improve, they discover they can stack blocks, roll a toy train or car, and mark up their world with a crayon. Provide a variety of these experiences for your child, and teach him to explore objects with all of his senses. Show him how the squeaking bear not only makes that surprising sound when squished but is also soft and cuddly to hold and feel. Better yet, make yourself a cause-and-effect toy, and make different silly sounds or facial expressions if your child touches your nose, tugs at your ear, or gently pulls your hair.

Using your senses game

This game teaches sensory exploration and provides an opportunity to practice labeling and understand cause and effect. Lay out several favorite cause-and-effect toys on the bed (such as a flashlight, pull-the-string stuffed animal, and windup toy). Have the child close his eyes as you put one in a pillow case. Let him feel it, and guess which toy it is. Or put several of his favorite toys in the pillowcase and see if he can pull out the toy you name, and then switch roles. Be sure to celebrate each identification by enjoying playing with the toy together. Nonverbal children can play this game using pictures, photos, or word cards instead of verbal speech.

TURN-TAKING BOARD GAMES

Children in Stage Four can often learn to enjoy turn-taking board games. Try classics such as "Candyland," "Concentration," "Chutes and ladders," and "Don't break the ice." They make great activities for lazy Sunday afternoons when you want to keep your child interacting and occupied with little effort. When Peter insists on watching a favorite movie for the twentieth time, I'll bargain with him. I'll turn on his choice of movie if he plays my choice of board game while we watch it.

REPRESENTATIONAL PLAY

Children usually start coming up with their own ideas to play out by imitating what they've experienced in real life. This is called representational play. My toddler grandson watches me talking on the phone, and the next thing I know I see him walking toward me holding a toy phone or real cordless phone to his ear, smiling and babbling. The other day I caught him in my bathroom swishing water in the toilet bowl with a brush because he had watched his mother cleaning the bathroom that morning. Our special kids may or may not automatically imitate us in representational play. You can encourage it by making the appropriate materials available in the right settings. For example, when you are cooking, you can place some toy or extra real pots or bowls and spoons on a little table in your kitchen (plus possibly items to cook like playdough, beans, or water) where your child can easily reach them. When sweeping, you might provide a little toy broom for your child to "help" alongside you.

Don't be discouraged or surprised if your child shows no interest. Try providing enticing materials like colorful playdough when pretend baking, or squishy bubbles when pretending to wash dishes. Use high affect and coordinated actions to get your child to imitate you as you roll out the playdough cookies together, or hand him one plastic dish after the other to scrub in his soapy tub. However, children with autism don't naturally get interested in something just because other people are interested in it, nor are they as inherently inclined to imitate others. So don't think there's something wrong with the way you're trying to play with your child or with the materials you're selecting.

When your child shows little enthusiasm for the activities or toys you've presented, don't be afraid to use them didactically to teach him how to use a roller, or wash dishes. It's okay to switch to ABA mode and even offer tangible rewards like edible treats for successfully completing the actions. Your child will have learned valuable motor sequences that he can use automatically when or if he decides he wants to.

What is automaticity?

Automaticity means being able to do a motor sequence without having to put in the effort to consciously think through each step. Developing automaticity saves a lot of energy. Remember how drained you felt after your first driving lesson? Every step required conscious effort and hypervigilance as you realized that a mistake could result in a collision. If you had to keep up that level of effort forever, most of us would find another way to get around. Therefore, automaticity is an important goal in itself.

Learning new motor sequences takes more effort for many children with autism than for neurotypical children. More repetitions are frequently necessary to develop automaticity.

Peter has brushed his teeth thousands of times, yet still has to count with me to make sure he brushes long enough on each side, and still requires monitoring to make sure he remembers to do each side. (He does learn more inherently rewarding routines much faster.) The point is that the more automatic you make the motor sequencing of play activities like putting LEGO or train tracks together, or "playing house" sequences like rolling playdough, or washing up, the more mental energy your child will have left over to create play ideas to insert those sequences into.

A person only has so much mental energy. Say you have a dollar's worth of mental energy to bake a cake. For us it might take 20 cents to get out all the ingredients, 25 cents to measure them out, 5 cents to mix them together, 5 cents to prepare the pans, and 20 cents to frost the cake. We still have 25 cents left over to add the finishing touches. For our children it might take 50 cents just to gather all the ingredients, and another 50 to remember how to pour and stir. The more practice they get with any motor sequence such as getting items out of the refrigerator or stirring, the more automatic it becomes, and the less mental energy it costs. If it only costs your child 10 cents instead of 50 cents to pour and stir, maybe it will be easy enough to be worth incorporating those actions into play. Play takes some effort, but the reward has to be greater than the cost to be fun.

When you learn to play the piano, you have to practice your scales so that the motor sequencing of your fingers becomes automatic. Then you can concentrate your energies on putting feeling and meaning into your music. The play circuits, games, and ABA taught play sequences are like scales. They provide focus and repeated practice of specific skills so that they become automatic. These specific skills include motor sequences, imitation, eye contact, gestural communication, coordinated actions, and anticipation. Your child can then incorporate them into the melodies of floortime play, in which his ideas and feelings are the music. As he experiments with all kinds of variations, themes, tempos, and moods, the hope is that he learns how to better create his own symphony of real life.

ADOPTING A FREE SPIRIT ATTITUDE TOWARD PLAY

What is play for anyway? It is an opportunity for your child to explore materials, actions, and ideas in a safe venue that allows for mistakes and repetition. It is an opportunity to explore different kinds of interaction with you, such as cooperating, turn taking, or competing. Most importantly, it is free time for your child to initiate and act upon his own ideas. If you are using the toy materials ABA style to teach action sequences like baking, or washing up, you are still accomplishing learning the use of materials, action sequences, and what the ideas of "baking," and "washing up," mean. In other words, you are accomplishing quite a lot. Later, as you make these enticing materials available, leaving them out on the table, you might find your child eventually does feel like initiating the use of them himself on his own time in his own way.

When you see your child initiating this way, be sure to take advantage of the opportunity to follow his lead and use your high affect to encourage him to act out his own ideas. Dr. Kasari and colleagues (Kasari, Freeman and Paparella 2006) designed a study at UCLA in which therapists spent the first part of each session showing children how to use toys ABA style, and then gave the children "free time" in the toy room with those same toys using more of a floortime model. Their studies on joint attention reveal the importance of the kind of play that floortime provides. Children who had 30 minutes of this kind of play (joint attention and symbolic play) for five days a week in addition to their 30 hours of ABA per week over five to six weeks had an average 15-month language gain at 12 months compared with a seven-month gain for children who had ABA alone.

Although it seems like hard work to be constantly looking for and creating all these opportunities for development, after a while it becomes second nature. Floortime becomes a way of life. Thinking of creative ways to engage and interact makes life interesting (and certainly challenging!). Taking that extra time to emotionally connect (catching that gleam in the eye or exchanging a warm smile) makes it beautiful, and even more so when you generalize it to all your relationships.

One key thing I've had to learn is to relax in my expectations. Do your best to provide enticing materials, teach your child the play actions, and then just make the toys and yourself available. If your child engages in representational play, that's great. If not, you may see those motor sequences you've taught emerge in real life as your child initiates and uses them to solve real problems and real needs. It's all good. The more you do with your child, the more places you bring him, the more of real life he experiences, the richer his repertoire of memories will be. He will draw upon these to reconstruct his own ideas someday, and put them into action when ready.

Playdates, anyone?

At this stage, your child should be fairly adept at following your lead, learning new play patterns and games, and tolerating variations. He should be familiar with turn taking and cooperative, coordinated interactions. He may be ready to play with other children.

Any of the games discussed in this book can be played with other children. I frequently pull a sibling to be Peter's play partner as I play the role of Peter's shadow. Depending on the play partner's personality, it may be important to have another adult around to coach him as well, to remind him to wait long enough for Peter to process and respond, and not introduce too much variation in the play circuits too fast. It works best if we play games Peter is familiar with in which interaction is built into the structure of the game.

If you invite another child with autism to play with your child, be sure to have enough help—both children will need a shadow. You will need to do some planning in terms of finding out the other child's interests and sensory issues to accommodate them. You should also try to match developmental levels and put together compatible temperaments. It would be very helpful to coordinate preparations with the other parent. Find out what kind of snack, games, books, and movies the children like. Practice the same games at home with your children so they are familiar with them. Practice a few goals of social speech such as greetings and thank yous/goodbyes. You might come up with a common visual schedule, so the children will know what to expect.

A reasonable playdate might last half an hour. Open with greetings at the door. Consider starting with a structured game with built-in interaction to begin with, such as hide and seek, or one of the treasure hunt variations (see pp.218–19), with the children taking turns hiding and finding the treasure. The games "Down by the bay" (p.143) and "Paying attention to the needs of others" (pp.194–5) demand a lot of interaction. You can select any game from this book or from the books in the References such as Gutstein (2002a, 2002b), Sussman (1999, 2006), or Miller (2007) depending on the interests of the play partner—for art or music lovers, consider some of the games mentioned earlier in this chapter in which the children copy or imitate each other's patterns. Lots of toys like blocks, put-together toys (LEGO, magnetic or snap-together animals and vehicles, etc.), and Lincoln Logs (www.lincolnlogs.knex.com) lend themselves to interactive play if the children take turns with one play partner playing the parts manager and the other the builder.

Use the same kind of cooperative model to have the children make a snack together, with one being the cook and the other fetching and handing ingredients from you to give to the cook. Popcorn or snack mix that goes in one big bowl to share works nicely. Close with reading a book together that's a common favorite, watch a bit of a video that the other child might bring over to share, or have a bit of free time outside. Have the children practice their goodbyes and thank yous, and give the other parent a big hug for a job well done together!

STAGE FIVE: THE WORLD OF SYMBOLIC THINKING AND PRETEND PLAY

By Stage Four, the child can create and hold ideas in his head to solve practical problems and accomplish concrete goals like fetching a stepping stool to climb up and get a cookie out of the cookie jar, or opening up several drawers or toy chests to find a favorite toy. The child begins to understand that different people have different ideas. By now he should have a repertoire of gestures to communicate with. He probably has a repertoire of coordinated actions such as imitating, cooperating, competing, turn taking, trading, and giving and receiving. He should be easy to engage, and able to complete multiple circles of interaction.

Moving from the concrete to representational to symbolic in language and play

The great leap that marks a child's entrance into Stage Five is the development of symbolic thought. The most obvious example of the use of symbols is words—a large part of teaching communication is teaching the use of symbols. Initially, when trying to find out if your child wants a cheeze-it cracker, pair the question with holding up a real one. Later pair the words with a photo of a cheese-it cracker, and then a line drawing (a representation), and finally just the written or spoken word. As you proceed in your teaching in this way, you are moving your child from concrete to representational to abstract or symbolic thinking.

Similarly, creative play starts with the use of real objects. Peter and I play store where I phone in an order using a real phone. Next we might use toy phones (representational play). Finally, we might play the game pretending a banana is the telephone or just using our hands. When you take a box of LEGO and shape it into an airplane and make it fly, you are teaching your child to move from the concrete to representational. That's why when building something together, whether an animal you snap together, a vehicle whose parts magnetically stick together, or a Lincoln Log house, be sure to make it become real in play. That way the child sees the function and fun of it, and practices moving from the concrete to the symbolic.

The important role of symbolic thinking in emotional regulation

One important reason to want your child to learn the use of symbols is that he needs to learn to use words to talk about feelings. Once your child has learned that the word "cracker" means that delicious yellow square he eats, and "car" means that vehicle that takes him places, he can learn that "mad" means that overwhelming bursting feeling in his chest or "love" means those warm, happy feelings of closeness he experiences when getting a hug and cuddle. It's important to learn to identify and label feelings and emotions. One of the most important tools we all have for regulating our emotions is to talk about them. Even the act of labeling the emotion immediately creates a space between having the emotion and acting it out. When I'm really angry, if I can say how I feel, suddenly the emotion is not me, but an idea called "mad." Now the thinking part of the brain called the neocortex engages with that limbic system, the emotional part of the brain. The neocortex has the potential to bring with it all the possible connections of memories of different experiences of anger, and presents alternative ways to deal with it. The first step in that chain of connections is the realization that "I'm mad."

Peter's teaching team started teaching him how to label emotions with ABA. We had him match word cards saying "happy," "sad," "mad," and "scared" with photos of people showing the corresponding emotions. Then Peter labeled our expressions as we acted out each emotion. Peter practiced labeling the emotions in picture books and videos. We would pause the action in Thomas the Tank Engine videos, and have Peter label the emotions expressed so clearly on the train faces.

But all this kind of teaching is just priming. As always, your child's best learning opportunities about emotions will come from real life, in situations in which his feelings are most relevant and meaningful to him, and his motivation is highest. Be on the lookout for those natural teaching moments. I remember sitting on the curb in Pasadena on New Year's day, waiting for the Rose Parade to begin. Peter looked at me with an enormous smile and started flapping his hands. "You're excited, Peter! I know, I'm really excited too!" I said. I wished I'd brought one of Peter's mini-whiteboards. It would have been the perfect opportunity to teach the word "excited" in written form as well as verbally.

Labeling the emotion when it's most intense not only reinforces the learning of it, but also has a magical therapeutic effect all on its own. When Peter was jumping out of the dentist chair, his panic visibly declined when I commented, "I know. You're really scared, Peter." When Peter's little brother grabbed the last cookie, I grabbed Peter's fists before they descended upon Luke's head, and said, "No, Luke! That's mine!" to model the words Peter could use instead of hitting. Then I said, "That made you mad, didn't it, Peter?" Feeling understood defused the emotion, and we were ready to negotiate sharing the last cookie.

Practicing emotional regulation through pretend play

Emotional situations in real life are the most powerful learning experiences for your child, but the problem is that those situations occur only erratically. Pretend, symbolic play can be a powerful tool for further practice identifying and dealing with emotions, and it's always available. In pretend play, you can use dolls, action figures, stuffed animals, or puppets to create any character, role, or situation you want in order to evoke a particular emotion. We have a dragon stuffed animal, alligator pillow, and wolf puppet that serve as villains. Winnie the Pooh has pretended to be Peter, the dentist, or the teacher in various play productions.

Representational toys are nice, but with symbolic play you can make any prop you need out of any materials you might have on hand. An open umbrella can serve as a tent. A little block serves as a chair, and a bigger stack as a table. A blue scarf makes a great lake. When we can't come up with a three-dimensional prop, we sometimes draw what we need and cut it out. Your child can try on any role from a dentist cleaning his dinosaur's teeth to a policeman directing toy cars in traffic. With play, you can try out different solutions to any problem. You can teach degrees of emotion by making a character a little scared, scared, or very scared.

I never dreamed Peter and I would get to the stage where he could understand or enjoy pretend, symbolic play. Since Peter loves food, I had been gradually trying to move into symbolic play from games that had included real food such as playing store with Peter as the customer ordering, and me as the storekeeper sending edible deliveries, or playing restaurant with stuffed animal customers. He only displayed a passing interest, as if trying to humor me.

What finally pulled Peter into the world of pretend play and got him truly engaged was the world of emotions. I discovered that if something of great emotional relevance happened to Peter during the day, re-enacting it or creating a drama with a similar emotional theme would capture his interest. We replayed scenarios that had made Peter happy or upset, and Peter readily engaged. Peter loves to ski. The morning after our ski trip, I piled pillows up by his bedside to make a ski slope. Peter enjoyed "skiing" his stuffed animals down the slope, and having Baby whale follow Mama whale as she made curves all the way down, just as we had done the day before in Peter's ski lesson.

We discovered that Peter also showed an interest in pretend play that contained elements and emotional themes he enjoyed in movies and books. For example, one afternoon in the library we read a nonfiction picture book about penguins. The next day, Peter was quite interested in drawing penguins together. We cut out his little penguin and made it talk. Then we re-enacted the story of his birth. Mama penguin, a stuffed animal, laid a plastic Easter egg and put it on her feet. The egg hatched, and the little cut-out penguin popped out and sat on her feet. Peter loved having Baby penguin cuddle with Mama penguin.

Your pretend dramas don't have to exactly match real life, and can mix settings, story elements, and characters from different sources. Peter loves the cozy, snowy setting of the silent cartoon, *The Snowman*. He also loves the story of *The Three Little Pigs*. So one morning as he lay immovable on the floor, we threw a heavy blanket over him, and built a story around Peter in a cozy cave with a windy snowstorm surrounding him. One by one, his stuffed animal friends would knock on the cave door, asking, "Little Peter, little Peter, let me come in!" Peter enjoyed peeking out of the cave and letting some come in and cuddle with him, but others he would throw out with glee.

Getting from here (Stage Four) to there (Stage Five)

At this point, some of you may feel doubts about your child's cognitive ability to understand symbolic play or to create ideas to manipulate and act out in play. Don't be discouraged! Every child develops at his own pace. Keep working on the previous stages. Play the sensory games your child enjoys, such as "Gotcha!" tickle, and clapping. Create practical problems for him to solve around his familiar routines such as "Where are your socks?" and go around looking in all the usual places his socks could be, or "What shall we pack?" for his lunchbox or his swimbag before going to the pool. Add humor to make it fun. You could end up finding the socks on Papa's ears. Every time you put in the effort to engage in fun interactions and create problem-solving opportunities for your child, you are working on and consolidating the fundamental levels of emotional and cognitive development, and providing the foundation for further growth.

Greenspan and Wieder (1998, pp.441–2) have a plethora of practical suggestions on how to gradually introduce symbolic thinking. *Give symbolic meaning to real objects.* Make beanbags into a "mountain" to climb down. Pretend the tire swing at the park is a rocket ship, and do a countdown. The bath tub is an ocean for toy fish. A blue blanket turns the bed into a swimming pool.

Greenspan also suggests *offering symbolic solutions to real problems.* When Peter lies down on the sofa, we cover him up with a heavy blanket and pretend he's a bear in a cave. When he wants to go out for a ride in the car, I hand him toy keys to the car. When he's thirsty, I pretend to pour imaginary juice from an empty pitcher into a pretend cup.

Play dual roles. If your child doesn't come up with his own response to an action in the drama, you can step out of being a character in it, and instead use your natural voice to whisper suggestions and choices on how his character might act. Alternatively, enlist another family member to serve as an assistant. For example, in the drama about Piglet and the predator visitors, someone else might ask Peter, who was making Piglet talk, "Should Piglet open the door, Peter? Or should he say, 'No, no no! Go away!'?"

Look for emotional themes in your child's play. If all your child is doing is banging his dinosaur on the table, make a guess and say, "Wow! That's one powerful dinosaur! Think he can take down this building (stand a shoebox up on its end)?" Aggression/power, anger, control, fear and anxiety, nurturing and dependency, curiosity, and pleasure/excitement are all common emotional themes in children's play (Greenspan and Wieder 1998, pp.206–8). Even if your child doesn't have the capacity yet to create his own pretend actions and plots, he might still understand and enjoy dramas you create around these themes.

Try to pick up on your child's current mood and select a matching emotional theme. The child intently banging his toy dinosaur might be interested in an opportunity to play out aggression. The child hiding under the covers might be feeling tired and overwhelmed. He might enjoy you pretending he's in a cozy cave, protected from a snowstorm. Have his favorite stuffed animals come quietly knocking one after another, so he can enjoy cuddling and comforting them in turn. Take advantage of what you know about your child. Did anything particularly good or bad happen in his day that made an emotional impact? Recreate an analogous drama or create one around the same emotional theme.

Expose, expose, expose. All the community outings you make to the library, post office, park, and grocery store, all the trips to the zoo, beach, and amusement park, and all the big and small social interactions you have along the way are potential material for play, as your child re-enacts his experiences. As another character in the drama, gradually and occasionally introduce new ideas. As your child responds to that new action or feeling, he's sharing your idea. Even if that response is not logical, pretend it is intentional, and create a meaning for it. Say Winnie the Pooh is cold and trying to get into a warm cave (under Peter's bed covers). If Peter throws Winnie the Pooh out of his bed, Winnie the Pooh might protest, saying, "Hey! You threw me back out into the cold! I'm going to find another way in!" As Pooh finds his way back under the covers, and keeps getting tossed out, before you know it, Peter is laughing and engaged in the drama of ousting Pooh even though his original intention upon throwing out Pooh might have been, "I want to sleep in. Go away." By treating your child's action as intentional and building a fun interaction upon it, you encourage your child to act intentionally the next time. As you respond meaningfully to each other's actions, you share ideas and create a pretend drama together.

Let's get real: It takes time

Try not to get stressed about this. I used to think of pretend play as some kind of absolute goal my child had to achieve, or we must be doing something wrong. Remind yourself that you are *not* responsible for growing your child's neural synapses. All you can do is offer the opportunities. You can lead a horse to water, but you can't make him drink. The best thing you can do for your child is spend a lot of time with him, enjoying him at the level he's at. If you know the next closest steps in development, you can ever so slowly and gradually introduce new elements. The key is to entice him into learning new elements by working them around his interests. You may not be able to make the horse drink, but you can make him thirsty.

Here's an example of a typical hour of play with Peter (age 11). You'll see how it takes a whole hour of warming up with Stage Three and Four interactions before we make a brief push into Stage Five—symbolic play.

> I usually start by putting out a few items like drawing paper and art supplies, a musical activity, and board games. He frequently eschews all of that, and heads for the kitchen for a snack. Although strictly speaking play methodologies like floortime and RDI try to get away from using external rewards, I am not a purist. One of my child's few interests happens to be food so I frequently build games around food. It's my way of making him "thirsty" for interaction.
>
> It was a beautiful day, so I grabbed the popcorn Peter picked out, and said, "Let's play outside." Dona, his floortime therapist, had come to play with Peter. "Let's play 'Keep up with Dona.' When I signal 'come,' you can come to get some popcorn from me, but you have to keep pace with Dona. If you get in front of or behind her, you have to go back to the beginning." I ran 50 feet in front of the two of them. When Peter looked up at me, I signaled with a "come" gesture. Dona playfully varied her pace, taking giant slow steps, then tiny fast ones, then dramatically stopped, etc. When the two of them made it to me, we celebrated and shared a handful of popcorn. Then I ran off another 50 feet to start the game over again. Peter loved the game, imitating Dona with a big smile on his face.
>
> After 20 minutes, I thought Peter might like to just enjoy being outside and get a chance to look around. I thought I might as well work in some language practice and get him to learn how to seek information. Since I still had some popcorn left, I started a naming game. I stood in front of or pointed to various interesting sights such as a flowering tree, bird flying, or Peter's little brother playing basketball. If he could name, describe, or comment on what we were looking at together, he'd get a piece of popcorn. If he couldn't think of anything to say, I'd remind him, "You can ask Dona." He would then turn to her and ask, "What is it?" and listen to her answer so he could repeat it to me and claim some popcorn. We moved from sight to sight rapidly, accepting and celebrating answers readily to keep the mood light. The game provided many opportunities for Peter to ask, "What is it?" and practice shifting his attention between his two playmates.

When all the popcorn was gone, it was getting chilly anyway, and we all went inside. Luke wanted to play too. We were ready for a "cool down," so we sat at the kitchen table with the art supplies. It was my birthday, so I suggested we try making birthday cakes. Luke got busy independently. For Peter, I had him imitate my lines and curves on the paper step by step, encouraging him to choose his own colors for each candle and decoration. When we had all finished our drawings, we put the three cake drawings side by side, and sang "Happy Birthday to Mama" with Peter filling in the blank for the word at the end of each line. Then I counted to three, and we pretended to blow out all the candles together. Peter laughed with glee. I thanked them all for a lovely birthday party, and Peter helped me hang up the cakes, assembly-line fashion. A good time was had by all.

In this play session we worked on a variety of social skills using an eclectic approach. The "Keep up with Dona" game was an adaptation of a Gutstein RDI game (2002b, p.91) aimed at teaching a child to synchronize his actions with his adult play partner. The naming game was done à la ABA. We introduced an element of pretend play, floortime style, in our birthday party, blowing out our pretend candles. I used tangible reinforcers in the beginning, to follow Peter's interest, but as he warmed up to the fun of interaction, was able to abandon them entirely in our last activity. We started out with a simple, gross motor imitation activity and ended working up to incorporate some Stage Five symbolic thinking. We also worked on naming, seeking information, and gestural language, all in the context of fun.

If I had tried to start out with pretend play around a theme of a birthday party, I don't think Peter would have been interested. He really just wanted a snack. We worked up from Stage One (food) to Stage Five (blowing out the candles), step by step. The structure of the games drew out interaction, which drew the group together. Peter had enough memories of birthday parties to understand blowing out the pretend candles we had all drawn on our cakes. What made it fun and meaningful was doing it together. Emotional bonding drives cognitive development.

Summary

In summary, pretend play grows out of the child developing the capacity to hold ideas in his head and move from concrete to symbolic thinking. Teaching language is terrific not only for communication, but also to assist the brain in separating perceptions from actions. When a child learns a label for a person, place, object, or feeling, suddenly that concrete thing becomes an idea, represented in his mind, that he can associate with other ideas. Pretend play makes those ideas come alive. The child can "play" with them, meaning learn to manipulate ideas using tangible symbols like puppets, stuffed animals, and toy cars. He can consolidate his memories by re-enacting them in play, try on different emotions and degrees of emotion safely, and explore different ways to deal with different emotion provoking situations. Pretend play is an excellent tool to help your child develop his inner world of ideas and emotions, and it is available at your convenience. Don't be afraid to try it.

Our children's dyspraxia in language and motor capacities is often unnecessarily rate-limiting. We think that because they have trouble talking or motor sequencing, pretend play is beyond their reach. But if you've worked with your child through the stages of engagement, multiple circles of communication, and problem solving, and he shows intent and understanding, he's capable of entering the world of ideas. Support each challenge and thereby flatten the obstacle course. Accommodate those sensory differences and motor challenges. Get around the speech dyspraxia with picture and gestural communication and AT. Support limited working memory using visual supports. Use your order of prompts to teach new things, and withdraw the scaffolding gradually as your child demonstrates ability.

When your child has challenges in multiple brain areas, you need to be eclectic with your methods and approach. The clear-cut presentations and drilling of ABA can prime your child's brain to retrieve and practice the vocabulary and motor sequences he might need in the activity choices ahead. The tangible reinforcers of ABA can add that extra bit of motivation needed for your child to put in that effort of getting started. Once he experiences the fun and warmth of playing with you, the interactions themselves become intrinsically motivating. RDI game frameworks provide the predictability and repetition your child might need to give him ideas of what to do next. Once your child has warmed up and you've got some momentum going, you can look for opportunities to encourage initiation, incorporating the child's ideas and variations, encourage perspective taking, and introduce elements of symbolic thinking. It may not look like the fluid pretend play of neurotypical children, but step by step, with all the supports in place, you can lead your child into the world of pretend and imagination.

Chapter 12

Higher Cognitive Development
Moving into Abstract Thinking

Peter and Belinda were working at school. Peter did not want to drink water at lunchtime, but he did want potato chips. Belinda poured a glass of water. She said, "You must drink some water first, and then you get a chip." She wrote "If ____, then ____" on a big piece of paper on the table. She put the glass of water on the blank after the word "if," and a big chip after the word "then."

Peter asked for a chip, but Belinda said, "Water first, then chip." Peter had an idea. He picked up the glass of water, carried it outside, and poured out the water on the grass. Then he came back to his chair and put the glass on the table. "Chip, please," he said.

Belinda said, "Nice try, Peter, but not what I want. You must drink water first, and then get a chip." She poured more water in the glass. Peter drank a very small sip of water, and held out his hand for a chip. Belinda said, "Little water, little chip." She put a very small piece of chip in Peter's hand. Peter ate the chip, but felt a little upset. "Big chip," he said.

Belinda said, "Little water, little chip. Big drink of water, big chip." She put a big chip next to the glass of water. "Let's work. If you want the big chip, take a big drink." At first Peter felt a little mad. He did not want the water. But as he was working, he kept looking at that big, delicious chip. So after 20 minutes, Peter stopped working. He took a big drink of the water. He drank half of the glass of water. Then he held out his hand, and said, "Big chip, please." Belinda gave the chip to Peter. It tasted delicious! Peter smiled, and Belinda smiled. Both were feeling happy.

Peter and Belinda wanted different things. Belinda wanted Peter to drink water. Peter did not want water; he wanted a big chip. Peter felt proud. He used his words to tell Belinda he wanted a big chip, not a little chip. He showed her that he did not want to drink all the water. But he did drink half of the water. So Belinda gave Peter the big chip. If two people want different things, they can tell each other what they want. Then each person can give up some of what

> they want, and get some of what they want. This is called "meeting
> half way," or "negotiation." When two people want different things,
> negotiation makes them both happy.

Peter went through a phase when he refused to drink water for long periods. But he really wanted potato chips. His tutor used the situation to teach him the if/then template. I wrote up this story called, "I can negotiate," to review with him later that day. It's one of many stories I write down for Peter to journal memorable life experiences and highlight moral or social lessons. I'm including it here to illustrate where you're headed next in cognitive development, which is to teach your child how to request and negotiate, to enable your child to get his needs and wants met.

REQUESTING AND NEGOTIATING: THE FIRST STEPS
TO SYMBOLIC AND LOGICAL THINKING

Consider how far your child has come by this point. After innumerable positive interactions with you, he's learned to readily engage with you, imitate you, and take his turn in your play/work patterns and communicative exchanges. He's moved from the concrete to representational, and hopefully to the symbolic in his mode of communication. He may have a vocabulary of a couple hundred or more words, whether spoken, written, PECS cards, or buttons on an AT screen. He's putting words together, and may be initiating his own communicative attempts, perhaps in requesting favorite activities, foods, toys, and people. Remember, affect (emotion) drives motivation that drives learning. Hunger for the favorite foods, toys, and sensory activities that give him pleasure will motivate your child to learn his first symbols, the words for what he wants, and a logical way to ask for them.

So observe your child to identify his wants and interests. Teach him how to indicate a choice clearly, whether that means handing you a picture card, verbally requesting, underlining or circling written choices, or pressing an AT choice button.

Next introduce your child to the logic of using a visual schedule (see p.113 in Chapter 8), and make use of it a habit. You'll be glad you did when the time comes when you need to prepare your child for a transition in activities, or inform your child of changes in his schedule or routine. For example, say a favorite activity like swimming is cancelled.

You can take it off your child's visual schedule, and show him several choices he can choose from to put up in its place, like "go to the park," "visit Grandma," or "get ice cream."

Teach your child the Premack Principle (or Grandma's law) right off the bat: "If you do this, then you get that." For example, post an "If ___, then ___" template in front of him. At dinner, fill in the blanks, "If you eat your spaghetti, then you get ice cream." On going out, write, "If you put on your shoes, then you may go outside." If you use the template frequently throughout the day, your child will come to understand the meaning of "If, then," another useful negotiating tool.

These three tools, a language system (pictures or words), a visual schedule, and an if/then template will empower your child to negotiate. He can choose what he wants and when to do or get it. You let him know your parameters by limiting his field of choices, and using the if/then template.

NEXT STEP: DEVELOPING ABSTRACT THINKING THROUGH STRUCTURED TEACHING, PRACTICE IN GAMES, AND APPLICATIONS IN DAILY LIFE

The next steps in cognitive development move into the realm of abstract thinking. Your child is now capable of forming ideas. Abstract thinking is the process of forming and manipulating those ideas. Greenspan and Wieder (1998, p.245) do a good analysis of different kinds of abstract thinking in their classic, *The Child with Special Needs*. They include the ability to answer and ask "wh" questions; categorize, compare, and contrast ideas; understand cause and effect; think both in terms of broad themes and details; manipulate and use concepts of quantity, time, space, and gradations ("er," "est," degrees of); and talk about emotions and feelings.

If you are able to remember all these kinds of abstract thinking, you will never run out of things to teach and talk about with your child.

First teach your child how to answer, and then ask "wh" questions. Basic "what" and "who" questions are usually the easiest to answer because the answers generally refer to tangible objects and people. As you work on "where" and "when," you're automatically working on those critical space and time concepts. Asking "why" requires an understanding of cause and effect. It's often taught in the context of talking about feelings. "How" can be taught in the context of breaking down tasks into steps, and introduces your child to the concept of organizing thoughts in terms of overall picture and details. "How much" questions address the development of quantitative and comparative thinking. More advanced "what" questions include "what kind" which prompts categorization, and open-ended questions like "what happened" which requires thematic, big picture thinking.

Take advantage of incidental teaching by sprinkling in "wh" questions whenever you spot an emotionally relevant context. "*What* do you want to eat for a snack?" you might ask as you hold out an orange in your right hand and a box of crackers in the other (or pictures of them). When your child asks for crackers, ask, "*How many?*" and have him count them out one by one as you place them in his hand. As your child pulls the covers back over his head when you try to wake him up in the morning, ask, "Do you want more time to sleep? *When* should I come back, in one minute or five minutes?"

Neurotypical children learn the meaning of "wh" questions through this kind of incidental teaching, but many of our children benefit additionally from a more explicit, concentrated approach. Tabletop exercises and games may provide the repetition required to effectively introduce a concept to your child. Once he gets good at these, he will require less prompting to answer your incidental "wh" and "how" questions, and will tolerate and enjoy more of them. Follow the same order of prompts discussed in Chapter 6 (see pp.71–2). All the games and exercises mentioned below can be done using verbal and written language, PECS, and/or AT (assistive technology) devices, including smart phone and tablet communication applications.

Brainstorming on how to teach "what"
STRUCTURED TEACHING

The most basic level of teaching "what" is in teaching labels. In typical DTT programs, the child becomes familiar with the word "what" from having to answer, "What is it?" and "What is he/she doing?" thousands of times as he is asked to label objects (nouns) and actions (verbs).

GAMES

You can consolidate your child's understanding of the concept of "What is it?" and "What is he/she doing?" by using these phrases at home in these games. I use the first two of these games when I see my child rummaging in the pantry for snacks or obsessing over some toy, and I want to slow down his consumption. If he has to have a snack, get your child to use words to tell you what he wants (such as crackers), and then place a small portion in a bowl. If he has to have a certain toy, tell your child he gets to play with the toy if he plays the game with you (use a 30-second timer). Both games require you, your child, and a third person, who I'll call Mr. Dictionary. I generally grab another family member who happens to be nearby. As you walk around your house for these games, it's perfectly all right to keep switching the person who plays the role of Mr. Dictionary.

The first game, "What is it?" goes like this.[1] Have your child follow you around as you point to various items in your house. As you point to, say, a chair, ask your child, "What is it?" If he answers "Chair," hand him a bit of a cracker (or whatever snack item he selected, or 30 seconds to play with his toy). Then point to another item. Start out asking him to label familiar items, so the pleasure of success hooks his interest. Then throw in an unfamiliar item. "What is it?" you say as you point to a vase, a new vocabulary word. No reply. Suggest to your child, "You can ask Mr. Dictionary." Provide whatever level of prompting is necessary to ask Mr. Dictionary, "What is it?" (If he reads, writing the phrase down on a card and letting him read it aloud is helpful. You may also prompt him to use PECS or AT/apps to ask.) Mr. Dictionary labels the item, "It's a vase." Have your child then tell you, "Vase" or "It's a vase," and promptly celebrate and hand him his reward. Continue your game, asking "What is it?" being sure to sprinkle in lots of familiar items with unfamiliar ones so as not to frustrate your child. This game is great for maintaining learned vocabulary and for teaching your child to seek information. He gets to practice both answering and asking "What is it?"

The second game, "What is he/she doing?" is similar. Instead of pointing to items for your child to label, stop in front of various family members doing various things like reading, eating, or cooking, and ask, "What is he/she doing?" Stop in front of his little brother watching TV. Ask your child, "What is he doing?" If your child answers, "Watching TV," terrific! Celebrate, and hand him his reward. If there's no reply, refer him to someone else nearby, also watching TV. "You could ask Daddy," you say. Prompt him to ask Daddy, "What is he doing?" Daddy answers, "Watching TV." Have your child turn to you and say, "Watching TV." Celebrate, and hand him his reward. This game allows the child to practice seeking information, and both answer and ask, "What is he doing?"

---

1   I learned this game from a brilliant Norwegian psychologist and consultant, Bodil Sivertsen, PhD.

A third game is centered round a favorite family activity. We play it when we go hiking or walking. I call it, "Asking 'what' with all five senses." It's a perfect opportunity to learn the meaning of "what" as well as practice tuning into the environment with all your senses as you stop to soak in the scenery, and take photos. "Hey, Peter, look at that! What do you see?" As you walk under a shady tree and hear the birds singing, stop and cup your ear. "I hear something. Do you hear it too? I wonder what that could be." As you pause to smell the roses, play a game. Cover your child's eyes, have him touch a soft rose petal and take a long sniff. "Can you guess what you're touching?" "The petal is _____ (soft), but don't touch these thorns! They're _____ (sharp)." "What do you think smells the best? This one or that one?" Take a photograph of that squirrel hanging upside down to grab a nut. Ask, "What's he doing?" Recollect these memories when you view any photos you have taken later that evening, or show them to Daddy when he asks how your walk went. Photos aren't the only visual record you can make—you could also draw a stick picture of your child. Draw arrows from his eyes, ears, nose, and hands pointing to his answers about what he saw, heard, smelled, and touched. If you stopped for ice cream, you can include what he tasted too!

Finally, a more advanced but all-round favorite language game to play is an adaptive version of "I spy with my little eye." Place several favorite toys, stuffed animals, or small edibles on the table. Say, "I spy with my little eye something you like. If you can guess what it is, you get it." Prompt your child to ask, "What is it?" Then tell him the category. "It's a kind of (food, stuffed animal, vehicle, etc.)." If the child can't guess the answer, prompt him to ask you more questions, like "What color is it?" "What size is it?" "What does it do?" "What does it eat?" etc. until he guesses correctly. Then let him eat the edible treat or play with the favorite toy (use a timer). Switch roles, and your child gets to practice naming the category and answering your attribute questions. Depending on his language skills, consider enlisting another family member to serve as an assistant to provide the necessary prompting. This game allows the child to practice categories and attributes as well as answering and asking "what" questions.

REAL LIFE

Ask "What kind…" questions to give your child practice in thinking in categories. When you go to the zoo, ask, "What do you want to see first, the farm animals or the wild animals?" When you go shopping and see bananas on the list, ask your child, "What section should we go to find this? Bakery, meat section, or fruits and vegetables?" If you keep in mind the question "What kind…?" you'll remember to look for opportunities to teach your child to organize his thoughts in terms of categories.

Brainstorming on how to teach "who"
STRUCTURED TEACHING

"Who" is another relatively easy concept to teach. Typical DTT programs will have already drilled your child on "Who is this?" as they show your child pictures of various important people in his life to teach him to name "Mom," "Dad," etc. Preschool circle time games are full of activities and songs using the word "who." There's usually an opening "Who is here today?" song, or "Who gets the ball?" type of games.

INCIDENTAL TEACHING

There are innumerable natural opportunities to practice using the word "who." When someone knocks on the door, have your child peek through the peephole or window to answer your question, "Who is it?" When someone comes up to greet your child, whisper, "Look, Peter, someone's coming to say 'hi.' Who is it?" so he gets a chance to retrieve the person's name from memory or get it from you to include in his greeting back. It's particularly easy to cue children using AT devices to answer "who" questions because all they typically need to do is push the button with some nametag or person icon to bring up a screen full of names of people.

TEACHING "WHO" WITH A TREASURE HUNT
VARIATION AND BY DELIVERING MESSAGES

I have a favorite game to give a child explicit practice in seeking information by asking a "who" question. A fun variation of the treasure hunt game is to hide the treasure in the pocket of another family member or friend in the house. Instruct them to carry on with their business, and give your child the opportunity to get their attention. After your child finishes his countdown, say, "I know *who* has your prize!" As usual, give him the least prompting necessary to ask you, "Who has it?" or "Who is it?" Answer verbally with the name +/- photo +/- written name of the person you gave the prize to, and prompt your child as needed to find the person. Prompt your child to get the person's attention by standing nearby and waiting, tapping his shoulder lightly if necessary. Help him ask for the prize by saying, "Prize, please," and make sure he says "Thank you" upon receiving it. Then celebrate, "You did it!" with a high five.

This game transitions easily into teaching your child how to deliver messages, a highly practical and useful skill. Start by having the recipient pocket a small prize for your child. Tell your child, "I know *who* has a prize for you!" Prompt him to ask, "Who is it?" Tell him the name of the recipient, but also hand your child a written note to deliver. Say, "Tell him 'Dinner is ready.'" The written note should say the same, and perhaps also have the name of the recipient written prominently on top to serve as an extra visual reminder to your child. When he gets the recipient's attention, your child will hopefully say or read off the note, "Dinner is ready." If he automatically says, "Prize, please," just have the recipient reply, "Oh, I see you have a note in your hand. Is that for me?" and prompt your child to read the message aloud. Then have the recipient warmly thank the child, and offer the prize. Gradually, the goal is to fade the prize as the whole process becomes less effortful and more automatic for him.

USING A VISUAL SCHEDULE TO TEACH "WHO"

A great way to routinely practice the concept of "who" with your child is to preview the day with him using a visual schedule. Try making a schedule like the following sample:

When?	Who?
Morning (place picture icon here of a sun rising up)	Miss Wendy (place a photo of the teacher here)
	Miss Belinda (place a photo of your child's tutor here)
Afternoon (place a picture icon here like a midday sun)	Miss Gabby (place a photo of the swim teacher here)
Evening (place a picture icon here of the moon in the sky)	Charlie (place a photo of the babysitter here)

Select the important people in your child's life who he will see that day, but don't put in every single person, or it's too much information to process. As you preview and review the day with your child, you'll have lots of opportunities to practice both the concept of "who" and "when."

Brainstorming on how to teach "where"
STRUCTURED TEACHING

The concept of "where" is usually introduced in a typical DTT program when prepositions are taught. The tutor places an item like a little bear inside, behind, next to, on top of, or under a box. The child is then asked, "Where's the bear?" and prompted to answer with the correct prepositional phrase. Another typical structured teaching exercise is to place a dollhouse on the table, and ask the child, "Where does this go?" as you hand him a bed, sofa, refrigerator, and other different kinds of furniture.

TREASURE HUNT GAMES

"Where" is relatively easy and fun to teach in games at home if you just think, "treasure hunt." The easiest version is a spin-off of the method used to teach prepositions. Take a box and hide a small treat in, under, or behind it, as your child covers his eyes and counts to ten. Prompt him to ask you "Where is it?" Answer "(under/in/behind) the box." The child gets one chance to look for the treat. If he doesn't find it, re-teach the preposition he missed, and start over again. Once your child gets good at this, reverse roles. He gets the treat if he gives you the correct preposition.

After your child gets good at this, vary the object you hide the treat in or around. Hide it under the chair, behind the box, or on top of the shelf. If your child is at a very basic level of language development, tie a long string to the hidden treasure, and give your child the free end so he can follow the string to the "sofa," "piano," "computer," or whatever other object label you want him to learn. It's helpful to place written labels on those objects and give your child a matching printed word card at the beginning of the game.

Then hide the treat farther away, perhaps in different rooms. "Your prize is in the (living room/kitchen/bedroom)." Initially you might help your child figure out which room is which using the same trick of tying a long string from the prize to your child, so he only has to follow the string to end up in the correct room. Consider also putting a sign on the door labeling the "bedroom," "kitchen," "bathroom," etc. Then disconnect the string from the prize so the child ends up in the correct room, but still has to look around for the prize.

The next level of difficulty is to actually hide the prize instead of placing it in an obvious spot in the room. That way, when your child goes to the correct room you named, he has another opportunity to ask you, "Where is it?" Then give a more precise direction with a preposition. For example, have your child count to ten while you hide a plastic Easter egg with his treat in it under his pillow in his bedroom. When he finishes the countdown, have him ask you (using the least amount of prompting required) "Where is it?" Reply, "Your treat is in your bedroom." Once he goes to his bedroom, he looks around and doesn't see the Easter egg obviously displayed. Wait for him to ask you, "Where is it?" Then say, "Your treat is under your pillow."

If you have another little one who wants to play, assist your child in reversing roles. Let him hide the treat for the other child, and answer when asked, "Where is it?" to give him practice giving directions naming rooms and using prepositional phrases.

There are an infinite number of variations to this game. Create problems for your child to solve like placing the prize in a clearly visible but hard-to-reach location such that he needs to find a stepladder or rake to help him, which can be placed nearby. Instead of telling your child which room or object his prize is hidden in, give attributes of the location instead, such as "where you sleep at night," or "the room with the microwave and refrigerator." Instead of hiding a treat, hide another person, and you've got a perfect transitional game to the classic, hide and seek.

Siegel (2003) describes a game that highlights how language logically connects thoughts or ideas. Have your child select a prize that you hide in a "treasure chest," and place several written clues in different locations around the house. Each clue tells the location of the next clue, the last telling where the treasure is hidden. At the end of counting down from 20, wait for him to ask you, "Where is it?" and reply, "The first clue is in the kitchen in the oven." Once your child finds that clue, it reads, "The next clue is in your bedroom under the green pillow." Once he finds that clue, it reads, "Your prize is in the room with the piano under the table." Such a game uses language to connect one idea to the next and also demands that your child pay attention to multiple attributes simultaneously.

The treasure in these games does not have to be an edible treat. You could place a favorite toy in a shoebox. Throw in a sand timer so your child will know how long he gets to play with the toy. Alternatively, you could just place one-minute sand timers without the toy in the "treasure chests" and teach the child to accumulate them to trade for time to play with his favorite toy. Similarly, you could use tokens, pennies, or promissory notes ("IOUs") to exchange for tangibles, time, or a preferred activity.

PRACTICING FAR AND NEAR CONCEPTS OF WHERE IN DAILY LIFE

"Where" is actually a big concept, as it includes all concepts of space. The answer to a "where" question like "Where is the book?" could therefore range from "on the table," to "in your room," to "at school," to "in Los Angeles," to "in the United States." Start with the most immediate and the most concrete conceptualizations like doing treasure hunts to look for prizes "on the table" and "in your room." Teach more distant places like "school" and "zoo" as you talk about your child's daily schedule and plan future activities. "Where did you go this morning?" "This afternoon we have some free time. Where do you want to go?" Make it visual, offering your child choice boards with words and pictures, such as cut-outs from brochures, photos, drawings, and diagrams. AT/apps and PECS books provide an automatic library of visuals, organized by category of place (rooms in the house like kitchen and bathroom, buildings like library and store, and places like the zoo and the park).

DIRECTIONS

"Where" also includes the concept of directions. When you do treasure hunts for hidden treats, give clues that use the vocabulary we use to describe distance. "You're getting closer!" "You're very close!" "You went too far!" Trade places and let your child hide the treasure with someone else to prompt him to say "closer" or "farther" or perhaps just hold up written cards that say, "Getting closer," or "Getter farther."

Teach your child "right," "left," "straight," and "back." Play the "Hokey, pokey," and learn "put your right hand in," and "your left foot out." Be the toy truck driver and make your child the policeman. Stand at one end of the room with him and have him "direct traffic" to tell you how to get to a target at the other end by turning right and left around the furniture. In the car, let your child occasionally be the navigator and give you directions for a five-minute cruise.

Teaching the use of maps

You can introduce the concept of following a map by hiding a treat under one of three cups you place on a table before your child, and giving him a "map" with three circles (the cups) on a rectangle (the table), the one over the treat being marked with an "X." Move the cups farther and farther away, till you have them on different pieces of furniture throughout the room that you've diagrammatically represented on the map. If you have someone else to help you, take turns hiding and finding the treat. When it's your child's turn to hide the treat, the other person can prompt your child on how to mark the map properly.

Gradually move the cups to different rooms. Eventually include mapping your back yard and front yard. The cups are useful at first because they show your child which piece of furniture matches your diagrammatic representations on the map, but once your child gets the idea, you can eliminate them, and just mark the location of the hidden treat with an "X" on the map. Then work toward making a neighborhood map you can mark off as you take walks.

Start using the maps you get at the zoo or amusement parks. Have your child circle the animals and rides he wants to visit, and follow the map as you go. When you take a long car trip, make a simplified map and mark off the distance you've traveled as you drive along. "See, we're half way there." "You can see we have only a little distance left to go!" Use your child's newfound skill to solve emotionally relevant problems. At the amusement park, "Peter wants the Big Wheel next. Luke wants the Bumper Cars. Which ride shall we do next? Let's look on the map and see which ride is closer."

Brainstorming on how to teach "when"

"When" is actually another big concept as it includes all concepts of time. As always, start by teaching the most immediate and concrete, and move up from there.

START TEACHING TIME SEQUENCE BY SIGNPOSTING CLOSURE

You can start teaching logical sequencing in everyday activities and interactions at a very early age. Greenspan and Wieder (1998) advise that in general, when you've got a fun interaction going back and forth with your child, keep at it for as many circles as possible until your child ends it. I used to think that advice was just to encourage parents to make as many circles as possible, but now I see another use for that rule. Letting your child end an activity provides an opportunity for him to learn how to signal completion. Whenever your child has had enough of an interaction and tries to end it, you have an opportunity to teach him to say or sign, "All done," rather than running away abruptly.

SIGNPOST THE BEGINNING AND END OF ACTIVITIES

The concept of time starts with the sequencing of events. Show your child that activities, jobs/routines, and stories have a beginning, middle, and end. Even though you're unsure how much your child understands of what you say, go ahead and use time sequence words in their usual contexts. Signpost the beginning and end of your activities—get your child used to hearing opening remarks like, "Once upon a time…" "Are you ready to play? Let's have some fun…" "It's time for bed! Let's get ready…" Say "The end" at the end of stories.

As your child gets older, insist he take an active role in signaling his transitions appropriately. Instead of allowing a child to aimlessly flit from activity to activity, insist on some closure. "Hold on Peter! Don't just walk away. Are you all done? Say, 'all done.'" Don't just shake your head and smile when your child's logic breaks down. Point it out. "Hey, I thought we were playing ball, and you ran off to the swings. Let's try that again. Are you all done with ball?" Even brief social encounters have a beginning and end. Don't let your little one just walk away while someone is in mid-sentence talking to him. Teach him how to end the interaction with eye contact and a hand wave or short phrase, even as simple as "Gotta go, bye."

TEACH TIME IN THE HERE AND NOW

A good place to start teaching time words is the practical "if/then" or "first/then" template like "First eat sandwich, then eat cookies." Once your child understands a sequence of two actions, he's ready to learn about longer sequences. Jobs and routines are a great context to teach time sequencing. "What do we do first?" "What second?" "What do we do next?" "What do we do last?" Take a series of photos of the steps involved in hand washing, and have your child put them in time sequence order. Tape them up on the bathroom mirror to serve as a visual reminder. Encourage your child to assume as much initiative as possible by giving long enough wait periods before you prompt, "What next?" Mark the end of the task with a high five and "We did it!"

Once your child understands time order for a simple sequence like that, go for something a bit more out of the present moment. Take photos and label them with the names of the steps in his morning routine like "Get dressed," "Eat breakfast," "Brush teeth," and "Put on shoes." Have him put them in time sequence order on a wall to remind him what to do, or on a visual schedule.

Here's what a short visual schedule of the morning's activities before school might look like.

When?	What am I doing?
First	Get dressed
Next or then	Eat breakfast
Next or then	Brush teeth
Last	Put on shoes

As the child completes each activity, have him cross it off. I actually sometimes like to write the activities on little cards with Velcro on their backs, so my child can peel an activity off the board when completed and place it in an "All done" envelope I attach to the bottom of the visual schedule. That way the visual schedule can double as a choice board, as Peter can choose the order of activities, and sometimes have a choice of activities to place on the board. The following story illustrates how a child can learn to negotiate using the visual schedule as a tool.

Peter had been working hard all morning at school, and started getting agitated. His tutor Belinda quickly created a visual schedule. On the wall next to Peter's desk was a board with five rows and four columns of clear plastic pockets. She quickly filled out cards to put in the pockets to let him know what to expect.

Next	break	
Next	work	
Next	car ride	
Next	lunch	at school
Last	go home	

She figured that if he knew a break and car ride were coming, he could get through another 20-minute work session. Peter did indeed calm down. Belinda said, "Time for break!" left Peter with a few sensory toys to choose from, and stepped out of the room for a minute. When she returned, she discovered Peter had his own suggestions about the rest of the school day schedule.

Next	break		
Next	work		
Next			
Next			
Last	car ride	go home	lunch

The card that said, "at school," was in the "All done" envelope at the bottom of the schedule. Belinda laughed. Peter smiled. He cheerfully completed his next 20 minutes of work, and then picked up his lunchbox to go home in the car. Which they did.

TEACHING CLOCK TIME

Once your child has an idea of chronologically sequencing current tasks and work, it's natural to proceed to explaining the concept of clock time. School days are already structured around the clock, so it may be possible to substitute clock time for first, next, next, next, and last on his visual schedule. Taking Peter's work schedule as an example, it might look like this:

When?	What am I doing?
8:00 am	Circle time
9:00 am	Work
10:00 am	Recess
10:30 am	Library
11:00 am	Work
12:00 pm	Lunch

As your child goes through each period, the tutor points out the time on the clock, has him match it to the time on his schedule, and has the child read aloud the next activity. As he completes each period, he crosses out that line or takes a detachable activity label off his visual schedule and discards it in an "All done" envelope.

You would be amazed at how children can actually pick this concept up, and how useful that can be. For instance, the clock came to the rescue for Peter at gymnastics one day.

> One of Peter's favorite activities is adaptive gymnastics. He eagerly looks forward to it twice a week. Once I made the mistake of leaving from another appointment much too early, and we arrived 25 minutes before class started. Peter was puzzled. No teacher in sight. The gym was unusually quiet. He flapped and squealed. He started getting agitated.
>
> "Peter, see the clock?" I said, as I pointed to the large round clock on the wall. Look, class starts at 3:30, and it's only 3:05." I gestured with my finger, drawing the distance the long hand would have to travel. "We have 25 minutes before class. We have time to get some gas. Let's go." To my relief, Peter smiled and brightened. He also seemed relieved. He readily followed me to the car. We went to the gas station and filled up the tank, and returned to gymnastics right before class began. Peter seemed to understand exactly what we were doing, and happily complied throughout.

TEACHING MORNING, NOON, AND NIGHT

Once your child has mastered a concept of time in this concrete and immediate sense, you may proceed to teaching him the slightly more abstract concept of morning, afternoon, and night. It's generally best to build new concepts upon prior knowledge, so clock time might be useful in teaching it. It's also generally best to teach using tangibles and visuals, so use drawings or icons of the sun and moon, and make the effort to go outside and point them out in the morning, afternoon, and nightime skies.

Try teaching your child these concepts by incorporating them into his visual schedule. Make a new expanded visual schedule listing each hour from 7:00 am to 9:00 pm on the middle column on a single sheet of paper. Divide the paper into three sections. Label the top section "Morning" on the left-hand column with an appropriate picture icon of the sun coming up. Label the middle section "Afternoon" with a picture icon of a midday sun, and label the bottom section "Night" with a picture icon of the moon. Shade the top two sections yellow and the bottom section blue to further distinguish day from night. Fill in the right-hand column with the major activities that mark the time of day.

Time of day	Clock time	What am I doing?
Morning (place picture icon of sun rising up)	7:00 am	Get up and get ready for school. Breakfast
	8:00 am	School begins
	9:00 am	
	10:00 am	
	11:00 am	
Afternoon (place picture icon of midday sun)	12:00 pm	Lunchtime
	1:00 pm	
	2:00 pm	
	3:00 pm	Go home
	4:00 pm	Exercise
	5:00 pm	
Night (place picture icon of moon in sky)	6:00 pm	Dinner time
	7:00 pm	
	8:00 pm	Get ready for bed
	9:00 pm	Bedtime

At the start of each activity, show your child this visual schedule, point out the clock time and time of day, and take a look out the window at the sky. Have your child cross off each activity as he completes it. Point out the next activity coming up, and ask your child, "When will it be time for (activity)?" Prompt him to answer, "(Clock time), in the (time of day)." For example, after swimming or gymnastics you might ask your child, "When will it be time for dinner?" Prompt him by pointing to the visual schedule and having him read aloud, "Six o'clock in the evening."

Once your child can use the visual schedule to tell you when certain activities occur upon questioning, you may want to fill in the more interesting events and activities that occur during the day as they occur. That way, by bedtime, your child may have one or two happenings to talk about with you at the end of the day. Try questions like, "So what did you do this morning?" or "Tell me about your afternoon." Prompt your child to refer to his visual schedule to remind himself of the day's events. Eventually, you may also be able to use the visual schedule to plan and negotiate future events.

TEACHING THE CALENDAR

For planning future events, try leaping into the abstract concept of the calendar. Starting in preschool, your child might be used to the teacher moving a marker from box to box on a calendar as each day passes. You might fortify this by having your child cross off each day on a calendar at bedtime, and point out the new month, date, and day of the week as he gets up each morning. But as usual, the best way to teach the calendar is to make it real and relevant by giving him the opportunity to actually feel time passing. If your child is looking forward to a special event like a trip to Disneyland in a week, mark the date on the calendar with a colorful sticker or cut-out picture of Mickey Mouse. At the end of each day, have him cross the day off on the calendar so he gets a sense of time as he sees the big day approach. Do a countdown "Only three days to go till Disneyland!" "Only two to go!" "Hey, guess where we're going tomorrow?" "Hurrah! Today is the big day! We're going to Disneyland!"

Do the same for big events like his birthday and Christmas. You can purchase ready-made Advent calendars with windows to open each day. A great typical preschool project is to have your child make a chain of alternating red and green rings cut out of construction paper at the beginning of Advent to hang up as a decoration. The child then tears off one ring at the end of each day, the last one on Christmas Eve. As you mark the days off, you can also talk about the meaning of the upcoming holiday or plans you're making for the celebration that he can look forward to and participate in. And use the calendar the day or week after to reminisce about the wonderful things you did *yesterday*, or *last week*.

TEACHING THE DAYS OF THE WEEK

For regular events, make a chart of Sunday through Saturday, and paste a picture of the main event that distinguishes it for each day of the week, like a photo of the aquatic center on Tuesday swim lesson day. When you say, "Good morning, Peter! It's Tuesday today. What are we doing this afternoon?" it teaches him to anticipate the future. It also helps give him a sense of duration of time. He'll get used to the wait period from Tuesday to the next, and learn how long a week feels. As he gets to know his days of the week by their events, you can say things like, "Sorry, Peter, I don't have time to take you today, but maybe next Tuesday," and he will have some real sense of how long that means he has to wait.

TEACHING YESTERDAY, TODAY, AND TOMORROW

As he gets used to associating days of the week with particular regular events, you can try this exercise to teach the concepts of "yesterday," "today," and "tomorrow." Say your child sees his occupational therapist Miss Diane on Mondays, goes swimming on Tuesdays, and gymnastics on Wednesdays. Make index cards with a photo of Miss Diane, "Miss Diane" written on one, "swimming" with whatever picture you use on your weekly calendar on another, and "gymnastics" and a corresponding picture on the third. Label three other index cards "yesterday," "today," and "tomorrow," and lay them down on the table. Say it's Monday. Give your child the picture/word cards and have him match them to the time (yesterday/today/tomorrow) cards. Then ask, "What are we doing today?" "What did we do yesterday?" "What are we doing tomorrow?" Finally, reverse the process and ask, "When do we see Miss Diane?" "When do we go swimming?" etc.

I'm a big fan of the iPhone camera. Take advantage of modern technology and take pictures of meaningful happenings and interesting things your child comes across in his day. Print out the pictures and have him sort what happened yesterday versus today. If you throw in brochures or pictures of special places you plan to go the next day, he can sort them into a "tomorrow" category.

Another way to teach yesterday/today/tomorrow is to break up tasks into projects that take several days to complete. This gives you a chance to talk about what we did yesterday, what we are doing today, and what we'll need to finish up tomorrow. Say you're planning a weekend outing. Mark your preparations on the calendar. The first day you might go shopping for things you'll need for the trip with your child (be sure to bring a list and have him check off items as you buy them). When you're all done, you can talk about planning to pack *tomorrow*. The second day you might pack together. (Also a great opportunity to ask, "What will we need?" and to use check-off lists.) Ask your child to help you pack the items you bought *yesterday*. When you're all done, talk about getting to bed early for the big day *tomorrow*. The third day wake him excitedly as you announce *today* is the big the day you get to go on your trip. As he brings you the duffle bags, thank him for helping you pack them *yesterday*. In the car talk about the fun things you plan to do *today* and *tomorrow*.

You don't have to come up with big projects to do this—little projects work just fine. Say your child wants jello. Mark your preparations on the calendar. Today the two of you go to the store to buy the jello. The next day you mix the powder with hot water and put it in the refrigerator. The following day you get to eat it. You can break up gardening projects into buying the seedlings the first day, preparing the soil the second day, and planting the third. And two-day projects also work. On the first day, talk about what you're doing today and tomorrow. On the second day, talk about what you did yesterday and what you're doing today. When you make the effort to break down tasks into steps, your child gets to practice the concepts of yesterday, today, and tomorrow while also learning some executive planning skills.

UNDERSTANDING THE PASSAGE OF YEARS

It's a great idea to keep a photo album/scrapbook of meaningful events in your child's life over the years. Insert little journal notes or social/personal stories you write for your child about these events as well as souvenirs and photos. And throw in an occasional daily schedule, especially when a particularly interesting event is recorded on it. Be sure to mark the dates prominently, including the year! That way, over the years, you and your child can enjoy reviewing happy memories as well as learn the meaning of seasons and years.

Brainstorming on how to teach "why?"

Answering "why" questions is part of a larger goal of helping your child understand cause-and-effect relationships. Your buzz words are "if... then," "what if," "because," "so," and of course, "*why*." Make an effort to use them as cues to articulate cause-and-effect relationships. You'll find many examples to point out in everyday life.

A note on teaching tenses

Neurotypical children pick up past, present, and future tense naturally from context. For Peter, we started out teaching action words, or verbs, as a category by adding the "ing" as a kind of tag or marker. We taught past and future tense by teaching him to modify the "to be" verb in front of the main action "ing" verb. We bought a book of photographs (Harrison 1994) depicting three-step sequences. For example, the first picture might show a baker standing in front of her ingredients to bake a cake. We prompted Peter to say, "She will be baking a cake." The next picture depicted the baker stirring the batter. "She is baking a cake." The last picture showed her proudly standing next to a beautifully decorated cake. "She was baking a cake." Nancy Kaufman (2006a, pp.109-17) describes a similar method in her dyspraxia workbook, which includes a section of useful picture sequences.

We had to change our strategy when Peter started using an AT device. The device lists each action verb without the "ing" with its past and present progressive forms next to it highlighted by an "ed" and "ing" in bold print on the keys. We switched from using past and future progressive tense at that point to traditional "ed" and "will (main verb)" forms of past and future tense. Possibly because he was primed to modify the form of the verb according to a sense of past, present, and future, Peter adapted to the new conventions quickly. The device itself is teaching him irregular and regular past tense verbs because it automatically displays them when he pushes "ed." We model the traditional tense conventions matching his AT device in our own speech, and he seems to be "picking it up" surprisingly naturally.

TEACHING "WHY" IN DAILY LIFE

"Do you want a hard push or a soft push? *If* I push harder, you'll swing higher." "Careful, that cup's awfully close to the edge of the table. *What* do you think might happen *if* you move your arm?" When it's raining, don't gather the umbrellas ahead of time. As you walk out the door, say, "Hey look, it's raining. *So* what should we bring?" As your child runs back into the house and finds his umbrella, ask, "I forget. *Why* do you have that umbrella?"

Greenspan (1998) points out that "why" questions are the most difficult to answer because they are the most abstract. If your child can't answer a "why" question, he suggests rephrasing it as a "what" question. For example, if your child can't answer "Why are you getting that umbrella?" try asking, "What do you want the umbrella for?" or "What are you going to do with the umbrella?" After the child gives his answer, say, "Oh, so that's *why* you're getting the umbrella," so he gets to understand the word "why" in context.

I have to confess that teaching Peter "why" is still very much a work in progress. I can't give you a tried and true recipe for success in teaching "why," but here are some ideas on how to make it fun.

TEACHING "WHY" USING NATURAL PHENOMENON

As usual, include your child's interests. Peter has lately become obsessed with the microwave oven. He also loves to play with and eat ice. These suggested a little experiment, an opportunity to teach the concept of "why."

> At the breakfast table, I handed Peter a cup of room temperature water, and poured myself a cup of hot water. Peter looked at me and said, "Hot." "That's right, Peter, my water is hot. Do you want your water hot?" Peter said, "Yes, hot." He proceeded to get up out of his chair to put his cup in the microwave. "Hey Peter, I see you're putting your cup in the microwave. Why?" I wrote "because" on an erasable whiteboard, and held it up. Peter read it, "Because," he said. "Because you want it hot or cold?" I prompted. "Because," said Peter, "You want it..." I prompted, "Hot!" said Peter, filling in the blank. "Twenty seconds," I advised.
>
> After ten seconds, Peter took out his cup. We put our hands around the cup. "Why is it getting hot, Peter?" I held up the board with the word "because" written on it. "Because," read Peter. "It was in the..." I prompted, "Microwave!" said Peter, filling in the blank. "Do you want it hotter, Peter?" I asked. "Hotter!" said Peter. He eagerly put his cup back in the microwave, and pushed the buttons for 20 seconds more. Afterwards he put his hands around the cup to test it. "Is it hotter?" I asked. "Hotter!" he replied. "Why is it hotter?" I asked, pointing to the whiteboard. "Because microwave," said Peter proudly. He took the initiative to put the cup back into the microwave with an excited gleam in his eye, happily squealing and flapping. He pushed the buttons for another 20 seconds. I took it out and felt the cup. Peter eagerly tested it. "Now it feels really..." I began, "Hot!" said Peter, completing the sentence with glee. "Why?" I asked. "Because microwave," he said.
>
> Next I brought out a big bowl of ice. "Peter, What do you think will happen if you put ice cubes in the cup?" I handed him a couple of ice cubes. Peter put them in his cup of hot water. As we watched them melt, I asked, "Why is the ice getting smaller?" I pointed to the whiteboard. "Because," said Peter, and paused, searching for the word. "Is it melting?" I prompted, as I wrote "melting" under

"because" on the whiteboard. "Melting," said Peter. "What if we put in more ice?" I asked, handing him several more ice cubes. Peter put them in his cup of warm water. Again I asked, "Why is the ice getting smaller?" I paused. No reply. "B..." I prompted. "Because," said Peter and paused, searching for the word again. I pointed to the whiteboard. "Because melting," said Peter.

"What if we put in more ice?" I suggested, handing Peter more ice cubes. He put them in. They were melting slowly. I put my hands around the cup. Peter put his hands around the cup, testing it. "Is it getting hotter or colder?" I asked. "Colder," said Peter. "Why?" I asked. "Because...ice!" said Peter, excitedly. "That's exactly why. We put ice in the cup, so it got cold." I gave him a high five, and we sat down to breakfast.

TEACHING "WHY" USING CHILDREN'S LITERATURE

A great book to use to practice the concept of "why" is *The Napping House* by Audrey Wood (1984). In the story a grandmother is napping in her bed, and a child, dog, cat, and mouse all pile up on her one at a time to enjoy the cozy warmth. Then a flea comes by and bites the mouse who scares the cat who scratches the dog who thumps the boy who bumps the granny who breaks the bed. Then they all go outside to play.

I first introduced the book to Peter one Sunday morning when he woke up but didn't want to get out of bed. I snuggled in next to him, and read the first half of the book, having him name each character sleepily piling into bed on top of the last character, as we enjoyed the cozy warmth of our bed too. "Why is the boy sleeping on top of granny?" or "Why is the dog sleeping on top of the boy?" I asked. Each time I prompted Peter to say, "Because it's cozy," as we enjoyed a cozy snuggle.

For the second half of the book, I acted out each action depicted on the page. "So what did the flea do to the mouse?" I asked Peter as I pretended my hand was the biting flea. "He b..." I prompted, "bit him," and delivered the pinch. "Bit him!" laughed Peter. "So what did the dog do to the boy?" I asked. "He th..." I prompted, "thumped him," and thumped Peter with a pillow. "Thumped him," echoed Peter. "So what did the boy do to granny?" I asked. "He bu..." I prompted, "bumped her," giving Peter a hearty bump with a little body slam. "Bumped her!" said Peter, joyously.

Next we read the whole book backwards. "Why did granny wake up?" I asked. "Because the boy b..." I started, "bumped her!" said Peter, filling in the blank. "Why did the boy bump her?" I asked. "Be..." I prompted. "Because," said Peter. "Because the d..." I continued with my prompting. "Because the dog," said Peter, completing the last word.

"Thumped him. Because the dog…" I prompted, "Thumped him!" said Peter quickly. We continued page by page. Because Peter had already read the book forwards using the word "so," he read the book backwards using the word "because" with few prompts. Priming him for word retrieval reduced the effort of reading it the second time, and increased his sense of success.

Another way to engage your child's interests and help him learn by doing is to use an element of pretend play. After we read *The Napping House* together, Peter still didn't want to get up out of bed. "Perfect opportunity," I thought to myself, as I gathered up several of his favorite stuffed animals. We re-enacted the story of *The Napping House* as Whale, then Penguin, and then Pooh sleepily crawled into bed on top of Peter to enjoy the cozy warmth. "That looks cozy, so here I come!" each one announced as he snuggled in. Then a toy bug came by and bit Pooh Bear. "Ouch!" exclaimed Pooh, as he jumped up and fell on Penguin. "Ouch! Why did Pooh fall on me?" cried Penguin, beseeching Peter. "Because Bug bit him," I prompted Peter to say. Then Penguin jumped up and fell upon Whale. "Ouch!" cried Whale. "Peter, why did Penguin fall on me?" "Because Pooh fell on him," I prompted Peter to say. "Are you getting up now?" asked Whale. As Peter lay immovable, Whale said, "Well, I guess that looks pretty cozy, so here I come again!" He snuggled back on top of Peter, and we repeated the entire process again. After the second round of the animals falling on top of him, Peter was ready to get up with a big smile.

Using a graphic organizer: Making cause-and-effect relationships visual with a flowchart

Illustrate this whole process to make cause-and-effect relationships visual for your child. I used the flowchart below to retell the second half of the story of *The Napping House* together with Peter. You can make flowcharts like this to illustrate cause-and-effect relationships in the plots of any story.[2] First I prompted Peter to retell the story from beginning to end to emphasize how one event caused the next. We repetitively used the word "so" to drill in its meaning.

flea → mouse → cat → dog → boy → granny → bed

---

2   *If You Give a Mouse a Cookie* series of books by Laura Numeroff and Felicia Bond (HarperCollins Publishers) also provide repetitive opportunities to explore cause and effect.

Above every arrow, I wrote the word "so." I put the flowchart on a big index card. As we turned each page of the book, I pointed to the next word on the flowchart. For example, I pointed to the word "flea" as we looked at the picture of the flea biting the mouse. I prompted Peter to say, "The flea bit the mouse." Then I pointed to the arrow. "So," Peter would say, turning the page to the picture of the cat waking up. I pointed to the word "mouse." "The mouse scared the cat," I prompted Peter to say. I continued prompting and pointing this way till we finished the book, the main emphasis being to learn the use and meaning of the word "so" in a cause-and-effect relationship.

Next we reversed the process, as we read the second half of *The Napping House* backwards to emphasize that that every effect/consequence has a cause/antecedent. We repetitively drilled understanding of the word "why" and use of the word "because."

	So		So		So		So		So		So	
flea	→ ←	mouse	→ ←	cat	→ ←	dog	→ ←	boy	→ ←	granny	→ ←	bed
	because		because		because		because		because		because	

Below every arrow, I wrote the word "because." I covered the top "so" words and rightward pointing arrows with a big white index card. As we turned each page of the book, I pointed to the next word on the flowchart, starting right to left. I opened the book to the picture of Granny falling upon the bed and breaking it. I pointed to the word "bed" on the flowchart and started, "Look Peter, the bed broke. Why did the bed break?" I pointed to the arrow and prompted Peter to say, "Because." I prompted Peter to finish, "Granny fell on it," as I pointed to the word "Granny." "Why did Granny fall on it?" I asked. I pointed to the arrow, prompting Peter to say "because" and turn the page to the picture of the boy bumping her. I continued prompting and pointing this way till we retold the story in reverse to the part about the flea biting the mouse. The main emphasis was to learn the use and meaning of the words "why" and "because." The reverse order emphasized the point that the word "why" is a prompt to think back to an antecedent cause, and the word "because" precedes the naming of it.

Flowcharts are an example of a "graphic organizer." This is a one-page form with blank areas to fill in that visually organizes related information. It also includes outlines, graphs, tables, Venn diagrams, flowcharts, concept maps, concept trees, and cause-and-effect maps. They are valuable for some children, especially visual thinkers. Consider experimenting with using various kinds of graphic organizers with your child. Even if your child doesn't seem to catch on to or benefit from a certain graphic organizer initially, he might find it useful later in his development. The whole point of graphic organizers is to make learning easier. (Google "graphic organizers" to find free educational websites like edHelper.com that display examples you can download and copy.)

TEACHING "WHY" IN TALKING ABOUT FEELINGS

The most emotionally relevant context to teach "why" is in discussing feelings. Talking about feelings is therefore your most powerful way to teach the cause-and-effect relationships underlying the concept of "why," and is obviously an important goal in and of itself. "Wow, you look really happy today. Did something good happen in school?" "Why do you think your little brother is crying? Do you think he's sad because he dropped his ice cream?"

Winner (2007, pp.166–7, 171) created a useful instrument called the social behavior map (SBM), a graphic organizer of cause and effect in relation to social behavior and emotions. It's very similar to a flowchart, and for your visual learner, it can be very helpful.

I tried it to deal with Peter's compulsion to tear up paper. I was working on getting Peter to restrict himself to tearing up junk mail that I would toss in a designated basket. Sometimes, he would forget and tear up other papers, which were sometimes important.

I drew the following SBM, which has been helpful. Consider making SBMs whenever either highly positive or negative incidents occur to review with your child. To make a SBM, draw in arrows left to right for each row. Use your "if…then…," "why," and "because" vocabulary as you explain the chart. Tape up SBMs of recurrent behaviors on the refrigerator door to have handy. When another negative incident occurs and you can feel your frustration level rising, pull it out and use it. It helps your child understand why you feel so mad, and thereby helps calm you down as well.

Behavior	→	How it makes the other person feel	→	Consequences you experience	→	How it makes you feel
I tear paper from INSIDE my basket	→	Mama feels happy ☺	→	Mama smiles	→	I feel happy ☺
I tear paper from OUTSIDE my basket	→	Mama feels mad! ☹	→	Mama makes me tape up the torn paper. If I tear up three papers, no car ride tonight	→	I feel sad ☹

"How does Mama feel?" (Point to the chart and use it to prompt him to say, "mad.") "Why is Mama mad?" (Prompt him to say, "Because I tear paper from outside my basket.") "So what do you need to do?" (Prompt him to read aloud, "Mama makes me tape up the torn paper. If I tear up three papers, no car ride tonight.") "How does that make you feel?" (Point to the chart if necessary to prompt him to say, "I feel sad.") SBMs help the child see how his actions cause effects on the feelings of other people. Those feelings result in consequences to him, that in turn impact his feelings. The arrows between the columns visually emphasize the cause-and-effect relationships.

Talking about feelings is a big topic that goes beyond a discussion of cause and effect. We'll take a more personal look at it in the next chapter on social and emotional development.

Using conversations and stories to practice "wh" questions
ASKING "WH" QUESTIONS ABOUT SOMETHING YOUR CHILD REALLY WANTS

We started asking Peter "wh" questions in the context of his requests. Indeed initially we started with a favorite request, "lunch." Peter would ask his tutor for "lunch," and she would ask him "why" he wanted lunch, and teach him to say, "because I'm hungry." She then developed a whole conversation about lunch, asking him "when" he wanted lunch, "what" he wanted for lunch, and "where he wanted to eat it," so he could practice answering a variety of "wh" questions.

PAUSING VIDEOS TO PRACTICE "WH" QUESTIONS

Stories from videos and books also provide great opportunities to teach your child how to answer "wh" questions. Videos are great for depicting actions and emotions. For example, pause a video of Thomas the Tank Engine falling into a ditch, and ask, "What happened to Thomas?" (fell down). "How does he feel?" (sad). "Why is Thomas sad?" (hurt, stuck, etc.). The facial expressions on the characters in the "Toy Story" series are also very clear. When Woody encounters Sid's ferocious bull terrier, Scud, pause the video and ask, "How does Woody feel?" (scared). "Why is he scared?" (mean dog, big teeth, etc.). "What's Woody doing?" (running away).

If it's too hard for your child to answer a "wh" question, try following it up with a fill-in-the-blank or multiple-choice question. "Thomas fell…" (down). "Does Woody feel brave or sc…?" (make a scared facial expression). "Woody is scared because the dog has big t…" (show your teeth). If multiple choice is too hard, try offering the correct answer against a funny or clearly wrong answer (Greenspan and Wieder 1998, p.247). "Is Thomas sad because he's stuck or because he has to go the bathroom?" Be sure to pace the frequency and difficulty of questions so that your child does not get too frustrated.

To make this excercise more fun, pretend you're the owner of the video "store." To "rent" the next half-hour video, your child has to give you ten cents. Offer him a cent for every question he answers correctly (even with prompting). Give your child a big glass jar to drop the cent in so he can easily see how many cents he's collecting. You might offer two cents for every question he asks you.

HOW TO PRACTICE "WH" QUESTIONS WHILE READING BOOKS TOGETHER

Picture books, especially nonverbal ones like the *Carl the Dog* series by Alexandra Day (1991), or old favorites like *Curious George* by H.A. Rey or the *Fred and Ted* Peter Eastman books (2005, 2007), are great because you can go at your own pace, forward and back, enjoying the visual images that stay put on the page for as long as it takes to process them. The great thing about books is that you can keep it fun by spending time on the pages your child is interested in looking at, and taking turns making comments.

Your comments can serve as a prompt for your child's next turn, especially if you incidentally drop in vocabulary you know your child will soon need but have difficulty retrieving. Say you are reading *Goldilocks and the Three Bears* together. You are reading the first page about the bears leaving their breakfasts to cool down while they take a walk in the forest.

Make a comment like, "Look, the bears are going *outside*. That's *where* they're going. *Outside*." Then turn the page and read about Goldilocks knocking on the door, and going inside when no one answers. Because you just made a comment about the bears going outside for your turn, for your child's turn to talk, you might ask him, "So *where* did the bears go?" Because you just primed your child with the words he needs in your previous answer, he has a better chance of coming up with the right answer.

Another way to help your child feel successful is to ask simple questions you know your child can answer such as "I see red flowers! Can you point to something red?" or "Look at all the chairs? Let's count them!" You can alternate these easier questions with your more difficult "wh" questions such as "What is Goldilocks doing?" or "Whose chair is that?" If your child answers these kinds of questions easily, you may want to challenge your child with harder, more, more open-ended ones like "What do you see?" "What happened?" or "Tell me about that." At all levels, it's helpful to have your child's PECS book or AT device handy to assist your child with word retrieval when it's his turn to answer a question. If he knows how to read, you can write down word menus of several choices on a dry erase board to help your child come up with the answer. If he's too tired to verbalize, he can point to or circle the answer.

DISTINGUISHING BETWEEN THE DIFFERENT "WH" QUESTIONS
Asking about one picture
A particularly useful exercise is to have your child answer several different "wh" questions about the same picture to make sure he is distinguishing the meanings of "who" (answer with the name of a person) versus "what... doing" (usually answered with an action) versus "where" (answered usually with a place or prepositional phrase) versus "when" (answered with a time word). Many children have difficulty distinguishing between these concepts. The concepts are abstract and the words sound similar and even look somewhat similar when written down. What do you do when you can feel as though it's hit-or-miss if your child is answering the correct "wh" question?

Using matching "wh" word menu headings
As mentioned in Chapter 9 (p.138; see also p.277), use matching labels with or without icons for your word menu headings and questions. That way, your child can find the answer to a "wh" question by looking

for it under the matching word menu heading. Say you're looking at a picture of Goldilocks sitting in Baby Bear's little chair, breaking it. Write "who" as the heading on one word menu and list "Goldilocks," "Papa Bear," "Mama Bear," and "Baby Bear" as choices. Write "doing" as the heading on another word menu and list "eating," "sitting," and "sleeping" as choices. Write "where" on another word menu and list "at the table," "on the chair," and "in the bed" as choices. Ask your child, "*Who* is that?" stressing the word "who" and writing the question down with "who" written prominently. Prompt him to look for the word menu with the matching heading, "who." Then all he has to do is choose between "Goldilocks," "Papa Bear," "Mama Bear," and "Baby Bear" to find the answer (Goldilocks). Repeat the procedure with "What is she doing?" and "Where is she sitting?"

As you ask each question for a given page of the picture book, at first provide your child with the corresponding word menu to prompt him. Once he answers questions easily that way, offer him more than one word menu to select from. It's helpful to draw in matching picture icons next to the printed "wh" word, such as a happy face next to "who" and little house figure for "where." (If your child uses AT/apps with icons, consider adopting the same icons used on his device for consistency; see p.278.) Make each icon a distinctive color to further assist your child in selecting the word list with the heading that correctly matches the "wh" word in the question. Deliver each question in verbal and written form (plus the matching picture icon) so your child has a matching visual aide to refer to for both the question and the answer. As your child gets good at matching icons to find the correct word menu to get his answer, try making the icons progressively smaller and less prominent (for example, remove the color) and emphasize matching the "wh" word. With time, you may be able to fade out the icons altogether. The next goal of course, would be to fade out the "wh" headings on the word menus. At that point, celebrate! Your child finally understands the difference between who, what, where, when, and why!

Using a "wh" table

It may also help your child to see the difference in meanings between the "wh" questions by displaying them visually in a table form. A table is another example of a *graphic organizer*. You can record your child's responses as he answers each question. "Who is that?" "What is (he/she) doing?" "Where is (he/she)?"

Picture you are viewing together	Who is that?	What is (he/she) doing?	Where is (he/she)?	Why?
Goldilocks eating porridge	Goldilocks	eating	at the table	because she's hungry
Goldilocks sitting in chair	Goldilocks	sitting	on the chair	because she's tired
Goldilocks sleeping in bed	Goldilocks	sleeping	in the bed	because she's sleepy
Papa Bear looking at Goldilocks	Papa Bear	looking at Goldilocks	in the bedroom	because he's surprised

Begin with asking just one or two "wh" questions for each page of your picture book. Start off your table with perhaps just one or two columns. Gauge the number of picture book pages (rows) to do by your child's attention span and interest. Don't start asking "why" questions before your child can even answer a "who" or "what" question. Add columns gradually, as your child works on one or two different kinds of "wh" questions at a time, and displays mastery. Don't feel obliged to fill in every column for every page; just use the questions that naturally suggest themselves to a given picture page.

The beauty of using a graphic organizer like this is that your child can actually see how all questions beginning with "who" are answered with names. All questions with the "doing" word are answered with an action word also ending with an "ing." "Where" questions can be answered with a prepositional phrase or place. The answer to a "why" question often begins with the word "because" followed by a description of the subject's feelings. Go down each column (cover up the other columns initially) as you ask the same "wh" question for each picture page to drive in the point. Then go down the next column similarly, so your child literally sees the difference.

The most interesting story to use is, of course, the story of the child's own life. In the next chapter (pp.277–8) we'll talk about recording the child's own story on his daily schedule or planner as a stepping stone to journaling.

Attuning to your child to get him to ask "wh" questions

Games give children more opportunities to practice words and concepts, and drilling is very helpful when learning something new. However, you don't have to constantly keep a list of games in your head—the best way to generalize learning is to apply it naturally. You will find many opportunities to help your child ask "wh" questions if you remember Sussman's simple rule (Sussman 1999, p.97), "Say it as she would if she could."

Attune to your child, and use what you know about his preferences, habits, history, and behavioral cues to guess what he wants to know. Say you see him wander into the kitchen while you're cooking, and it's been a long time since snack time. As you see him look at the pot cooking on the stove and sniffing, try asking, "Do you want to know *what's for dinner?*" Pause, then prompt him to ask that "what" question. When you see his favorite Thomas train in a corner and him searching for it, don't just hand it to him. Instead say something like, "You look like you're looking for something important. Do you want to know *where is Thomas?* I know where he is." Pause, and if he doesn't say anything, prompt him, "Try asking me *where.*"

Brainstorming on how to teach "how"
INCIDENTAL TEACHING

Greenspan and Wieder (1998, p.246) say "Children often learn how… because they relate to functions children experience, for example, 'How should we get there?' 'How should we fix it?' 'How does it go?' 'How does it work?'" There are many opportunities to incidentally teach the meaning of "how" if you keep it in mind to signpost the word when you explain how to do things to your child.

Instead of singing "This is the way we brush our teeth/comb our hair/wash our face/put on our shirt" to the tune of "Here We Go Round the Mulberry Bush" while teaching your child the steps of his morning routine, perhaps substitute the word "how" for "the way." Any time you do a "task analysis" and break down a task into steps, you have the opportunity to write and say the word "how" before you begin. Before showing your child how to microwave his lunch or fold a shirt, signpost the concept of "how" and preface your demonstration with phrases like, "This is *how* to use the microwave," or "Let me show you *how* to fold a shirt."

Also try to keep in mind giving your child opportunities to ask "how" questions. If his toy runs out of batteries, and he brings it to you, don't just fix it. Try asking, "Do you want to know *how* to make it go? Then ask me," and prompt your child to ask, "How does it go?" or even just "How?" Then say something like, "It needs a new battery. Do you want to know how to change the battery?" Prompt him to ask, "How?" or "How (do I) change (the) battery?" (You might just say the words in parentheses for your child and only prompt him to say the main words outside the parentheses.) Then say, "Okay, then I'll show you how. This is how you change the batteries." In this short exchange, you've managed to give your child multiple opportunities to hear and say the word "how."

Remember the section on breaking down projects big and small into two- and three-day activities to teach the concepts of "yesterday," "today," and "tomorrow"? These same opportunities can be used to teach the concept of "how." When you announce your upcoming weekend outing to your child, tell him, "We'd better get ready. *How* shall we plan?" and sit down with him to mark your calendar as you plan your preparations together. Similarly, when he asks for jello or wants to make cut-out sugar cookies, do the same. "Great idea! *How* shall we do it? Let's write down what we need to do."

GAMES

In case your child needs more practice than he can get incidentally, here are a couple of games that will enable your child to practice using the word "how." One game is a simple adaptation of the "Directing traffic" game (see p.222). I call it, "How do I get there?" Pretend you are the delivery truck driver trying to deliver a toy truck with a treat in it for your child. Your child stands at the opposite end of the room. He orders a treat he likes from you, and gives you his address to deliver it (you may do this over the phone if you want to also practice telephone manners and social language). Then you tell him you don't know how to get there. Ask him to tell or show you *how* to get there. Then your child can give you directions around the furniture/obstacle course verbally or nonverbally, depending on what you want to work on. (Verbal directions for left and right have to be reversed if you are standing at opposite ends of the room, but may be good practice in perspective taking, if your child is ready for it.) You may then reverse roles, or better yet, have another child play the customer while you shadow/coach your child. This game obviously practices a lot of language and communication skills, but also emphasizes the point that answering a "how" question means describing a process or task step by step.

Another "how" game is called "Robot Mom" (see also p.184). I initially created it to encourage Peter to initiate requests, but later adapted it to teach the meaning of "how." For the version of the game that teaches "how," the child gets to choose something that requires at least several steps to put together. Robot Mom says, "I am Robot Mom, your wish is my command," or "What do you want?" The child makes his request. Robot Mom asks, "How do I make/get that?" The child then has to tell her by gesture, words, or whatever means of communication he uses how to fulfill his request, step by step.

When you play "Robot Mom," you can offer your child a choice of anything that requires steps to make. Offer a menu of foods that require steps to prepare, like a fruit salad or peanut butter and jelly sandwich. There are great toys on the market consisting of sets of vehicle parts that you can put together in different ways to make different vehicles. You may offer your child a choice of which vehicle he wants you to build. Lay out the parts in front of him, have him select a vehicle from the pictures on the box, then ask him how to build it. He gets to tell you which part to pick up, but only Robot Mom can touch the parts and put it together. (When done wordlessly and without gestures, this is a great game for teaching a child to point with his eyes; see p.152.)

"HOW" AS AN INTRODUCTION TO THEMATIC THINKING

When you think about it, learning the concept of "how" is a step into an advanced kind of abstract thinking. The child learns how to think ahead and practice some executive planning. He learns to start with an overall goal or concept and then break it down into steps. A common problem for individuals with autism is to distinguish the forest from the trees, or getting the "big picture" of a process. In that regard, games like "Robot Mom" work on an important cognitive skill. The child gets to practice identifying the big picture first, the goal, the destination, the request. Then he practices breaking it into steps. In other words, he learns to distinguish the theme from the details. We discuss more ways to work on this critical thinking skill at the end of this chapter (see pp.253–4).

Brainstorming on how to teach "how much"

INCIDENTAL TEACHING

The concept of "how much" is vast as it encompasses quantities, measurements, and comparisons. Most parents introduce these concepts naturally in the course of their everyday interactions. "Luke, you grabbed most of the French fries. Look how *few* Peter has! Now come on, you need to share." "Wow, look how big you've grown. Your old shorts are too small. We'll have to go and get some bigger ones!" "Do you want *one* cookie or *two*? No, no, you can't have *five*. That's too *many*. Don't eat too *much*, it will be dinner time soon." In general the best way to teach abstract concepts is to start with concrete examples in the context of emotionally relevant and meaningful situations for the child (Greenspan and Wieder 1998).

The problem is, many of our children don't seem to pick up these quantitative concepts naturally. Therefore, sometimes more directed and explicit teaching may be helpful. Once some basics have been learned at the tabletop, generalizing with incidental teaching opportunities like those described above will become effective and important.

STRUCTURED TEACHING

So how do you start teaching quantitative concepts? Peter's DTT program started out by trying to teach big versus little. We used various interesting objects like a giant and doll-size sunflower, big and miniature Thomas trains, giant versus small stuffed animal whales and penguins, a Hoberman Expanding Ball (www.officeplayground.com/HobermanSphere), and balloons we would blow up to different sizes. We tried offering Peter a big piece of beef jerky versus a very small piece, or a lot of popcorn versus a little bit. Surprisingly and discouragingly, it took months of drilling "big" versus "little," "a lot" versus "a little" for Peter to acquire even an emerging understanding of quantity.

DTT programs usually include exercises in sequencing and seriation. An example of a sequencing exercise is to string different color beads according to a repetitive pattern such as blue-green-red, blue-green-red, blue-green, etc. Later, the child is taught how to sequence more complex patterns such as the steps to getting dressed or washing hands. Turning on the tap is followed by wetting the hands, which is followed by rubbing on soap, etc. Educational supply companies offer picture cards and other materials to order in sequences.

Seriation is a sequence ordered according to a certain characteristic like size, intensity, or age. Typical exercises to practice this concept include ordering a set of blocks from shortest to tallest (nesting toys work well for this exercise), ordering a set of photos of people from youngest to oldest (rummage through photo albums to find pictures of your child at different ages from a baby till present, or of Grandpa from childhood to old age), or ordering a set of blue paint samples from light to dark blue.

USING THE LEFT SIDE OF THE BRAIN TO SUPPORT GROWTH OF THE RIGHT

I was never sure if Peter was really catching on to the concepts of sequencing or seriation, or just memorizing how to order the materials he was given. He could order a set of puzzle pieces shaped like thin crayons from short to tall within the frame, but seemed lost when I dumped them out of the frame, and tried to have him order the crayons without it. When we tried to teach him how to count from one to ten, he memorized the order of the numbers relatively quickly. However, when I would ask him for one little plastic bear versus two bears, he was lost.

What was going on in Peter's brain? It is commonly known that the left hemisphere of the brain is the place where language is processed in the great majority of people. The left side also names numbers and calculates. However, the right hemisphere, in particular the right inferior parietal lobe, is activated in brain imaging studies when participants compare numbers. When split brain patients who have a surgically divided corpus callosum (the mass of fibers that connect the two hemispheres) are shown sums to their right hemisphere, they can only approximate. They can't calculate, although they know that obviously wrong sums such as 4+6=23 are incorrect. So it seems that the right hemisphere approximates while the left hemisphere calculates—the right side seems to be the place where the mind approximates, and has a concept of quantities (Blakemore and Frith 2005).

Peter was able to readily learn number identification and counting, so his left hemisphere was working well. Perhaps the more intact left side could help the right, which was clearly struggling with a sense of quantity. So we taught him the sign language for one to five, holding up the corresponding number of fingers when we would say or write the numeral. When he had mastered that, we got little cubes that stuck on our fingertips, and would have Peter tell us if we were holding up one versus two cubes on our fingers held up in the proper sign language configuration.

After he mastered that, we were able to put the cubes on the table instead of on our fingers, thereby fading away the sign language prompt. That was how Peter was finally able to tell us if there were one or two cubes on the table, and give us the number of cubes we asked for.

Once the numbers got higher than five, the sign language configurations didn't lend themselves to this method, so we switched to touch math, where each numeral is associated with that number of dots arranged in a certain configuration upon the numeral. When we would ask Peter for a certain number of items, he would first just match items one to one upon the configuration of dots we drew upon the numeral. After many repetitions, he was able to memorize the configuration of the dots such that we did not need to actually draw them upon the numeral. If we asked for five bears, we placed a large numeral five upon the table, and Peter placed five tiny bears upon the numeral in the exact configuration that the dots used to be in. Finally, we were able to fade the numerals as well. If we asked for five bears, Peter was able to count them out by placing them on the table neatly in the same configuration he had learned. It was as if he were imagining a big numeral five with the five dots arranged upon it lying on the table.

At this point Peter can count out any quantity of items up through 20 or more. He can count up to 100 cheerios by grouping them in tens as he goes as long as you help him keep his piles separate with an egg carton or other organizer. He no longer arranges the objects he's counting out according to his touch math dots, but instead puts them into a random pile. When we used to ask him how many crackers he wanted, he always answered "one" or "two" by rote. Now he'll get a mischievous gleam in his eye and ask for "five" or "a lot." When he sees me reaching into a bag of beef jerky to get him a piece, he spontaneously reminds me to make it "big." He also readily asks me for "bigger" if the piece I give him is not big enough, or "biggest" if he sees a bigger piece available than I'm reaching for. But it took this stepwise process with the left brain supporting the right for him to get there and truly grasp an understanding of the concept of quantity.

HANDS-ON IDEAS FOR TEACHING MEASUREMENT

Miller (2007, pp.247–9) describes some brilliant exercises to teach concepts of quantity, measurement, and comparison using body perceptions and tactile learning. He has different children fill clear bottles with marbles, some half full, some with a little, and some with a lot. He has the children identify which bottles have more and less, and figure out how to transfer marbles from the bottles with more to those with less to make all the quantities about the same. I've tried this idea with Peter, having him pour water for the family to different levels in clear plastic cups, and then try to even them out, as we talk (and write) about too much, too little, more, less, and the same. Peter frequently pours for the family, taking requests for half, full, a lot, and a little. Once in a while he gets to hear a protest about someone he's missed having an *empty* cup.

Miller teaches measurement and comparisons by having children line up against a blackboard, and mark off their heights, discussing taller and shorter. Then he has the children figure out how many one-inch slabs they need to stand on to get as tall as the tallest child, and see how they're a certain number of slabs or inches shorter.

As a family who loves to garden, we planted amaryllis and corn plants to teach Peter how to measure and compare lengths. We had Peter read the back of the seed packages and use a ruler to help us measure off the distances between plantings and rows. Each day, we matched the height of the plant with a length of masking tape, which we taped to a graph. Peter could see and measure the growth of the plant as the tapes got longer and longer with each passing day. You can match the graph of length of the corn plant (taped right to your paper) against time with photographs of your child standing next to the plant to give him a visual demonstration of progression over time.[3]

HANDS-ON IDEAS FOR TEACHING COMPARISONS AND DEGREES

Gutstein (2002a, 2002b) describes a number of hands-on games to practice the concept of comparative degrees. Children practice varying degrees of force, throwing a ball back and forth. They modulate the loudness of their voices, whispering and shouting across progressively increasing distances. They practice rating their degrees of happiness from ice cream happiness to going-on-vacation happiness.

You can practice similar kinds of comparison games with your child. Make walking to and from places with your child into a game. Take turns being the leader and calling out instructions to walk slow,

---

3 Miller (2007, pp.249–51) also uses body perceptions to teach a sense of time. He has children compare how many seconds they can fully extend their arms holding up a one pound weight. He helps them learn the passing of minutes by having them do a task for a progressively increasing assigned number of minutes that they have to self-monitor, announcing to the teacher when time's up.

fast, and faster. When you race to the car, and he wins, use comparative language and say, "I'm fast, but I guess you're faster!" When he's across the room trying to talk to you, playfully pretend you can't hear, and say, "Louder, please. What's that? How 'bout even louder? Still can't hear you! Try your loudest, please!"

Practice throwing and catching at progressively farther distances. As you step back, call out your instructions, "One step farther!" When you miss, order, "One step closer!" Gutstein (2002b) recommends actually marking or measuring the distance you can throw and catch reliably for, say, ten times in a row, and monitoring progress over time as you practice. In general, look for opportunities to show him how to monitor and notice change and progress such as marking his height upon a growth chart on the wall, the number of laps he can swim or bike, or level of difficulty in the books he reads. Teach him to be aware of and monitor his own degrees of improvement. The following story demonstrates that learning the concept of gradations can be fun, even for the reluctant learner.

> All Peter wanted to do was tap a stack of five long strips of papers he'd ripped from a magazine that were stuck together. I sat on the couch next to him and started imitating his taps. We shaped that into a game where I'd tap a short pattern like tap-tap-tap and then he'd imitate. Then he would pick a pattern, like tap from the front, tap from the back, and tap so hard the whole end of the paper would fly around like a tether ball held by the fulcrum of his fingers. Then we'd move the whole arm and swish the paper right, then left, then in a circle. Peter really enjoyed this game.
>
> Next we substituted colorful scarves for the paper and imitated one another's patterns. Last we practiced "degrees of" with a science experiment. First we experimented with blowing a scarf off of one's face with different degrees of positioning the face to the vertical. Next we tried it with heads back with different degrees of blowing. Next we tried to see if it was easier to blow off the scarf if it was folded as opposed to spread out, or if we stacked two scarves together. Last we had a contest to see how far we could blow a scarf, and marked the distance with Peter's tapping papers. Peter labeled who blew the closest and farthest.
>
> Peter got an idea of the concept of gradations by blowing harder and harder. He got to practice using comparison language. He learned to experiment. Best of all, he turned a compulsion into a purposeful, fun game.

TEACHING QUANTITATIVE CONCEPTS IN REAL LIFE

Opportunities to make concepts of quantity, measurement, and gradations relevant and meaningful abound in real life. When your child asks for juice, ask how much. A little bit, half a glass, a full glass? If he has five cookies, and his little brother asks for one, have him count out how many he has left, and teach him to write the math sentence 5-1=4. If his little brother also gets a cookie from you, point out how the little guy has now made off with 1+1=2. Shopping at the grocery store is rich with opportunities to work on quantities. "Oh no! I asked Luke for five apples, and he only put three in the bag. How many more, Peter?" "That watermelon is small. Can you find a bigger one? How about finding the biggest one?" "Give the lightest bag to Luke to carry. I'll take the heaviest."

Cooking provides great opportunities to learn measurements, quantities, and sequences, with a tasty reward at the end of the learning process. Cake mixes provide the directions for the sequence, visually in pictures right on the box. Board games like "Sorry," "Monopoly," and "Quirkle" are full of math concepts. Say you're playing a game of Quirkle where you lay down as many bricks as you can in your turn that match a sequence, then draw more bricks to refill your hand of six. For his turn, you can ask him, "How many bricks do you need?" For your turn, you can ask him, "May I have some bricks?" and wait for him to ask you, "How many?" or count out the number of bricks you need himself. If you look for opportunities to ask "How much?" your child will get lots of hands-on, meaningful opportunities to develop the right side of the brain and grow in the abstract realm of quantitative and comparative thinking.

"What happened?" Seeing the forest from the trees with open-ended questions

"Hey, how was your day?" "What happened this afternoon?" "Tell me about it." Even neurotypical kids often reply in monosyllables if at all. "Okay," "Nothing," "I don't know." Open-ended questions are hard to answer. Answering requires recalling a lot of information and distilling it into a summary that emphasizes what's important. That takes a lot of abstract thinking. It requires seeing the forest from the trees, understanding the big picture, and synthesizing and organizing details into themes.

I approach this topic with trepidation because we are only just beginning to approach it with Peter. Therefore, I include this section more as an invitation for you to keep this kind of thinking as a goal for your child rather than to share a finished experience. It's a work in progress. Abstract thinking is difficult to teach to our little ones, and cannot be forced. They have to develop into the capacity for it. Open-ended questions are the most difficult kind of questions for many children, and certainly mine. Here are possibilities and ideas you may want to experiment with that seem to be working with Peter.

INTRODUCING "BIG PICTURE" THINKING BY SIGNPOSTING THE NAME OR PURPOSE OF YOUR NEXT ACTIVITY

As mentioned in the section on teaching "how" (see pp.243–5), a great place to start teaching what I'll call "big picture" thinking is to remember to signpost the overall purpose or name of what you are about to do together at the start of a functional task. "Time to wash hands," you might announce before ushering your child to the bathroom. "Let's get dressed." "Better get ready for school." Then go through the steps with your child.

It's fine to signal the end with a comment like "Good job!" but sometimes consider signposting the end of the activity by reiterating the big picture theme. This can be as simple as substituting or adding the name of the activity you just did for or after the word "job." "Good washing hands." "Good job getting dressed." "Great job getting ready for school." You don't have to sound scripted. "Those hands look clean. Nice washing." "You got all dressed! You look nice." "Wow! Done with getting ready for school in record time. Let's go!"

You articulate "big picture" thinking every time you name an activity. You demonstrate organizing your thinking by theme every time you organize your activity into steps for a purpose. "Time to go swimming. What do we need?" "Let's have a picnic. What shall we pack?" "Better go shopping. Let's make a list."

Look at packaging on cake mix boxes, seed packets, and put-together toys with your child. Point out the big picture of the cake, the plant, or the completed toy on the cover of the package. "Let's make that (the cake, the toy, or grow the plant)!" you might say. Then turn the box over and follow the steps together. Take advantage of good packaging to make the concept of theme/details, big picture/steps visual.

USING WRITING TEMPLATES TO MAKE "BIG PICTURE" THINKING VISUAL

Another way to make "big picture" thinking visual is to create writing templates. As your child reads books or watches videos, try to help him organize his thoughts by theme by writing them down in outline form. He can then literally see how to categorize details under themes and subjects. Say your child just read a book, *The Wonderful World of Dolphins*. Here is one sample template (questions in quotation marks) followed by sample answers (enclosed in parentheses).

"What is the book about?"

(The book is about dolphins.)

"Tell me three facts you learned."

1. (They swim in the ocean.)
2. (They eat fish.)
3. (They jump high.)

"Tell me one thing you liked or thought was interesting, and why."

(I like dolphins because they are fast.)

You can customize your templates to provide as much support as your child needs.

Fill in the blank.

What is the book about?

The book is about _____(dolphins or lions?).

Tell me three facts about dolphins.

1. They _____ (swim or walk?) in the ocean.
2. They _____ (eat or cook?) fish.
3. They _____ (jump or dance?) high.

Tell me what you like about dolphins.

I like _____ (dolphins or lions?) because they swim fast.

Of course the most interesting story of all for your child to think and write about is the story of his own life. (We go over using big picture thinking templates to journal your child's own story in the next chapter, pp.281–3.)

PRACTICING "BIG PICTURE" AND EVALUATIVE THINKING THROUGH JOURNALING

For now, I just want to make a pitch for journaling by making homemade books, either by hand or electronically with an app (such as "StoryKit," created at the University of Maryland). When you go on a outing, take your pictures and souvenirs and tape them into a little book entitled, "My trip to the park," "Mommy and I go shopping," or "My family vacation." Make a "big picture" opening and closing statement like "This book is about our trip to the beach," for the opening, and a simple emotionally relevant evaluative statement at the end like, "The beach was really fun."

There is no better place to apply big picture thinking than in journaling your child's own story. Being able to recall and retell those stories when given an open-ended question like "How was your trip?" enables your child to take his turn to talk in conversations. In learning how to do this, he develops his ability to think abstractly in terms of themes and facts, subject and details, a critical skill in the organization and communication of ideas. It's also the start of creating an interior world of reflection and feelings about experiences and events.

SUMMARY

We've come a long way together in the discussion of cognitive development, teaching your child how to connect ideas in a logical and meaningful way, not just to express bodily and sensory perceptions and desires, but also in more abstract ways.

Shepherding your child through cognitive development is hard work for you and very hard work for your child. So pace yourselves—cognitive development cannot be forced. The great majority of your time and effort and that of your child should be spent consolidating whatever level he's at presently. Listen to your child, and he will teach you the pace at which you should progress.

One day I truly thought I had pushed too far. After school, I worked on planning a three-day project making sugar cookies with Peter (his idea), marking the steps we'd do each day on the calendar. We wrote how tomorrow we would make and refrigerate the dough, and the next day we would roll it out and cut out our cookies. We made jello jigglers and talked about cause and effect as the powder dissolved and the ice cubes melted. We played restaurant and took orders from customers big and little brother who wanted their two green jello jiggler stars or one big and one little red jello jiggler hearts delivered to them. Peter looked exhausted as he stretched his brain to understand all the concepts and keep up with all the demands.

But Peter always surprises me. Afterwards we went on a car ride to a fun, easygoing social group date. But when Peter's therapist tried to take him away to play, Peter wouldn't budge. "Mama!" he said repeatedly, pointing to me, whenever she tried to take his arm. I walked arm in arm with him to the playroom, and assured him I would sit right outside the door for a few minutes in case he needed me. He braced himself and pulled me close so he could give me a giant snuggle and kiss, as though he were saying goodbye before going off to war. Then he determinedly plunged into the room.

A child is so forgiving. You may believe you've pushed too hard beyond his limits and he'll never want to be with you again, and lo and behold, discover that he still loves you. Enjoy and revel in his love as you explore the realm of abstract cognitive thinking and tackle its challenges together. Remember your "wh" and "how" questions, and you'll never run out of things to learn, teach, and talk about with your child.

Chapter 13

Advanced Social and Emotional Development
Exploring Inner Worlds

"Okay, Peter. We're here. Time to get out of the car." I tried to sound cheerful and confident, but I knew we were in trouble. I could see him through the rear view mirror shrinking into his seat. Peter was developing more and more anxiety as he grew into the preteen years. It was getting harder and harder to get him out of the car, particularly to go to potentially noisy, crowded public places. I got out of the car and opened his door. "Here we are, honey. Let's go grocery shopping!" Peter would not budge. "I can see you're scared, Peter. Don't worry, Mama's right here. We'll go together, and you'll see it will be fine." No response, just more shrinking down into his seat. "Okay, Peter, let's just practice getting out. See that tree nearby? Just touch the tree, and you can come back into the car." Peter readily took off his safety belt, ran to the tree ten feet away, touched it, and dived back into the car. He clicked his safety belt back on, gave me a big smile, and slammed the door shut.

On the way home, I started talking about yesterday when he managed to come out of the car to go shopping at Target with me. I reminded him how much fun it had been to buy the Easter candy, and how delicious the hot, buttery popcorn had been that we bought at the end. The grocery store also had great snacks, even barbeque potato chips. I wondered if maybe he'd like to go back and try again.

To my shock, I heard a soft, "Okay," from the backseat. We turned around, and parked in the supermarket parking lot. As soon as I turned off the engine, I heard a click. Peter decisively and quickly unbuckled his belt, sprang out of the car, closed the door, and ran to the grocery store. He hesitated a minute in front of the automatic doors that made that scary whoosh sound from the negative air pressure. He collected himself, and plunged inside.

We had a perfectly calm shopping trip after that, with Peter helping me get items off the shelf per our routine. He loved his little bag of barbeque potato chips. "Good thing you're so brave, Peter!" I congratulated him, as I handed him the bag. He accepted it proudly with a big smile.

This is what Stage Six and above may look like in our kids. Peter demonstrated an understanding of past events (the successful trip to the store), cause and effect ("if I go into the store, I'll get a treat"), and an ability to reflect on past experience to make a choice for the future despite a present cost ("I have to be brave and get through that door"). Who would have guessed he could come this far? Peter has autism, OCD, anxiety, noise hypersensitivity, Tourette's, severe speech dyspraxia, auditory processing disorder, problems with visual, auditory, and working memory, problems with word retrieval, medical issues, and the list goes on and on.

My point is to be encouraged. We as parents see all the challenges our children face, and the outward appearance of all the disabilities can be overwhelming. But remember that those disabilities are just the outward appearance. They are not your child's heart. You will discover who your child is, and your child will grow as a person, developing that heart and inner world, as you patiently enable your child with learned skills and supports to make choices and act upon the world.

ACTING UPON ONE'S FEELINGS: EXPLORING THE POSSIBILITIES IN STAGE FIVE

It's important to see how far your child has come. During Stage Five development, a child develops the capacity of symbolic thinking. He applies this capacity to practice identifying feelings and acting out little dramas with themes of emotional relevance. This is the stage in which with your help, he may explore a range of emotions. When Mr. Wolf comes by, does Piglet get mad or get scared? He forms ideas about a range of possible actions he could take in response to that emotion. If Piglet is scared, should he cry, hide, or ask Winnie the Pooh for help? He learns that one character's behavior affects how another feels. Winnie the Pooh can comfort Piglet with kind words, gestures, and tone of voice. He can frighten and chase the wolf away by using a loud voice and pushing him out the door. During Stage Five, a child learns how to identify his emotions, those of others, and think of different actions. By exploring those different courses of action in play, he gradually learns that different actions have different consequences—he begins to learn about cause and effect in an emotionally meaningful way.

It's important to understand the significance of this kind of learning. The connection between emotion and action is weak in many children with autism, which is one reason why we see so much meaningless activity, from flitting around distractedly to self-stimulatory behavior to obsessive compulsions. As Greenspan and Wieder (1998, p.116) put it:

> The autistic spectrum disorders…appear to involve a deficit in this core capacity, that is, in the connection between intent or affect and the different component parts, especially the ability to sequence motor patterns (motor planning), behavior, words, and spatial configurations. Autistic spectrum disorder represents an extreme example of what happens when there is a deficit in the ability to connect intent or affect to the other capacities of the human brain and mind.

In Stage Five interactions, the child learns how to talk about feelings and emotions, and to make a critical link between them. He learns that he can act upon those feelings, form ideas about different courses of action, and change the outcome: "I care about this wolf because he scares me. If I hide, I still have to be scared. If I chase him, he'll go away." In other words, he learns to act meaningfully and purposefully according to how he feels. Every time you identify the emotion, explore various options for action, and point out the emotional consequences in real life or pretend play, you are strengthening this critical link between emotion and action. You are remediating a core deficit of autism.

That is why it is so important to spend lots of time in Stage Five interactions. If sensory integration, motor planning, language, and praxias (knowing how to do sequences such as combing hair or opening a jar) are the component sections of the orchestra, and your child's intent or will is the conductor, affect is the music he plays. It is your child's emotions and feelings. Affect defines meaning for the child, and therefore drives his choices and actions: "I'm scared of the wolf, so I'm going to hide or get Mama to chase it away."

A child with autism requires a lot of practice understanding his emotions and acting accordingly. With practice, he learns that his behavior does indeed change his situation, which reinforces intentional or purposeful behavior. With experience and explicit teaching, he also learns that his situation includes the feelings of other people. He comes to understand that his behavior changes the feelings of others, and that their behavior changes his. The development of this kind of logical cause-and-effect thinking defines Stage Six.

WORKING ON THE COGNITIVE BASIS OF EACH STAGE OF SOCIAL AND EMOTIONAL DEVELOPMENT

Greenspan describes Stage Six as the stage of logical thinking with emotional meaning. At all levels, social and emotional developments depends in part upon a corresponding level of cognitive ability. Stage Three, circles of interaction, depends upon the child being able to actively respond to his parent's overtures—to understand his parent's overtures and motor plan an intentional response. Stage Four, problem solving, depends upon the child being able to hold ideas in his head and sequence them. Stage Five, pretend play, depends upon the capacity for symbolic thinking.

You can work on cognitive and motor skills not just with floortime and RDI but also with ABA, pivotal response training, speech therapy, occupational and physical therapy. Different methods lend themselves better to teaching certain skills. Occupational and physical therapy methods lend themselves to helping children improve their motor planning. ABA, pivotal response training, and speech therapy are all great for developing language, written and spoken. Floortime and RDI put everything together and make use of all the child's perceptual, motor, and cognitive capacities in order for the child to interact socially in an emotionally meaningful way. Conversely, by harnessing the child's motivation to explore his own interests and ideas and to enjoy the warmth of loving interaction, floortime and RDI play push forward cognitive development, just the way Peter learned that Piglet and Pooh could symbolize real people because their dramas helped him deal with emotionally relevant situations in his own life.

STAGE SIX AND BEYOND: A MAP FOR HIGHER SOCIAL AND EMOTIONAL DEVELOPMENT

So what are the kinds of cognitive capacities that you are trying to develop at Stage Six, using all these teaching methods? What's the social utility of abstract thinking? How does it help your child make friends? And what comes after "Stage Six"?

Stage Six is the stage of developing logical and abstract thinking. In Chapter 12 (p.214), we outlined the different kinds of abstract thinking (Greenspan and Wieder 1998, p.245). These cognitive skills enable your child to build an inner world, a stable understanding of himself he can use as what's called "an internal organizing principle." The goal is for your child to develop a sense of his own needs, interests, preferences, abilities, and values so he can interact and act upon the world accordingly (see pp.266–283).

As your child discovers himself, the goal is for him to also discover other people. And the first step is to understand that other people have different minds, perspectives, and their own inner worlds. The next is to discover that it is useful, interesting, and fun to share these inner worlds. Children learn emotional bonding through sharing perspectives in conversation, working together toward a common goal, and co-creation such as in the arts, sports, or work projects. I go more into how to make use of these kinds of opportunities for emotional bonding later (see pp.284–9).

I can't emphasize enough how important emotional bonding is. You need to make interaction with you worth your child's effort—fun, love, and joy are the juice of life, and you need to get your child addicted to it. So when your child takes the initiative socially, even looking at you to see your reaction or to get information, make sure you reward it by highlighting your affect and providing a satisfying emotional response. As the connection between interaction and pleasure grows more robust, try to create as many opportunities as possible for your child to develop that connection with others. Adults and peers can be coached to give that extra waiting time and highlighted affect your child needs to experience the reward of social interaction.

Once your child becomes genuinely interested in interacting with others, he's more motivated to do the work of learning how to do it better. Instead of automatically demonstrating an understanding of his thinking, play dumb in small degrees at first, ever increasing the work he needs to do to show you what he means. He needs to learn that "seeing leads to knowing," that is, others may not see what he sees, and won't know unless he tunes into their perspective and makes an appropriate adjustment. Begin to explicitly teach social skills such as how to read and express himself through body language, and how to enter and exit groups and conversations. Most importantly, he needs to learn how to listen in order to carry on a conversation that is meaningful and interesting to his conversation partner.

Next children learn about the difference between the interior and exterior world, and begin to realize that internal thoughts, feelings, and ideas are more important than exterior appearances. They learn that in this game of minds, people are always forming impressions based upon their perceptions, which may be very different from reality (such as the wolf fooling Red Riding Hood in *Red Riding Hood*). Start teaching your child how to start thinking about what other people are thinking about him, and how to act so that others perceive him in the way he intends. In other words, start explicitly teaching principles of social interaction like forming impressions, the "social fake" (acting polite when you don't feel like it; see Winner 2007), and learning to observe nonverbal clues like social context, past history, and body language to deduce another's true intentions.

In addition to real life, literature and movies become important sources of material to practice deducing the hidden feelings or false beliefs of the characters, and understanding their inner worlds. Asking, "What would you do next?" and "What do you think the character will do next?" gives your child the opportunity to make inferences and judgments, and allows him to practice shifting into another person's perspective. Pretend play, and eventually drama and theatre, are further means of exploring the perspectives of another, sharing another's inner world, and practicing sending social messages and forming impressions.

As your child discovers the joy of emotional bonding, he begins to value membership in groups and friendships. He learns to reference group members and peers frequently to determine if his actions strengthen his acceptance by others. In time, he learns to find true love and friendship with others who value his inner self and want to share theirs. He learns how to make friends by taking a sincere interest in other people. He learns how to make memory files in his head about the interests, cares, preferences, strengths and weaknesses of his friends. He learns the requirements of lasting friendship such as sincerity, altruism, and forgiveness.

Friends need to be able to empathize. Your child needs to identify the emotion of the other person, care about it, and learn to express that caring and understanding. He needs to learn to guess the cause or multiple causes, and think of different ways to either change those causes or otherwise affect his friend's feelings to increase his joy or reduce his sorrow. There is a lot of abstract thinking involved here. Furthermore, the more developed an individual's self-concept is, the richer it becomes with values, virtues, and experience, and the more he has to offer to others. He will be a better friend if he has more to share.

At this point, you may be either very excited to see the panorama of possibilities for your child in the future, or you may be thinking, "Sounds like a very long journey to me." I can relate to both points of view. It is a long journey, for everyone, and takes a lifetime. I don't know how far my child will proceed on this road, but the more important thing is heading in the right direction. A level of social connection and emotional regulation are possible at every stage of the journey. Happiness is possible at every stage if your child feels loved and useful. However, knowing what the next step is and helping your child grow in that direction will only further enable your child to develop an ever richer emotional and social life.

RESOURCES FOR GAMES AND EXERCISES

So now that you have this map of social and emotional development, how, practically speaking, does one travel down it? There are many outstanding resources available to give you practical ideas on how to take the next step.

Fern Sussman's books *More Than Words* (1999) and *Talkability* (2006) give ideas on how to move your child along the developmental social skills and communication ladders using play, routines, music, books, toys, and playdates. It's easy to use her books, as she organizes her suggestions by the child's developmental level. She gives easily understood descriptions of each stage and color-codes the pages accordingly. You can turn to the chapter on how to use play, music, books, or whatever modality to help your child progress, find the pages with the color corresponding to your child's developmental level, and try out the ideas one by one.

Steven Gutstein has written outstanding manuals that describe interactive games to try with your child. His books *Relationship Development Intervention with Young Children* (2002a) and *Relationship Development Intervention with Children, Adolescents and Adults* (2002b) systematically teach all the individual skills necessary for that complex symphony we call social interaction. He starts from the fundamentals of attending and engaging to referencing, coordinating and anticipating actions, to adding variations and improvisations. He divides social development into five levels and 24 stages. How fast your child progresses through the games in each stage and level depends on his particular neurologic profile, meaning his cognitive, language, and social strengths and weaknesses.

Peter's RDI consultant told me that Peter was the slowest of all her students to make progress, and it has taken us nearly ten years to get Peter through 6 out of the 24 stages. However, his progress is real and beautiful to see. Take ideas out of the book at your child's level, see which ones appeal, and then modify and vary them to match your child's interests and abilities. Once you have some of these fundamental social skills down, like ready engagement and referencing faces for information and shared emotions, your child's life is so much the richer as he uses that new capacity throughout the day, in all his interactions and activities.

Michelle Garcia Winner creates a social curriculum for children with Asperger's syndrome and less severe autism. Her books *Thinking About You, Thinking About Me* (2007) and *Think Social—A Social Thinking Curriculum for School-Age Students* (2005) are full of great games and tools to use to improve social understanding and practice. I've taken several ideas from her books and modified them to use with Peter, such as her SBMs (see pp.237–8) and people file diagrams.[1]

So now hopefully you have some idea of where you're heading and how to get there. There are a plethora of resources and books full of more ideas you can glean from in the References at the end of this book. Let's now get down to some practical examples now—let me take you down the road the few steps more that Peter and I have travelled.

INSTRUMENTAL INTERACTION VERSUS EXPERIENCE SHARING

Recall how in Chapter 11 we discussed how the first place for your child to learn and apply symbolic and logical thinking is in getting his basic needs met. Teaching a symbolic communication system, visual schedule, and logical negotiation to get your child's needs met are priorities to avoid frustration and meltdowns.

> *Peter loves to ride in the car, and give directions. He has a favorite route he frequently directs me to. At one point the road forks right or left. Peter loves going left because the road makes a wide detour that goes through a pretty part of town. I prefer going right to save on gas and time. I love listening to music in the car. Peter prefers quiet. As we drove along, I turned on the radio. Peter immediately protested, "Turn off." I complained, "But I love music. If you get to pick the route, I get to listen to music." Peter insisted, "No music. Turn off." I turned off the music, and said, "Then I get to pick which way we go." Several blocks from the fork in the road, I heard*

---

1   This idea helps your child remember the interests and special talents and abilities of others. Draw the person on a piece of paper with lines connecting their hands with a list of hobbies they do with their hands, like "play the piano," "cook," or "fix things," and lines connecting their feet with a list of favorite activities they do with their feet, like "soccer," "hiking," or "biking." You might draw a line connecting the head with a list like, "loves movies and reading mysteries," and a line connecting the heart to a list like, "loves me, her baby brother, and her dog, Spot."

> a quiet voice in the backseat speak up. "Music. Turn on." "Thanks, Peter!" I said, and turned on the radio. Immediately after, Peter said, "Left." I moved into the left lane. After another few seconds, Peter said, "Turn off." "No music?" I asked, incredulously. "No music," he replied emphatically. I turned off the radio. Then I moved into the right lane. "I get to pick the route then," I said. By now we were very close to the fork in the road. "Turn on!" said Peter quickly. I turned on the radio. "Left!" he cried. I pulled into the left lane, and just made the turn. I left the radio on the rest of the way home. Peter didn't seem to mind. He settled back contentedly and enjoyed the scenic route home. It had been a successful negotiation, and we both enjoyed the ride.

This conversation is an example of an instrumental interaction—a real conversation with each partner taking turns talking, listening, and relating what is said to what has just been heard. But the point of the exchange is instrumental, to get a need or want met. Your child may demonstrate the best of his cognitive skills in instrumental interactions because getting what he wants is highly motivating.

However, you want your child to communicate and have a relationship with you beyond the *instrumental*, meaning to get something from you. Gutstein divides interactions into the instrumental and *experiential*. You want your child to interact with you experientially as well, to interact just for the pleasure of experiencing the interaction. If unrestrained in a restaurant, my two-year-old neurotypical grandson will walk up to the waitress and neighboring tables to smile and "chat" with any potential friend. Outside on a walk he points to squirrels and birds and looks back at me to make sure I enjoy the experience with him.

In *Engaging Autism*, Greenspan (Greenspan and Wieder 2006, p.96) discusses interaction and communication as emotional signaling, a way to feel close to another person through an exchange of gestures and/or words. As Greenspan puts it,

> …the child begins to value communication not just as a means to getting a cookie or hug, but because communication itself feels as good as a cookie or hug. Imagine yourself at a cocktail party with someone who is empathetic and warm, who nods and glows as you're talking, and who seems to value your every word. It's not just that the person seems to understand and agree your ideas; you feel a primary sense of connectedness, a sense of belonging and of being appreciated at a very core level, the same way a four-month-old

baby feels when she smiles at Mommy and Mommy gives her a big smile back.

Is it possible for our children to connect emotionally with others at this kind of primal level? To want to be with us just to be with us? Experience sharing is interacting for no other goal than to share each other's interior world of emotions and ideas. By nature it's spontaneous, dynamic, unpredictable, and creative. However, to keep such interactions flowing, each person must read the other, and create his own response while modifying it depending upon the other person's feedback. A child can only share what he has. We need to build up the child's inner world, so that he has more ideas, experience, and understanding about his own feelings to share.

We also need to build the child's desire to tune into the perspectives, thoughts, and feelings of other people. He needs to become interested in the inner worlds of others as well as to share his. This takes learning on the part of our children because the connection between affect and interaction, relationship and emotional gratification is hardwired to varying degrees. The neural connections in those more highly impacted with autism can be sparse indeed. It is definitely possible to strengthen those connections, but to do so requires a lot of intentional positive experience sharing.

The more highly impacted the child, the more practice he will need. The catch is, of course, that frequently the more highly impacted children are also those with more cognitive challenges, and frequently more motor, sensory, and emotional challenges as well. Therefore, the more difficult it is to create repertoire to practice positive experience sharing.

We take our neurotypical children on community outings to the park, library, store, zoo, and farmer's market, and they automatically create memories and ideas about their experiences that they act out later in pretend play. We read them books and show them videos and see them take the same initiative. Do the same with children with high functioning autism with lesser degrees of cognitive impairment, and you'll still see them develop interests and create their own ideas. These form the repertoire or content of their actions. Work with this content, playfully inserting yourself into your child's actions to transform them into interactions. Greenspan and Wieder's classics *The Child with Special Needs* (1998) and *Engaging Autism* (2006) detail their techniques of playful obstruction and expansion beautifully.

But for our children with comprehensive and severe autism, they need a lot of help to learn how to form their own ideas. Their interests may be restricted to the purely sensory, such as food, swinging, or self-stimulation behaviors. If you want to go beyond purely sensory-based interactions, you need to work on both their cognitive as well as their relationship development.

That's why it's so important to work on the cognitive in conjunction with the emotional and relational. Use every tool you've got, not just DIR and RDI, but also ABA, pivotal response training, occupational and physical therapy, to improve your child's ability to think and act upon his environment.

Explore books, videos, and the real world together to add to his knowledge base and experience of different environments and activities. Explore the arts together by taking him to shows and concerts, and experiment with learning a musical instrument, drawing, and crafts. Do constructive work projects together like cooking, baking, gardening, and building. Especially when he's little and easier to handle, introduce him to different kinds of movement and sports like swimming, skiing, biking, gymnastics, yoga, and dance. All these experiences and activities form contexts in which you can work on your goals of cognitive and relationship development. They are also the seeding ground of potential interests your child may develop as he grows in his cognitive capacity and emotional self-awareness.

Try not to get discouraged with the slow pace of progress in your more highly impacted little one—you have a lot more work to do than parents of children who are impacted less comprehensively. Developing a functional communication system takes years; it has taken Peter nine years to develop a spontaneous verbal vocabulary of less than 200 words, though his expressive vocabulary on his Vantage (AT device) and receptive language skills are greater (more comparable to those of a five-year-old). But if you teach with love and skill, it is possible to help your child build an inner world, learn to tune into the perspectives of others, and enjoy experiential interactions.

BUILDING AN INNER WORLD

For a child to develop true friendships and intimacy, he needs to be able to both share his thoughts and feelings and care about those of others. He needs to both talk and listen to a certain kind of story. This story is not about external facts or events, but about the heart. Every person has a story of the heart, about an inner world of thoughts and feelings that identify who he is and define his character and personality. This section is about how to help your child develop a sense of himself, an internal organizing principle, a self-awareness and identity, an inner world, that he can share with others. The next section will discuss how to teach him how to tune into and care about others and their inner worlds (see "Teaching your child how to tune into others, pp.284–292).

What are the ingredients that comprise a person's inner world? What makes you, you? A young child first starts distinguishing himself from others by his desires, preferences, and interests. If you listen in on the conversations little children have with their friends, you hear them talking about their favorite toys, movies, places, activities, and foods. They also start talking about what they're good at, their talents, and accomplishments. Gradually they start talking about their experiences, feelings, and important people in their lives. With time and experience, they become cognizant of their strengths and weaknesses, virtues and vices. As adults praise them when they're good and correct them when they misbehave, they eventually develop a sense of morals and values.

You build this kind of self-awareness and character development in your child with autism in the same way. The process is just slower, more deliberate, and takes more repetition and explicit teaching. The key is to strengthen that connection between affect, the child's emotion, and its cause, so that the child learns what he likes, what he's good at, and how to behave. As with all children, you can shape his interests, abilities, and values to some extent, but in general the process of developing an inner world is a journey of discovery you make together. Your role is to encourage and nurture.

Self-awareness: What do I like, and what am I good at?

So when your child eats something he likes and starts smiling and squealing, say, "You really liked that peach, didn't you? Mm…peach. Delicious. Peaches make me happy too!" After a great ride at an amusement park, look at each other and stretch the moment. "Wow! That was such a great ride! Wasn't it fun, Peter?" Sit with the emotion for as long as your child wants to, and don't hurry on to the next activity. Make the most of that happy moment to enjoy it together, and talk about it, identifying the feeling and the cause. You are creating ideas about the peach, and the ride, memories he can refer to later. With each memory, you add a piece of identity to him. "I love fast rides, and I love being with Mom." He becomes aware of his own preferences, interests, strengths, and abilities.

Affect tolerance: Learning to understand and cope with emotion

Similarly, don't be afraid to sit with and acknowledge negative emotions. If your child hits his little brother who starts wailing, point out, "Look, Peter. Poor Luke. He's crying. He looks sad to me. What do you think?" As you comfort the little brother, let your child experience how sad you and the little brother both feel. That uncomfortable feeling may motivate and prepare him better to learn the next steps of reconciliation ("Say, 'I'm sorry, Luke'"), repair ("What can we do to make him feel better? How about we get some ice and tissue together?"), and recompense ("Let's give Luke the next turn").

Conversely, if his little brother breaks a favorite toy, and your child starts crying, don't rush to repair or replace the toy. Comfort your child, but give him the opportunity to experience the sadness so he learns he can survive it. As you commiserate with him, acknowledge and verbalize his emotion, and speak to him soothingly; he will also learn *how* to survive it. He will learn the idea of sadness, what it means, and how to identify and label it. That idea will create a space between his emotions and acting out because of them. The next time he's sad, perhaps memories of this past experience will come along with the identification of his feeling sad, and he may remember how you calmed him down.

Emotional regulation: Learning how to calm down

You can reinforce the memories of those calming strategies and elaborate on them with explicit teaching. Use the concept of the emotional thermometer to your child (see pp.164–5). Next to each level of emotion, add a calming strategy. We started using these thermometers to teach Peter to self-manage his sensory challenges. The three levels of "Not so good," "Upset," and "VERY UPSET!" corresponded to "A little loud," "Loud," and "Too loud." Next to each of these levels was an arrow pointing to a strategy to deal with it. "A little loud" led to "I cover my ears." "Loud" led to "Headphones." "Too loud" led to "Let's go!" An emotional thermometer for fighting with his little brother might have had the following levels and strategies: "A little mad" → "Say, 'Stop it!' and count to ten" →

"Angry" → "Say 'Stop it!' and walk away" → "VERY ANGRY" → "Cross my arms and get Mom."

But an emotional thermometer only goes so far. It increases your child's awareness of his own emotional state, and gives him concrete steps to temporize, but ultimately, the only way a child learns how to deal with emotion is by experience.[2] He learns by watching, absorbing, imitating, and identifying with the way you experience one emotional storm after the other together with him. As you acknowledge his feelings and label them, he learns to express his feelings with words and gestures instead of destructive actions. "Wow, I can see you're really mad. Not just a little mad, but very, very, super dooper mad!" When you give him a punching bag or pillow to hit, take him out for a brisk walk, or teach him how to count to ten or take a few deep breaths, he learns how to discharge his anger more appropriately. "Now, hold on there. Grab onto my hands, that's it. Now push hard against my hands, push, push, push. Let's do ten, come on, let's count…" As you talk calmly to him with reassuring words, he learns positive self-talk. "There, you see. Feeling a little better now? Do you need more pushes? Shall we go outside and get some air? I can see you really wanted to hit Luke, but you didn't. That was great. You see? You can do it. You don't need to hit. You can be mad, but you'll be okay. Come on, keep walking. You're doing great."

Finally, once the emotion has dissipated, and you feel reason has returned, the two of you can talk about what happened, why it happened, different solutions, and go back to reconcile and negotiate with the little brother.[3] But you can't skip any steps in emotional regulation. You have to deal with the emotion first. In dealing with it in a calm and positive way, you teach your child how to deal with it.

As he experiences these big waves of emotion with you there buffering him with your calm demeanor and patient acceptance, your child will learn to see himself through your eyes. He will learn that the negative emotions are not him, but something he has that passes. With a lot of practice watching you and absorbing your reactions, especially your calm acceptance, in time your child may learn to accept and understand his feelings, but not let them control his actions.[4]

---

2   This discussion assumes the child has also had instruction in the basics of identifying and expressing emotions. See Chapter 10 for activities to teach this (pp.157–9).

3   Winner's (2007) SBMs might be useful in these kinds of discussions. See pp.237–8.

4   Calm acceptance of the emotion is coupled with redirection and reformation of the action. See Chapters 15 and 16 on challenging behaviors.

I would especially work on teaching your child how to monitor and become aware of his emotions early on, before they grow to an unmanageable size. The best way to regulate emotions is to start dealing with them at the lower end of the emotional thermometer. Self-awareness is the key to successful emotional self-regulation. In the beginning, expect to do a lot of prompting, as you walk your child through the steps. "I see Luke is being loud right now. Are you feeling a little mad?" Say Peter replies, "Mad!" "Let's tell Luke, 'Hey Luke, see how Peter's feeling?' How are you feeling Peter?" Peter reiterates, "Mad!" "What can we do, Peter? Want to tell Luke, 'Quiet, please'?" Peter says, "Quiet." (Then usher noisy Luke out of the room.) "There, you see, Peter? You used your words, and now it's quiet. Feeling better?"

Teaching morals, values, and virtues

You can teach your child morals, values, and virtues essentially the same way. The main way your child learns is by absorbing your reactions and responses to life situations. This is the same way neurotypical kids learn how to behave. Say you've just had a vigorous bike ride around the park, you make a comment like, "Wow, that was really something Peter, we did five miles today! Are you tired too? Wasn't that fun though? You should be so proud of yourself for sticking with it. I sure am." A comment like that teaches the child several things. "I can be tired and have fun at the same time." "Mom's proud of me for sticking with it. I feel good about trying hard." He learns to want to persevere.

If your family has ties to a religious faith, consider making participation in those traditions part of your child's education. As he learns about his family's faith tradition, he receives explicit instruction on shared values and community norms. He comes to understand the good and the love that can stem from that faith tradition.

Look for opportunities to catch your child being good. Point out the positive practical consequences. "You shared with your little brother, and see? Now he's sharing with you." "Good thing you helped me bring in the groceries. Those popsicles would have melted. Would you like one?" In your praise, use concrete words and be specific. "I saw the way you gave your brother a piece of your cookie. I love the way you shared." Reinforce the praise later during conversation. Let your child overhear you as you tell Papa how he shared with his brother. If you have a habit of conversing as you put your child to bed or a tradition of bedtime prayers, try to bring up at least one good thing your child did that day. He'll both learn to listen and look forward to that special time of recollection together.

Reflection: A tool for inner growth and a lifelong habit worth making

That brings me to my final point. A key tool for building your child's inner world is reflection. As each opportunity arises to point out a preference, interest, ability, or virtue, by all means point it out and celebrate with your child. But our children tend to have short memories. As much as your child can relive the experience by reflecting upon it and talking about it, the better you consolidate those positive memories. So highlight the high points in your child's day in your conversations and recollections at the end of the day. Make it a habit and part of his daily routine. Compile a book of stories with drawings and/or photos of times you caught him doing good, and he'll have his own book to proudly review.

The same goes for the low points. Whenever an emotionally relevant incident occurs in your child's life, take the opportunity to talk about it both immediately, at the time of the incident, and later in reflection. Often a child learns the most from his mistakes. Peter has a book of reflection stories, which retell the meaningful events in his life, both good and bad. The book is divided into two sections entitled, "Hurrah!" and "Oops!" What follows is a sample story from the latter section.

> *7/5/10 "I fixed the cake"*
>
> *Mama, Stephen, and I baked a cake. It was beautiful. It looked yummy. I was digging into the cake to eat it. Then the cake was ugly. Mama was mad. But I helped Mama fix the cake. First we put whipped cream on it. Then I passed strawberries, blueberries, and raspberries to her. She put them on the cake. The cake was beautiful again! Mama and I were happy again too. Next time I want cake, I will ask Mama first.*

At the preverbal stage, your recollection might just be to play a few rounds of a new interactive game your child learned and enjoyed that day, or to sing a song that he heard and seemed to get excited about at big brother's school concert. Once your child develops more of the capacity to form ideas and hold onto them, bring out photographs or souvenirs you collected over the course of the day, and see if he seems interested. Later in development, when he understands symbolic play, you can re-enact a particularly meaningful event in your child's life or its emotional theme with stuffed animals, dolls, or puppets in pretend play.

For your more advanced child already working on abstract thinking, here are some practical suggestions for how to do recollections using symbolic communication (written and spoken words, PECS, AT device) and journaling. These exercises will develop your child's abstract thinking while helping him build an inner world.

HOW TO DO A DAILY RECOLLECTION
The first step: Walking your child through it

Retelling and talking about stories in general is a great way to teach your child about the inner worlds of different individuals and characters, and practice his abstract thinking, such as how to answer "wh" questions (see pp.238–42) and organize his thoughts by time sequence. Recollections are a great place to begin, as you talk about and reflect upon the most interesting and meaningful story your child knows, the story of his own life.

As your child goes through his day, highlight the most memorable moments with a bit of conversation. At breakfast, for example, "Wow, you got chocolate chip pancakes! Isn't that your favorite?" During a walk in the afternoon, you might point out, "Look at that! What do you see? Those squirrels are chasing each other. Do you think they're playing?" At an evening game of Chutes and Ladders, his little brother might get upset. "Poor Luke, he looks mad to me. I think he really wanted to win, don't you?" Journal these moments in a paper or electronic notebook, using AT/apps like "StoryKit." Collect souvenirs like acorns or sticks you collected on a walk, brochures and maps of places you visit, programs, and tickets.

Having prepared your child with all these prior mini-conversations, and armed with all your memory joggers, your child is now ready to practice organizing his thoughts in sequential time order. At the end of the day, do a little recollection and retell the story of your child's day together. Use spoken or written language, PECS, AT/apps, or whatever communication mode your child prefers to talk.

Say, "How was your day today? Tell me about it." You might start out by asking fill-in-the-blank questions. Present your photo of your child happily eating his chocolate chip pancakes, and ask, "In the morning, you ate your favorite chocolate chip _____ (pancakes)." You can relive the memory, pretending to pour the syrup, eat the pancakes, and say, "Yum!"

together. Then present your picture of the squirrels perhaps, and say, "In the afternoon, we went for a walk. What did you see? _____(Squirrels playing.)" Or present the acorns and sticks he collected, and ask, "What did you do in the afternoon?" or "I wonder where these great acorns came from?" Finally, take out your Chutes and Ladders gameboard, and ask, "In the evening, Luke got upset. Remember what happened when Luke lost the game?" Remind him how he helped. "It's true—Luke was crying. He was sad because he doesn't like to lose. But then, remember? You made him feel better! You brought him a _____ (tissue), and played another game with him." Finish with an evaluative statement like, "So what do you think. Was it a good day, okay day, or not so good?"

Once in a while, try writing down your child's responses for him as you go, and read the story together at the end, which you can keep in his journal, along with the photos (and acorns) taped to the page. If your child communicates on an AT device, simply re-read your child's stored responses together. Many devices also allow you to print them. What follows is a sample of what the finished story might look like.

> *"In the morning, I ate my favorite chocolate chip pancakes. In the afternoon, I went for a walk. I saw squirrels playing. In the evening, my little brother got upset. He was crying. He was sad because he doesn't like to lose. But then, I made him feel better. I brought him a tissue, and played another game with him. It was a good day."*

The next step: Getting your child to do more by teaching him how to organize and retrieve memories in "wh/how" categories

These kinds of recollections help your child grow in his self-image and identity by affirming his preferences, interests, abilities, and values. However, at this level, you as the parent are doing all the work of recalling the memories and organizing the thinking. Your eventual goal is for your child to make reflection a habit of his own. How do you enable a child to get there? To begin with, prompt your child to answer simple multiple-choice, fill-in-the-blank type questions as a way to engage him and get him to actively participate in the recollection. Then sprinkle in some harder questions. Prompt your child through the recollection by asking "wh" questions, which are the next level up in terms of difficulty. Apply the "wh" table (such as on p.241) to teach your child how to organize his thoughts and memories about the events in his day. The trick is to make it visual with a graphic organizer.

Say you and your child are going through a day like the one described above. Recall that you make a bit of conversation at the time of each meaningful event to point the event out to your child and mark it as memorable. "Wow, you got chocolate chip pancakes! Isn't that your favorite?" After breakfast, instead of jotting down the event yourself, journal it together with your child, using a "wh" table format.

When?	Who?	What...doing?	Where?
In the morning at breakfast	I	ate chocolate chip pancakes	in the kitchen.

As you point to the "What...doing?" heading, ask your child, "What were you doing this morning?" and have him fill in the blank. He can write his answer down himself, or he can dictate and you can record. Then point to the "When?" heading, and ask, "When did you eat those yummy pancakes?" Again record. Finally, point to "Who?" and with a little tickle ask, "Who was the lucky guy who ate those super yummy pancakes?" You don't have to ask a question for every column, nor elicit all the information for any one question. If your child answers "morning" for "When?" that's great. Write that down or jot down the more complete answer, "in the morning at breakfast." Ask as much and only put in as much as your child tolerates. You want to keep this fun.

By the end of the day, your "wh/how" chart might look like this (optional information to be elicited is enclosed in parentheses):

When?	Who?	What... doing?	Where?	Why?
In the morning at breakfast	I	ate chocolate chip pancakes	(in the kitchen)	(because I'm hungry.)
In the afternoon	Mama and I	saw squirrels	on our walk.	
In the evening	Luke	cried		because he lost.

These "wh/how" tables may look complicated on first glance, but consider how the information would look to your child written out in longhand. It actually summarizes an enormous amount of history in a format that's simplified and condensed. Most importantly, the format enables your child to literally see how to organize his thinking. It also provides your child with a one-page "cheat sheet" to use as a reference in his conversations with you later, as you recollect the day together.

A technical tip on using matching icons to distinguish between "wh" questions

It's helpful to place icons of your choice (ones that match your AT device if your child uses one) for "what," "who," "where," and "when" alongside each question. If your child uses an AT device, all he has to do is match the icon to receive an automatic prompt from his device, as the icon will lead him to that category of vocabulary. For example, if you put whatever action word/verb icon your device uses after "What were you doing?" and your child reads it as a prompt to push that button on his AT device, the device will automatically bring your child to verbs. If you put the icon for people after "Who did you see?" the device will show a choice of relevant people that have been pre-programmed into it. Put the icon for places after "Where did you go?" Put the time icon that brings you to a menu of time words after your "When did you do it?" question.

As mentioned in Chapter 12 (p.241), if you don't have an AT device, you can do the same thing in written form by providing lists of words marked with headings and picture icons that match your "wh" questions. For example, make a list of time words like "in the morning," "in the afternoon," or "in the evening" under the heading "When?" with a drawing of a little clock next to it. When you ask your child, "When did you do it?" draw the same little clock after the word "When?" Then all your child has to do is match the little clock drawings to select the correct list to find his answer in. As he gets good at this, make the clocks smaller and the word "When?" larger and more prominent till you fade your picture icons. In time, the goal is to fade the "When?" heading on your time word list entirely. At that point, celebrate! Your child understands the meaning of the word, "when."

Use this same format as your child goes from one activity and event to another in his day, and fill it out together as a routine. With enough repetition using this chart format in many different contexts, your child will eventually understand the difference between what, who, where, and when. Use the same procedure described above to fade the use of the icons and teach your child how to directly match "Who?" with his list of people, "Where?" with his list of places, and "What...doing?" with his list of verbs.

Next step: Bringing in the feelings by adding evaluative comments

So far, your "wh" table is giving your child lots of practice organizing his thinking about the events in his day, and helping him understand the abstract concepts of what, who, where, and when. But you also want him to reflect upon those events, and to do that he needs to learn how to tune into how he feels about them. How you feel about the events in your life are what give life meaning and value. Ultimately those emotional evaluations drive motivation and therefore your actions. The beginning of this kind of important emotional thinking is for your child to become aware of how he feels about what he does and what happens to him.

Start a new "How do I feel?" column on that "wh" table. Ask your child how he feels about each event in his day, or if he likes or doesn't like an activity. Let him select a yellow happy face or blue sad face to stick in his feelings column. Also ask him "Why?" or "What did (or didn't) you like about it?" Record his evaluation and reasons for making it on the "How...feeling?" and "Why?" columns, respectively. The goal is to increase both his emotional awareness and understanding of why he feels the way he does.

Our children with autism also need a lot of help in developing a sense of proportion and perspective where emotional matters are concerned. It therefore may be helpful to your child to have him put one, two, or three happy (or sad) faces next to things he likes (or dislikes) a little, quite a bit, or a lot, to work on degrees of emotion. This will help him recall his favorite or worst part of the day. The proportion of yellow happy faces compared to blue sad faces also gives him a visual perspective on the day so he can tell you if he's had an overall good or bad day.

You can take emotional thinking to a whole new level if you also talk with your child about how his actions impact the way other people feel. (See pp.237–8 on SBMs.) Once your child gains an understanding of how he feels about events, start getting him to take the next step and think about the feelings of others. "Why did you dig into the cake Mama baked?" you might ask. "Because I was hungry," he might reply. "How did Mama feel about that?" you query. "Mad," he replies. "Why did she get mad?" you ask, as you follow through. "Because that made the cake ugly," you prompt him to realize.

Your "wh/how" table may now look like this, as you add questions like, "How did you like the pancakes?" and "How did Luke feel?" (Optional information to elicit is enclosed in parentheses.)

When?	Who?	What... doing?	Where?	How... feel?	Why?
In the morning at breakfast	I	ate chocolate chip pancakes	(in the kitchen.)	☺☺ I loved them!	(because I was hungry.)
In the afternoon	Mama and I	saw squirrels	on our walk.	☺ I liked it	(because the squirrels were funny.)
In the evening	Luke	cried.		☹ Luke was sad	because he lost.

Armed with your "wh" chart, iPhone photos, and any tangible souvenirs you've collected during the day to use as additional memory joggers, you are now ready to recollect the day with your child on a whole new level. Now you can refer your child back to his own comments on the "wh" chart if he needs help answering questions. You may also "preview" the chart, going over it line by line, to prepare your child before even beginning to ask your recollection questions. The goal is to enable him to answer your questions with the least amount of prompting, so that the answers come more from him and less from you.

Making the leap from visual schedule to journal

Now you're ready to morph your child's visual schedule into a journal/ diary. School, with its regularity and routines, provides a perfect context in which to do this. A child's daily schedule may start out looking like this:

When?	What am I doing?
8:00 am	Work on words and numbers
10:00 am	Recess: Play outside
10:30 am	Music class: Play the drums
12:00 pm	Eat lunch
12:30 pm	Work on reading books
2:30 pm	Car ride home

Eventually, adding one column at a time, the chart may morph into something like:

When?	Who?	What... doing?	Where?	How did I feel? Why?	How did he/she feel?
8:00 am	Belinda and I	worked at math and words	at school	☺ okay because I worked hard	☺happy because I worked hard
10:00 am	I	had a break	outside	☺happy	
10:30 after break	I saw Mr. Wulff	played the drums	music class	☺☺ very happy because I like the drums	☺happy
12:00 pm	I	ate lunch rice, nectarine, chicken	outside	☺☺ very happy because I like nectarines	
12:30 pm after lunch	Belinda and I	read a story about a girl and her kite	at school	☹ not so good because it was too hard	☹ The girl was sad because she lost her kite.
2:30 pm time to go home	I	had a car ride	to home	☺happy	

This basically teaches your child to organize his memories into categories of people ("who"), activities ("what...doing"), time ("when"), place ("where"), and feelings ("how did I/he/she feel about this occurrence?"). This makes information easier for your child to remember and retrieve. When you ask him *what* he was *doing* at music class, prompt him to remember by looking down his "what...doing" column. If he wants to know *when* he gets his recess break, help him retrieve the information by looking down the column under the "when" heading.

Emotional categories

It's worth emphasizing that one of the most important kinds of categorizing to teach your child is emotional. The most socially relevant categories are actually the emotional categories. That's why those happy, neutral, and sad faces, and how many there are, are so important to add to the chart.

Practice this kind of emotional evaluation and categorization in all kinds of settings, and let your child hear others do it. Driving home with the family from an outing, ask what each person's favorite animal was at the zoo, or favorite ride at the amusement park. What was the most interesting thing they learned or saw at the museum? At the dinner table when people start talking about a book, movie, or performance they just read or saw, ask about their favorite parts or characters. In real life conversation, when people ask how your day went, they don't want a list of your activities–they want to hear about what was emotionally relevant to you. So be sure to work on this kind of categorization with your child.

> *We were driving in the car back home from a family vacation in San Diego. I asked the kids what they liked the best about the trip. "Surfing!" said Teddy. "The aviary (at the San Diego Zoo)," said Stephen, who always appreciates a fine scientific collection. "Candy!" cried Luke, who had spent all his money at the hotel concessionary when he discovered candy in the shape of LEGO. Following the rhythm of the group, Peter softly chimed in "Boat." Sure enough, the last thing we had done before leaving for LA was to let Peter pick our last stop at Sea World. He had pulled us over to Oscar the Grouch's big swinging boat ride in the Sesame Street Amusement Park section where he had a glorious time rocking back and forth in ever enlarging arcs in the giant boat-shaped swing. "He really understood!" I whispered to my husband. I reached over to the backseat to give Peter a high five. "Oscar's boat ride. I loved it too, Peter."*

The next step in learning how to reflect: Answering open-ended questions

Once your child gets good at answering "wh" and "how" questions about his day, you might venture into open-ended questions. These include, "How was your morning?" "Did you do anything fun or interesting at school today?" "Tell me about your field trip." Answering these kinds of questions often draws a blank from even neurotypical children because it requires an advanced kind of abstract thinking, seeing the forest from the trees, the subject from the facts, and the themes from the details. Once again, use of a graphic organizer might help (see Chapter 12, pp.251–4).

Why use graphic organizers?

If you go into a typical kindergarten classroom, you can see how carefully the environment is set up. There's usually some kind of cubby system where the children enter. You might see cubbies consisting of tall open cupboards, with a shelf above perhaps for a take home folder, a couple of hooks underneath to hang coats and backpacks, and a bin on the bottom for a lunchbox. The teacher usually places a big homework basket on a table next to the cubbies, so children can open their backpacks, place their homework in the basket, and then put their folder in the top shelf, backpack on the hook, and lunchbox down below. The structure of the cubbies silently instructs the child how to organize his belongings. Placing the homework basket on an adjacent table silently reminds the child how to order his actions as he enters the classroom. With repeated practice, organization and orderliness become routine and habitual, at least regarding these first actions of the school day.

Graphic organizers work the same way. All they are really is your instructions and prompts built into the design of the page. They provide a structure and framework upon which your child can hang his thoughts. He can literally see how to organize his thinking. As your child puts down information in the same format over and over, the goal is for him to learn how to organize his thoughts that way automatically, as a matter of habit. Hopefully he will continue to maintain that order and structure in his thinking, even without the graphic organizer.

A table, flowchart, and writing form or template are visual aides for how to organize thoughts. Unlike verbal instruction that comes and goes and may vary slightly every time, graphic organizers provide the consistency that fulfills a need for repetition and the permanence that accommodates slow processing. They enable a child with limited working memory to hold onto ideas so he can manipulate them.

Don't be afraid to use graphic organizers as reliable teaching aides and learning supports.

Write your open-ended question at the top of your template. "What did you do this morning?" "Tell me about your walk. What did you see?"

These are theme statements, followed by prompts on how to respond. Your child's answers are the details. An example follows:

What did you do this morning? (Prompt your child to rephrase this as an opening statement.)

Tell me three people you saw and what you did with each one.

1.

2.

3.

How was your morning? Was it good, okay, or not so good?

Sample answer:

This is what I did this morning.

I saw Miss Kristen for speech. I said a lot of words.

I saw Mr. Wulff for music. I played the drums.

I played Uno with Zack.

I had a good morning.

Put the written template in front of your child like a cue card. The purpose of the template is to give your child a structure to follow with more specific instructions on how to answer the opening open-ended question. He can either write his answers directly on it, or refer to it while giving you his answers verbally, with PECS cards, or with his AT device. He should have his "wh/how" chart in hand.

Customize your template to match the content of your child's day. If your child went on a field trip to the zoo in the morning, instead of listing three different teachers he saw, you might instruct him to tell you three different animals he saw.

You may also customize the template to provide more prompting if necessary. For example, if the prompt "Tell me three people you saw and what you did with each one," is still too open-ended for your child, substitute more specific "wh" questions.

1. Who did you see for speech? What were you doing at speech?

2. Who did you see for music? What were you doing at music?

3. Who did you play with after music? What game did you play?

If your child has trouble with the "wh" questions, you can move to fill-in-the-blank questions. If these are still too hard, try multiple choice. If he needs even more help, make one choice the correct answer, and the other a ridiculous choice, either because it's funny, clearly wrong, or uses words the child doesn't even know. For example, here is a template with a high level of prompting to answer the question, "What did you do this morning?"

This is what I did this _____ (morning or night).

1. I saw _____ (Miss Kristen or Luke) for speech.

   I _____ (ate or said) a lot of words.

2. Then I saw Mr. Wulff for _____ (music or skiing).

   I played the _____ (drums or French horn).

3. Then I saw _____ (Zack or Sponge Bob).

   We played _____ (Uno or Rugby).

I had a _____ (good, okay, or not so good) morning.

Making the evaluative statement at the end is often the most difficult step for a child. It requires him to recall and synthesize a lot of feelings he's had over time. If he recorded his feelings in happy or sad faces, he can translate the number of them into an evaluative statement. More happy faces than sad might translate to a "good" day. An equal number might be an "okay" day. More sad than happy faces might make the day, "not so good."

These templates prompt you to work on several important goals. They make your child practice organizing a logical answer to an open-ended question. By visually laying out the activities of the morning under the heading of what he did that morning, he gets a chance to literally see how to categorize details under themes, an important abstract thinking skill. By ending with an evaluative statement, you are teaching your child how to talk about feelings, and to think reflectively. "I felt mad." "Mama thanked me. She was happy." "It was a good day." "I liked it because…" Each time you make your child think about feelings and form opinions, you teach him how to create meaning. As he counts up the happy versus sad faces on his journal to evaluate his day, he learns to balance the good and bad. He learns how to emotionally process life, and develop perspective.

Summary: Helping your child build an inner world

So what is a child's inner world? It is his interior life. It includes his thoughts, feelings, and values. As you point out and celebrate your child's preferences, interests, abilities, and virtues as he demonstrates them throughout the day, and recollect them again in conversations, journaling, and reflection, you build your child's self-awareness. He starts forming memories and ideas about himself that form his self-image or identity.

As you help him tune into his emotions and identify them, he becomes aware of an inner world of thoughts and feelings.

That consciousness allows him some control over his emotion as it becomes an idea he can bring other ideas to bear upon and modulate, such as memories of past experience, alternative responses, and your loving interventions. With time and repetition, he learns to internalize and imitate your attitudes, coping strategies, and emotional reactions. His capacity to emotionally regulate himself grows with each new experience of successful coping.

As you affirm his ever greater efforts and ability to tolerate frustration, patience, perseverance, and self-control become part of his internal standard. As you celebrate positive accomplishments and review lessons learned, that internal standard grows along with a sense of values. He develops an idea of who he is, a self-concept that will form the basis of moral character. You create a habit of inner reflection where he learns to evaluate his actions against standards you set. His own internal standard thereby grows with each recollection.

That internal standard will become a powerful modulator of affect someday, and his actions and decisions will reflect it and filter through it. Emotions drive motivation which drive cognitive learning, but the converse is also true. Engaging that frontal lobe by thinking reflectively and against an internal standard is the basis of emotional regulation. Helping your child build a strong interior life will protect him against his own stormy passions and mood swings, and guide him to make decisions to live a purpose filled and meaningful life.

TEACHING YOUR CHILD HOW TO TUNE INTO OTHERS

If friendship and intimacy result from a sharing of inner worlds, your child must learn how to listen as well as tell. If the first goal is to help your child build an interior life, the second goal is to increase your child's desire and capacity to tune into the feelings and perspectives of others. Work on this second goal concomitantly with the first as most activities provide ample opportunity to do both. Children have varying degrees of inclination to attend to the needs and feelings of others. Perhaps some have a larger helping of mirror neurons than others, and naturally find more pleasure in helping and pleasing. For our children, you have to build that desire to tune into others. So make it worthwhile. Almost any activity you do together can be turned into an emotionally bonding experience if you're intentional about it.

Creating warm interaction in every activity

When you do daily chores and routines, work projects, play activities, outings, sports, and arts together, make it interactive, then highlight the mutual fun and enjoyment with your high affect and celebratory endings.

The great folding sock race: Expanded version

Almost any activity can be done interactively. Take folding the laundry.

To do it assembly-line fashion, your child could take articles out of the dryer one by one and hand them to you as you fold them and put them into piles. If you want to work on understanding possessives, make boxes labeled with each family member's name, and switch places. You take each piece of clothing out of the dryer, fold it, and hand it to him, saying, "That's Daddy's," or "That's Mama's," etc. and let him place it into the correct box.

To use a turn-taking framework, consider taking turns folding. Mama could say, "Fold something red (or big/small, a shirt/towel/pants or other type of laundry, or belonging to a certain family member)." The child would have to select something with that attribute, and then fold it (with help if needed). Then the child gets a turn to tell Mama what to get.

To use a competitive model, try having a race to see who can finish folding several pairs of socks together first (see "The great folding sock race" on p.175).

Think of Miller's categories of interaction, cooperation, turn taking, and competition. You can usually build one of these kinds of interactions into your activity. That's your framework.

As you and your child work or play interactively, put in the payoff, which is the warm looks, tones of voice, and gestures. When you put love and fun into your interactions, your child will tune into you to receive it. At that point, you can add in some teaching.

Introducing perspective taking into your child's daily life

Start teaching your child about perspective taking by simply pointing out the different preferences of other people. Make shopping for a birthday present for Daddy a fun game. Ask your child what Daddy likes to do or eat, and what color he likes to wear. Incorporate his ideas into your choice for a present, and coach Daddy to point out with delight those features your child selected. "Peter, this is my favorite color!" "How did you know I love this kind of cookies?"

You can also teach your child that tuning into the thinking and perspectives of others is rewarding because it's fun and interesting to see things differently and learn something new. When you go on a walk or an outing, stop once in a while if you see something interesting. Ask your child what he sees or hears, then point out what you did. Flip through colorful magazines together and take turns pointing out and cutting out pictures of things that make you happy, find funny, or like to do. You can make theme books of places you want to visit, foods you'd like to try, or favorite animals to find at the next trip to the zoo. You can label alternate pages with "Mama's favorite…" versus "Peter's favorite…" Take turns pointing to favorite pictures in the family photo album, and telling stories you recall about them.

Using games and stories to practice perspective taking

For more advanced thinkers, there are some classic games that make perspective taking fun. Look up at clouds together and take turns sharing what animal or other shape each person identifies. Make a random squiggle, and then have each person draw a picture incorporating it. Compare what possibilities each person saw in the squiggle. Gutstein (2000, p.138) offers other fun games on perspective taking such as interpreting inkblots and making up silly captions to magazine pictures together.

After reading a story together, help your child process what happened to the character using a template like the one below:

What is the story about? Say, "The story is about _____ (who)."

1. Tell me the beginning (setting).

2. Tell me the middle (the problem).

3. Tell me the ending (solution).

How did the main character feel? Who did you like or not like and why?

The story is about Goldilocks and the three bears.

1. The three bears went out for a walk.

2. Goldilocks came into their house. She ate their porridge, sat in their chairs, and slept in their beds.

3. The bears saw her sleeping in the bed. She woke up and ran away. The three bears were mad.

Goldilocks was scared. She did not ask first. That was bad.

Here's another sample answer about another familiar story:

The story is about three little pigs.

1. Three pigs were building houses.

2. A wolf was trying to blow them down. He wanted to eat the pigs.

3. He could not blow down the brick house.

The pigs were scared. The wolf was bad. I don't like the wolf.

The evaluative questions that come last make your child practice thinking about the feelings of others. Repeated practice at this is a first step in teaching your child empathy. Asking your child how he feels about other characters is a step even more abstract than empathy, as he has to judge a character's actions against an internal standard.

If your child needs more help to understand fiction, create templates that provide more prompting in the form of questions presented, from open-ended to "wh" to fill-in-the-blank to multiple choice (see pp.253, 281–2). The story below describes Peter's first encounter with the three bears:

"Peter and the three bears"

First Peter and I read a picture book version of Goldilocks and the Three Bears together straight through. I took out Peter's stuffed animals, a doll, and props, and we acted it out the second time. Peter played the part of Little Bear, so he got to act "happy" when going out on a walk with Mama and Papa Bear, "mad" when he discovered his porridge was all eaten up, "sad" when he saw his broken chair, and "surprised" when he saw Goldilocks sleeping in his bed. He tried hard to act out all the emotions, showing his teeth in a contrived grin for "happy," grimacing for "mad," rubbing his eyes for "sad," and widening his eyes for "surprised." Though he only managed to hold each expression fleetingly, he acted out each emotion appropriately.

Later at night during his usual bedtime car ride, we talked about the story of The Three Bears. He required little prompting to answer my fill-in-the-blanks questions about the story. But I was floored with how he answered my questions about how Little Bear felt—"Happy," about the walk, "mad" about the porridge, "sad" about the chair, and "surprised" about seeing Goldilocks in his bed. He nailed every one!

The next morning, we reviewed by reading the story through and acting out the different parts in the mirror. Then I made a table of "wh" questions. I picked four key pages from the storybook that basically captured the beginning, middle, and end of the storyline, and asked Peter various "wh" questions about each page. I recorded the answers he gave me on his Vantage on the chart. When we finished all the questions, this is what the filled out chart looked like:

Who?	What…doing?	Where?	Why? Or How… feeling?
Three bears	are walking	in the forest.	
The girl	is eating porridge	in the house	because she is hungry.
The girl	is breaking it and sitting	in the chair.	
Three bears	are looking at her	in the bed.	They are mad. She is scared.

Finally, I prompted Peter through open-ended questions. I gave him the chart and said, "Tell me the story of The Three Bears, Peter." I opened the book to each of the four pages and said, "Tell me

> *about this page." Then I prompted him to read the corresponding sentence he'd constructed by filling out the "wh" table. Whenever he mentioned an emotion like "hungry," "mad," and "scared," I held up the mirror to him and both of us acted out the emotion together. Peter acted out and retold the entire story of The Three Bears, and even finished saying, "The end!"*

Working on theory of mind

Sussman (2006, pp.79–84) explains how to use happenings in real life and stories in books to develop your child's theory of mind. Help your child understand different points of view: "You like oranges, but Daddy doesn't like oranges. If you put an orange in his lunchbox, he'll be sad."

Help your child understand different perceptions. Our kids frequently don't realize that other people don't automatically see or know what they do. Don't automatically adjust; protest! "I can't see the page. Turn the book so I can see the picture too!"

Point out the difference between how a person may feel on the inside and act on the outside by helping him understand hidden feelings. "Aunty said not to bother, but it's such a hot day, I think she really wants a drink. Let's get one for her."

Show him that people may have false beliefs because of what they don't know. "Let's hide, so when Daddy walks in he'll think we're not here. Then we can jump out and surprise him!"

If the intricacies of teaching theory of mind seem overwhelming, let it go for now. Give your child time to develop the cognitive capacities to access your teaching. For children naturally gifted with the capacity for high levels of abstract thinking, there are some great resources. Greenspan and Wieder (1998) have chapters on how to teach multicausal, triangular, gray zone (relative), and reflective thinking. Greenspan and Greenspan (2010) wrote an entire book to guide your child through these upper levels. Gutstein (2000, 2002b) and Winner (2005, 2007) give outstanding specific exercises for individuals and groups to improve social thinking, including perspective taking, theory of mind, and development of group identity and friendships.

Let your child set the pace

The key to successful social teaching is to find whatever level your child is at, and stay there as long as it takes. Don't get so goal driven that your play sessions feel like drilling sessions where you fire off one challenge after another. When you feel like you're doing all the work of the interaction, and forcibly pulling your child out of withdrawal, sometimes you're working at too high a level. It's better to introduce higher level activities more gradually, as your child develops that broad base of cognitive development to support it. Do probe with little forays into higher level activities as your child warms up. Keep them fun and brief initially. Your child is your best teacher. Look for his feedback. The smiles, happy chuckles, and natural eye contact with that joyful gleam and sparkle tell you that you're on the right track. As your child develops, doing more higher level activities for longer periods will feel natural, as what you do matches his ability.

Do work with your child intentionally. Work through the stages of emotional responding, circles of interaction, and solving problems together. You bond as together you play games, explore the inner world of ideas and imagination through pretend, explore the outside world through books and outings, and work to create something worthwhile, whether it be a garden, new game, or improvised piece of music on the piano. Your child will learn that tuning into you results in pleasurable fun interactions, learning and seeing interesting new things, and the joy of collaboration and co-creation. Talk about how his actions make you feel. Gradually he will learn to care about what you are thinking and feeling because making you happy makes him happy. He will tune into you because he loves you.

That's not to say this kind of work on social and emotional development will be all fun. Expect to overshoot once in a while. You have to take risks and make mistakes to learn and grow. It's true that every fun interaction with you strengthens that association of relationship with pleasure. But it's also true that every time you push your child to do a bit more while keeping it rewarding in the end, you stretch his capacity to wait and to work. If you push a bit too hard or for whatever reason the child has a meltdown, ride it out with him. With your calm and reassuring presence, you teach him to accept and tolerate his big emotions. As Greenspan puts it, "The only mistake you can make is not to try" (Greenspan and Wieder 1998).

CREATING JOURNAL STORIES TOGETHER

It's fun to make books for your child about memorable outings and events in his life. Create books that match the cognitive developmental level of your child. Although now the stories I record for Peter are mostly text with a few line drawings, I didn't start out writing them that way. Children progress from the concrete to the representational to the abstract. I started out making books in which each page was mostly filled with either a souvenir or photo taped to it, and only a short line of text. I progressed to making line drawing picture books with a sentence or two for each drawing. Books full of tangibles and visuals still hold the most interest for my child. Think scrapbook, but simple and clear. Start out by limiting your visual images and related thoughts to one of each per page to reduce visual processing demands and focus the child's attention.

Say you're making a book about a trip to Disneyland. Collect souvenirs such as the stuffed Eeyore toy you bought, brochure/maps you used together, the stubs of the tickets he handled, and the candy wrapper off of his Mickey Mouse lollipop. Look at the photos you took together and take turns pointing out items of interest. "Frontload" memories of your trip by enjoying all these tangible memoirs together. Then write a personal story about the trip, writing one line of text at the bottom of each page. Leave most of the page blank to make room for each visual memento. Lay out your souvenirs and photos, and have your child select and tape in the corresponding one as you read each line of text. Make it a game. Limit your field of choices to as few as your child needs to keep this activity fun and successful. Let your child actively participate in this storytelling/recollection as much as possible.

After you complete the book, you can do it a second time in the opposite way—show your child each page illustrated with a souvenir, photo, or picture, and have him read the text. As a more advanced variation, cover the text, and have your child retell the story as he makes comments about each page. You might prompt him with "wh" questions like "What happened?" "What color?" "What did you see/do/eat?" "How many?" "Who's that?" Add easier questions to ease the effort required, like fill-in-the-blank or yes/no questions, or take turns making comments. Write down each person's answers and comments. Finish with some evaluative statements, like what each of you liked or didn't like the most. Practice the distinction between theme statements and details by beginning your story with a big picture statement like "This story is about our trip to Disneyland." Then re-read the story you created together.

But take your time. As always, take your lead from your child in terms of content and timing. Follow your child's interests in terms of what rides, characters, photos, and souvenirs you talk about most and what questions to ask when you need to prompt. You don't have to cover every photo or souvenir in one sitting (or at all). Each time you read the story, you may be changing it each time, adding more comments to your blank or partially filled pages. Your book can grow with each retelling, and your single line texts may turn into paragraphs. Your child can read it differently each time as well, selecting different pictures and comments to talk about. I let Peter add to the "artwork" as well. He often helps color in the pictures I draw. Sometimes he adds happy or sad faces to the text, depending on if he liked or didn't like what it describes. He uses colors sometimes to highlight texts he feels strongly about, yellow for happy, red for mad, and blue for sad. "We waited too long!" might get underlined in red. "Peter was driving the little car," might get highlighted with a yellow happy face.

Creating personal stories like this gives your child lots of practice with the higher cognitive skills discussed earlier, such as theme/details, talking about emotions and feelings, using time/space concepts, and sequencing. You can practice comparisons, degrees of feeling, cause and effect, and other concepts too depending on the questions you ask and the comments you make. "Which train was bigger, the Casey Junior or Grand Canyon train?" (comparisons). "What was more fun for you, the merry go round or the roller coaster? I liked the merry go round, but the roller coaster was really exciting!" (degrees of feeling). "Look what happened to Luke! Why did he get all wet?" (because he sat in front—cause and effect). "Remember the ice cream? The line was really long. We waited a long time. I didn't like that. How about you?" (time concepts). "Let's see. Remember when we were at the carousel? Luke wanted to go to 'It's a Small World' next, but you wanted to drive the cars. Do you remember why we went to 'Small World' first?" (because it was closer—space concepts and comparisons).

In real life I would not ask as many questions in a row. It's better to observe your child, give him plenty of time to come up with his own comments, and make more comments on the visuals he appears more interested in, throwing in questions only occasionally.

The most important goal is for your child to learn the fun of sharing perspectives and creating something together with you. He learns to reflect upon his own life, build happy memories, and develop a self-concept by identifying his likes and dislikes, interests, and feelings. When you write down the stories about when he is helpful, brave, and caring, he develops values. When you write down the stories about the challenging or difficult experiences he survives, he learns perspective. As you express delight and humor pointing out what made you happy, sad, or mad, liked and didn't like in the pictures and souvenirs, he learns that your reactions are interesting and fun. He tunes into you because he enjoys it. You are teaching him to truly listen to you. This is a critical step toward true conversation.

SOCIAL AND EMOTIONAL DEVELOPMENT: IT'S ALL ABOUT CONVERSATION

What is a conversation?[5] It is not just about taking turns talking. The critical step is to actually tune into and listen to what your conversation partner is saying. Your reply has to logically connect to what you just heard for the conversation to make any sense.

Sussman offers a practical rubric for parents to help their children learn this process. Her books *More Than Words* (1999) followed by *Talkability* (2006) are beautifully laid out "how to" manuals for parents to work on communication skills with their children, organized by developmental level. A good strategy is to study the sections applicable to your child's current level, and read on as your child progresses. Here we will review her general principles that apply to every level.

Staying in the conversation: The parent's turn

Sussman's (2006, p.52) rubric *for the parent's turn* in the conversation is to *include, interpret, introduce,* and *insist* (see p.127). Include your child's interests, ideas, and words in your play and conversation as the "hook" to motivate engagement. Interpret the way you think he meant it. Introduce a new idea by talking about past memories or future plans, feelings, and beliefs, adding details and explanations, making comparisons, or imagining and pretending (Sussman 2006, p.103). Insist on a logical reply. You can insist playfully, but be persistent. Children are good at sizing up your fortitude—regardless of your past history with your child,

---

5   Technically, a conversation entails at least 60 percent commenting and no more than 40 percent answering questions. I use the term "conversation" here in the more colloquial sense of a back-and-forth exchange.

if you start making a habit of being persistent, eventually he will put in more effort as he learns it takes more effort to resist you than comply.

Staying in the conversation: Helping your child with his turn

For the child's turn in the conversation, Sussman (2006, p.87) gives an excellent *order of prompts or cues* from the least to most help in assisting your child in his response. The goal is to only provide as much scaffolding (prompting, cueing) as is necessary, and to withdraw it systematically to work toward independence. Ask a question (an open-ended question like "what happened?" or a "how" or "why" question, and if that's too hard, a closed "wh" question such as who, where and when), ask an easier question to answer (like a fill-in-the-blank question, yes/no, or multiple choice), give a hint or make a suggestion, and finally tell your child what to say.

Some children may need additional prompting such as signing, shaping your mouth to form the initial sound of the first word(s), giving the initial sounds of each word, or saying all but the last word as a fill-in-the-blank exercise. You can facilitate a longer and more pleasurable and productive conversation with your child if you have the time to provide all of his accommodations, such as paper and pencil, keyboard, or AT device, and memory aides (journal notes, photos, and souvenirs). Adjust the level of cueing that you start with to your child's level or just one order higher to prevent frustration.

Keep the rally going

For children with advanced cognitive skills and perspective taking ability, Gutstein (2000, p.154) describes an ingenious game to practice the rules of conversation. He likens conversation to a game of tennis. Player One serves by introducing a topic. He wins a point if he asks something the other player is interested in. Player Two answers. He gets a point if he then tells and asks something the other player is interested in. Players win as a team if they manage to rally back and forth for, say, five minutes. Modifications of the game include "conversational volleys" in which the game ends if one of the players makes a comment off the original topic. To incorporate a concept of Winner's (2007, p.78), if the referee knows the players well, he can give extra points for implementing what she calls a good "social fake." This is when a player is known to have no interest in a particular topic, but feigns interest well in order to be polite and stay emotionally connected to the other player.

Affect is the reason

Ultimately, no matter how much skill practice creates, there has to be that desire for emotional connectedness. You must establish that connection between pleasure and interaction, emotional gratification and relationship. It begins with developing the capacity of the child to respond emotionally to the parent's overtures, and grows with each level of ability to engage joyfully in circles of interaction, and then to coordinate, anticipate, initiate, transform and co-create new interactions. As the child learns the joy of interaction, he learns to tune into his play partner, and eventually enjoy the perspectives of other people. He learns how to listen to the perspectives of others, even seek them out, and then impact them. In other words, all the steps we've been discussing are necessary for making true conversation. Conversation at its best is a genuine meeting of minds, and a sharing of souls. Social and emotional development is all about conversation.

What makes you and I as neurotypical, social beings want to talk? Sometimes we talk to share information about a subject of mutual interest or knowledge. But emotional bonding occurs primarily when we talk about events, people, and ideas that impact our emotions, that evoke feelings we share with conversation partners who may increase our joy or decrease our sorrow with their responses. When I ask you how your day went, I don't want you to give a report listing all the events on your schedule that day. I expect you to select those happenings that impacted your emotions, the high points and low points. In talking about those moments, you get to relive and enjoy again the happy moments, and call upon me to help support you and help you process your difficulties (therapists call this *emotional coregulation*).

This is not all beyond our children's reach. Broaden the range of your child's emotions by creating play scenarios with a variety of emotional themes, from aggression to nurturing, anger, fear, excitement, and pleasure. Stretch your child's capacity to tolerate emotion by allowing him opportunities to practice emotional regulation. Don't give in at the slightest sign of distress; instead challenge your child to one more minute of waiting, work, or effort with a big reward in sight. Don't be afraid to walk that line between challenge and success. That's how your child makes progress. Tune your child into identifying his own feelings, and teach him healthy self-talk to accept mistakes, balance the bad with the good, and look for the positive. Teach him to forgive. Teach him to be grateful. Highlight all the times he shows fortitude, helpfulness, patience, kindness, and hard work. Retell the story of your child's life to him each night in a daily recollection, in which he has the opportunity to reflect on the meaning of his daily life events. That's how your child will build a strong interior life, a sense of values and positive self-concept.

Love gives it meaning

Our children may not be able to converse fluently with us about their joys, but they may brighten with happy squeals and flaps when we walk through the door. They may not be able to tell us their sorrows, but may burst into tears when they see us after a tough day of holding it all together. Peter may not understand all my joys and sorrows, but he increases my joy when he spontaneously pulls my head down to give me a kiss. He decreases my sorrows when I see him quickly hand his prized cookie or chip to my crying grandson. Our children are beautiful. We only need the eyes to see it.

> Do everything for Love. Thus there will be no little things: everything will be big. Perseverance in little things for Love is heroism. (St. Josemaria Escriva 1981, v.813)

Chapter **14**

Learning to Learn, It's a Beautiful Journey

I was concerned as I dropped off Peter one morning. I had pushed him pretty hard at a piano lesson, and then declined his request for a sixth piece of bacon at breakfast. He looked frustrated and on the verge of hitting when I handed him over to his tutor, Belinda. "Mama said no more bacon for now, but we'll take it in to work with us. If you like, we can work for it," she told him.

I needn't have worried. When I returned a few hours later, Peter was all smiles. Only half the bacon was gone. He had happily worked the whole several hour session for half a slice of bacon!

Peter doesn't need much extrinsic reinforcement to do the work of learning, because at this point learning isn't so much work as it is a joy. He truly loves to learn. It's actually regulating for him. There have been times he's been upset over reflux pain, and we give him a choice of activities to do while waiting for his medicine to work. He generally picks "work." Peter has found that if he concentrates on learning, he's distracted from the pain. He likes to work through it.

How do you get a child to want to learn? How do you teach learning skills, so that a child learns how to learn?

HOW TO HELP YOUR CHILD THROUGH THE LEARNING PROCESS

Learning is fun when you use appealing materials, work your lessons around your child's interests, and make it relevant by engineering opportunities for your child to apply what he learns in real life. Throw in some fun rewards and lots of warm encouragement, and you might think you have a recipe for success. But sometimes, learning is hard. Not every lesson can be presented in such an interesting way that the child feels motivated to put in the hard effort to learn it.

Ultimately, the key ingredient to motivate your child to learn is to enable him to be successful. Our children require a lot of support to learn. There are many steps in the learning process. A child may experience difficulty at any one step or multiple steps along the way.

Addressing your child's physical and sensory needs

Before your child can learn anything, he has to be calm and regulated, so always start with Stage One goals, and take care of those preliminary essentials. Your tools are *observation, context,* and *history* to attune to the needs of your child. *Sensory integration* and *exercise breaks, sensory accommodations,* and *environmental adaptations* may be helpful. It may be as simple as giving your child a good breakfast and checking to find out the last time he went to the bathroom. Many parents pass a *communication book* between home and other places like school and afterschool programs to keep such data as well as notes on what was done that period for later conversations.

Allowing your child to emotionally attune to you

Next your child needs to notice you. Don't be in a hurry to rush to the material you want to teach. Think Stage Two goals, and take a moment to motivate your child to tune into you. Do you learn better or more from someone you like or someone you're mad at or afraid of? Have you ever frozen in front of a particularly critical or negative teacher? This is what psychologists call, the "affective filter." Your emotional reaction to the teacher filters out what you can learn from her. So make the relationship work in your favor instead, and take the time to greet and interact with the child. Establishing that *affective bond* is the purpose of the polite niceties we begin most social interactions with. With your child that might look like a few affectionate words, and maybe a little tickle exchange or "Gotcha!" game with sneaky fingers.

Getting your child's attention by reducing environmental and internal distractions and using motivational methods

Then your child needs to pay attention. The best way to get a child's attention is to *include his interests*. Use all the motivational tools covered in Chapter 7, including using *appealing materials, intrinsic and extrinsic reinforcement*, and *shared control*. Make use of visuals like *choice boards* and *visual schedules* to allow your child to negotiate. Show him the reward he is working for to raise motivation, and ease him into initiating his work by starting with easier content till he warms up. Remove environmental distractions. Train his attention by teaching him how to get into "learning readiness mode" such as a "Three–Two–One" countdown, and how to inhibit his stims (for a refresher of DRI, DRA, DRO, and using positive reinforcement for increasing time intervals versus the *shrinking reinforcer method*, see pp.314–6). For your child, this might mean putting him in a quiet, uncluttered room with his back to any windows, allowing him to order a few learning activities on his visual schedule, choose a sensory or exercise break to put at the end, and doing a countdown.

Getting information into working memory by accommodating auditory and visual processing deficits

The next step is to get information into the brain. In psychology lingo, that's called putting stimuli into working memory. The working memory capacity of a child may be quite limited. Think of a juggler juggling several balls in the air—he can only juggle so many at once. If a child has a very limited working memory, you can help him keep more balls in the air by *breaking problems into little chunks or steps* and by providing *visual and auditory supports*. Say you have a child with auditory processing disorder trying to learn what two dimes and three pennies equals. He has to remember what a dime is, what a penny is, how many of each there are, and the operation he has to perform. Plus he has to decipher all the words you just said and make meaning out of all those sounds. That might be too many balls to juggle.

Help input the information more effectively into his working memory by bypassing the auditory processing and language deficits, and writing down the problem in symbols. Further help him by breaking the problem into steps, and having him first figure out the value of two dimes, then the value of three pennies, and then put them together.

If your child has a visual processing deficit and struggles to decipher written symbols, provide auditory supports by highlighting important information by repeating it, "Remember that's two dimes and three pennies." You can also help him hold onto his correct responses along the way as he's processing the problem. If he says, "Let's see, two dimes is twenty," you might repeat "Twenty." Then he might say, "Three pennies is three," and you might say, "Three." If he seems lost, after an adequate pause to give him time to solve the problem independently, support his working memory, and say, "So twenty plus three makes…" In doing so you help him hold twenty and three in his working memory so he has another chance to manipulate them into a sum.

Using multisensory teaching methods and tangibles to support processing

Multimodal teaching may also facilitate the next step in learning, which is processing the information. In our math problem example, this would be the step of the actual learning of the addition operation. Your tools to help with processing are the principles of *breaking down problems* into small enough steps to be doable for your child, moving up from the *concrete to representational to the symbolic* in steps, and using a multimodal approach.

What this might look like in our example above is by writing "2 dimes=?" and having him exchange each dime for a stack of ten cents, counting the cents, and then writing "20" in place of the question mark. He might do the same for three cents, then put the two piles together as you point to the "+" sign, and finally add up all the cents. You could repeat the addition operation of 20+3 with various other small objects as well, and if necessary spend a lot more time on the concept of grouping objects into tens before you add back the layer of coin identification. In this example, you are breaking up the problem into steps, making use of concrete tangibles, and using spoken, visual, and tactile teaching modalities.

Keeping your child balanced on that edge between challenge and success: Fading prompts systematically except for essential accommodations

The key principle to motivate your child to do this hard work of learning is to keep him feeling successful. That's why in DTT you provide immediate feedback at every step. If you adjust the level of support and size of each step up or down according to your child's feedback, you can keep him balanced on the edge of challenge and success where learning takes place. Remember, "What fires together, wires together." It's important to correct your child's mistakes quickly, and increase your level of prompting or decrease the level of difficulty so that your child practices the correct responses repeatedly. As your child learns a new concept, *fade your supports systematically* to give him the opportunity to develop as much independence as possible, leaving in place only essential accommodations. In our math example, your child might be able to fade use of the tangibles, but always need to write down the problem.

The principles of multimodal teaching, breaking tasks into little steps, and fading supports systematically applies to all kinds of learning. A *task analysis* breaks down functional skills like cooking, making a bed, and getting dressed into steps which can be taught systematically by *forward or backchaining* (see p.359). You can use forward and backchaining to teach your child the steps of a functional skill or chore, a game, or math problem and follow the same *order of prompts* (physical, demonstration, gestural, verbal) to get through each step.

Use it or lose it: The importance of generalization

No matter how well a child learns something in a teaching setting, for the learning to go into long-term memory, the concept must be *generalized.* In other words, "Use it or lose it." Your child needs to use the language and math he learns at the desktop in real life, solving real life problems. Once he sees how the learning is relevant and meaningful to him, it has a chance of going into long-term storage. Every time Mom gives him two crackers, Dad gives him three more, and he adds them up to five, he's consolidating that math fact. When he and his little brother put in the cents they've earned doing chores to see if they can buy a five-cent sundae from you to share, they consolidate their math even more.

Provide multimodal supports for retrieval

Even after a child has knowledge he's learned and stored, he may still need your help retrieving and expressing it. Your tools are the same principles of providing *multimodal support* and *scaffolding*, providing the minimum assistance necessary for your child to be successful and stay motivated. For the child with speech dyspraxia, word retrieval may be supported by offering a choice of several PECS cards, written *word menus* you scribble down on a piece of paper, or an AT device. If you've been eclectic and flexible in your teaching, your child will find some way, through the spoken, signed, written, or electronic word, to communicate in all kinds of situations.

HOW TO TEACH LEARNING SKILLS

Ultimately, you want your child to learn how to learn on his own. This is a slow process. Begin by developing in him a love for learning. Go for the twinkle in his eye, as you plan how challenging you're going to make that next step you teach, and how much support you're going to give. When you get the balance just right, your child will show you in his desire to work and need for decreasing amounts of extrinsic reinforcement. Read your child's responses to pace your teaching according to his speed of processing. Inject your warmth, enthusiasm, and encouragement. Your child will develop a taste for success and sense of pride in mastering concepts. Every successful teaching session feeds that addiction for learning, so try to end each one on a positive note.

Accommodating sensory needs, inhibiting stims, and initiating learning readiness

Learning independently requires many skills. Exercise your child's ability to inhibit distracting stimming by demanding it incrementally and intentionally in more settings, such as work sessions, doing chores and routines, during play sessions, and outings to quiet public places like church, or the library. Fade your prompts on his "Three–Two–One" countdown (see p.101) so he learns how to pay attention whenever you begin a play or work session with just a look from you or perhaps a *hand signal* like holding up three fingers. The goal is for him to learn to focus his own attention at the start of every endeavor. Teach your child how to access his own sensory accommodations such as noise cancellation headphones, or closing the door when he begins work.

Developing self-monitoring skills

Teach your child to make choices and set up his own visual schedule, and check off boxes or put his word/icon labels of each activity in an "All done" envelope so he learns to monitor his own work completion. This is the beginning of *self-monitoring skills*. Organize his work in consecutive drawers or file folders so the environmental set-up suggests and reminds him of the next step. You can use such a set-up to create an *independent work station* (see p.90). That may be your child's first step toward learning how to study on his own. Create worksheet exercises in which the goal is to find and correct mistakes you include intentionally, so your child learns how to *check his work*.

Seeking information and using references

Encourage your child to *write things down* to support his own working memory. Teach him to use *references* by constantly referring him to his PECS book or AT device so he'll learn to seek it out and use it independently. Teach him to refer back to his own completed work as well, such as pointing out where he's previously spelled out a word he's now looking for. Teach him how to *seek information* with "who," "what," and "where" games, and look for opportunities to generalize that skill in getting what he wants in daily life.

Encouraging initiation

Most of all, reward his spontaneous imitations and initiations with your encouragement and attention. *Wait* long enough to give him time to process and explore on his own, but if he seems to be forgetting his original intention, assist him in shaping his actions into something purposeful and rewarding.

For example, once Peter and I were setting the table together. I put down a napkin, and he placed a fork upon it at each place at the table. The phone rang, and when I came back, Peter had placed many napkins down on the table with forks on each one. They were bunched up in the middle of the table, but he had taken the initiative to complete the table setting on his own. Of course I praised him warmly. Rather than undoing his work, we incorporated it in our procedure by laying the plates next and then having him spot which plates were missing a napkin and fork and taking them from the supply he'd already created in the middle of the table.

The best way to reward a child's initiative is to *incorporate his ideas.*

REFLECTIONS ON THE PROCESS
Stepping back to encourage independence

Stepping back to wait and accepting calculated risks to allow your child to learn by making mistakes is hard. Sometimes, all that's required is patience. I'm teaching Peter how to change batteries on his flashlight and headphones by just patiently waiting as he puts them in with the wrong orientation, and uses *trial and error* to keep switching them around until his equipment works. Sometimes the calculated risk is a bit more annoying to accept, such as when he wastes Gatorade powder by putting a ton in his glass of water, and then realizes it's undrinkable, and starts all over putting in a bit less. Sometimes accepting the risk calmly may qualify you for sainthood, such as letting your child experience the consequences of not getting to the bathroom in time, to teach him to tune into his body signals. At those times, just remember that one lesson you have many opportunities to teach is to accept mistakes graciously as a part of life.

It's a beautiful journey

It's not easy to help a child learn how to learn, but with time and patience you can encourage your child to imitate, initiate, and explore. It's a worthwhile goal to be intentional about teaching your child learning skills. You are teaching a child self-awareness when you teach him how to access his own sensory accommodations and check his work for mistakes. You're teaching him how to set goals when he makes choices on his visual schedule. He learns to be proactive as he accesses his references and supports. He learns perseverance as he monitors his own work completion in his independent work station, and self-control as he learns to focus his attention and inhibit his stims. Your child learns how to access and build a support system as you wait for and direct him to seek information from you and others. As you keep him on that edge between challenge and success, you stretch his tolerance for frustration and improve his capacity for delayed gratification. These qualities are his future keys to success.

A long-term study on attributes of success

The Frostig Center, a school for children with learning disabilities in Pasadena, California, conducted a 20-year longitudinal study on children with learning disabilities, normal intelligence, and no sensory deficits or emotional disturbances (Raskind, Goldberg and Higgins 2003). They discovered six qualities that were correlated with future success, as assessed by a variety of psychosocial measures. They are "self-awareness" (knowing what you need, building on your strengths, and making provisions and accommodations for your weaknesses), "goal setting" (planning), "proactivity" (doing what you plan and promise and getting what you need), "perseverance" (fortitude), "building and accessing support systems" (asking for and getting help), and "emotional coping strategies" (developing patience and a positive attitude).

These study results are being applied in classrooms across the country. In order to explicitly teach and encourage the development of these attributes various strategies are being employed. Some teachers put these qualities on laminated "keys for success" and highlight them by presenting them to students who display these qualities or point them out in others or characters in literature and history. At our kids' level, you might consider making laminated stars or keys with simpler labels like "I know what I need," "Good planning," "I'm a doer," "Good worker," and "Good asking." Hand your child a star when he acts like one, and celebrate!

Chapter 15

Challenging Behaviors

We were late to swim class. I parked the car, got out, and opened the car door. "Come on, Peter, time to go!" I tried to sound cheerful and confident, but getting Peter dressed for swimming and out of the house had already been a slow and sluggish process. He looked at me, but didn't move. Peter usually enjoyed swimming. "Come on Peter. It's a beautiful day for swimming, and Miss Gabby is waiting!" Peter looked down at his feet and slapped his hands down hard on his lap. "You may not feel like swimming right now, but you'll feel better once you're moving. Let me help you." I held out my hand. "Move your feet over here, and take my hand. That's right. This foot down, then the other. That's it. Okay. Now you grab this (handle on the swim bag), and I'll grab that (the other handle). Good! Let's walk!" I closed the door, and off we went. "Right, right, right, left, right!" After a jerky start, Peter got into the rhythm of walking to my chant. It wasn't long before I heard him whispering softly along "Right, right, right, left, right." I stole a glance at him out of the corner of my eye, and smiled. He caught my glance and smiled back, as we continued our march to swim class.

Many books include extensive sections about remediating maladaptive behaviors. You can find many good suggestions in Greenspan and Wieder's (2006) book, *Engaging Autism*, and Bryna Siegel's (2003) book, *Helping Children with Autism Learn. Teaching Activities for Autistic Children* by Eric Schopler *et al.* (1983) details behavior management strategies for a wide range of specific problem behaviors, including spitting, slapping, head banging, perseverative loud noises, biting, and screaming. The purpose of this chapter is not to comprehensively cover every challenging behavior, but to help you understand your child, and offer some helpful strategies to deal with some of the more common behavioral problems stemming from neurological differences due to autism.

THE NEUROLOGICAL BASIS OF SOME CHALLENGING BEHAVIORS

Our children have a plethora of challenging behaviors. Many have a neurological basis such as sensory integration and basal ganglia issues, inattention and distractibility, obsessions and compulsions, anxiety disorder, cognitive limitations, and frustration from an inability to communicate. But my child is also slowly developing a sense of himself as a separate person, with his own desires. Emerging is a realization that those desires sometimes differ from what other people want him to do. So along with the challenges of autism, we are now also dealing with the opposition that typically develops at age two. How do you recognize and deal with all these variables?

The opening story to this chapter illustrates how what may look like disobedience or defiance at first may actually be due to a neurological issue related to autism. I knew Peter usually liked swimming, and I knew he had been moving sluggishly earlier. So I guessed the problem was not with the prospect of swimming, but possibly "basal ganglia" issues. Perhaps he was frustrated with being hurried when he couldn't get his body to move. Therefore, I broke up getting out of the car into small, easy steps with short, simple words and gestures, called "action-oriented directions." Chanting helped create a rhythm to pace Peter along. Grabbing the other handle on the swimbag gave Peter a physical marker to follow as we walked to the pool, and made it more fun because we were doing it together. But I didn't know if I had guessed right until I tried the solution and it worked.

There are plenty of times when I don't guess right, and Peter continues or escalates his protest. (We cover the more extreme escalations in our next chapter on self-injury and aggression.) For now, say your child is protesting, but still able to negotiate. What's a parent to do?

My first suggestion is to take a few moments to reflect. That moment of recollection helps you to be more objective. Sometimes we personalize our child's behavior and believe he must be thinking, "How can I make life difficult for Mom right now, and drive her as crazy as possible?" The reality is our kids don't have the perspective taking and social thinking capacity to scheme like that. Their behavior is their best attempt to communicate or satisfy an unmet need.

When you don't understand why your child is misbehaving or you've guessed wrong, my suggestion is to go back to basics. Try to figure out what the problem is from the child's point of view, and respond accordingly. What is my child's behavior communicating? What is my child trying to say? Why is he upset? The first step toward developing an effective strategy to change challenging behaviors is to attune to your child.

FUNCTIONAL BEHAVIORAL ANALYSIS

Behavioral therapists call this kind of assessment a functional analysis because the goal is to determine the function or goal of the problem behavior. If you can determine the goal, you can help the child learn alternative, more appropriate or adaptive ways to meet his goal. Another name for functional analysis is an ABC assessment for antecedent, behavior, and consequence. The antecedent is what happened prior to the behavior and what may have triggered or precipitated it or give you clues as to the cause. A simplified list of causes includes sensory needs, self-stimulation, trying to get some preferred tangible, or trying to escape from a nonpreferred activity. The behavior is the problem or target behavior you want to change. The consequence is what happened after the behavior, and how you can reshape your response to teach the child a more adaptive or appropriate substitute behavior.

Say a child is going out the kitchen door to go on a bike ride. He opens the door, suddenly stops, and starts flapping and squealing. His little brother squeezes by and gets hit on the head. What do you do? The problem behavior in this case is primarily the hitting. The cause of the hitting might be accidental, incidental to the flapping. It might be a general expression of frustration because he can't find the words fast enough to tell you what he wants. Plus along comes little brother squeezing past and thereby making him feel more hurried and frustrated. The sudden stopping and stimming may be primary, just due to an automatic unknown need of the body to stim, or it might be due to something else. A secondary cause includes anticipation of impending stressful sensory bombardment, the bright light outside. Another might be suddenly spying a favorite edible (say a cherry) left on the kitchen table and not knowing how to ask for it, or not really wanting to go bike riding and not knowing how to protest it.

Address the hitting. You need to create a space between hitting and getting his needs met, so he doesn't learn that one leads to another. Hold your child's hands and say, "Watch your hands. Look at your brother. It hurt when you hit him. Say, 'Sorry.'" (You might also say something to his little brother about not squeezing past.)[1] Then go with your best guess. "Are you worried about the bright light outside? Say, 'too bright.'" After he says "Too bright," get his sunglasses and put them on. If you guessed right, he'll go right out the door. If not, explore the other possibilities and teach him to communicate, "I want cherry" or "No bike riding." By considering all the possible causes, you have a better chance of providing a helpful response that teaches your child an alternative behavior to use next time.

Sometimes the cause of a problem behavior is not as simple as a sensory need or communication problem. What follows are some of the behavioral and relationship-based strategies that have been found to be helpful when challenging behaviors are caused by neurological problems associated with autism. We also talk about frustration with work, and strategies to increase cooperation, as this is such a common problem. Let's start with a discussion of underlying medical issues. These may not be directly related to autism, but unveiling them is most definitely more of a challenge because of the communication difficulties due to autism.

UNDERLYING MEDICAL ISSUES: REVEALING THE CULPRIT

The need to consider the possibility of an unrecognized medical problem is a point worth emphasizing. When Peter was a toddler, he would pound fiercely on his chin. We thought it was a self-stimulatory behavior, but finally took him to the dentist and discovered he had several deep, painful cavities between his teeth. Years later, Peter developed sudden episodes of agitation and aggression without any apparent external precipitants. One moment he would be fine, doing his math, and the next he'd be lying on the floor, moaning, banging his head on the floor, and trying to hit anyone who intervened. We eventually discovered that Peter has gastroesophageal reflux. Stomach acid was refluxing back into his esophagus, causing pain. Putting Peter on long-acting medication to block stomach acid production resolved the emotional outbursts.

It's sometimes tricky to figure out if a medical culprit is causing your child's agitation. Peter had an acid-detecting probe placed in his lower

---

1   If your child is too upset to reconcile with his little brother right away, address the frustration first so he knows you understand him, such as, "Did you want that cherry?" If you guessed right, and he seems eager to have the cherry, have him say, "I want cherry." Then reassure him that you will give him the cherry. You might even hold it in your hand so he knows it's coming. But before giving it to him, proceed with having him reconcile with his little brother to address the hitting.

esophagus to look for spikes in acidity, indicating reflux. The hospital read the printout as mild, with reflux occurring less than 5 percent of the day. When I asked for the actual data, however, I noticed several brief acid spikes correlating exactly when he had demonstrated agitation and aggression on a chronological diary I kept simultaneously. Nonetheless, I tried taking Peter off of his acid-blocking medicine, thinking I might be able to get by offering him antacid tablets for temporary relief as needed. Peter's episodes of agitation and aggression recurred markedly. Antacid tablets used as needed would take the edge off temporarily, but it was exhausting for Peter to struggle with the discomfort episodically and unpredictably over the course of each day. The battles ceased upon resumption of the original long-acting acid blocker. My point is that medical testing can give you helpful information, but interpret it thoughtfully. It often can't give you a definitive answer. Your conclusions should depend upon careful observation of your child.

Furthermore, some medical disorders are only partially understood. Gluten enteropathy, or celiac sprue, is a specific autoimmune disease. Reasonably accurate testing is available for it. However, some individuals do not have gluten enteropathy, but do demonstrate milder problems with gluten ingestion, called gluten intolerance or sensitivity. Gluten intolerance or sensitivity is not well characterized or understood by medical science at this time, but that doesn't mean your child can't have it. Peter had mysterious bouts of diarrhea and abdominal cramping for years if he consumed more than a small amount of wheat. Despite a negative antibody test for celiac disease (gluten enteropathy), when we put Peter on a gluten-restricted diet, his gastrointestinal symptoms resolved. We confirmed his gluten sensitivity when we removed the gluten restriction for a period of time, and the symptoms recurred. Symptoms that I previously attributed to irritable bowel disease have resolved back on a gluten-restricted diet.

When medical science can't give you a definitive answer to a potentially medical problem, sometimes the best you can do is to take a scientific approach to investigate further. Figure out a way to track and measure your child's symptoms as objectively as you can before and after a biomedical intervention, whether in order to decide whether it's worth continuing. Even if you decide the intervention is helping, you might want to confirm your decision with further testing periods off and on the intervention, especially if the intervention carries any risk of side effects. The improvements are less likely to be coincidental if they are repeatable. Suspect a medical culprit when you see your child display inexplicable, erratic, or uncharacteristic behaviors, and do your best to use a scientific approach to rule out the possibilities.

WHAT TO DO WHEN "STIMMING" IS TAKING OVER YOUR CHILD'S LIFE

Sensory issues are big in our kids. Peter seems to have an inborn insatiable urge for sensation. It has taken various manifestations over the years, including flapping, rocking, tapping, tearing things like paper, twigs, and leaves, squealing, and picking at his lips and skin, sometimes to the point of minor self-injury. Even when self-injury is not an issue, "stims" are sometimes problematic. They consume the child's attention and energy, distracting him from learning and interacting. They disturb and distract other people, especially in quiet public places like libraries, or waiting rooms. If the child is stimming on objects, such as paper and twigs, destruction of property becomes an issue, such as picking and tearing stims on Papa's bills, brother's homework, or the neighbor's garden. How can we help our children reduce or at least contain their stims to specific times, objects, and places? Is it possible to decrease their need for stims, or teach them to inhibit them?

Why do they do it?

I've heard accounts by individuals with autism who give different reasons for their "stims." One young woman with autism described her stims as a way to generate sensory input under her control to drown out the external sources of sensory bombardment on her nervous system. We have noticed that Peter does indeed stim more when in crowded, noisy environments. Using his noise cancellation headphones does help decrease stimming behavior in those situations.

One person said he flapped in order to figure out where his body was in space, as if to compensate for an undersensitive proprioceptive sense. Some occupational therapists prescribe a regular "sensory diet" to help satisfy this kind of need. For example, you might give the child "sensory toys" like squeeze balls or exercise resistance bands to use at regular periods between academic work. You can even create a label called "Sensory break" with or without a picture icon to place on your child's visual schedule. If he knows when he can look forward to the next sensory break, you might have better luck demanding he inhibit his stims during work times.

Beware of tolerance

You have to be careful with not overdoing these kinds of breaks, however. Too much may exacerbate the need for more, the way scratching leads to more itching. Years ago, when trying to get Peter to sit through Mass with me in church, I tried bringing a bag of sensory toys for Peter to tap and squeeze. Instead of decreasing his need to wiggle, flap, squeal, and tap, the more he played with the sensory toys, the harder and louder the tapping and flapping would get. It's as if the body gets used to a certain level of stimulation, and then needs more to satisfy it. This is called "tolerance," a common neurologic phenomenon, in which the body adjusts to a certain level of stimulation or medication, and then needs more to get the same effect.[2] Indeed many occupational therapists working on sensory integration will continue a particular kind of sensory activity such as swinging a child, bouncing him on a big ball, wearing a weighted vest, or pulling against a resistance band for no more than 20 minutes at a time. Now I restrict sensory breaks to no longer than 20 minutes and usually only a few minutes, using a timer, and rotate the sensory toys I offer as choices.

What are sensory toys?

Sensory toys and activities satisfy a child's interest in experiencing favorite sensations. There are toys of all different kinds of textures and consistencies. Koosh®, gell, and bumpy squeeze balls, stretchable nylon and rubber strings, and all kinds of beaded necklaces with knuckley and clickable joints help satisfy the desire for tactile sensation. Flashing tops, pinwheels, light sticks, and light-up gell balls satisfy a need for visual stimulation. Bounce ball seats, trampolines, doorway chin-up bars, and resistance bands (thick elastic bands used for resistance training when working out muscle groups) give the proprioceptive input many children with autism crave. Weighted vests, sandbags to place on the lap, heavy blankets and body socks to crawl under and into help provide pressure. Balance boards and balance beams, playground structures, and rock climbing walls are options for the child who loves climbing and balancing challenges. Regular, tire, platform, and netted swings and spinboards help satisfy a need for vestibular stimulation.

---

2   The proposed mechanism is a down-regulation of neuronal receptors when saturated with a neurotransmitter.

To find sensory toys and equipment, google "sensory toys for autism" where you'll find popular commercial websites like funandfunction.com or autismsuperstore.com. Some parents put a few sensory toys in their child's backpack for quick access to use as a reinforcer or stress reliever as needed. As usual, be sure to rotate the toys periodically to avoid satiation.

How to reduce the need to stim

Overall, we found that the best way to reduce stims is to provide lots of regular physical exercise to calm the body, and lots of positive engagement with work and other activities to distract the mind from sensory seeking. In general the CDC (Centers for Disease Control and Prevention) recommends at least 30 minutes of intense enough exercise to raise the heart rate to roughly 60–80 percent of the maximum calculated heart rate (220 minus age in years) daily for adults, and at least 60 minutes for children.[3] It's especially important to apply those rules to those with autism, to keep stimming at a less distracting level. Your child doesn't have to get in all 60 minutes at once, though. One possible schedule is to do 30 minutes of concentrated exercise such as swimming, gymnastics, biking, or working out on the exercise machines at the gym, and a cumulative 30 minutes of vigorous, big amplitude exercise breaks between academic work at the table, alternating with sensory breaks.

Exercise breaks

Some examples of big amplitude exercises include big jumps, jumping jacks, ball slams (holding a weighted ball with both hands, raising the arms, and throwing the ball down upon a pile of towels), pushups, squats, tug-o-war, stretching exercises with resistance bands, snake jumps (jumping over a rope laid on the ground), frog jumps from a squat, and full sit-ups in which the child ends up standing on his feet, giving you a high five at the top.[4] You can work on both social interaction and physical exercise with most of these activities if you do them together with a sense of fun.

---

3   www.cdc.gov/physicalactivity/everyone/guidelines/adults.html
4   Dr. Gwennyth Palafox, Pasadena: www.meaningfulgrowth.com

Restricting stimming to certain objects, places, and times

Lots of exercise may decrease stimming behavior, but it won't eliminate it. A more reasonable and realistic goal is to reduce the child's need to stim with exercise and distraction, and teach your child to restrict his stimming behavior to acceptable objects, places, and times.

It takes persistent redirecting, but it is possible to teach your child to restrict his stimming to certain objects. At one point in Peter's life he would stim on lamps by shaking them so hard that the light bulbs would break. We introduced a backpack of sensory toys for him to shake, rattle, and roll instead. He picked leaves and branches off of the neighbor's trees, and we had to redirect him to restrict his foraging to sticks and leaves that had already fallen on the ground. He developed an insatiable urge to tear up paper, including Papa's bills and his little brother's homework. We set up baskets in every room with scratch paper and junk mail he could tear up. When he would tear up anything outside his baskets, he would have to tape it up and write a sorry letter to the victim whose property was just destroyed.

You also sometimes need to restrict stimming to certain places. When Peter was small, he had an urge to climb every bookshelf and counter. We even had a hard time keeping him off the piano. He would climb so high up trees in the park that once I just couldn't reach him and had to wait an hour for him to climb down. I would have to drag him off the furniture and take him outside to climb on the play structure. We learned to avoid getting near the more easily climbable trees, and let Peter perch on top of the playground structures in the park instead.

We have already touched upon trying to set limits on acceptable times to stim by placing it on your child's visual schedule. If you suspect that stimming is distracting your child from concentrating on his work, do an experiment. Make labels for "sensory break" and "exercise" and alternate them with "work" periods. During the "work" periods, insist on inhibiting stim behavior. You might find that your child concentrates much better on his work without the stimming.[5] You can even put up a large sign that says, "Work Zone: Quiet voice, hands, and body." Flip it over during break periods.

---

5   Some children seem to concentrate better with some low level of provision of sensory-seeking outlets, such as soft background music, a resistance band tied between the front legs of the chair, or a Koosh ball to squeeze on the desk. Others escalate their sensory seeking when any is allowed.

How to teach inhibition

At this point, you may be wondering how on earth you can insist on inhibiting stimming behavior. Say it's time for a work period, and your child is stimming like crazy. How do you get him to stop? First it might help to discharge some of his excessive energy with a short interactive sensory activity like a clapping or jumping together game.

Then consider trying a "Three–Two–One" countdown (see p. 101). Initially you might have to offer a reward just for successfully executing this work readiness routine. Rewards include social praise, a treat like a tangible prize or time doing a preferred activity, or a token that can be exchanged for a treat. After your child's got the countdown routine down, the next time you do it, try withholding the reward until your child has also completed a very short, easy piece of work like a familiar worksheet or puzzle. If your child starts stimming during his work period, stop the work activity, and start over with your countdown procedure. As he demonstrates success, gradually lengthen the work period before rewarding to stretch your child's capacity to inhibit stimming.

The technical term for this procedure is called "differential reinforcement of alternative" (DRA). Encourage the desired alternative behavior, working, by rewarding it upon completion. You are also inhibiting the undesired target behavior, stimming, by doing a "differential reinforcement of incompatible" (DRI), in your countdown procedure. Your child can't stim if his hands, feet, and voice are quiet. Your countdown procedure furthermore lengthens the time the child has to wait before receiving his reward.

If that's not enough to reduce stimming, highlight the "differential" consequences of your child's behavior not only by positively rewarding the alternative behavior, working, but also by creating even more pronounced negative consequences for the targeted behavior, stimming.

Set a relatively easy "maintenance" task before your child, like a puzzle or familiar worksheet. Show him a reinforcer like several pistachio nuts or a piece of fruit cut into several pieces. If he completes the task without self-stimulatory behaviors, he gets to enjoy the whole reinforcer. But each time he starts squealing or tapping, sternly sign "quiet" and gesture with open hand, palm up, for him to give up a piece of his reinforcer. I call this the "shrinking reinforcer" method.

The final method to get your child to inhibit stimming is called "differential reinforcement of other" (DRO). You reward the child for not doing the targeted, undesired behavior for a given period of time. (It's called differential reinforcement of "other" because as long as he inhibits the targeted behavior, any "other" behavior earns a reward.) Say a child tends to stand up, flap, and squeal. Say he does this on average every five minutes. Start rewarding him for, say, every four minutes initially that he inhibits this behavior and stays in his seat, using a sand timer or other visual timer that he can track himself. Gradually lengthen the number of minutes he has to inhibit the stim to earn the reward until he gets through a reasonable 20–30-minute length of time for sitting and working.

Of course, you may use any of these techniques to help your child inhibit stimming not just during work periods, but *at other times he needs to concentrate*, such as when performing his daily self-help routines, doing chores, and playing with you. For some of these situations, if your child starts stimming, doing a simple countdown may be all you need to do to motivate your child to inhibit further stimming. Continuing the activity may serve as a reward in itself. Mealtime involves food, bathtime involves bubbles and bath toys, and play interactions are usually inherently fun or include some pleasurable sensory payoff in the circuit. For chores, you can withhold preferred activities until task completion.

Summary of strategies to help your child inhibit unwanted behaviors
These strategies don't only work for inhibiting stimming, but for *all kinds of unwanted behavior*, from getting out of his seat at the dinner table and wandering, to hitting. Give the child something else to do which is physically incompatible with continuing to carry out the misbehavior. Reward a preferred alternative behavior. Shrink the reinforcer if he displays the misbehavior. Reward for increasing lengths of time the child inhibits the undesired behavior.

The following story illustrates my attempts to use all these strategies to get Peter to stop stimming in church.

> Peter loves to tap and tear up paper, especially paper of a certain thickness and crisp texture. Unfortunately, he discovered that our church bulletins fulfilled those criteria perfectly. Sunday after Sunday he would insatiably tap and then tear up my church bulletin as we sat in the pews.

My initial strategy was to keep his hands busy with sensory toys (differential reinforcement of incompatible), so he wouldn't tap and tear loudly, but it didn't work. Peter worked himself up to a frenzy tapping the toys, rocking back and forth in the pew, and eventually squealing. Next I tried bringing puzzles, worksheets, and put-together toys with us to church. I gave him tiny pretzels, raisins, or grapes as rewards for doing his work. This strategy (differential reinforcement of alternative) worked well for years. However, we would take up an entire pew laying out all our activities, and continued to serve as a distraction to others. Besides, at some point, Peter also needed the opportunity to pay attention and listen to the service.

With Gwen's advice, Peter's psychologist, we came up with a DRO (differential reinforcement of other) strategy to help Peter inhibit his tapping/tearing sensory seeking in church. I wrote: "Goal: No tapping paper in church," on the top of a piece of paper placed in a plastic sheet protector. Underneath I wrote: "Do this:" and drew ten little boxes. At the bottom of the page, I wrote, "I Earn: One church bulletin to tap or tear up outside."

I brought two three-minute sand timers to church along with that goal sheet. Every time Peter made it through a three-minute sand timer without stimming, he checked off a box on his goal sheet. If he started to stim, I reminded him to be quiet, and had him start over that time period by turning over a new sand timer. After he checked off ten boxes, he got to go outside to tap and tear up the church bulletin.

When we first started this DRO strategy, we used one-minute timers, and additionally rewarded every time he inhibited stimming for the whole minute with a tiny piece of pretzel. We gradually worked up to a three-minute timer, and faded the edible rewards. We left it to Peter to remember to turn over the sand timer and check off the boxes, so he would learn the pivotal skill of self-monitoring.

It was a grand day when we made it all the way through Mass with no rewards till the end. Peter grabbed a bulletin as we walked into church. I gave him a look, and he handed it back to me. I drew 15 boxes on an envelope and told him he could have the bulletin to tear up after he checked off all the boxes. Peter used my smart phone timer and checked off boxes every three minutes for quiet behavior. Every time that timer went off (vibration mode), he looked up at me with a proud smile, clicked that pen open, and checked off a box. After 15 boxes, Mass was over, and he got the bulletin. He received it with glee and tore it up immediately (outside the church).

Self-monitoring

It's important to note that none of these inhibition strategies, DRI, DRA, or DRO, are supposed to be secret weapons that you as the parent use to manipulate your child's behavior. Rather, the greater the transparency, the greater the chance your child will internalize these strategies and thereby develop a critical executive function skill, that of self-monitoring.

Therefore, go ahead and tell your child what you're up to. Let him share the goal and own the problem and solution too. Tell him your DRI strategy up front, "Look, son, people get scared when you flap your hands in their face like that. They might think you'll hit them. So next time you feel like flapping in front of a lot of people, put your hands in your pocket. Then they can't be out and flapping."

Similarly, if you see him rummaging in the pantry, let him in on why you're proposing a DRA strategy. "Peter, you just had lunch. You can't be hungry. It's not good to eat too much. Let's take just a few of those chips and use them to work." Then put a few of the chips in a bowl and break them up to use as reinforcers as you read a book or practice the piano together.

Have your child engage those frontal lobes to monitor his own behavior as the two of you implement a DRO strategy. Say he's squealing periodically during a Christmas concert. During intermission, propose a DRO game. "Hey, Peter, would you like a snack? Let's play a game. I have these five pieces of jerky (make them small). You get one after each Christmas carol if you're quiet. But if you squeal, you have to take one and give it to the Grinch to eat." You can pretend to be the Grinch, or draw a face on a paper bag and label it "The Grinch." If he forgets to "feed" the Grinch when he squeals, open the bag playfully, and prompt him to transfer a piece of jerky into the Grinch's "mouth." The nice thing about this game is that it not only makes your child pay attention to his squealing, but also to the performance, as he has to monitor when each carol ends to take his reward.

Advanced self-monitoring

I close this section with a fascinating concept I learned about self-monitoring. Apparently, just having your child self-monitor the frequency at which he engages in a target behavior changes that frequency. Having a child who talks to his neighbor give himself a checkmark every time he does that decreases the frequency he chats during class. Engaging those frontal lobes to pay attention apparently also hires them to do their job of inhibition.

Initially reward the child as long as his counts match yours, even if he's talked to his neighbor multiple times. Say you give him tokens he can accumulate for five minutes of computer game time each. If the frequency of his talking during class doesn't decrease on its own, offer a second reward system in addition. Give him an additional token every class period in which he's checked off less than three boxes. However, let him know you'll still be doing spot checks on his self-monitoring. If the number of boxes he checks doesn't match yours, he doesn't get any tokens.

BATTLING THE OCD MONSTER

What do you do if stimming starts spiraling into a compulsion, and you can't get your child's attention to do anything else? Sometimes you can find a way to break through by joining in—engage those frontal lobes by turning the stim into a game.

> Peter was batting a long strip of paper incessantly. I said, "That looks like fun. Can I play?" I started batting the strip alternately with him. Then I turned it into a fun math game. "You start. Tap one" I let him tap the strip once, and then placed my hand on his tapping hand gently. "Okay Peter, my turn." Then I tapped the paper once. "One tap plus one tap makes…" Peter filled in the blank "Two!" "Okay Peter, you get two taps." We kept on going, adding one more tap each time until he got up to ten. Then back down again tapping one less on each turn. By the end of the game he no longer required me to place my hand over his to inhibit tapping.

However, you can't always count on being able to think of a fun and playful way to end a compulsion, especially when it's a full-blown rather than an emerging compulsion. Sometimes Peter got a crazy gleam in his eye and then had to start climbing on the very narrowest and most precarious branches of a tree or the highest shelves at home, walk on top of the piano, or have to pluck off and tear apart leaves from the neighbor's trees. At those times, redirection to more acceptable places to climb or objects to pick up were met with fierce resistance.

When Peter was small, we found the best way to deal with these compulsions was to firmly nip them in the bud, and consistently break the compulsion, no matter how stormy the resistance. For Peter, that required bodily removing him to an entirely new environment away from the compulsion trigger, which meant dragging him out of the park away from the trees or away from the piano for a soothing ride in the car. We found that giving in even occasionally to letting him indulge in a compulsion only "fed the compulsion monster," making the compulsion stronger and harder to break the next time.

Now that Peter is older and bigger, dealing with OCD requires a more nuanced approach.

> The other day we were in the drugstore. Peter was really into tearing up paper, and discovered a stack of brochures. He grabbed a handful. "No, Peter, only one. One per customer. That's it. You don't need more." Peter looked very distressed, and the wild gleam started up in his eyes. Fortunately I'm still bigger than he is, so I took immediate action. I took all but one brochure from his hand and replaced the rest. I decided to cut my shopping trip short, and left my cart. Taking Peter firmly by the arm, I started walking out of the store, talking in a firm but reassuring tone of voice. "You will be fine, Peter. You don't really need those papers. You have enough. It's all in your mind. It's the compulsion monster, telling you that you have to have them. We'll fight it together. You don't really have to have them all. You'll see. We will get out of this store, and you will be fine." In this way, we managed to exit the store, and then Peter really was fine.
>
> We celebrated by buying a treat from the store next door, and recorded the story in his journal. The next time we walked into a store with brochures, Peter grabbed a handful, then looked back at me and put them all back, except one. Of course we celebrated again.

Expect your child to backslide at times, and test prior set boundaries. As I mentioned before, we place baskets of junk mail and scrap paper around the house, and Peter knows he is allowed to tear up paper only from those baskets.

> The other day he saw a nice, juicy piece of paper. It was a resume, typed on high quality, thicker paper. He looked at me, and I saw that crazy gleam in his eye. Despite my "No!" he snatched the paper and started ripping it up. I grabbed the ripped paper, grabbed Peter's arm, and firmly led him to the table. "Was that paper in your basket, Peter?" "No," he said. "Were you supposed to tear it up?" "No." "How does that make Mama feel?" "Mad." "How does that make Peter feel?" "Sad." I brought out tape, a piece of paper, and a pencil. "What do you need to do?" We taped the resume back together. Then Peter wrote a sorry note to his father, to whom the resume was addressed. "Where can you get paper next time, Peter?" We walked arm in arm through the house and stopped before each pile and basket of paper. "Can you get it here?" "Yes," he said if we stopped in front of one of his baskets. "No," he said if we stopped in front of paper that was not in one of his baskets. I took a paper out from one of his baskets. "Do you want this?" "No," he said. I put the paper in my purse, and we hurried off to catch Mass.

> *At church, I was dismayed to see a big pile of papers at the entryway. The congregation was saying a long set of communal prayers that day for some special intention. Peter saw the papers, lit up, and grabbed a juicy set stapled together. Then he looked into my eyes, handed me the stapled stack, and took the paper I had previously offered to him out of my purse. We sat down. "You didn't tear up the paper outside your basket. You took the paper that was inside your basket." I beamed with pride and held his hand. "How does that make Mama feel?" "Happy." "How does Peter feel?" "Happy!"*

Cognitive behavioral strategies have been proven useful in helping individuals manage their OCD, and many can be adapted even for young children (see March 2007). I want to encourage you to keep talking to your child, to help him recognize obsessions and know you are his ally and supporter. If you detect a compulsion when it's just emerging, you might be able to turn it into a turn-taking game that brings it under the control of the child's own frontal lobes. Teach him to resist the compulsion monster by modeling self-talk ("I don't need to do this. I don't want to do this. I can stop, and I will be fine"), introducing deep breathing and relaxation exercises to weather milder compulsive urges until they pass and fade, exercising his resistance by delaying, shortening, or modifying stronger compulsive behavior, and removing him if necessary from totally overpowering and irresistible compulsion triggers. Either way, be as consistent as possible in enforcing the limits you set, and work on "response prevention," not allowing your child to experience the misleading momentary relief of totally giving in to a compulsion. Get your child off that merry go round of repetitive thoughts by interrupting it as early as possible. Obeying and even colluding with compulsions allows them to grow stronger until they consume all your child's energy and attention. You only get more resistance when you delay tackling the compulsion monster.

GRAPPLING WITH ANXIETY

Anxiety is a common symptom in individuals with autism. It can be disabling when it prevents a child from trying new things or being able to adapt to the unexpected. Some of the anxiety no doubt stems from sensory integration problems. The senses are bombarded with information that may be processed with disparate speeds through distorted channels. Dealing with it all day may make a child feel exhausted and defensive.

Peter's anxiety is palpable when we venture into crowded or noisy environments, especially unfamiliar ones. He tucks his head down and grabs onto my arm for dear life.

It's painful to watch your child struggle with disabling anxiety. I'm reminded of a time we were standing on top of a snowy ski slope. Peter loves to ski, but the wind had picked up a little, and the snow blowing in his face was just too much for him. You could see how much he wanted to ski down that slope, but how anxious and terrified he felt. He stood there, frozen and immobile. In that particular situation, I pulled out a tiny dose of an antianxiety medication called lorazepam from my pocket. Peter eagerly took it, as he was familiar with its effects from occasional past use when travelling to novel places or trying potentially scary new activities. Fifteen minutes later, I had a new child, gleefully gliding down the slope on his skis. The dramatic contrast gave me pause, as I wondered what life would be like for Peter without constantly having to struggle with anxiety. So for now, we work on educational and behavioral methods to support Peter and help him deal with anxiety.

One way to picture what goes on in the brain regarding big emotions like anxiety is a seesaw. On one side are discharges from the emotional areas of the brain, like the limbic system and amygdala, the latter structure being particularly involved in generating fear and anxiety. On the other side to balance these emotional discharges are the frontal lobes which send inhibitory fibers that modulate the final experience of emotion from past memories, judgments, and analysis. In anxiety disorder the balance is tipped far over to the emotional side, as the experience of anxiety is oversized and out of proportion. What our role is as emotional regulators of our children and teachers of self-regulation is to strengthen the input coming in from the thinking side.

Your best weapon against anxiety is preparation. Before a potentially anxiety-provoking situation, frontload all the information, practice, and role-play, so the signals will be there to send on D-day, when frontal lobe input will be desperately needed to balance the panic signals coming in from the amygdala.

Before a visit to the health care provider, go to the library and find reassuring picture books to read to your child about visiting the doctor or dentist. Get a toy doctor kit and play doctor, switching roles as doctor and patient. Line up the stuffed animals for your child to practice on as well. Ask if you can visit the doctor or dentist's office when it's quiet to rehearse coming into the waiting room, and maybe look at the equipment as a kind of field trip. Perhaps an understanding doctor or dentist would be willing to come out for a moment to meet your child, say hello, and pose for a photograph you can show your child later, right before the real visit. Bring transitional objects like a favorite stuffed animal, one who had perhaps served as one of the patients your child played doctor on.

The same procedure goes for starting in a new school or vacationing in a new place. Pull out any photographs, books, or brochures you can find to show your child the new vacation spot. Take a "virtual tour" on the internet. Tour the new school when it's quiet before school starts and figure out where his classes are. Make a visual schedule of some potential activities your child might play before a playdate, and role-play with puppets, dolls, or stuffed animals before (and after). The following story highlights the importance of frontloading to get through a highly anxiety-provoking situation—a date in the operating room.

> I'm often struck by our narrow escapes. Life with Peter is like whitewater rafting down a stream rated a notch or more above my skill rating.
>
> Yesterday Peter, Belinda, and I went to the children's hospital for a combined case of dental work and an upper endoscopy. It had taken quite a bit of planning and coordination to get as much done under anesthesia as possible–dental X-rays and procedures his dentist wanted, and several GI (gastro-intestinal) procedures the gastroenterologist wanted.
>
> The children's hospital is great, but overbooked and overworked; it takes many calls and dogged follow-up to pass on information from one person to the next. I did my best to do the appropriate dietary and medication manipulations prior to Peter's biopsy date. I tried to tell the nurse practitioner at Peter's pre-op that he wouldn't take the Versed® syrup they use to induce anesthesia–Peter has an aversion to taking liquids on command. When I mentioned the problem with even drinking water, I knew I had told her too much–she looked at me as if I were a lunatic mother, especially when I told her he was much better at swallowing pills. What can I say? Our kids never follow the usual developmental progression.
>
> My far-sighted husband came home a week before the operation date and tossed me a green anesthesia mask. "Just in case you want to practice with Peter," he said. I sighed to myself, thinking, "More work on top of everything!" but realized that Peter probably wouldn't take the Versed syrup. So just in case, I got started. Belinda and I worked with Peter ABA style to get him used to the mask. First we worked with the mask alone, disconnected from any hose. Our goal was just to get Peter to touch the mask to his face by himself. Then we waited to reward him until he positioned it over his nose and mouth. Then only if he would hold the mask snugly over the nose and mouth. Then only if he would allow us to hold the mask with him. Then holding it on till he counted to ten. Then connecting a hose to it.

Then turning on an oxygen tank to 0.5 liter/minute, and increasing the flow rate in 0.5 l/min increments with each subsequent trial so he would get used to hearing and feeling the flow of air through the mask, and learn to breathe it in. We used Winnie the Pooh as the patient, and had doctor Peter administer the sleeping gas so Peter could see that the gas made Pooh fall asleep so the dentist could fix his teeth.

When the big day came, we packed a big bag with books, games, Pooh, and the anesthesia mask. We alternately played games, read, and practiced with the mask on Peter and Pooh as we waited at the hospital. Peter loves to tear up his father's glossy magazines, and fortunately, I had brought one of them along as a reward. We needed it to persuade Peter to change into his hospital gown. When the nurse gave Peter the Versed syrup to drink, sure enough he refused—he had been practicing administering pretend oral medicine to Pooh through a syringe, pushing a plunger. He got as far as accepting a tiny taste. But then he just couldn't make himself swallow the bitter liquid, though he tried for many minutes. We tried using a tiny syringe, offering ice chips after each tiny sip, but Peter finally refused the ice chips and started to bolt out of his chair.

I had to make a decision at that point. I could have forced the issue, as Peter really was trying to cooperate, and squirted that medicine down his throat all at once. Even if he spat most of it out, maybe enough would go down to make him sleepy so the doctors could more easily perform a mask induction. But what if we ever needed to come back and do more procedures? If I used force, I might lose Peter's trust and cooperation the next time. No point in winning the battle to lose the war. Right now, I still had his desire to cooperate. But we had to change tactics—he had done his best with the Versed. The bolting indicated he was clearly done with it.

"Peter, come back and get into this bed, and you won't have to drink the medicine," I said, putting the medicine down on the table. I held up my empty hands to prove my good intentions. Peter looked at me and immediately hopped into the transport bed. "We're going to take a ride, and then use the sleeping mask, just like we practiced," I said. Belinda had neatly packed away the practice mask. The nurses were wheeling away Peter, but I ran back to grab it with only a vague intuition that it might be helpful. I expected the OR would have its own equipment to use, but maybe I could show Peter the mask if necessary as a reminder of our analogous past practice. Seemed like a long shot, but, oh well. I ran to catch up with everyone.

In the OR, the nurses gave Belinda and I soothing warm blankets to put over Peter and tuck under tactfully to serve as mild restraints. Peter was looking into my eyes, unsure, but trusting, trying hard to cooperate. But when the anesthesiologist brought the clear plastic mask forward with the anesthesia gas flowing, Peter got a wild look in his eyes, and started to try to sit bolt upright. Instinctively, I whisked out the green familiar mask he'd practiced on, and said, "Look Peter, here's your mask. Come on let's practice again. Peter saw the familiar mask, relaxed visibly, and laid back down, his eyes still unsure but trusting. I quickly handed the mask to the anesthesiologist who discreetly switched the hose to the gas from the OR mask to Peter's green mask. Then Belinda and I placed the mask over Peter's nose and mouth, while Belinda put her face close to Peter's and started counting with him as they had practiced many times before. After one last brief struggle to open his eyes and lift his head, Peter quietly succumbed to sleep. Belinda and I quickly exited the OR, emotionally exhausted, but deeply grateful. Peter had made it! He finished the course without losing control.

What happens if, despite all your preparation, your child panics? Is there any hope of salvaging the situation? There have been innumerable times Peter and I have found ourselves in difficult situations without adequate preparation. One year we went to a fall festival at a pumpkin patch on the spur of the moment. I had not even taken the time to show Peter the website advertisements of this new place. It turned out to be extremely crowded and noisy. I had to coax Peter out of the car with his favorite snack, beef jerky. He gripped my arm, tucked his head into my shoulder, and could not move his feet, he was so terrified.

In such a situation, step one is to verbalize your child's emotion. You thereby show him you acknowledge and understand how he feels plus you model the number one way neurotypical people regulate their emotions, to talk. "I can see how anxious you are, Peter. I'm going to help you through this. I know once you try it, you will like it a lot. It's really fun in there." As always, body language conveys a more powerful emotional message than the words themselves. Your warm, reassuring tone of voice and smile, cheerful affect, and confident body language are the most powerful antidote to your child's overwhelming sense of anxiety.

The next step is to try to engage the frontal lobes, the master of illusion and distraction. Remind your child of successful similar experiences in the past. "Remember last year when we went to the other pumpkin patch? All those orange pumpkins as far as the eye could see. I wonder if we'll see even more here. Think you can find some even bigger ones?"

If all the above fails, consider giving simple action-oriented directions and easy goals. "Think we can make it over there to touch that big pumpkin? Looks like ten steps. Here we go. Right, right, right, left, right!" "I see a carrot! Can you point to the carrot? That's right. Let's just see if we can find ten interesting things. Then we'll see if you still want to go." If you run a few steps ahead of your child to point out the next item for him to touch, you may coax him to go a bit farther and endure the situation he's afraid of a bit longer, as he's moving toward you, toward safety. You are partnering your child to exercise his courage (see Burns 1999, p.252).

Then, as soon as you see a potentially highly reinforcing activity or treat, go for it! In the case of that particular trip to the pumpkin patch, we were fortunate to stumble upon the hay ride as soon as we entered. We hurried onto the tractor before Peter realized what was happening. As he loves any kind of ride, once that tractor started moving, Peter visibly relaxed and started looking around. We were in! Of course, my next option would have been the barbeque corn.

We ended up having a lovely day at the pumpkin patch. We took plenty of photographs and bought pumpkins and treats as souvenirs. When we came home, we enjoyed reviewing it all, and recording another adventure for his journal. This last step of recollection is your investment. The more positive memories your child collects of successfully overcoming anxiety and fear, the better equipped he'll be to deal with future anxiety-provoking situations. "Good thing you're so brave, Peter! What a great time we had!"

The techniques we use are bread and butter common sense. They do work. They just take time, patience, and energy. In learning how to cope, Peter has had to use his memories, rely on relationships of trust, and think ahead. He's also learned to be truly brave.

LIVING WITH INERTIA

In chemistry they call it "activation energy." In physics they call it "inertia." Psychologists call it "task initiation." Whatever you call it, getting our kids to get going is a big problem for many of us parents. Getting your child out of bed, into and out of the bathroom, getting ready for school, into and out of the car to get to an appointment on time, moving from one classroom to the next, getting him off of the couch, and even getting him to take his turn in a game or conversation can each feel like a minor battle.

Our kids can drive us crazy with this problem. I've heard of two cases of children who actually developed full-blown catatonia, an inability to get moving at all. One was temporarily helped with a medication called a benzodiazepine, but quickly developed tolerance to it. The other managed to pull out of it nearly completely with a high energy behavioral approach (the mother employed strategies like putting paper footprints on the floor between the bed and bathroom to help the child get his feet to move from one place to the other).

Why is it so difficult to get our kids to move and transition? Is it stubborn willfulness or defiance? Seeing how hard Peter tries to cooperate and do the right thing despite all his challenges, I truly do not believe that, though it may play a contributing role sometimes, depending upon the child's personality and temperament. I believe that the problem primarily lies within the basal ganglion, that part of the brain that controls starting and stopping actions. A deficit in this part of the brain would explain the widespread problem of lack of initiative we see in individuals with autism. Of course, sensory integration and cognitive processing difficulties may also contribute toward fear of change, lack of adaptability, and desire for routine and sameness. To initiate or cope with a change or transition requires a nimble brain, able to integrate lots of new information coming in from the senses, assess new situations, access memories from which to create a menu of potential responses, and imagine their future consequences. Besides all that, the body has to move when the higher brain centers command it to, but that takes extra effort when the basal ganglion is dysfunctional.

My point is that there are no simple solutions to inertia. The way to help your child is to support each one of the deficits mentioned and constantly work toward developing each domain of the brain responsible for each of these mind capacities. Therefore, as always, support your child's sensory integration problems with appropriate accommodations— remember those noise cancellation headphones and sunglasses if you need to get your child to transition to a noisy and bright outdoors.

Help your child access his memories of past successful experiences reviewing personal stories and photographs of events similar to the upcoming one. Help prepare him for a future event by showing him brochures and pictures of the upcoming activity or place you plan to visit, read stories about it, and make use of rehearsal and pretend play, as discussed earlier (see pp. 162–3, 323–6). Again, the more stressful the upcoming event, the more preparation (frontloading) you need to do.

Offering a transitional object may be helpful in some circumstances. The classic teddy bear is an example of a transitional object. It may be even better to use a stuffed animal somehow associated with the upcoming event. You might offer your child a stuffed toy whale before visiting Sea World, a Toy Story® action figure before going out to see the next Toy Story movie sequel, or the dinosaur with big teeth that he played dentist on before the real visit. Any prop or visual aide associated with the upcoming event might prove useful as a transitional object. If your child has music class and enjoyed playing the drums the last time, offer your child a drumming stick. If he loves picking up sticks during walks, offer him a nice big stick off the ground outside when it's time for a walk.

Of course, one of your most powerful tools for helping your child anticipate the future is the visual schedule (see pp.225–6). Give your child time to mentally prepare for an important transition by showing and pointing to the event on the schedule as the appointment draws closer. "We leave in an hour… Half an hour left… Get ready, you have five minutes…"

Despite providing all these supports and preparation, what if your child still resists a transition? What if you still can't get him off of the couch or out of the car for the next activity?

All action takes some effort. We act because the effort is worthwhile in order to get something we want. In other words, all action is the result of the motivation being higher than the effort required. Something appears to be wrong in the brains of our slow-to-start kids that makes the effort of initiation so much greater. They frequently need extra support to increase their motivation or decrease the effort required to act.

To increase motivation, start with the positive. Remind your child of something he likes about the activity you want to transition him to, so he has something to look forward to. The best way to get Peter out of bed in the morning is to show him his plate of breakfast. You can also try to increase your child's motivation to move on to the next activity by using the principle of shared control. Try offering your child some choices for the next activity if possible. If you have something already scheduled, you can still offer choices by letting him choose an activity to put on the visual schedule after his appointments. "You want to rent that new video? Great, if you get up and go to swimming, we'll go the video store right after."

If positive reinforcement doesn't work, you might need to go to the negative. Create a cost for continuing to lie on the couch or stay in the car. Sometimes there's a natural negative or logical consequence you can take advantage of. The heat may persuade a child to exit the car on a summer day if you have a few minutes to wait. Boredom from you turning off the TV or video game might help get a child off the couch. Parents are typically pretty used to creating negative consequences when natural or logical ones don't suggest themselves. These include all the typical methods parents use to motivate their children to do things they don't want to do. "Get up on the count of three, or else!" The "or else" may vary from tickling a child till he gets up, threatening to remove a privilege such as his TV or computer time for the day, setting an alarm clock, to calling for help to physically carry off the child.

The *shrinking reinforcer method*, introduced earlier (see p.314), is a particularly helpful tool to help your child overcome inertia. It provides both positive and negative reinforcement. Offer a reinforcer, something he really likes, if he gets off the couch. For Peter that might be a big piece of paper to tear up or favorite edible like a piece of beef jerky or nectarine. That's the positive reinforcement part. However, if he doesn't get up within some specified amount of time, like the count of three or a timer set for a minute, *make the reward smaller.* Tear off a section of the paper. Cut the beef jerky or nectarine in half. That's the negative reinforcement part. Shrinking the reinforcer creates a cost for not getting up. Warn the child again, have him help you set the timer, and if the timer goes off and he doesn't get off the couch, halve the reward again. Keep repeating the process, and hopefully your child will get the idea and finally learn to hurry up.

> Peter loves rides in the car. He looks forward to the car ride home from school. However, he is extremely slow to walk from the classroom to the parking lot. Peter's tutor decided to work on the motivation side of the equation. Warm praise for when he'd pick up the pace did not work. Peter slowed down to pick up sticks and would just stop and rest at will. His tutor didn't want to go as far as to offer food rewards, though she knew that would be motivating for Peter. Instead, she decided to create some logical consequences. "Peter, if you walk faster, we'll have extra time for a longer car ride." Peter usually took a long 20 minutes to make the walk from the classroom to the parking lot. "If you make the walk in ten minutes, we'll have ten extra minutes to ride in the car," she said as she set the visual timer.[6] The results were amazing. Peter walked so fast that he had time to use the bathroom (in which he didn't dawdle either for a change) and make it to the parking lot before the red color in the visual timer ran out! "You did it!" cheered his tutor, "You get ten extra minutes in the car!"

---

6   We use a "Time Timer" which looks like a clock with remaining time in red that disappears as the hand moves down the minutes.

Sometimes, it's hard to think of a logical or natural consequence to use as reinforcement. You might need to go with a tangible reinforcer. The less preferred the activity, the stronger the reinforcer you'll need to select. We bike laps around the block for exercise. There are some days Peter does not want to do it. He rides so slowly that it's hard to stay upright on the bike, and he stops frequently. I made a deal with Peter that if he could make it to the next landmark without stopping, he'd earn a four-inch long thin strip of jerky. If he stopped before the landmark, however, I would eat an inch of the jerky each time. It only took a couple of stops and seeing that strip of beef jerky getting shorter and shorter for Peter to get the idea. After he was able to make it from landmark to landmark without stopping, I chose landmarks farther and farther apart. He was able to do the last lap without any stops.

Increasing motivation is one side of the equation to get your child to move. You can also work on the other side by decreasing the effort required to initiate a transition. Sometimes the activity you want your child to transition to just looks too hard or overwhelming to him. Make it easier by making your goal smaller or breaking it up into smaller steps. In the bike riding example, I told Peter he could have the beef jerky if he made it to the next landmark, which was a tree 50 yards away. If that was too hard for him, I could have made the target something like 50 feet away, or even closer. As he got successful with the shorter distances, I could always make them progressively longer as tolerated. When Peter really doesn't want to get out of the car to go shopping with me, I sometimes promise to just buy one thing. Once he was so anxious about going into a restaurant that I told him he only had to make it to the front door. After he tapped it, we turned around and went back home in the car. I figured that even though it was a small step, it was a step in the right direction.

Even once your child buys into the idea of moving on, it may take a lot of effort for him to get his body to do so. Whether the cause is a dysfunctional basal ganglia, problems with motor planning, or some other problem with the brain, many of our kids have problems with getting their bodies to do what they want. Actually, all of us could use some help in this regard from time to time. Have you ever had a bit of low back pain or arthritis and had trouble getting out of a low chair, especially one with soft cushions you sink into? You learn to choose to sit down in higher chairs with firm seats, back supports, and arm rests.

Do the same with your child. Reduce the effort to act. Say your child is slow to put on his shoes. Help lower the effort required by practicing with him till tying his shoes becomes more automatic, or get him Velcro ties instead of shoelaces. If you expect him to concentrate, prepare his work environment with a chair and table at the right heights that make it easier for his body to get into position to pay attention. To reduce the effort required to get off the couch, when selecting living room furniture, try staying away from beanbag-like couches and chairs that the body just sinks into. If you're concerned your child isn't keen about the next activity you're driving him to, park closer to your destination to reduce the effort of the transition.

To help your child with motor planning issues, use *action-oriented directions*. This is one time when clear directives are superior to declarative comments.[7] "Roll to your side. Swing the legs over. Give me your hands. Up we go!" is superior to "I wonder what you might like to do next? We might make it to that appointment on time if we hurry." When the basal ganglia (involved with the initiation of movement) or cerebellum (involved with motor planning) is not doing its job, the last thing the child needs is more complicated language to process. He needs simple, clear directions he can get his body to follow, broken down into doable steps.

Often a child may "warm up" to an activity, so try not to let the initial inertia discourage you. It may take ten minutes of stop and go to get Peter out of the driveway on his bike, but once we get started, he can ride for miles on his bike without a pause. Even if your child is moving so slowly that you think it's hopeless, try using these principles.

Summary of tools to get your child to cooperate

Prepare your child for the upcoming activity with his visual schedule see pp.225-6). Lower the effort required by accommodating his sensory issues. If the upcoming event may be stressful, rehearsal and role-playing in pretend play may lower anxiety. If necessary, use action-oriented directions, and make the target activity easier or break it down into smaller steps. Raise motivation by using stories, pictures, and transitional objects to remind him of past successes in similar situations, or of something he may like and can look forward to in the upcoming activity. You may also raise motivation by offering choices, giving positive and/or negative reinforcement, and using the shrinking reinforcer method.

---

7   When trying to make conversation, making open-ended comments encourage more talking and sharing than direct questions and imperatives.

As the child warms up to the new activity, raise the effort. In the biking example, that would mean making the child ride farther to get any beef jerky. Lower the rewards. As the child gets to enjoy biking, fade offers of beef jerky. Before your child realizes what's happened, he's doing more on less reinforcement. In other words, he's doing what he's supposed to do. You will have conquered inertia together, at least till the next round.

Observing my child interact with other people, it's fascinating to see how he'll do so much more for some than for others. Your child develops a history with every person, and that history sets his expectations. Therefore, do your best to be consistently persistent. If your child learns that Mom is an eternal pest who does not give up, he will also figure out that in the long run it's less trouble to just go along and cooperate with her than to resist. Every skirmish and minor battle with inertia is therefore worth winning.

Do select your battles well, however. You need to respect your child's pace and not schedule too much in too little time. As stated before, a turtle is a turtle and there's only so fast he can process and move. Set realistic, respectful expectations, and be patient with yourself and your child. Show your enthusiasm for what's coming up to increase your child's motivation, and encourage him to bolster his efforts. With your warmth and a sense of humor, you'll be the most important positive factor on both sides of the initiation equation.

FRUSTRATION WITH WORK

Peter knew a dime was worth ten cents. He knew a penny meant one cent. He could count to a hundred by tens and ones. But trying to get him to count out 15, 24, or 69 cents with dimes and pennies seemed impossible. Peter patiently worked on it during math for days, but it was taking more and more breaks to get him to cooperate, and he wasn't making progress. It finally dawned on us that Peter probably needed a firmer foundation in breaking two-digit numbers into groups of tens and ones. We gathered bags of all different kinds of small tangibles to practice on, including Rice Krispies®, raisins, popcorn, and toothpicks. Peter spent many hours happily grouping them into tens and ones, until giving us any two-digit number of objects was automatic. Although he had fun eating some of the edible tangibles at the end of math sessions, he no longer needed any breaks or other reinforcers to happily cooperate.

Because it's so common, I just wanted to share a few useful principles about preventing frustration with work. These principles apply to school work, chores, tasks, or any expectation you put upon your child that he doesn't choose to do himself.

Match expectations to ability

It goes without saying that you need to match your goals and expectations to your child's ability. If you've ever been to an annual review/ Individualized Education Program (IEP) meeting, you know the mantra. Set your goals based upon your child's baseline knowledge or skills and expected rate of progress, not on standards based on age or grade.

The same principle applies to the task at hand. If you sense that the work you're presenting is too hard, immediately give more support (a stronger level of cueing or prompting) to get the child to successfully complete the task at hand. Then drop down to an easier task so that the child experiences success. You might need to work a while longer at a lower level and more gradually introduce more challenging instruction, or present the concept differently, in smaller, more learnable steps. Stay at one level as long as it takes for new knowledge to get consolidated and new skills to become automatic. I like to think of consolidation as moving horizontally instead of vertically.

If your child can't make the jump to dimes and pennies, perhaps for now it's just too much to both remember the worth of a coin plus grouping into tens and ones. That would be adding another ball to juggle in the air, an example of vertical progress. If you meet with frustration and resistance, try moving in a different direction. Move horizontally by expanding his experience with grouping. Explore that concept with all kinds of fun and interesting tangibles. Once grouping becomes automatic, it will feel much easier to juggle that extra ball in the air. Learning then takes less effort, and resistance decreases.

If the work is boring, even if not yet mastered, you might need to move on to different material temporarily, while you figure out how to present it in a different way, perhaps with more interesting materials or in smaller doses. Just be sure the child finishes the task at hand before moving on so that the child does not learn to fuss and whine his way out of work. Either give more support and prompting to get your child through it, or redefine the task to one he can tolerate. Say you're trying to get a child to practice writing the letter "A." You see that the child is getting frustrated as his writing gets sloppier and sloppier. It's better to get a child to give his best effort to make a few legible letter "A's" than slog through a whole line of sloppy "A's." So if the child was going to get five minutes of computer if he finished two lines' worth of "A's," you might offer the five minutes instead if he gives you just three letter A's representing his best effort.

In addition, use the opportunity to teach the child how to communicate his needs more appropriately. For example, teach him to say or hand you a card saying something like "It's hard. Help." Then redefine the task or provide extra prompting support. We are actually teaching Peter to use a work frustration thermometer with happy, straight face, and unhappy faces corresponding to "The work is okay," "The work is hard. I need more time," and "The work is too hard! Help!"

Sometimes the problem with work is that it's too easy. It's important to check your data or reassess your child for mastery, because the very reason for poor performance may be boredom from having to repeat work he already knows. I recall one ABA supervisor who insisted on teaching colors over and over despite the fact that Peter had demonstrated perfect mastery with another tutor. She felt that unless he could label his colors with her as well, he had not really generalized his learning. In fact, Peter was bored and therefore would not cooperate. Rather than making work a test of wills, it is sometimes better to move on for the moment, and reassess the child for that particular task at another time when he's in a better mood, and your relationship with him has improved.

Teaching is always a balancing act. You want the child to take you seriously and follow instructions, but you also have to really listen to him. Hence if your child resists circle time, you need to ask yourself why. Perhaps the level is too high for him, and the teacher might adopt a layered teaching approach where she begins with easier activities he can participate in or think of easier questions to direct toward him, and then dismiss him early. On the other hand, if the level is too low, the teacher might have to add more challenging material and/or involve the child as a helper or leader, especially in social games. The children might have such disparate levels of ability (which may all vary according to subject), that the best solution might be to form separate circle times for different levels of ability, and different groups for different subjects. Special education teachers have a formidable task trying to keep each child balanced on that edge of success and challenge.

Establish your credibility

Every child, especially the strong-willed child, will test you at some point. Does she really mean what she says? Do I really have to follow that instruction? Say Peter just decided he was tired of swimming lessons. He doesn't understand the importance of being "pool safe." From his point of view, playing with those swim toys just isn't worth getting his head wet. Or say you asked your child to sit in his chair at mealtime, but he continues to run around the house. Or say a child at circle time refuses to attend even when appropriate accommodations have been made. If you've accommodated for sensory differences and adjusted the rewards up and the demand down as far as you can reasonably go, you're at one of those testing points. I should say "opportunity," because this is an opportunity for your child to learn that you do mean what you say.

It is critical that he learn this lesson early on. The longer the history you have with your child getting his way over yours, the longer it will take to change his understanding of your relationship. The more unpleasant testing he will do, and the more hard work of following through you will need to do. Furthermore, when your child is physically small, follow through is a lot easier. You can carry him into the pool with you. You can pick him up and place him in his chair, rewarding him for every few minutes more he stays seated. For attendance at circle time, an aide can seat herself behind him to place her hands on his shoulders or wrap her arms around him like a safety belt if necessary for gradually increasing lengths of time. Of course, your emphasis should always be on making pool time, mealtime, or circle time interesting and fun.

CONSIDERING OTHER VARIABLES

Not all of our children's misbehavior is due to autism. Motor planning deficits may contribute, but sometimes a child may not pick up his toys because he simply doesn't feel like it. Poor communication over a toy may be a problem, but sometimes he may hit his little brother just to experience power. Sensory issues may make the bike helmet feel tighter than it is, but sometimes he may refuse to wear it just because it's a bother.

Go ahead and employ the usual limit setting and enforce natural and logical consequences the way you intuitively would for a neurotypical child.[8] Put those favorite toys he won't pick up in a box, and high

---

8   For an outstanding book on setting limits and the use of natural and logical consequences, see MacKenzie (2001).

enough so he can see it but can't reach it. When he asks for his toys, make him finish cleaning up first. Scold him for hitting his little brother, show him how sad his little brother feels, make him sign, say, or write sorry, and hand over the toy for his little brother to take the next turn. Put away the bike until he decides to wear the helmet. Children need to experience limits and parents need to establish their authority and credibility regardless of whether there's a diagnosis of autism. Failing to enforce limits from the beginning when the child is little and easier to handle results in stronger resistance later.

Some popular disciplinary strategies don't work as well in our children with autism, however. Time-outs lose their punch in a child who prefers social isolation. A child with cognitive deficits won't necessarily understand the connection between losing a distant privilege or doing unrelated extra chores and his misbehavior. Rewards and punishments may need to be more directly connected with the misbehavior, and occur more immediately. If he throws his food on the ground, have him clean it up right away. If he won't wear his bike helmet, put away the bike. If a negative consequence that your child can understand does not present itself naturally in a situation, the shrinking reinforcer method may create one.

SUMMARY

Our children have so much to be frustrated about. It's hard to make sense of all the sensory information bombarding them, including language, verbal and nonverbal. Half the time, they don't know what they want themselves, and can't identify how they feel or even what hurts. Even when they have an idea of what they want and don't want, their dyspraxias prevent them from expressing themselves. Inertia makes it hard to initiate action. They are often expected to spend a lot of time and effort learning things that they can't understand or have no interest in. Their bodies betray them with a constant need for sensory seeking or "stimming." Deficits in attention, auditory and/or visual processing, and working memory impair their thinking. Anxiety and OCD overwhelms their emotions. The frontal lobe connections that normally regulate and modulate emotions by experience and judgment are weak. The social instinct that enables one to draw strength and support from others is also weak.

Our children need us to make up for all these deficits with our support and accommodations. The most important intervention for challenging behaviors is therefore for you to attune to your child so you can offer the right support when and where it's needed and set expectations appropriate to your child's abilities. The loving and trusting relationship he has with you will be his greatest help.

The most helpful strategy you can employ to reduce challenging behaviors is to teach him a basic communication system so he can make his wants and protests known. Teaching him how to use a visual schedule so he has some means of negotiation is also critical. To move your child along the path of someday being able to emotionally regulate himself, teach him to identify emotions. Show him how to use an emotional thermometer.

For your part, prevent frustration by attuning to your child's strengths and weaknesses. Designing a curriculum with goals and expectations that match the child's level is the key to gaining cooperation with schoolwork. The same reasonable expectations should determine the chores, self-help skills, and leisure activities you plan for time at home.

The heart of effective management of challenging behaviors is understanding your child, and having a solid, loving relationship with him. All your hard work in filling your child's emotional bank account with loving, pleasurable interactions is a worthy investment. Extrinsic rewards only go so far—some children have few interests strong enough to motivate them to do what they don't want to.

You are also your child's most important emotional buffer and regulator. He is able to absorb your positive and calming emotions to the extent that he loves and trusts you. He will also learn to want to be good because he enjoys your warm affirmation and is saddened by your disapproval. Through your modeling and teaching, he learns how to regulate himself by communicating, taking self-soothing actions, and looking for help. Again, the stronger your relationship, the more he will learn from you on how to self-regulate.

The tools we use to regulate our children's behavior are not different from those we employ with our neurotypical children. We just need to employ them more deliberately and intensively. We need to work harder to attune to our children because they can't tell us what they need or get it themselves.

The ultimate solution for challenging behaviors does not lie in intelligently dealing with individual behaviors, but in the child's development of emotional self-awareness and self-regulation. To that end, working on the fundamentals of communication and relationship development are essential. There is no superficial solution to challenging behaviors.

Chapter 16

Self-Injury and Aggression

It was music class. When the teacher walked toward him playing his guitar, Peter jumped up and squealed with a distressed look on his face. He started swinging his arm, and nearly struck the child sitting next to him, but his tutor, Belinda, deflected the blow. He then struck his own chin. When Belinda tried to grab his hands, he fell to the ground and started banging his head against the floor. Belinda tried to stop him. Peter hit her with an open hand. The teacher, aides, and students were aghast and stared in shocked silence. Peter had never had such an outburst in school. After another long minute of struggling, the head banging subsided, and Belinda asked Peter if he wanted to go. He got up and walked out with her to their usual classroom, which was now empty and quiet. He sat down and sobbed. Belinda talked to him soothingly and applied gentle squeezes to his arms and hands. After 10–15 minutes, the sobs subsided. Belinda offered to take Peter home, and he got up and walked quietly to the car with her.

Children with autism display a plethora of challenging behaviors. Meltdowns such as the one described above are painful and distressing to everyone, especially the child. Physical self-injury and aggression are especially frightening. Why do children resort to it and what can you do about it?

MANAGING THE ACUTE SITUATION

Tell yourself to do what you would do in any emergency—don't panic. The first priority is safety. Frequently, the people around will be willing to help, but won't know what to do. Be prepared to provide direct instructions. Ask other adults for help to move everyone to a safe place. Sometimes that may mean asking another adult to help you remove your child to a quiet room. If that is not possible, you may need to ask for cushions, pillows, or rolled up clothing to place under your child's head if he's banging it on the floor. Another adult may need to usher everyone else to another room. You don't want more targets for your child to strike, and you don't want an audience. If you have a stronger, larger child, you might want to check into some formal training in crisis prevention and management to learn how to de-escalate a violent meltdown. If you have to use physical restraint, you'll want to know how to use it safely.

It's common to feel helpless and frustrated when trying to help your child at moments such as these. Sometimes your child's emotions are so overwhelming that he seems unreachable. You may feel as though you might as well not even be present, as he doesn't seem to calm down no matter what you say or do. To some extent, even with nonautistic individuals, the best you can do is ride with them through the storm. The emotions take over for a while. The experience is just bigger and longer with children with autism because their capacity for emotional self-regulation is more limited, as is their ability to reference and to take in your calming influence.

I physically restrain Peter if he's trying to hit himself or others. I hold his arms down, and get help to do so if necessary. You can immediately say, "No hitting," as you are restraining your child, but keep your tone of voice calm and supportive, while firm. Try not to make derogatory remarks like, "You're going crazy!" or "Why do you have to do that?" as it only makes the child feel worse about something he cannot control. Instead, use words and a tone of voice that show you're on his side, and help him see you as an ally and protector. "I'm not going to let you hurt yourself. I'm going to help you through this." Acknowledge your child's feelings so he knows you understand. "You're hitting because you're upset. That music is too loud. When it's too loud, it hurts, doesn't it?" Then try to talk him down, "It's okay. Music stopped. It's quiet now. I've got you. No one's going to get hurt. No hitting. You'll be okay..." Again, verbalize his feelings and choose words that reassure him of your support. Once the physical resistance abates, I try to tie calming with release, saying something like, "I like the way you're not hitting anymore. I'm going to let go now."

If your child needs more soothing, upon moving to a more private and quiet location, I then immediately offer alternatives to hitting like squeezing in a body sock, deep pressure, or covering up under a cozy, heavy blanket. Children have their individual preferences for what they find regulating and calming. I would include at least some talking, as verbalization is the major way most people learn to self-regulate their emotions. Even if your child cannot talk yet, it's worthwhile to model the process. For some children, chatter can be irritating, so just use enough words for your child to be able to tune into the tone of your voice, and understand that you're there to support him. Other children respond better when you keep talking, as they seem to tune into your words and use them to calm down faster. Just a change in environment is often helpful in breaking the momentum in a meltdown. My son loves car rides, so I will frequently invite him for a ride in the car. He calms down more quickly as he's watching the scenery go by out the car window and listening to his favorite, soothing music.

Once the storm has passed, it's helpful for everyone involved to mark its resolution. For other witnesses, a brief poke of the head into the room to smile and say, "Peter's okay now," may suffice. Depending on your plans, you might follow that with, "May he join you all in a few minutes?" and/or "We'll talk about this tomorrow," so everyone knows they'll have an opportunity to better understand the situation. (Of course, later you do follow through with a short discussion and perhaps a book about big emotions such as *When My Autism Gets Too Big!* by Kari Dunn Buron, 2004.) To your child, you might say something like, "Wow, that was a big one. You okay?" Then give a reassuring smile, rub on the back, or hug.

RECONCILIATION AND REMEDIATION

Now that the emotion has been defused, and your child is calm, you can work on reconciliation. "Okay, we are going to leave music class. But first, look at your tutor. See, how do you think Belinda feels? (sad) Do you know why? (hurt) That's right, Belinda is feeling sad because you hurt her when you hit her. What can we do?" Prompt your child to say sorry, or offer a gesture like signing sorry, patting the victim gently on the hand, getting her a tissue or ice bag, and/or writing a sorry note (this can be done later if the timing isn't right at the moment).

Then remediate by giving your child the proper substitute behavior. "Next time, tell Belinda, 'Too loud! Let's go!'" Have your child imitate the more appropriate behavior, and then immediately reward by giving him what he needs, such as leaving the music class. If he's already in a different location, you can role-play, saying, "Let's pretend. Say, 'Too loud! Let's go!'" and then get up and walk out the door. If his mood allows it, you can even try to practice this alternative behavior several times to make it stick. In behavioral parlance, this is called "positive practice overcorrection."

RESTORATION

What you do next depends on the level of effort you judge your child can tolerate. The goal is to make your consequent activities sufficiently restorative, but not so rewarding that you create "secondary gain" for your child. You don't want to inadvertently reward having a meltdown. If your child is up to it, return to your prior activities, such as returning to the music class with headphones on after a little walk. Other examples include saying, "You okay? Shall we go get a drink of water?" If you feel your child needs a more preferred activity to restore him further, try to delay the timing of it so that there's a longer time lag between the meltdown and any positive consequence. If the child was doing math before music class and the meltdown, you might say, "Let's finish up two more problems, and then it's snack time." Make sure you choose reasonably easy math problems. Select a task that you know the child can be successful at completing without undue effort. You are trying to warm up the child to return to his usual activities, but you need to constantly assess and accommodate for his level of emotional regulation. A key principle is to *time the reward or "reinforcement" immediately after the behavior you want, and not after the behavior you don't want.* Making snack time contingent upon finishing those two math problems makes it clear to the child that he's getting a snack for finishing his work, not for the meltdown.

APPLYING A FUNCTIONAL BEHAVIORAL ANALYSIS

Once your child is calm and back to his routine, take a deep breath. Get someone to take over so you can take a break if possible. Collapse in a chair, take a walk, turn on some music, or do whatever works for you. The most important part is to give yourself time to think. If you want to decrease the frequency of these meltdowns, you need time to reflect on what happened, what to do if it happens again, and how to prevent it. Go through your "A, B, Cs" as discussed in the last chapter (see pp. 307–8). What caused, triggered, or preceded the incident? What exactly was the behavior you would like to reduce or replace? What did the child get out of the behavior? What was the result or consequence? The analysis is helpful because it distills the experience into the concrete actions that took place. Children frequently tune out words, but pay attention to actions. Functional analyses may therefore help you to see the experience through your child's eyes.

Identifying the behavior

Let's go through the above example step by step. First identify the problematic behavior. Clearly in this case the behavior was hitting himself and trying to hit another child. If you weren't doing a functional analysis, you might stop here and just try to punish the behavior to eliminate it. But behavior is not random. It's driven by some cause. Misbehavior is frequently the way our children communicate because language is so difficult for them. Punishment for misbehavior without trying to understand what your child is communicating is therefore both unfair and ineffective, as it ultimately increases frustration. If you want to effectively modify misbehavior, you need to know the cause so you can provide an acceptable substitute.

Analyzing the antecedent

As discussed in the previous chapter, some of the common causes or antecedents of misbehavior are unmet sensory needs, interfering with a compulsion, or communicating pain, protest, or frustration. You need to "listen" to your child. That means even if he can't talk, try to figure out the cause from his point of view. In this case this would be an increasing sensitivity to sound. Upon reflection, we realized it had been building up for weeks. The final trigger was the sound of the guitar playing and singing getting louder and louder as the teacher approached.

We realized the meltdown was triggered by sound hypersensitivity because lately Peter had been covering his ears more and more with any loud sound such as when someone turned on the blender or vacuum cleaner, or on hearing an audience clap after a show. Music class used to be one of his favorite activities, but in recent weeks he had been covering his ears more and more. In retrospect, we realized that he had shown some reluctance to enter the music room that day.

Intervention options at each stage in the meltdown process[1]
"ANXIETY"

Although our kids sometimes go from calm to meltdown instantly, usually there's some warning. Usually kids go from anxious to defensive, and then act out. If we had recognized that Peter was getting anxious with

---

1   Terms derived from Crisis Prevention Institute, Inc. (2005) *Nonviolent Crisis Intervention Training Program*, www.crisisprevention.com, 1-800-558-8976.

his reluctance to enter the room, we could have used that opportunity to deflect the meltdown by addressing his needs while he could still reason and communicate. For example, we could have stepped back out of the room, knelt down to Peter's eye level, and asked, "Is something bothering you, Peter? You're covering your ears. Is the music too loud?..." This stage is your opportunity to use words to ascertain and acknowledge your child's feelings, and for your child to use all his communication skills and options. It's a great learning opportunity in a way because your child is highly motivated to communicate and negotiate with you. In our scenario, the tutor could ask, "Peter, shall we ask Mr. Wulff to start out with a softer song? Would you like to sit in the front or back?" A supportive body posture, tone of voice, and cadence are just as important as the words you say.

Ultimately, Peter's hypersensitivity to noise did motivate him to learn an important skill. We used the occasion to teach him how to use an "emotional thermometer" (see pp.268–9). Peter quickly learned to size up the loudness level and carry out the appropriate action steps independently. What took a year was for him to learn to put words to the process. Now he can spontaneous vocalize "Too loud!" which is an important step in emotional self-regulation (see pp.167–8 on social emotional development). So getting away from loud sounds ended up motivating Peter to learn how to become aware of and identify his emotional state, communicate how he felt, and learn strategies to regulate himself.

"THE DEFENSIVE STAGE"

If you don't recognize that your child is getting anxious early on, or if your child's anxiety is escalating too fast, you might find yourself dealing with the next stage. The defensive stage is when your child is so upset that he loses his ability to negotiate, but may still be able to understand simple directions and make a choice. In our scenario, say Peter is squealing and covering his ears. One appropriate intervention at this step might be to say, "Peter, the music is too loud for you. Put on your (noise cancellation) headphones, or we're leaving." By this stage, too many words and questions may just be irritating. Clear, firm directives or simple choices work better with immediate action to follow through.

"THE TENSION REDUCTION PHASE"

Even if you haven't been able to deflect a meltdown during the anxious and defensive phases, your child may still learn a lot from how you deal with the "tension reduction" phase—that is, what you do as your child is calming down. In fact, your child is sometimes most open to learning from you at this stage. Since reason is finally returning, he might remember most clearly what you do and say at this point. Try to maintain that "therapeutic rapport" to the very end, remaining calm, concerned, and positive. The first thing your child will hear as he emerges from his emotional storm will be your calming voice, and he will eventually learn how to talk to himself as he's hearing you. Hopefully, the first thing he'll see as he turns around to look at you is your positive and reassuring smile, as you invite him to transition back into an understanding world.

Analyzing the consequence

At this point we've analyzed the trigger (antecedent). We have some strategies to accommodate Peter's sound sensitivity and substitute "good" (socially acceptable, effective, "adaptive") behaviors for the maladaptive behavior (meltdown) to get the desired function (ending the loud sound). We now discuss the point after de-escalation at which your child has regained his reason. He's primed to learn from the consequence you select.

MINIMIZING SECONDARY GAIN

Choose and present this consequence carefully, lest your child learn lessons you did not intend to teach. In our example, the consequence of Peter's meltdown was leaving music class and a car ride home. Going home was an understandable choice as it was Peter's first aggressive outburst, and everyone needed time to recollect and restore. But what if Belinda continued to take Peter home every time he had a meltdown? Peter might well learn that an effective way to get to go home early is to have a meltdown. We call these inadvertent, unintended rewards "secondary gain." The best way to avoid secondary gain is to choose consequences appropriately. If the antecedent is sensory overload, the appropriate consequence is indeed to remove the overload, in this case, removing Peter from music class. But what if the cause is not wanting to come in from recess or another preferred activity? In that case, the appropriate consequence after calming would be to return to music class, with more supports during the transition (for example, use of a warning timer, visual schedule, and/or transition object such as a drummer's stick if the child likes to play the drums in music class).

Another way to reduce the chances of secondary gain is to be careful about your timing. How you execute the consequence is important as well as the consequence you choose. If you think your child can tolerate it, have him make amends and practice a more appropriate substitute behavior before he gets a positive consequence. Doing so lengthens the time between the inappropriate behavior (hitting) and the positive consequence (car ride home), reducing the chance that your child associates the two. Conversely, time the positive consequence (car ride home) immediately after you get your child to demonstrate the desired, more appropriate behavior (using words, "Too loud! Let's go!"). Consistently pairing an appropriate behavior with a positive consequence helps create an association that sticks.

Even if your child is too upset to make an apology at this time, do your best to highlight the behavior you are reinforcing with your words and timing. For example, picture these two scenarios. In the first scenario, Peter is having a tantrum on the floor. Belinda says, "Poor baby! You're really upset. Let's go home!" Even if initially the cause of the tantrum was noise hypersensitivity, if this sequence was repeated a few times, Peter might well learn that having a tantrum results in getting to go home early. In the second scenario, Belinda soothes Peter with words and deep pressure, not with the prospect of going home early. *As soon as the sobs subside,* she says, *"Good calming down!* I think you're ready for a car ride home!" In the second scenario, there's at least a chance Peter might learn to associate calming down rather than having a tantrum with the car ride home. If Peter needed holding down during the meltdown, once he stopped trying to hit, Belinda could say, "I think I can let go now that you're not hitting. If you keep those hands down for a minute, we'll have a car ride." It's worth reiterating the importance of establishing a clear connection between getting calm and getting free.

TEAMWORK

Teamwork is essential. Soon after this incident, the school's special education staff held a meeting with us where we discussed strategies for future outbursts so Belinda would not feel she needed to bring Peter home. We came up with a plan that involved adjustments for both Peter and the staff. We would provide more "frontloading" or preparation even before Peter entered the music room. Belinda would read a personal story I wrote to Peter about him entering music class, feeling surprised about the loud music, and deciding to put on his headphones. Belinda would show him that music class was coming up on his visual schedule, and make sure he put the headphones in his backpack where he could find them fast in case he needed them.

The music teacher might start out class with a softer volume of music, and perhaps some of Peter's favorite songs so that he could at least make it through the first part of music class. The hope was to engage his attention and draw him into the fun of being with the other children and enjoying the music to gradually stretch his capacity to tolerate sound volume. To assist him in tuning into and identifying his own internal state, we decided to try the emotional thermometer method described earlier. An additional strategy was to teach Peter to raise his hand and ask the teacher for "Softer music, please. Not so loud" (written on a card).

In case these strategies failed, and Peter continued to escalate into a full-blown meltdown, we decided to offer a milder reinforcement *upon calming* such as, "It's good that you stopped the head banging. You're calming down so I don't need to hold you down anymore... (Pause to make sure the hitting is over.) Okay, Peter, if you're ready, let's go. How about the swings for ten minutes?" Instead of the swings, the next time we might try returning to Peter's regular, quiet classroom to do ten minutes of yoga, and the next time perhaps try reading a story. Eventually, Peter might even be ready to return to music class (with headphones). We would work toward selecting a consequence least likely to create secondary gain, but just sufficiently restorative.

SHAPING AGGRESSION INTO A MORE ADAPTIVE RESPONSE

It's even more important to be wary of inadvertently rewarding misbehavior in cases where the reason for the misbehavior is defiance or trying to get out of a nonpreferred activity. For example, I observed a child with autism hitting a gym teacher because he did not want to follow the teacher's instruction to do a sit-up. The teacher held the child's hands and firmly said, "No hitting!" but then allowed the child to skip his turn.

Do you think the child tuned into the teacher's words ("No hitting!") or actions (allowing him to skip his turn)? It would be better if the teacher could at least make the child repeat after him, "I don't want to!"

and then reward the use of words by allowing him to skip his turn. Just try to remember to insert the prompt for the more acceptable substitute behavior before you provide or allow a consequence that could be perceived as rewarding.

Again, picture the teacher holding the child's hands after the hit, looking him in the eyes, and saying, "No hitting. Instead say, 'I don't want to!'" The child says, "I don't want to!" and the teacher says, "Good use of words! Okay," and compromises by giving the child an easier exercise to complete (providing a substitute), providing help or shortening the task (fewer sit-ups). If the teacher doesn't feel the child can tolerate any demands, he may just decide to move on after getting him to use words to say "no." The next time it's the child's turn, the teacher anticipates the strike, and grabs hold of the child's hands while they're still up in the air *before* they've come down. The teacher prompts, "I don't want to!" The child repeats, "I don't want to!" and the teacher again rewards, saying, "Good use of words. Okay," and either compromises or moves on. Perhaps on the third turn, the teacher grabs hold of the child's hands in the air, and can pause expectantly, giving the child the opportunity to spontaneously say, "I don't want to!" Children who have less verbal skills may present an "I don't want to!" picture/word card instead or learn to shake their head and/or say simply, "No!"

Once the child has learned to substitute words for hitting, you should move on to bigger goals such as negotiating cooperation. In the example above, the teacher might give children who do a certain number of sit-ups a smiley face sticker to collect on a chart. A certain number of smiley faces might result in a reward meaningful to the child. Skipping your turn therefore results in an opportunity cost. Such a system also prevents other children from imitating the child's "I don't want to" behavior, so introduce it as soon as possible. The idea is to gradually stretch the child's capacity for cooperation step by step.

SUBSTITUTING WORDS FOR HITTING

With Peter, we try hard to catch his hands before a strike comes down. We give him the words he needs to substitute, he repeats them, and gets the reinforcing consequence. For example, say Peter is tapping on a paper. He drops it. I take the paper. Peter raises his hand to hit me. I catch his hand, look him in the eyes, and give him the words he needs, saying, "No hitting! Say, '*My* paper.'" Peter repeats, "*My* paper," and I hand him the paper. If you reward immediately after a desired behavior, the child is more likely to learn that behavior. Peter is learning that words get him what he wants.

But what if I'm not fast enough? Peter hits me before I can catch his hands. The axiom about neurons firing together, wiring together works the other way too. The longer the time interval between the behavior and the reward, the less likely the child will associate the reward with the behavior, and the less likely he is to learn the behavior. Therefore, if you don't want your child to learn that hitting leads to getting what he wants, insert as many steps as you can between the hitting and the getting.

Let's return to our scenario. Peter hits me after I place the paper in my purse. I look at him, hold his hands, and say, "No hitting! Next time say, '*My* paper,' and I will give it to you. But now you hit me, and that hurt. What do you say?" I have him sit down and write, "Sorry Mom. No hitting," two or three times. If your child can't write yet, you might try setting a timer for a minute or some other tolerable time period, saying, "If you hit, you have to wait to get the paper back. Next time ask." Have the child push the start button on the timer.

After the child has finished his sentences or the timer has gone off, go back to the scene of the incident. I point to the paper and say, "Do you want the paper? Say, '*My* paper, please.'" Peter repeats, "*My* paper, please," or says on his own, "I want paper, please." Either way, I cheerfully hand him the paper.

When I feel he can tolerate it, I will sometimes practice the correct sequence several times over, in a playful, game-like way, to give him more opportunities for those neurons to fire together. Positive practice overcorrection is an excellent tool for correcting all kinds of behavior, not just disciplinary. For example, say I'm trying to teach Peter how to make a bed neatly. He throws his pillow haphazardly toward the head of his bed. I might show him how to straighten it out, and then return it to the crooked position he threw it in and have him straighten it out several times in a row. This kind of learning allows the neurons to fire together repetitively right in the context where the learning is meaningful and therefore most likely to stick.

SUMMARY OF PRINCIPLES

The first step in heading off aggression and self-injury is good observation. Occasionally our kids will go from calm to meltdown with no warning, but usually you'll notice phases. Kids get anxious, then defensive, and then act out. Your intervention differs depending on how early you catch your child in the meltdown process as he becomes progressively more emotionally overwhelmed and less able to reason. If you manage to maintain your therapeutic rapport throughout, your child will learn something positive even if you can't deflect the meltdown. The goal of a functional analysis is to understand the reason for the behavior so that next time you can try to accommodate the child's needs and/or teach the child an alternative more adaptive and appropriate way for him to get his needs met. It's the most important step, as it enables you to prevent future occurrences.

Preparing the child before a potentially stressful event is called "frontloading." The greater the potential stress, the more frontloading you need to provide. If your child gets anxious despite frontloading, support him with your calming body language and supportive tone of voice to review his alternative behaviors, and prompt him as needed to follow through with his choice. If he gets defensive, be directive and provide him with the words and actions he would or should be using or doing if he could. Quickly support him through them so he feels the immediate success of those more appropriate actions. If a strike occurs despite your best efforts to prevent or avert it with frontloading and negotiating alternative behaviors, you need to deal with the injury. Your first priority should be safety for everyone concerned. The child may need to be physically restrained or contained from causing himself or others further injury. The victim needs attending to. You will need to get help and delegate these essentials.

Before any learning or remediation can occur, you must then deal with the emotion. Calming the child is restoration, or emotional regulation. Sometimes, the strike itself defuses the child's emotion, and he appears calm and even sometimes remorseful immediately after. Sometimes it takes a while to calm your child down. Trying to punish before the child is calm is usually counterproductive, as it may provoke more frustration, anger, and aggression. Think restoration and remediation instead of punishment. Choose words that convey reassurance and protection. Acknowledge your child's feelings so he knows you understand. It goes without saying that the inciting stimulus must be removed or your child removed from it, whether that be music that's painfully loud or an item your child is obsessed with.

Once calm is restored, help your child learn how to initiate a reconciliation. Prompt your child to say sorry, or offer a gesture like signing sorry, patting the victim gently on the hand, getting the victim a tissue or ice bag, and/or writing a sorry note.

Then give your child the proper substitute behavior. Have your child imitate the more appropriate behavior, and then immediately reward by giving him what he needs. Timing the reward to follow immediately after the behavior you want to teach is critical. Conversely, do your best to lengthen the time between the misbehavior and any positive consequence. Work toward selecting a consequence that rewards the behavior you want to teach, and creates a cost or at least minimalizes secondary gain for maladaptive behavior, especially when the reason for the misbehavior is getting out of a nonpreferred activity. In appropriate circumstances, "positive practice overcorrection" (better termed "let's try it again") helps children substitute the right for the wrong behavior by giving them many opportunities to practice.

THINGS DO GET BETTER

In closing, I want to encourage you to take heart. Every child melts down occasionally, whether they have autism or not, and adults do too. In fact, the principles and techniques discussed in this chapter work equally well for neurotypicals. Our kids are just a lot more challenging because so many seemingly small triggers set them off, and they don't know how to calm themselves. Self-regulation can be learned, however. When I feel exhausted helping Peter ride through one emotional storm after another, I try to remind myself of the progress he's made. At times I'll see him lift his hand ready to strike, and he'll look into my eyes and put his hand back down to his side. Rather than striking himself or others, frequently he'll take my hands to indicate he needs me to hold his and squeeze them. He readily puts his noise cancellation headphones and sunglasses on because he knows they help him.

A silver lining: Strong affect, even negative, may drive learning

Every challenge is also an opportunity. Dealing with stress has helped Peter develop some problem-solving and planning ahead skills. The other day Peter had to get through a noisy, crowded room to get to the playground beyond it. He and his tutor staked out the situation outside, looking through the classroom window. "Okay, Peter, it's noisy in there. We don't have your headphones. If you want to get to the playground, you'll have to walk through fast," she said. Peter replied, "Okay." He drew himself up, picked a path, and walked determinedly and quickly through. He made it!

In order to avoid the loud sound of the toilet flushing, Peter learned to put on his headphones before entering a public restroom. Natural consequences are the most efficient teachers. One day before flushing, he ran out of the bathroom to put his headphones on. Unfortunately, the bathroom door automatically locked after him, and he had to wait for someone to get a key to open the door for him to complete his bathroom routine, flush, and wash his hands. After that one experience, Peter learned to think ahead and get those headphones out of his backpack himself and put them on before entering a bathroom. Dealing with a sensory challenge motivated Peter to demonstrate his first executive functioning skills!

Truly, affect drives learning. Learning to deal with these strong negative emotions can actually push your child up the developmental ladder. So far I've given you an approach to dealing with meltdowns that is largely behaviorally based. But I need to mention another approach that you can use in addition.

Try a little play therapy

I mentioned in Chapter 11 (pp.164–5) how the need to deal with strong emotion was what got Peter interested in pretend play, another example of affect driving cognitive development. Since then, whenever he has a meltdown, I try to do a little pretend re-enactment of the scene later in the day, but with a positive ending to show him an alternative way to handle stress. For example, Peter had a head banging meltdown the other day after his tutor broke a compulsion taking paper that belonged to other students. Later that day when Peter was enjoying tapping away on some paper, I had Winnie the Pooh say how much he just had to have that paper, and grab Peter's paper away to tap himself. Tutor Rabbit insisted that Pooh return the paper to Peter. Pooh did, but then started talking about how he had to have the paper again and grabbed it once more. We repeated this sequence several times till Peter clearly felt frustrated with Pooh's compulsion. "Peter, help Pooh fight this compulsion monster! Tell him 'Pooh, you don't need that paper! You just think you do!'" I asked Peter what he could do to help Pooh, and Peter got up and threw away the paper out of Pooh's sight. "Thank you, Peter!" said Pooh, relieved. "You helped me fight the compulsion monster!" "Welcome!" said Peter, cheerfully.

Dealing with grief

Still, dealing with self-injury and aggression can be a painful, emotionally draining business. We tell ourselves over and over that our little ones aren't intentionally hurting us, and that they aren't malicious. We know they can't help a lot of what they do because of autism. Those inhibitory frontal lobe neural connections just aren't as well developed, but with patient teaching, they will grow stronger. But still, every time Peter hits me, it hurts deep down. Not just the superficial physical pain, but deep down emotionally.

Just last week Peter wasn't feeling well, but I had to take him with me to take his little brother to a piano lesson. It was a hot summer day. By the time we got there, Peter was tired, and didn't want to come out of the car. I couldn't leave him in the car because it was much too hot, so I insisted, and pulled him out.

I saw the whap coming, but didn't react fast enough. It came down upon my head. I felt stunned, and deeply sad. I went through the motions of having Peter take note of how I felt and writing a sorry note to me. I did a positive practice overcorrection, teaching him to slap his hands down upon his lap instead of another person's head. Next time I know I need to prepare better and bring a transition toy or activity with me, or let him experience the natural consequence of the heat to persuade him to leave the car. Peter accepted all the steps, and looked into my eyes sincerely when he said he was sorry. Although I remained calm throughout the process, inside I was shaking.

It helps to know what to do to help your child navigate through these meltdowns, but what do you do about yourself? It's the proverbial easier said than done to tell yourself not to take your child's aggressive actions personally. Your child desperately needs your unconditional love and understanding. I can testify that this kind of problem does indeed improve with practice. Peter resorts to hitting rarely now. Still, the heart of a parent is strong, but not made out of iron.

So the last step of this process is an essential one. Take the time to restore yourself. Find some respite care, and schedule in time for recollection and regular exercise, to see friends and do things you truly enjoy. If you mess up occasionally dealing with these meltdowns, give yourself some slack. Nothing is lost or hopeless. There's always time to rethink your strategy. Our kids give us plenty of opportunities to practice. As long as you keep getting up to try again, over the long haul, your child will learn he can trust you to be there for him, as ally, coach, and as his calm in the storm.

Trust your intuition

"Peter, put on your shoes. You're going bike riding with Charlie," I said over my shoulder as I rushed along trying to get out of the house. "I have to pick up Judy from the doctor's office." Time to pick up my daughter and newborn grandson from the doctor's office. I ran out the door, closing it behind me. But it took me several minutes to figure out how to buckle in the new car seat.

As I finally got into the driver's seat and turned on the engine, Peter emerged from the house with his aide, Charlie, behind. Peter glanced at me briefly, then continued on his way. "Let's go, Peter! Time to go bike riding!" Charlie said, urging him on. They passed my car. Suddenly, I heard two sharp whacks. "Hey! What did I do to deserve that?!" yelled Charlie. I turned off the engine, and ran out of the car. Peter was standing face to face with Charlie with his fists clenched and hands by his side. "Peter! What's going on?" I put my hand gently on Peter's arm. I waited, but no words emerged. Peter hung his head, with a furrowed brow. "Did you want to go with Mama?" I asked.

It was like the sunshine breaking through a cloud. He looked up at me with a big smile and shining eyes. "Yes!" he said enthusiastically. "Peter, you need to use words, not hitting," I said. "Say 'sorry' to Charlie." "Sorry," said Peter quickly, then turned to race to my car. "Not so fast," I said, gently restraining his arm with my hand. "Say, 'I want Mama,' to Charlie, so he knows what you want." "I want Mama!" said Peter promptly. Then he looked at me. "Okay, Peter," I nodded. He took off like a lightening bolt, dove into my car, and shut the door. "Let's all go pick up Judy and see the new baby," I announced, and we all took off together to our next adventure.

Sometimes our kids hit because they experience a strong emotion, and can't process it fast enough to come out with a more appropriate action than a protest/hit. I believe Peter saw me in the car, and really wanted to be with me. I'm not even sure he had crystallized a thought "I want Mama." He probably experienced a wave of longing and frustration, and only knew that something was wrong with this picture of Mama driving off without him when he wanted to be in that car too.

Neurotypical children and even us adults may also need may also help to process our emotions. Later that evening, I saw my 14-year-old son sitting on the couch, dejected. I passed by several times over the course of about 20 minutes as I ran around preparing for the next day, and noticed him sitting there in the same position. Finally, I stopped and sat on the couch next to him. "Teddy, is something bothering you, honey?" I asked. Then it came out. He was feeling bad about himself because he had forgotten to hand in his volleyball uniform. He talked about it, and came up with some executive planning strategies. I could see the relief on his face at the end of our conversation because he got something he needed. And I don't think what he needed so much were the executive planning tips, though they will be helpful in the future if we follow through.

What he needed most of all was to feel accepted. If he could see in Mom's face that being absentminded didn't make him any less lovable or acceptable, he could believe that himself, and still love and accept himself. We parents are mirrors for our children. They see themselves through our eyes. Oftentimes, we assume our children know we love them, and skip straight to the "fix it" step. But they are reading us all the time. When your child "messes up" you have a great opportunity. Even my neurotypical child needed help, and did not know how to ask for it directly. He did not automatically talk to me about his feelings, or know that might help him.

How much more so is this common problem magnified in our special needs kids. Use your body language, tone of voice, and touch to make your child know you want to understand, and that he is accepted unconditionally. Separate the problem from the child, and work on the problem as allies together.

Things happen fast. I wish I was better at quickly coming up with the words to give my child to express his emotions. I have to make myself take the time not to skip the words, along with the tone of voice and gestures. "Peter, I know you didn't mean to hit. You just didn't know how to tell us. I will let you come with me. But first let's fix this. Look at Charlie—see how he feels…" Then proceed with getting him to say sorry and use words and/or gestures to communicate instead of hitting. "Teddy, it's good you care so much. I can see you want to be responsible. I am absentminded too. Let me share some strategies that have helped me. We'll work on this together if you'd like."

Thank goodness I can always revisit the issue later. The next morning, I playacted the scene with Peter with his stuffed animals, and had Mama bear tell Peter bear that she understood why he hit because he was afraid she would drive away.

To know how to effectively help a child, you need to use your whole mind and heart. Use context, past history, and everything you know about your child's personality and desires to guess his intent. That is intuition. Then act as your child's peripheral brain. Help him fill in the gaps and communicate and act upon that intent appropriately. Acknowledge and verbalize his feelings so he feels understood and creates a space between himself and those feelings. Most importantly, when you calmly and lovingly accept his shortcomings while helping him correct them as his ally, he learns to love himself and to correct his mistakes instead of fearing them. When you encourage him to talk to you and try to express himself, you give him the tools to learn emotional regulation. Eventually, he will learn to talk to himself the same way, and be the stronger for it.

Chapter 17

Working on Self-Help Skills and Making Use of Routines

Peter and I have been practicing his bathing routine for several years. We'd gotten to the point where he could get through the whole routine from head to toe by imitating me as I would go through the motions standing outside the shower, without any physical prompts. It took some practice, but Peter finally learned how to even roll up the bath tub mat, pick up the bath tub toys, and hang up his towel with a few gestures as reminders. One day, I left to go answer a phone call. By the time I got back, I was astonished. Peter had finished his bath, dried himself, got dressed, and hung up his own towel. "You did such a great job" I beamed. As I saw the bath toys neatly stacked and tub mat rolled up and tucked away in a corner, I truly meant it as I said, "Better than any of your brothers could have done!"

I never imagined I'd see the day when I could make a comment like that. After hundreds of repetitions, you get to start thinking, "Why bother?" Surely if hundreds of repetitions haven't worked yet, this next one won't make a difference. There is a great temptation to give up teaching self-help skills and do everything for your child, as at that moment it would truly be the faster and easier way. However, I'm here to testify that even if hundreds of repetitions aren't enough, thousands may do the trick.

WHAT ARE SELF-HELP SKILLS?

Self-help skills refer to all the basic skills of daily living such as toileting, bathing, hand washing, feeding oneself, dressing, and brushing teeth. It also includes more advanced life skills such as making one's bed, folding and putting away laundry, setting the table, sweeping the floor, fixing simple meals, washing the dishes, and cleaning up toys after play or school supplies after working. More complex skills include checking out a book from the library and helping with shopping for and putting away groceries.

ATTITUDE

All of these routines may take a long time to learn with lots of repetition and patience. Peter has taken ten years and over 20,000 trials to learn how to go to the bathroom and wash his hands mostly independently, and then I still have to qualify the word "independently" because if I'm not keeping an eye on him, he'll still only rinse his hands for three seconds, which is not even long enough to get all the soap off. However, because we have relentlessly worked on these routines, I can at least say he has made progress on all of them, and I still consider myself sane.

The first point is attitude. Relax. Your personal goal should not be a certain achievement in your child, because biologically he may not be capable of reaching it, and it is absolutely not your fault, nor his. I learned this after massive frustration with my son's bowel incontinence that we struggled with for over ten years. Peter simply took a long time to develop the body awareness to know when he needed to go. Sometimes you have to remind yourself of progress—if you're still cleaning up four or five times a week, but your child has several bowel movements a day, remind yourself that he's 80 percent continent. The best you can do in these frustrating situations is to provide the support your child needs at the level he's at while regularly giving him the opportunity to learn.

What would not be helpful would be to give up and forever leave him in diapers, letting him grow accustomed to feeling wet, and never learning to tune into his body sensations. What would be harmful would be to get upset at him with every episode such that he felt bad about himself or grew anxious about toileting. You need to be persistent about offering your child the opportunity to learn, and be prepared to accept the consequences in a calm, objective manner.

The key to success is to keep the motivation high for your child to do his best during those opportunities. Say you believe your child is ready for potty training because he is clutching himself when he's about to go or has wet himself, or starts the need-to-go dance. When you believe the timing is right, and you place him on the potty, be sure to have a terrific reward waiting for him (see the box on Siegel's potty training method in Chapter 7, pp.91–2).

You can also turn on the motivation by creating a cost for not cooperating. Let your child feel the discomfort of wet or soiled pants at least occasionally. Have him help you clean up in a calm and sensible way—you do the big things while giving him something mildly unpleasant like the final scrubs, but not so big a task for him that it will create too much more work for you.

The general strategy is to offer just enough support, and withdraw it systematically and determinedly as your child shows greater capability. If you steel yourself to accept your child's inevitable mistakes with grace, every episode is an opportunity for him to learn to trust you. He will also learn that mistakes are a part of learning, and to accept them with grace and good humor.

SET REASONABLE GOALS

It's a good idea to pace yourself and your child. If you work on too many self-help skills all at once, you will both feel overwhelmed. So make yourself a list of skills that match what you developmentally believe he can succeed in, and just work on those.

Different self-help skills require different levels of motor planning, body awareness, memory, and judgment. It takes time to develop all these capacities, but practicing the steps in your child's routines actually helps him develop them. Select the routines or parts of routines that you feel your child can handle or are within his reach. As you practice those parts, he'll become more capable, and you'll be able to advance to harder steps. Once certain steps are mastered or you reach a plateau, keep them up or maintain them while you add more.

It always feels best when you pick the routines to work on that he has the best chance of success with—those that match his skills and interests. So with Peter, we began with a hand washing routine because he likes water, and with setting the table because he loves to eat.

HOW TO TEACH SELF-HELP SKILLS

Once you've decided what to teach, how do you teach it most efficiently? There are some useful tools to help you teach systematically and efficiently. Those conceptual tools are called task analysis, forward and backchaining, and positive practice overcorrection. Visual aides and music may also help your child tremendously if he's a visual learner and likes music. A systematic way to teach hand washing might start with presenting your child with a sequence of pictures depicting the various steps of turning on the taps, wetting the hands, using soap and rubbing the hands together, the final rinse, turning off the tap, and drying hands. That process of breaking down a task into its individual steps is called a *task analysis*.

Forward chaining

Point to each step as you label the action verbally. Provide your child with just enough support to carry out the step, following the usual order of prompts. *Forward chaining* is when you teach each step of the task analysis beginning from the first to the last.

Backchaining

Backchaining is when you teach the last step first, then the next to the last step, and so on until you've taught all the steps in backwards order in the task analysis. The beauty of this method is that the child has a built-in automatic reward in carrying out the last step (drying hands)— completion of the task (hand washing) and being able to go off and do something else (like eat!).

Combining methods

All this sounds much more complicated than when done in practice. In real life, you frequently combine the methods naturally. When introducing the visual picture sequence, do a forward chain to emphasize how the order of the steps matches both your song and picture sequence. But you might not want to fade all your prompts before moving on to teaching the next step. Fade your physical prompts, but continue pointing to the corresponding picture and/or continue singing through the entire forward chaining procedure, so your child has enough repetitions to memorize the song or learn to refer to the visual picture sequence on his own eventually. When you feel he's got reading the picture sequence down or knows the song, backchain fading your pointing or singing, starting from the last step to the first.

My point is that it doesn't really matter exactly which procedure you use, as long as you prompt sufficiently and then fade your prompts systematically and inexorably. The key is to pause long enough to give your child the opportunity to demonstrate his capability, but not so long that he forgets what he's doing and gets distracted.

"Do-overs," or positive practice overcorrections

If your child tries a step independently, but does it wrong, immediately correct him, showing him the right way with whatever level of prompting is necessary, so he doesn't get used to doing it wrong. Then try positive practice overcorrection, or "trying it again." This means "undoing" the step one or more times to give the child more opportunities to practice what you just taught him.

MAKING USE OF ROUTINES TO TEACH COORDINATED ACTIONS, TEAMWORK, TURN TAKING, LANGUAGE, INITIATIVE, AND REPRESENTATIONAL AND ABSTRACT THINKING

Since there are many ways to do a routine, each represents a wealth of potential educational opportunities. Make a bed together with your child on one side (initially with the other parent as coach) and you on the other. This is a perfect set-up to learn synchronized actions, as you imitate each other picking up one layer of bedding at a time, tugging at the same time to get rid of the wrinkles, and pulling that layer up to the head of the bed together. Your child can learn cause and effect as he sees that a pull in one direction but not another will smooth out a wrinkle.

Peter loves having a lot of stuffed animals on his bed. What a great opportunity to practice all the coordinated and synchronized actions necessary for catching and throwing. We started out with just a few animals, and stood a few feet apart. I gently threw them and Peter caught them. At this point, we have a dozen animals scattered around the room; I throw several, and then Peter throws several, or we start alternating throws. I purposely throw them from different angles at high speed so Peter has to pay attention. Sometimes we make it a language game, and I ask him if he wants the big or little penguin, the bunny versus the dog, or the gray or white seal. Or I ask him to throw me a particular animal, again staging it so that he has to pay attention to more than one attribute (for example, among a group of big and little whales and penguins, I might ask for the little penguin). Sometimes the stuffed animals get mischievous and play peek-a-boo so Peter gets to practice saying "Hi" and "Bye," or exchange places with the animals in his brother's adjoining bed, prompting Peter to protest "Mine!" or "Not mine!" Peter gets to practice coordinated actions, turn taking, pretend play, and language all in the context of making his bed.

You can work a fun interaction into almost any chore or routine. When Peter was first learning how to brush his teeth, we did a "Follow the leader" game where we would brush together in front of the mirror, and he had to follow my lead as I brushed one quadrant systematically after the next for 10 seconds each. We'd start and stop together. Once he learned the routine, I faded my cues, first by just gesturing and counting instead of actually brushing, and then just verbally saying up or down, left or right when he'd forget to do a quadrant. What started out as an RDI game became a self-help skill.

Setting the table, sorting utensils, loading the dishwasher, and sweeping with the broom/using the dustpan are all great opportunities to practice coordinated teamwork and switching roles. At times the whole family can get in on the act and create an assembly line to set the table or put away dishes or groceries.

Routines provide nice opportunities for the child to make the jump from concrete to representational thinking. When setting the table we made use of Peter's visual learning strengths and drew a plate, utensils, napkin, and cup on a laminated placemat which he could reference as he laid the items right on the placemat. Getting dressed was a fun opportunity to practice initiative and a bit of representational thinking, as we made a big laminated paper boy doll with Velcro tabs, and let Peter choose which piece of clothing to Velcro onto the doll. He then put on that corresponding underwear, t-shirt, pants, shirt or sweater on himself, while we sang, "This is the way, we put on our…(pants, shirts, etc.)" with each piece of clothing. A self-help routine became a bridge to pretend play.

Because they are repeated ad infinitum, routines make great opportunities to signpost beginnings and endings, to teach labels like "time to get up," "bedtime!" or "let's set the table, " and to mark closures with a celebratory high five or "thanks, good job!" Routines teach your child how to sequence and practice time words like first, next, then, and last.

Because your child develops expectations of what comes next, routines provide the perfect context to introduce unexpected, surprising actions and mistakes to get your child to initiate with corrective language and action.

Of course the repetition is also what makes routines a great opportunity for teaching language in general, as you pause and wait for the child to ask you for the pants or shirt, plate or spoon, and have him put away shopping items in the refrigerator, pantry, bathroom, and bedroom.

WORKING ON MOTIVATION

Sometimes, your child might get stuck, and even though you suspect he is capable of doing a self-help skill, he just doesn't seem motivated to try. For example, a child might show all the signs of toilet training readiness like knowing things go in certain places and dancing around when he needs to go, yet not be willing to sit on the potty. Or he might have the motor skills to put on his shoes and socks, yet not be willing to do it himself. When motivation is the problem, remember the principle of maximizing the power of a reinforcer (see pp.86–95).

WORKING TOWARD INDEPENDENCE AND AN ATTITUDE OF HELPFULNESS

Learning self-help skills can be fun and a source of pride for your child. Furthermore, as you consistently expect your child to do his part, and he enjoys the satisfaction of working as a team with you and feeling your warm thanks and praise, he will learn an attitude of helpfulness.

Teaching these skills does require a considerable degree of determination and organization on your part. A useful picture to have in your mind is constructing a building. You need scaffolding to build, but it is removed as each level is completed. Be determined to systematically withdraw supports as your child masters each tiny step of his routines.

DELEGATING AND COMMUNICATING

You also have to be organized in terms of delegating and communicating with your child's other helpers in his life. It's important to delegate some of this teaching to older siblings, babysitters, or respite workers, or you will spend your entire life getting through a day's worth of self-help routines with your child, and no one can do this amount of repetition and stay sane. When you do delegate, communication is crucial so that everyone knows what your child's level of capability is, and is determined to set similar expectations. Otherwise, someone else might be constantly undoing the independence that you are working so hard to build, as it's much easier just to do everything oneself than to demand it of the child.

Of course, no one can be totally consistent, and sometimes your child will be upset or feel ill, and you'll need to temporarily reduce demand. Be gentle on yourself and your child, but like a gentle stream, wear away along the same path, and you and your child will make progress together.

Chapter 18

How Can I Do This?

There's a scene at the end of "The Two Towers," the second film in the trilogy, "Lord of the Rings," in which the protagonist, Frodo, exhausted from his quest, sinks onto the ground and says, "I can't do this." His faithful friend and supporter, Sam, then reminds him of the noble reason for their quest. Those words of encouragement, along with Sam's tireless devotion, are enough for Frodo to pull himself together and get up to try once again.

There might be many times you feel like Frodo and say to yourself, "I can't do this." Parenting a neurotypical child these days is challenging enough, but meeting the needs of a child with a major disability can feel overwhelming. The needs of children with autism are great, and depending on the severity of the disability, the amount of energy and time required to meet them often exceed what parents can provide alone. Even if you've developed a working educational plan for your child, how do you go about implementing it? How do you build a team of tutors and develop a network of support to assist you in the overwhelming quest of educating your child?

ROUND UP THE USUAL SUSPECTS

Every local community has its own situation in terms of resources available to assist families with children with special needs. California has regional centers as the first source of government funding and guidance families generally turn to. In the United Kingdom, most public special education is funded through Dedicated Schools Grants which local authorities in consultation with their Schools Forums distribute to local schools. In the U.S., the local school district is also the main source of educational support for children with special needs, often providing schooling, speech, and occupational and physical therapy beginning in the preschool years.

But since every child is so unique and resources scarce, it is unlikely that public resources will suffice in terms of expertise, programs, and personnel available to completely meet your child's needs. And private health insurance companies in the U.S. often have very restrictive terms for coverage of autism treatments, and very broad definitions of what they consider "experimental" and therefore uncovered treatments.

PREPARE YOUR SCHEDULE

You can avoid a lot of frustration if you accept that educating your child is going to take a lot of your time and input. You can't depend on experts, and you can't depend on funding. Listen to your doctor, school district, and other specialists available to help you. Contact your local parent support groups and autism organizations to find out the best resources available in your area. Those are all important things to do. But the most worthwhile thing you can do for your child is to start working with him yourself. Try some of the ideas in this book and others, and don't be afraid to make a mistake. Funding can take weeks to months to come into place, but you do not need specialists and consultants to get started.

A regional consultant for special needs students enrolled in public schools once came over to my home for a get-together of families with children with autism. She asked me what I do with Peter. I was being completely honest with her when I told her, "I don't do anything different for Peter than what I've done for the rest of my seven children. Just more." In truth, you use the same principles of childrearing. Try to make things fun, get them to help, keep stretching them, and be persistent. It's called parent power! What ultimately gets through to these little ones is your warmth and love. No one loves your child like you do, which qualifies you as the best specialist for your child. Start with some of the "people games" in Sussman's *More Than Words*, or early exercises from Gutstein's *Relationship Development Intervention with Young Children*. Just start. That way, when your resources and funding start coming in, you'll be prepared to make the best decisions and choices, because you will know your child better.

Even once you get your school programs for your child together, you may find you need help to handle the "downtime." I encourage every parent to look into a home-based social and emotional development program like floortime, RDI, and/or the Hanen Program (Sussman 1999), so you will get training for yourself and can start training assistants to work with your child at home. Regular exercise should be a component of that home program, whether you check out a book on yoga and do it together at home, or look to see if there's an adaptive recreational program locally available in swimming, gymnastics, or other sports.

No matter how much help you find though, don't ever give up working with your child directly. Carve out special time everyday to get to know, interact with, and enjoy your child. It doesn't have to be a big chunk of time all at once. Perhaps you could start by working with him 20 minutes several times a day around your family's daily routines such as when you get him up for the morning, upon returning home from work or school, and when you put him to bed. Make the most of the brief "passing" moments of the day to connect with your child, such as giving little tickles or roughhousing, or a few minutes of floortime. I have a friend, Nene, who is a mother of ten. I asked her how she manages to give each child individual attention. She replied, "When I have to do something for one, like brush her hair or give him a glass of milk, I put my affection in there. In all the little things I do with them or for them." When Nene is with one of her children, she is really present in that moment with that child, communicating her affection with her attentiveness, gestures, and eye contact.

A word about guilt

Guilt is that gnawing, uncomfortable sadness you feel when you're not doing what your conscience tells you that you should be doing. As parents, it's common to believe that it is our job to provide everything our children need to become independent and happy. This is a problem for a parent of a child with a severe disability. Sooner or later you come to realize that you cannot possibly provide everything your child needs. Even if you sacrificed everything else in your life, you might not get there, and then you would feel guilty about the other people and the goals you abandoned along the way!

My advice to you is to surrender. Your dream that your child will somehow find a way to get his needs met throughout his life and learn how to be happy is absolutely right. The misconception is that you are responsible for making that happen, or you are not doing what you should. No one should bear the burden of controlling the future. It's simply not true that any one of us has such control, not even over our own lives, let alone those of others.

On the other hand, the love you put into all your little interactions with your child adds up. Don't underestimate what you can do. Read this and some of the other books in the References on how to teach. That way, what you do, you can do well. You can make all those little bits of time and energy you can muster throughout the day count for a lot. Because each one of those interactions will carry with it the beautiful and transforming power of love. So rein in that overactive imagination that anticipates everything that could possibly go wrong in the future, and "let the day's own trouble be sufficient for the day" (*Matthew* 6:34). We all have limited resources. Just do your best, and be at peace.

ON FINDING GUIDANCE, SUPPORT, AND RESOURCES

You'll need some guidance and support. Find a good special needs library or look online. Books are empowering, and you don't need to read them cover-to-cover all at once. Just read the sections most relevant to your child at the stage that he's at or for the particular problem you're facing, practice what you read, and then move on.

Going to conferences is a great place to find consultants who can help you with your home program. When you hear a speaker you really like, go up afterwards to talk to him. Even if he doesn't do private consulting, he may know where to refer you. Your developmental pediatrician or local parent support group are also good sources of referrals and support.

A good independent consultant, usually a licensed psychologist specializing in autism, who you like and trust, can help you in many ways. That person can help you put together and troubleshoot for your home program, assist you with parent training and perhaps even help you train your home volunteers, be another objective observer of your school program, and provide references to other specialists and tutors. It's helpful to have a credentialed, objective person to bounce your ideas off of to make sure you don't go off the deep end, to be your child's advocate with other agencies, and offer you support and encouragement.

ON TEAM BUILDING

When building a team of people to help you with your child, it is helpful to have the attitude of reasonable expectations. There are many fine people, professionals and volunteers, who may be willing to work with you and your child, but they, like you, have their limitations. I remember another parent asking me for a floortime referral once. When I mentioned the name of a talented floortime specialist to him, he shook his head. She had developed a reputation of being late. "I don't need to deal with that," he said. I felt it was a loss for his child because it was probably the same easy going, laid back personality that made her chronically late that also made her so remarkable at floortime. My point is to be flexible. Don't burn your bridges.

Everyone brings their unique set of talents, interests, and strengths. Much of your job will be team building, matching the right person to work with your child in the right part of his program. Therefore, a bubbly, energetic teenager might be a perfect assistant coach to do interactive floortime and RDI games with you and your child, but you'd better ask a more disciplined and organized acquaintance to take over parts of your ABA program.

My older sons find one-on-one tabletop work tedious. Though I still made them learn how to do it so they could help me out here and there in a pinch, I mostly ask them to take Peter out biking or skateboarding. The better you can match a person to a task, the more fun everyone will have, and the longer your helpers, paid and volunteers, will last. For me personally, I found I was a lot better naturally at some teaching methods than others, but was able to "grow," albeit a little painfully, into a reasonable level of competence, even in the areas that were originally harder. Autism has a way of stretching you, and parents grow along with their child.

A word of caution

It goes without saying, of course, that you provide appropriate training and supervision for everyone who works with your child. That can be as simple as being within earshot, or at least making a habit of spot checking briefly and randomly to see how your child is doing or if he or your helper need anything. Catch a problem before it gets so frustrating that your child reacts with a challenging behavior. Establishing procedures and boundaries such as spot checks, working in common areas, periodic supervision and coaching, and not delegating bathroom assistance also discourage the potential of abuse. Having helpers at home does free you substantially to do other things, but not completely. The safety of your child depends upon your making your presence felt.

DEVELOPING A WIDE CIRCLE OF FRIENDS

Professor Mary Falvey wrote a book called *Believe in My Child with Special Needs!* (2005, pp.57–61), in which she explains a concept of helping your child develop a "circle of friends." Your child is part of a larger community. You can help your child enormously by helping him build a community of people around him who know him and care about him. There's the inner circle of immediate family, then extended family and good friends, then casual friends and acquaintances, and finally professionals who are paid to work with your child. For the family members and close friends who want to commit to even small regular "playdates" with your child for a period, teach them limited repertoires of games, activities, and teaching methods that match their interests and personalities. Each one will develop his or her own style and relationship with your child—vive la différence!

A little repertoire goes a long way

Peter's big brothers are now in high school and college, and have very busy schedules. I ask each of them to just make the attempt to do a few circles of interaction with Peter a day. I give them an easy repertoire that's fast, discreet, and convenient. As they mill around the house in the evenings, I'm sure there are moments they can catch Peter rummaging in the kitchen looking for snacks or watching a bit of TV. So when they see him watching TV, they can sit next to him for a couple of minutes, make comments about the program, and pause the video now and then to ask what emotion is depicted on one of the character's face. When they catch him foraging in the pantry, they can have him use words to request his choice of snack, take a small portion out, and use it to play a few rounds of a language game with Peter. (See Chapter 11, pp.191-5 and Chapter 12, pp.215-23.) Sometimes I'll grab a big brother to work as a team with Peter loading the dishwasher or sweeping the floor. One rinses, the other loads. One sweeps, the other handles the dustpan. The point is to make the repertoire short, convenient, and easy. Keep it interesting by varying the activities you teach and request family members to do with your child. After a while, if you're reasonable and persistent, everyone will get used to being asked, and interact naturally and habitually with their special sibling.

Make an effort to introduce your child to the "community helpers" in your neighborhood, so your local librarian, store clerks, and even firemen and policemen if possible know your child's name. Some of them may occasionally pause to get a hello or high five from your child in passing. Similarly introduce your child to neighbors and acquaintances at church so there are many people who know his name and can wave to or greet him, or at the very least know to whom to return him if he ever gets lost. Many churches can recruit volunteers to help you set up a special needs Sunday school class, and some of these people may also be willing to do some part-time tutoring afterschool for your child. My child's level of disability makes it very difficult to develop peer friendships, but in recruiting the older children of my best friends to do part-time tutoring and babysitting, at least Peter has a circle of friends of his generation who can be part of his community as they grow up together.

Sandee, a friend of mine, sent me an email the other day. Here's what she wrote:

> A friend of mine has an autistic adult son, probably in his 40s. He lives in an apartment with two roommates. I had seen him a couple times with them, and when I was in Barnes & Noble one day, I passed him in the aisle, and said, "Hi Mark." He whirled around and put his arms across his chest (hands on shoulders) and had the most shocked and scared look on his face. He bent backwards a bit and just looked at me. I quickly added, "My name is Sandee, and your parents are friends of mine. We are in a Bible study together." He relaxed a bit, smiled and nodded. I waved and said, "Nice to see you," and went on my way. I don't remember that he said anything to me. The next time I saw his mother, she said, "Mark said he saw you in Barnes & Noble." So, when he saw his mother, or called her, he remembered my name and said that he saw me.

Our kids sometimes react to unfamiliar people in a way that discourages interaction. Mark may have looked startled and appeared discomfited with Sandee's overture, but the fact that Mark told his mother about their meeting demonstrated that it meant something to him. How much friendlier and warmer the world would seem to our children, if many people were like Sandee, and made the effort to connect. There are many people of good will around who no doubt would like to be helpful, but don't know how. Another way to help your child is to make the effort to build this outer circle of friends as well. Be outgoing, and don't be shy about introducing him, modeling and coaching both his responses and those of the person trying to interact with him.

GO TOGETHER

You truly are an ambassador between two worlds, the world of special needs children and the world of neurotypical thinkers. That leads me to making the point that the way you go about getting your child's needs met matters. If you treat your school district and other providers collaboratively and reasonably, they will be more likely to treat the next family with a child with special needs with openness and flexibility. If you introduce your child to others with openness and ease, and gently coach them along as the situation warrants, they will feel more comfortable engaging your child and asking you questions on how to do it better. They may lose some of their shyness in approaching the next person with a disability. When people see you love, accept, and enjoy your child, they may realize that there is a beautiful treasure under all those layers of disability for those who make the effort of discovery.

Helping your child up the developmental ladder should not be a lone quest. Welcome your friends and family into your child's life, and build a community. Be flexible and open to the talents and personalities of others, and build a team. The best people in Peter's life didn't come with experience or credentials. They did, however, come highly gifted in love, patience, and the humility to be willing to learn. Those are the qualities to look for in the people you recruit to work with your child. And don't worry, you don't have to be good at everything. You will find the people who can balance you. The most important thing you can do is love your child for who he is. That is the most essential ingredient in the education of your child.

Conclusion
A Toolbox of Slingshot and Stones

The story of David and Goliath is one that we sometimes see repeated in our own lives. Peter faces Goliaths of daunting proportions. Take his OCD. One morning he was tapping and tearing paper to the point of frenzied madness. I keep a special magazine hidden in the back of the car that has just his favorite thickness of paper to tear. I pull out one page at a time when I need a reward to motivate Peter. He was going through my car trunk looking for that magazine like an addict looking for drugs. I spent the day keeping this Goliath at bay by working hard to keep Peter busy.

But then it was time for evening Mass. I had been helping Peter practice a self-monitoring activity for weeks to keep him from tapping and tearing paper in church. He was getting pretty good at this activity, and knew the procedure well. But would it work on a day like today, when Goliath was huge? As we entered the church, I felt like I was sending David into the arena with nothing but a slingshot and stone.

Yet there at Mass he sat doing an absolutely excellent job of self-monitoring. He remembered to keep turning a three-minute sand timer, checking off one of a series of boxes I'd scribbled on a sheet of paper after the sand ran dry, and even recapping the pen each time. He did it all himself, and very politely asked me for a piece of a crisp seaweed snack I kept ready after he checked off each box. After finishing all the boxes, he looked at me to make sure it was okay to get his final reward, taking the piece of paper outside to tear it up. Who would have guessed that such huge madness could be contained with such a simple procedure and idea?

Echolalia is another one of Peter's Goliaths. Every evening he asks me for a car ride before bed. As we drive around the city, I ask him questions about his day. Typically, I offer him a fill-in the blank or multiple-choice question to make word retrieval easier. Sadly, most of the time, he answers with whatever word choice I last said.

But one night, after his bath, I thought I'd try something new, and sat on the couch with Peter and his AT device. I wrote the questions on his Vantage, and he answered them with my help. I was pleased and surprised that many times he would find the proper icons before I could. Then in the car, I pretty much repeated all the questions plus some extras with comments sprinkled in between. To my delight, Peter was echolalic only once. He answered the other six questions correctly, using single words, and sometimes whole phrases.

"Why did you write a sorry letter this morning?" "Because I tore paper," he replied spontaneously. It was Papa's bill. "What kind of muffins did we bake, banana or corn?" "Corn" he replied. That might have been echolalia, but he did say it clearly, fast, and loud, as if he were sure. "What kind of exercise did Papa, Mama, Luke and Peter do this morning?" "Rode bikes." "What kind of laundry did we fold? Towels, shirts, and…" "Underwear!" replied Peter. We both chuckled. "Who did you work with this afternoon?" "Miss Jeannette." No problem with that one. He loves Miss Jeannette. "Why did we go to Papa's office? What was Papa doing?" "Look eyes." "How were your eyes?" "Good!" "Where did we go after Papa's to buy things?" "Shopping store." "What did we buy?" "Mel… ('on' I prompted) Melon!" "Did you like our walk after dinner?" "Like it!" "What color was the sky?" "Rosey." I was getting goosebumps. A real conversation in the car with Peter talking to me from the backseat!

So previewing our conversation on the Vantage defeated Goliath that night. Peter always surprises me. Autism can look so hopeless, with all the inertia, crazed OCD behavior, and echolalia, but once in a while, we have our triumphant moments. Don't hesitate to try that little slingshot. We use simple ideas, like checking off boxes to learn to wait and previewing to assist word retrieval, but with a little persistence, insistence, and affection to make it clear we're on the same team, these are powerful and empowering tools for Peter. There are times my little David can conquer Goliath.

I hope I have not overwhelmed you with all the information in this book—autism can feel like an overwhelming disorder. Everything takes effort for our children, and everything requires teaching.

My goal in writing this book is not to make your job any harder, but to help make it possible. Without knowledge and tools, our children are just too hard to raise. To unlock them from this devastating condition requires a multimodal, holistic educational approach, utilizing insights and methods gleaned from a variety of approaches to work on every affected part of the brain.

No single teaching methodology can provide the motivation, repetition, and generalization required to rewire the brain when a child is comprehensively and heavily impacted. But each method has its great insights. DTT provides the systematic breakdown of cognitive concepts into tiny learnable steps. RDI does the same with social and emotional development and provides the frameworks to focus on one fundamental social skill at a time. Floortime (or DIR) principles remind us to constantly make relationship and emotional attunement central, forging the connection between relationship and emotional satisfaction and regulation, affect and motivation. Sussman's Hanen Program (see p.75) maximizes one's ability to provide incidental teaching in the home to develop communication skills. The TEACCH method explains how to create strong visual supports in the environment. Pivotal response training emphasizes the development of pivotal skills such as motivation, initiation, and self-monitoring. Rather than competing with each other, the different teaching methodologies complement one another.

Fortunately, you don't have to memorize this alphabet soup of educational approaches. They all boil down to some common principles that form a toolbox of common sense for parents who want to teach their child with love and skill. Teaching is really all a matter of conversation. Consider what you yourself do when you want to communicate with someone (Sussman 1999, pp.92–109, 2006, p.87).

The first step is to observe and listen. Attune to your child with your whole mind, heart, and intuition, using what you know about his preferences, personality, and history to read his mood and anticipate his needs. No one can productively learn and interact when the spirit or body is upset because of anxiety, frustration, exhaustion, pain, hunger, thirst, or the need to use the bathroom. Your tools are *accommodations for his sensory and body needs, and affective bonding* to calm and soothe those upset feelings. It doesn't work to try to skip this step. You must get your child into a "regulated state" before he can learn anything. Since many of our children can't regulate themselves (though they get better at it with patient training), we parents find ourselves spending a lot of time and energy at this step, and coming back to this time and time again. Get good at sensory integration and patiently buffering your child's moods, and it will pay off in spades.

The second step is to respond to what you've heard. Let your child know you've listened and understood him by *interpreting* or translating what he's tried to say, or *imitating* or responding to his actions, while trying to shape his words and actions into something meaningful and purposeful. Showing that you've attuned to him is the best way to motivate him to attune to you, which prepares him for the next step.

The third step is your turn. This is your opportunity to introduce something new. The best way to encourage your child to listen to what you have to communicate is to *include his interests.* The genius of *incidental teaching* is to creatively engineer or take advantage of all the naturally occurring teachable moments in daily life to motivate your child to learn when he's intrinsically interested in what you have to teach. When you can't think of a way to incorporate *intrinsic reinforcement* into your teaching, you can still include your child's interest using your tools of *extrinsic reinforcement, shared control,* and *limited choices.*

The content of your turn otherwise depends on your child's level of cognitive and social development. At the earliest stages of development, your turn may be the start of a simple sensory game like peek-a-boo or tickles. Later that might be imitation games or teaching actions in a play circuit. Once your child develops a capacity for symbolic thought, you might teach language or quantities. Eventually, you may be developing your child's ability to think abstractly, introducing concepts of cause and effect, time, space, categories, comparisons, and feelings. Analogously, regarding social development, initially you may be working on the fundamentals of teaching your child how to coordinate and synchronize actions with you, read facial expressions and body language, and develop a repertoire of gestures. Later, your child will learn to compete, to initiate with variations to your games, and then learn to transform them, and co-create new ones.

Your tools for this step of taking your turn in the conversation are to *break down concepts or skills into steps as small as necessary* for your child to be able to learn them, adjusting the size of the steps and the level of support or prompting you provide according to *constant feedback* elicited from your child at every step. Use the principle of *moving from the concrete to representational to the symbolic* in your teaching, and provide *auditory and visual supports* as needed to circumvent processing disorders. As Sussman puts it, "Say less, stress, go slow, and show" ("the four S's"; see p.146 and Glossary).

The last step to complete one circle of conversation is to invite or elicit a response from your child. Your greatest tool is patience, as you *pause and wait* to allow your child time to process. Playfully and gently *intrude and insist*, prompting your child as needed to complete that circle of interaction. The *order of prompts* (Sussman 1999, pp.114–23; see also Cooper *et al.* 2007, pp.401–4; Miltenberger 2004, pp.198–206) is a useful tool for systematically withdrawing the level of your prompting or support to guide your child toward independence, while being cognizant that sometimes continued support may always be needed. The goal of every teaching method is to keep a child on that edge of challenge and success such that he feels successful and motivated to keep learning that next learnable concept or skill, whether that is the next vocabulary word in his DTT program or following eye gaze in an RDI exercise.

As with any conversation, aim for as many circles of listening, reflecting, talking, and again listening to your child's response as is meaningful and fun, in the case of a social interaction, or until you've finished communicating what you need to, in the case of a lesson teaching a concept or skill. Keep the conversation going with good *timing, pace,* and *rhythm* according to the processing speed and attention span of your child. Keep up your child's motivation by making the curriculum interesting, relevant, and useful to him at the level he's at, by providing adequate support to make the effort required manageable for him, and of course with your enthusiasm and warm encouragement. Your child's relationship of love and trust with you will become his strongest motivator.

Affect (emotion) does drive motivation and attention, and therefore learning. For any learning to stick, it must be *generalized.* Consolidate a newly learned concept or skill by applying it in all different settings, locations, and positions with different people, using different objects. Stay at one developmental level for as long as it takes your child to master it, knowing that development is built one level upon the other, and real progress is possible only upon strong foundations. Your child will show you if you've got the balance right between challenge and success by the twinkle in his eye.

I realize that my child has biological limitations. When I see him struggle to motor through the complex coordination of breath control, tongue and lip positioning and laryngeal contractions needed to produce intelligible speech (speech dyspraxia), forget what he wanted to say while looking for the person he wanted to tell (short working memory), or pound his chin so hard that he cries (compulsive self-stimulatory behavior to the extremes of self-injury), I doubt he will ever lose the diagnosis of autism. I've come to accept that. What we really want for our children is for them to be happy, and we assume that their capacity for happiness only increases with their capacity to think, relate, and act upon their environment.

In Peter's case I can testify that that assumption is true. When I see him smile widely with pride and give me a "See, I did it!" look on doing his work well, spontaneously slap me a high five after making the bed together, or laugh with delight when one of those light bulbs goes on and he understands a new concept, I think of how profoundly human it is to have this love of learning and accomplishment. When he first learned how to ride a two-wheeler bicycle, I remember watching him ride fast around and around with glee. It was so worth those hundreds of laps we made holding onto his handle bars and letting go for microseconds at a time (we actually started with a "buddy bike," an adaptive sort of tandem bike).

Peter always surprises me. The other day I was walking my bike and reached the gate that was closed. I looked over at Peter who was 20 feet away, and he came over and held the gate open for me to walk my bike through. When getting ready to unload the groceries from the car, I'll be hollering for the big kids to come over and help me, and there will be Peter, already standing there by the trunk, waiting to carry in the bags. I was teasing one of my older sons one night, pointing to my cheek and asking for a kiss while he groaned and protested, and the next thing I knew, I felt two warm little arms around my neck and a gentle kiss on the cheek from none other than my quiet Peter.

There is so much going on inside of these beautiful, precious children, but sometimes they can't let us know or we don't see it because their challenges loom so prominently in our minds. My point is that working off of hope is better than working off of doubts and preconceptions. I love Greenspan's inspiring perspective of never assuming a ceiling or fixed deficit, but moving one foot forward after the next to see where the developmental journey takes you.

My father asked me why I would bother writing this book, because he said so few parents have the luxury of quitting their job to spend as much time and energy as I have in working with my child. But my goal in writing this is to help parents so perhaps they will not feel so desperate and compelled to quit their jobs (though if you do, you will have only so much more experience enjoying your child). If you understand what's wrong with your child, the general principles of treatment and the fundamentals of the various treatment modalities, and know enough about the developmental process to know where you're going and what to aim for next, you can design your child's treatment program better, even if other agencies and providers are doing most of the hands-on implementation. And you can convert your despair time with your child into productive quality time—because you have the tools to connect with your child and have fun with him as well as help him along in his development.

Consider gathering a library of outstanding references like the ones cited in the References. Read and try the activities presented for each level as your child develops. You don't have to know it all at once, but learn as you go, and your child will teach you as you go. The resources listed are the ones I use, but you know your child the best, so I encourage you to read on your own and choose your own favorite references. We parents are so fortunate to live at this time in this country, with all the outstanding contributions made by brilliant minds for the benefit of our children, and the ready availability of information from books and the internet. I really encourage you to tap into the power of reading, to mine the fantastic amount of information and ideas circulating to try out the ones most likely to work on your child.

You know your child the best. You know his sensory preferences, interests, strengths, and challenges better than anyone else. You spend the most time with your child, and have the opportunity to work with him in all kinds of settings including your daily routines at home, working in the kitchen or garden together or while watching a video together, during community outings, and during special times you carve out for one-on-one playtime or reading time together. You have the most motivation to help him because you love him the most, and you have the greatest potential to bring out the best in him because he loves you the most.

There are many of us families with children with moderate to severe autism, and not enough experts and providers to meet the needs of all our children. The good news is that you are the most important teacher your child will ever have. If you know what you are doing, you can start intervention immediately and constantly as a way of life. After a while, the principles will seep into your brain and become a habit, and you will automatically be doing "floortime, all the time" (Greenman and Wieder 2006, p.186). I think you'll find it's fun, especially if you pace yourself and give yourself enough time to refresh, recollect, and maintain your other important family relationships by training enough babysitters and gathering enough supports.

I've been down your road. Having all these tools has been like having a compass, machete and water on a trek through a jungle. Without them, I probably would have lost my way, and my son to his own impenetrable world. Instead, he is joyful and connected, with a great love of learning and pride in his work and helping around the house as a team. Such is the power of knowledge and understanding, applied to even as implacable a foe as autism.

I've introduced a lot of slingshots and stones in our journey together through this book. I hope you find them useful skills to employ in the education of your child. But it's really the power of love that will enable your child to conquer his Goliaths and move up the developmental ladder. Bring lots of friends along with you. By delegating one small game or activity for them to do on a regular basis, you'll be building your child's community of friends and future supports, and allowing one more person in on the treasure who is your child.

> Give, and it will be given to you; good measure, pressed down, shaken together, running over, will be put into your lap. For the measure you give will be the measure you get back. (*Luke* 6:38)

Glossary

ABA (applied behavioral analysis): A technique of analyzing behavior, its causes and consequences, in order to improve it through positive and negative reinforcement.

Accommodation: Addressing needs by providing for them or supporting them.

Action-oriented directions: Short, clear, imperative instructions given to assist an individual with motor planning issues with the least amount of verbiage to process.

Affect: Emotion, feeling.

Affect regulation: Modulation or buffering of affect to achieve a calm, focused mental state.

Affect tolerance: The capacity to feel big emotions without losing control.

Affective bond: Emotional bonding.

Affective filter: The effect of relationship and emotion on perception and learning.

Amygdala: A part of the limbic system, or emotional center of the brain, that performs a primary role in the processing and memory of emotional reactions, including fear and anxiety.

AT/apps (assistive technology/communication applications): Dedicated communication devices/computer software that are often run on a smart phone or tablet; both are designed to help a child communicate by making manual choices.

Attention deficit: Difficulty with focusing and paying attention.

Attunement: Listening to and observing another person in order to understand his feelings, needs, and what he's trying to express.

Auditory processing disorder: A deficit in comprehending and remembering auditory input.

Autism spectrum disorder: A neurological, developmental disorder characterized by repetitious behaviors and deficits in social relating, communication, and sensory processing.

Automaticity: The ability to perform with little conscious effort because a skill is either innate or thoroughly mastered through practice.

Backchaining: Teaching the steps of a procedure in backwards order to harness the motivating power of task completion.

Basal ganglia: A part of the brain involved with attention, and starting and stopping action.

Big picture (or *Gestalt*) thinking: The ability to see the forest from the trees, and organize thoughts in terms of subjects, topics, and themes.

Block trials: A series of teaching trials in discrete trials training (DTT) in which the same item to be learned is presented repetitively in blocks before switching to another item that the student has to discriminate it from.

Broca's area: A part of the brain responsible for expressive language (speaking).

Cerebellum: A part of the brain that controls the rate, rhythm, force, and coordination of actions.

Circle of interaction: A back and forth interaction in which an initiation is met with a response which circles back when the initiator then responds meaningfully to that response (for example, baby smiles, parent smiles back, and baby laughs in delight).

Communicative intent: Having something to say, the desire to communicate.

Consolidation: Practicing at the same level of prompting until learning is fully mastered and performance no longer effortful.

Conversation: A back and forth exchange in which each person's response depends upon the other.

Corpus callosum: A mass of neurological cables that connect the right and left sides of the brain.

Differential reinforcement: Rewarding more for greater effort or achievement.

DIR: The developmental, individual-difference, relationship-based interventional model that uses floortime (Greenspan and Wieder 1998, 2006).

DRA (differential reinforcement of alternative): A method of inhibiting a misbehavior by reinforcing an alternative behavior (for example, keeping a child busy coloring a picture in a doctor's waiting area so he doesn't just sit there and stim).

DRI (differential reinforcement of incompatible): A method of inhibiting misbehavior by engagement in a behavior incompatible with the misbehavior (for example, getting a child to string beads to keep his hands out of his mouth).

DRO (differential reinforcement of other): A method of inhibiting misbehavior by rewarding the child for not doing it for predetermined periods of time.

DTT (discrete trials training): A technique used in applied behavioral analysis (ABA) in which teaching is broken down into trials, or tiny steps in which an instruction is given, and feedback from the child elicited to demonstrate learning.

Dyspraxia: Partial loss of ability to perform coordinated actions.

Echolalia: Answering by repeating the last word or words heard.

Emotional coregulation: The work of emotionally buffering and calming another person.

Emotionally regulated state: A calm, focused state of mind.

Engagement: A state of paying attention to and being involved with another person.

Executive function: A set of mental processes that helps connect past experience with present action, used in planning, organizing, strategizing, paying attention to and remembering details, and managing time and space.

Expanded trials: A series of teaching trials in discrete trials training (DTT) in which the target item is presented in successively lower frequency between presentations of distracter items.

Experience sharing interaction: Interaction for the sake of sharing thoughts and feelings rather than to get a need or want met.

Expressive language: Talking via any of a number of different modalities such as sign, picture exchange communication system (PECS), AT/apps, verbal or written speech.

Extrinsic reinforcement: Rewards that are unrelated to the action being rewarded, such as giving a skittle to a child for correctly naming an animal.

Field: The choices presented from which the student has to select his answer.

Floortime: A teaching method used in the developmental, individual-difference, relationship-based interventional (DIR) approach in which the child is drawn into circles of interaction as the therapist follows his interests and lead.

Forward chaining: A method of teaching the steps of a procedure in order from beginning to end.

"Four S's": A pneumonic created by Sussman (1999, p.194)—"Say less" means to simplify what you say, using short sentences. "Stress" means to use your tone of voice and vocal inflections to emphasize key words. "Go slow" means to give your child time to process your words. "Show" means to use gestures, visuals, and tangibles to provide multimodal cues.

Frontal lobe: A part of the brain responsible for planning, inhibition, impulse control, and judgment.

Frontloading: Pre-teaching, priming, or preparing the individual before an event or a learning task.

Functional behavioral analysis: An analysis of the antecedents and consequences of a target behavior to determine what function the behavior serves so that more adaptive behaviors may be substituted.

Gestalt: An integrated understanding of a set of data, big picture thinking.

Graphic organizer: A visual aide like a table, flowchart, or graph that pictures how thoughts may be organized and related.

Gyrus: A fold in the brain.

Hanen Program: A teaching method that gives parents the tools to help their children communicate using everyday activities and visual supports.

High affect: Being animated, energetic, and expressive.

Hypersensitivity: Oversensitive.

Hyposensitivity: Undersensitive.

Icon: A simple line drawing or small pictorial representation to be read instead of or to supplement written words.

Ideation: The ability to form ideas as opposed to perceiving and responding automatically.

Incidental learning: Learning within a natural context, using the teachable moment as opposed to planned lessons.

IEP (Individualized Education Program): A term used in the U.S. to signify an educational program designed collaboratively by parents and school educators and uniquely for a particular child that includes goals and objectives, accommodations for any disabilities, and a specific plan of services to help meet the goals; in England and Wales, the loose equivalent would be the Statement of Special Needs construed at an annual review meeting.

Inertia: Difficulty starting or initiating action.

Instrumental interaction: Interaction for the sake of getting a need or want met.

Intrinsic reinforcement: Rewards that are a natural consequence of the action being rewarded, such as giving a skittle of a certain color to a child naming that color.

Intuition: 1) Immediate knowledge without the conscious use of reason; 2) Using what one knows about the history, situational context, and personality of another person to read or guess their intent.

Joint attention: The ability to get another person's attention, direct it to an object of interest, and check back to ascertain the person's reaction.

Limbic system: The parts of the brain involved with generating emotion.

Maintenance activity: Already mastered activities to be maintained in repertoire.

Mass trials: A type of discrete trials training (DTT) trial in which the same item and instruction is presented repeatedly, such as repeatedly saying, "Give me ball" and having the student hand over a ball to introduce the label "ball" to the student.

Meltdown: Irrational, disruptive behavior caused by an uncontrolled emotional outburst, usually preceded by anxious (agitated but able to reason and negotiate) and defensive (self control barely retained, but still able to make choices) phases and followed by a tension reduction (calming down) phase. Terms derived from Crisis Prevention Institute, Inc. (2005) Nonviolent Crisis Intervention Training Program, www.crisisprevention.com, 1-800-558-8976.

Multisensory teaching: Engaging more than one sense in teaching such as using tangibles to teach addition that may involve auditory, visual, and tactile components.

Negative reinforcement: An unpleasant stimulus that motivates a target behavior in order to be relieved of it, such as a ringing alarm clock that makes the sleeper wake up.

Neocortex: The most highly evolved part of the cerebral cortex.

Neurotypical: Normal, not having a neurologic disability or deficit.

Occupational therapy: Interventions aimed at enabling a person to perform daily activities (occupations), particularly fine motor and sensory integration.

OCD (obsessive compulsive disorder): A mental disorder characterized by preoccupation with nonfunctional repetitive thoughts and actions.

Order of prompts: A ranking of prompts from strongest to mildest; a typical hierarchy is physical to demonstration to verbal to gestural to position/proximity to previously learned responses.

Paraphasic error: An involuntary substitution of an incorrect word for the correct one.

Pathophysiology: The physiologic mechanism of a disease or disorder.

PECS (picture exchange communication system): The child hands over a card with a picture representation of a desired item or activity in exchange for the item or activity.

Perspective taking: The ability to guess or understand another person's perceptions, thoughts, and feelings.

Physical therapy: Therapy aimed at improving movement and motor planning.

Pivotal response training: A treatment approach that emphasizes the teaching of "pivotal" or key behaviors that are central to wide areas of functioning, including initiation, motivation, and the ability to respond to multiple cues (Koegel and Koegel 1995).

Play circuit: A pattern of play interactions that can be repeated and therefore anticipated.

Positive practice overcorrection: To repeat a reparative or corrective action one or more times in order to solidify learning the right over the wrong way.

Positive reinforcement: A reward given to increase the frequency of a correct or desired behavior.

Praxia: The ability to perform purposeful motor sequences fluently like opening a jar or combing one's hair.

Priming: Pre-teaching or preparing.

Proprioception: A sense of the relative position of different body parts (for example, arms and legs) derived from sensory receptors in the muscles, joints, and ligaments.

Random rotation: A type of discrete trials training (DTT) trial in which the target item is presented in random order with other mastered items.

RDI (relationship development intervention): An intervention designed to systematically teach relational skills in a developmental progression (Gutstein 2000, 2002a, 2002b).

Receptive language: Comprehension, understanding of language.

Reconciliation: The step in the process following a misbehavior in which the perpetrator attempts to make amends to injured parties.

Reinforcement hierarchy: Ranking rewards in order of preference so that the most intensely desired rewards can be reserved for the greatest achievements or to motivate a child to perform the least preferred tasks.

Reinforcement schedule: The frequency of rewarding; it can be continuous (given every time a correct response occurs) or intermittent, given in fixed or variable ratios or at fixed or variable intervals.

Reinforcement survey: A search for information regarding what can be used as rewards for a particular student, conducted by offering a variety of items, observation, and speaking with other people who work with him.

Reinforcer: A reward; it can be tangible like a sticker or edible, an activity like tickling, swinging, or bubbles, or tokens to be accumulated and exchanged for larger prizes or time spent doing a preferred activity.

Remediation: 1) Addressing deficits by trying to correct or repair them; 2) the step in the process following a meltdown in which a more appropriate behaviour is taught to substitue for the maladaptive behavior.

Scaffolding: Providing the correct level of support or prompting, and withdrawing it systematically as competence is demonstrated.

Secondary gain: Unintended rewarding consequences resulting from misbehavior.

Self-monitoring: Tracking the occurrence of one's own target behaviors.

Self-regulation: The ability to calm oneself.

Self-talk: Talking to oneself; it may support memory such as repeating a parent's directions and may relieve stress such as by recalling past successes in similar situations or focusing on the positive.

Sensory integration: Putting together information from the various senses to gain a coherent understanding of the environment.

Sensory seeking: Engaging in activities that stimulate one or more problematic sensory systems.

Shaping: Reinforcement of successive approximations of the desired behavior.

Shared control: The therapist giving the student some choice in what to do next.

Shrinking reinforcer method: Presentation of a reward to be given after a set interval of time that shrinks with each target misbehavior that occurs within that time frame; alternatively, presentation of a reward to be given after a certain task is accomplished that shrinks with the additional passage of time if the task is not completed within a set time frame.

Social behavior map (SBM): A tool created by Michelle Garcia Winner (2007) to help an individual see the cause-and-effect relationships his behavior has upon how others feel, the consequences to him, and how that subsequently makes him feel.

Social referencing: Looking to others to assess their emotional reactions.

Speech and language pathologist: An expert in teaching language and communication.

Speech dyspraxia: Difficulty speaking because of faulty word retrieval and deficient motor planning of the muscles responsible for the articulation of speech.

Stereotypy: Repetitive actions that serve no functional purpose.

Stimming: Self-stimulation, repetitive behavior that serves no functional purpose except to satisfy a sensory need or habit.

Structured teaching: Planned lessons to teach goals systematically.

Syntax: The rules that govern the ways in which words combine to form phrases, clauses, and sentences.

Tactile: Related to the sense of touch.

Tangible reinforcer: A reward item that can be touched such as a sticker, edible, or toy.

Task analysis: The process of defining all the steps necessary to learn a specific task.

TEACCH (Treatment and Education of Autistic and related Communication-handicapped Children): A program developed for the state of North Carolina in 1966 that employs individualized structured teaching and lots of visual supports.

Theory of mind: The intuitive understanding that other people have different thoughts, knowledge, and feelings and the ability to guess, understand, and track their different points of view.

Three-point eye gaze: Looking at another person to get his attention, looking at the object of interest to draw his attention to it, and then looking back at the person to see if he understood.

Three–two–one countdown: A learning readiness procedure, "Three: Sit up tall. Two: Quiet mouth. One: Quiet hands and feet."

Triangular thinking: The ability to think of multiple ways to achieve a goal or result, including indirect routes.

Vestibular sense: How the body senses rotation and movement via sensory receptors in the inner ear.

Visual processing disorder: A deficit in comprehending and remembering visually presented information.

Visual schedule: A critical teaching tool in which activities are pictorially represented or written down in the order they are to be done so that the student knows what to expect.

Wernicke's area: A part of the brain responsible for receptive language (understanding).

References

Awh, E. and Vogel, E.K. (2008) "The bouncer in the brain." *Nature Neuroscience 11*, 5–6.

Blakemore, S. and Frith, U. (2005) *The Learning Brain.* Malden, MA: Blackwell Publishing.

Burns, D. (1999 *The Feeling Good Handbook,* New York: Penguin Group. (First edition 1990.)

Buron, K.D. (2004) *When My Autism Gets Too Big!* Overland Parks, KS: Autism Asperger Publishing Co.

Cardon, T. (2004) *Let's Talk Emotions.* Shawnee Mission, KS: Autism Asperger Publishing Co., p.15, A2-6.

Cooper, J.E., Heron, T.E. and Heward, W.L. (2007) *Applied Behavioral Analysis.* 2nd edn. Columbus, OH: Pearson/Merrill Prentice Hall.

Day, A. (1991) *Carl's Afternoon in the Park.* New York: Farrar, Straus and Giroux.

Eastman, P. (2005) *Fred and Ted Go Camping.* New York: Random House, Inc.

Eastman, P. (2007) *Fred and Ted Like to Fly.* New York: Random House, Inc.

Emberley, E. (1970) *Drawing Book of Animals.* New York: Little, Brown & Co.

Emberley, E. (1972) *Make a World.* New York: Little, Brown & Co.

Emberley, E. (2002) *Complete Funprint Drawing Book.* New York: Little, Brown & Co.

Escriva, St. Josemaria (1981) *Friends of God.* London: Sceptor, Ltd.

Falvey, M. (2005) *Believe in My Child with Special Needs!* Baltimore, MD: Paul H. Brooks Publishing Co.

Fovel, J.T. (2002) *The ABA Program Companion.* New York: DRL Books, Inc.

Gladwell, M. (2005) *Blink.* New York: Little, Brown & Company.

Greenspan, S. and Wieder, S. (1998) *The Child with Special Needs.* Reading, MA: Perseus Books.

Greenspan, S. and Wieder, S. (2006) *Engaging Autism.* Philadelphia, PA: Da Capo Press.

Greenspan, S. and Greenspan, N.T. (2010) *The Learning Tree.* Philadelphia, PA: Da Capo Press.

Gutstein, S. (2000) *Solving the Relationship Puzzle.* London: Jessica Kingsley Publishers.

Gutstein, S. (2002a) *Relationship Development Intervention with Young Children.* London: Jessica Kingsley Publishers.

Gutstein, S. (2002b) *Relationship Development Intervention with Children, Adolescents and Adults.* London: Jessica Kingsley Publishers.

Harrison, V. (1994) *Verb Tenses.* Bicester: Winslow Press Limited. Available at www.superduperinc.com, accessed on December 5, 2011.

Kasari, C., Freeman, S. and Paparella, T. (2006) "Joint attention and symbolic play in young children with autism: A randomized controlled intervention study." *Journal of Child Psychology and Psychiatry 47*, 611–20.

Kaufman, N. (2006a) *The Kaufman Speech Praxis Workout Book, Treatment Materials and a Home Program for Childhood Apraxia of Speech.* Gaylor, MI: Northern Speech Services, Inc. National Rehabilitation Services.

Kaufman, N. (2006b) *Speech Praxis Treatment Kit for Children*. Gaylor, MI: Northern Speech Services, Inc. National Rehabilitation Services.

Koegel, R. and Koegel, L. (1995) *Teaching Children with Autism*. Baltimore, MD: Paul H. Brookes Publishing Co.

Koegel, R., Schreibman, L., Good, A., Cerniglia, L., Murphey, C. and Koegel, L.K. (1989) *How to Teach Pivotal Behaviors to Children with Autism: A Training Manual*. Unpublished. Send requests to Robert Koegel, PhD, Counseling/Clinical School Psychology Program, Graduate School of Education, University of California, Santa Barbara, CA 93106-9490.

Koziol, L.F. and Budding, D.E. (2009) *Subcortical Structures and Cognition: Implications for Neuropsychological Assessment*. New York: Springer.

Leaf, R. and McEachin, J. (1999) *A Work in Progress: Behavior Management Strategies and a Curriculum for Intensive Behavioral Treatment of Autism*. New York: DRL Books, LLC.

MacKenzie, R. (2001) *Setting Limits with your Strong-Willed Child*. New York: Three Rivers Press.

March, J. (2007) *Talking Back to OCD*. New York: The Guilford Press.

McNab, F. and Klingberg, T. (2008) "Prefrontal cortex and basal ganglia control access to working memory." *Nature Neuroscience 111*, 103–7.

Miller, A. (2007) *The Miller Method: Developing the Capacities of Children on the Autism Spectrum*. London: Jessica Kingsley Publishers.

Miltenberger, R.G. (2004) *Behavior Modification*. Belmont, CA: Wadsworth.

Mukhopadhyay, T. (2003) *The Mind Tree: A Miraculous Child Breaks the Silence of Autism*. New York: Arcade Publishing.

Myers, C.A. (1992) "Therapeutic fine-motor activities for preschoolers." In J. Case-Smith and C. Pehoski (eds) *Development of Hand Skills in Children*. Rockville, MA: The American Occupational Therapy Association.

Partington, J.W. (2006) *The Assessment of Basic Language and Learning Skills—Revised*, Pleasant Hill, CA: Behavior Analysts, Inc.

Raskind, M.H., Goldberg, R.J. and Higgins, E.L. (2003) "Predictors of successful individuals with learning disabilities: A qualitative analysis of a twenty year longitudinal study." *Learning Disabilities Research and Practice 18*, 4, 11/03, 222–36.

Schopler, E., Lansing, M. and Waters, L. (1983) *Teaching Activities for Autistic Children*. Austin, TX: Pro-Ed.

Schultz, R., Gauthier, I., Klin, A., Fulbright, R.K., *et al.* (2000) "Abnormal ventral temporal cortical activity among individuals with autism and Asperger syndrome during face discrimination." *Archives of General Psychiatry 57*, 331–40.

Shapiro, L. (2003) *The Secret Language of Children*. Naperville, IL: Sourcebooks, Inc.

Sicile-Kira, C. (2006) *Adolescents on the Autism Spectrum*. New York: Penguin Group.

Sicile-Kira, C. (2008) *Autism Life Skills*. New York: Penguin Group.

Siegel, B. (2003) *Helping Children with Autism Learn*. New York: Oxford University Press.

Sussman, F. (1999) *More Than Words*. Toronto: The Hanen Center.

Sussman, F. (2006) *Talkability*. Toronto: The Hanen Center.

Williams, D. (1999) *Like Colour to the Blind*. London: Jessica Kingsley Publishers.

Winner, M.G. (2007) *Thinking About You, Thinking About Me*. San Jose, CA: Think Social Publishing, Inc. (First edition 2002.)

Winner, M.G. (2005) *Think Social—A Social Thinking Curriculum for School-Age Students*. San Jose, CA: Michelle Garcia Winner (information@socialthinking.com).

Wood, A. (Illustrated by D. Wood) (1984) *The Napping House*. Orlando, FL: Harcourt Brace Jovanovich.

Young, E. (2002) *Seven Blind Mice*. New York: Penguin Putnam Books for Young Readers.

Index